Policing, Security and Democracy:
Theory and Practice

Edited by

Menachem Amir
The Hebrew University, Jerusalem, Israel

and

Stanley Einstein
The Middle Eastern Summer Institute on Drug Use

The Uncertainty Series

Copyright 2001 by the Office of International Criminal Justice(OICJ),
Box 1819, Huntsville, TX 77342-1819, USA
Telephone: (936) 436-9454 — Fax: (936) 436-9483
e-mail: books@oicj.org — www.oicj.org

Opinions expressed in this publication do not necessarily reflect the views of the
Office of International Criminal Justice.

ISBN: 0-942511-91-3 Paperbound
ISBN: 0-942511-92-1 Hardcover
LOC: 2001092261

Copy Editor: Nathan R. Moran
Cover designed by Ronit Berson

Contents

A Prologue to the Series

UNCERTAINTY is an international, interdisciplinary series of topic-focused books publishing invited state-of-the-art analyses one or more times a year. Each volume will contain a minimum of 10-15 review articles. They will focus on an issue, problem or process which remains unresolved. The topics will be ones which significantly affect the quality of life of the individual and the nature and effective functioning of our institutions, communities, and of society-at-large. Authors will help you, the reader, to move from concepts, definitions, theories, paradigms and their 'demands' to the implications of current generalizable empirical data, to the future of the issue's topic, noting remaining unresolved issues, the barriers to their understanding, planning and implementation and suggesting future research.

Each issue will include:

* *ABSTRACTS*
* *REFERENCES*
* *GLOSSARY*
* *RESOURCES*: Lists of selected printed, auditory, and visual materials from governmental and private organizations which the interested reader can write to for further information.
* *GRAPHICS:* Graphic materials, designed to help you, the reader, 'see' the issues, their parameters, 'demands' and (inter) relationships.

UNCERTAINTY, the series, is designed as a forum for minimizing individual and systemic uncertainties, to promote exploration of selected vital human concerns and to maximize the needed openness for preventing premature closure as we examine, think about, and create new paradigms of change. In our increasingly complex world in which solutions all too often raise, or themselves become, problems, the paradox of the lawfulness of unpredictability is our reality; notions of *control, predictability* and '*cause and effect*' are mythical messages. In our complex world the concept of predictability changes. The answer to the question 'Tell me what will happen?' *always* has some degree of uncertainty. 'Tell me what is plausible, likely, to anticipate is reasonable.' The answers could be the same, scientifically speaking, but the meanings will be different. In our complex world, the dynamics of reality do not play dice, even though to all appearances, and to 'common sense,' life and reality is experienced as a dice game.

UNCERTAINTY is and can be a stimulus and tool for you.

Both the authors in each volume and the editors welcome queries and feedback.

The Editors

Acknowledgments

Many people have made it possible for this volume to move from an 'interesting idea' to an actual publication. The willingness of professionals, friends, colleagues and strangers to take the necessary time from their busy personal and professional responsibilities for this project continues to serve as an ongoing source of joy to both of us.

Working with known and experienced professionals in this transnational, globalizing volume has resulted in a most satisfying meld for the editors...and hopefully for you, the reader. We have learned a great deal.

Yossi Gadot (Department of Psychology Lab., Bar Ilan University), Ralph Amelan and Gil Shimon (American Center - Jerusalem), the Abstract translators–Marina Barham, MA, Palestine National Authority, (Arabic), Valery Gafurov, Ekaterinburg, Russia and Vitale Ustinov (Russian), Dr. Fu Hua Ling, The University of Hong Kong, (Chinese), Paulo De Mesquita Neto, (Portuguese), ,Isobell Hermant, Medicins du Monde (French), Dr. Maria Alaniz and Dr. Jonny F. Andia, NDRI, NYC (Spanish), Prof. Minoru Yokoyama, (Japanese), and the graphic designer of this volume and of the Uncertainty series, Ronit Berson, was and remains beyond what the editors expected. We are most grateful to each of them.

Our families and friends were most patient as we attempted to meet the demands of this volume. Their support made it possible for us to continue.

And of course this volume, and The Uncertainty Series, would not be possible without Dick Ward, who continues to demonstrate his belief in two colleagues and their dream.

Lastly, this book is dedicated to our grandchildren and to the whole young generation who may inherit a better world and better qualities of life through advancing and protecting democracy by and with a democratic police and democratic policing.

List of Figures

List of Tables

List of Contributors

Menachem Amir, Ph.D., is a member of the permanent faculty and a Professor of Criminology at The Institute of Criminology, Hebrew University, Jerusalem, Israel.

William Bratton, President of the New York City based consulting firm, *The Bratton Group LLC.*, served as Police Commissioner for the New York City and Boston Police Departments and re-engineered five major police agencies.

Stanley (Shlomo) Einstein, Ph.D., clinical and social psychologist, researcher, academician, lecturer, journalist, radio interviewer, author, editor, consultant, and conference organizer is the creator and co-editor of "The Uncertainty Series."

Nigel Fielding, Ph.D., Professor of Sociology and Deputy Dean of Human Studies at the University of Surrey, Guildford, England.

Hualing Fu, SJD., Associate Professor of Law at the University of Hong Kong.

Andrew Goldsmith, Ph.D., Professor at the Law School of Flinders University, Adelaide, South Australia.

Ahti Laitinen, Ph.D., Professor of Criminology and the Sociology of Law, University of Turku, Finland; responsible for the academic training of police officers in the field of criminology and the sociology of law.

Peter K. Manning, Ph.D. is Professor of Sociology and Criminal Justice at Michigan State University.

Gary Marx, Ph.D., Professor Emeritus of Sociology at M.I.T. He has taught at the University of California at Berkeley, Harvard University, and the University of Colorado.

Paulo de Mesquita Neto, Ph.D., is senior researcher at the Center for the Study of Violence at the University of Sao Paulo and Executive Secretary of the Sao Paulo Institute Against Violence.

Mark Shaw, Ph.D., is a Research Fellow at the South African Institute of International Affairs based at the University of the Witwatersrand, Johannesburg, South Africa.

Clifford Shearing, Ph.D., Professor and Director of the Centre of Criminology at the University of Toronto, Canada, and coordinates a Community Peace Programme at the School of Government, University of the Western Cape, South Africa.

Lawrence W. Sherman, Ph.D., is Director of the Fels Center of Government and Albert M. Greenfield Professor of Human Relations at the University of Pennsylvania.

Eli B. Silverman, Ph.D., is Professor in the Department of Law, Police Science and Criminal Justice Administration at John Jay College of Criminal Justice, City University of New York.

Lt. Col. Alexander Yelin, Deputy Chief-of-Staff of the Sverdlovsk Oblast Regional Interior Department, one of the largest regional divisions in the law enforcement system of Russia

Minoru Yokoyama, Ph.D., is a Professor and the former Dean of the Faculty of Law at Kokugakuin University, Tokyo, Japan.

Ugljesa Zvekic, Ph.D., Criminologist, Regional Advisor, Crime Prevention and Criminal Justice, UN Office for Drug Control and Crime Prevention, S. Africa; Scientific Counselor, Institute of Criminological and Sociological Research, Belgrade, Yugoslavia.

Introduction

This is the second volume in **"The Uncertainty Series"**. This time we turn from crime to the social, official, public and private reaction to crime, but as it is related to the first link in the criminal justice system, the police. Being aware of the complexity of this issue we, in a sense, made it more complex by seeking to explore the relationships between police reactions to crime within the context of 'democracy' as dynamic, ongoing political arrangements, processes and as a value system.

We invited papers from scholars and practitioners asking them to write about the relationships between police, security and democracy. In addition, we posed for them two sub foci: discuss this subject with attention being paid to 'democratic policing' and 'democratic police organization'.

Sadly, for us, we had to reject papers which were far removed from the targeted issues. We found ourselves categorizing those articles which were accepted because of their broad diversity. We are fully aware that the processes of categorizing are as loose or as tight as the agendas or interests of the categorizers as well as the theoretical-conceptual milieu at the time. We decided to divide the contributions into five sections which you, the reader, may not agree with. These are:

- articles centered upon the *theory of the relationships* between police and democracy;
- *community policing* as the supposed apex of democratic policing;
- police and *policing in stable democracies;*
- police and *policing in societies that are in transition* from repressive regimes towards democratic political systems and/or free market economies, and
- *special issues* which democratic police and policing have to consider either because of technical or social developments or because they are inherent in the processes and essence of police and security forces exercising their mandates.

We have continued the tradition created in the first volume of this series *"Organized Crimes: Uncertainties and Dilemmas"* of asking the contributors and selected other practitioners and scholars to share their views regarding: *What is the Most Critical Unresolved Issue Associated with Contemporary Democratic Policing?*

We wish you, the reader, a stimulating learning experience and pilgrimage as you journey through the complex concepts, processes, paradigms, areas and issues, the 'actors' and the necessary conditions which make up contemporary democratic policing and security-related issues and concerns in various parts of our continued globalizing world.

The Editors

Section I
Introduction
Some Theoretical Aspects

Some Theoretical Aspects

Lawrence Sherman, in the tradition of liberal democracy, views the basic concern of democracy being to guarantee and promote human and civil rights. These rights are protected through arrangements about the 'rules of the (political) game' and by *consent*. This 'consent' is most important in societies which are characterized by *diversity* (cultural, ethnic, class, etc.) Therefore inherent in all policing is variability and diversity. Police, as any organ of the State can function efficiently in protecting both the individual's and group's rights if its policies are also based upon consent which is achieved by adherence to the law and by proving that police officers behave both fairly and morally. Police can educate the populace to obey the law by showing integrity and law abiding behaviors. But most importantly police need to obtain *consent* and *legitimation* for its policies as well as functioning efficiently.

Sherman contends that by inculcating obedience to the law and by being fair and moral we can create a 'master-identity' of a democratic-oriented policeman

In a tightly written paper Gary Marx shares with us that democracy is a condition, a content of values and processes, that include systems of rules and procedures designed:

- to protect but also to change the rules,
- by democratic processes, and
- protect democratic values of human dignity and civil rights.

'Democratic police' and 'democratic policing' are characterized by being subjected to control, transparency, accountability, political neutrality, adherence to the law and to due process in carrying out its mandate.

The mandate of the police, in every political system, is to control crime and to maintain public order. But unlike totalitarian regimes, these functions are performed within the context of public accountability.

Unlike totalitarian regimes there is an adherent tension, a conflict between liberty and order, so that there are regulative laws and procedures in order to maintain a balance between them. Inherently some liberty must be sacrificed for order; order become a process guaranteeing freedom and rights.

Police discretion to deprive, however temporarily, people's rights, in order to protect democracy, may also become a threat to democracy. This paradox becomes sharper and more critical even in the more democratic context of community policing. This reality is increasingly more prominent because of the new technologies of surveillance and extraction of information which calls for more stringent rules and mechanisms of control over the police.

Eli Silverman interviewed the well known former New York Commisioner of Police, William Bratton. Mr. Bratton also invokes the tension between liberty, security and order. The assumption is that the citizen is ready to forgo a little liberty for public security and order

Community policing is the new philosophy that came closer to democratic policing. But because of the police's legal authority to infringe upon civil rights and their permission to use force, police forces must be under control. In a democracy this means *transparency, accountability* and *accessibility* of the people to the police. Such external control is added to the internal control which sometimes fail or are insufficient. Better police cadet recruitment policies, training and teaching them the problems associated with policing a multi-ethnic, class and cultural society and the mechanisms which are needed in order to inculcate police to obey the law while policing the people and their public and private communities democratically.

Menachem Amir discusses the relationship between police, the State and Civil Society. For him the police mandate is to protect the

- interest of the State and its stability, and
- the civil society, especially the rights of individuals, groups and the whole community, however this latter entity is defined.

There is a built-in imbalance in the relationships between police, the State and society. All-too-often police relate to 'them' as if the latter individuals and systems impede policing by erecting obstacles which hinder efficient policies which are designed to protect the State and society at large. In democracies the State and civil society may object to achieving and/or maintaining democratic goals by non-democratic means. The State and civil society often feel threatened when police serve sectorial, vested interests (economic, political, ethnic, class etc.)

The relationship between police, State and society must be evaluated on the basis of and within the context of

- conflicting social and political interests, and
- conflicts between the role of defending individual rights and the need to protect the security and order of collectivities and the whole social order.

These posited assumptions, conditions and processes are valid for the various types of democracy: liberal, consensual, conflict and crisis types. It is an accepted 'given', for all types of democracy, that police operate

- within the framework of the democratic rules,
- under the control of the law and
- under the arrangement of *transparency* and *accountability*.

Police, however, unlike other government organs, need *more controls* because

- of the mandate to enforce laws which at times lack social consent or support for State policies of their enforcement;
- of the possible detrimental consequences of some police actions for the people, and
- the organization of the police and their work conditions create the norm of 'secrecy', and occupational subcultural ambivalence towards the law and of law violations by policemen.

When any of these occur police can be viewed as their being a threat to society on a micro to macro level as well as to democracy and to themselves.

Nigel Fielding's paper is difficult to summarize. It is a concise, revealing paper about the relationships between police and community which is exemplified through three models of policing. These models are compared by using various criteria. Given this volume's focus- police and democracy- the three models are compared in terms of police legitimation, police and politics, the politics of police control and accountability and the role of the community. Fielding warns us that the police are vulnerable to corruption, law and civil rights violations in each of these three models. And because of this reality both internal as well as external ongoing controls are critical.

Clifford Shearing's paper is about redefinitions and of new conceptual approaches to police and to policing. Policing, Shearing notes, is no longer in the 'business of crime prevention'. Crime is only one type of *risk* which confronts modern society. Objective risks and the sense of risk are handled by the 'security industry' which is guided by new theories of crime and crime prevention (e.g. routine activities, rational choice and situational crime prevention), and new theories of marketing and management of customer service.

Crime, from these perspectives, is not only the illegal or the immoral, but it is also that which causes 'loss'. If this position is accepted the criminal justice system, including the police, are redefined as to their roles. Considerations of efficiency, of cost effectiveness also mean an actuarial account which views future developments, anticipations, possibilities and opportunities for risks. The human elements remain within the considerations of *restorative justice* rather than being only a retributive reaction. Police, under these developments and conditions, adopt new principles as part of the necessary context for creating security and preventing 'risks'

- efficient management and
- society is defined as a 'collectivity of customers'.

Policing 'risks', Shearing contends, has not been the monopoly of the State and its policing organizations for quite some time. The apparatus of policing and security, including public space, has increasingly become the responsibility of private industries of security and safety. The official, public police - the blue line retains their monopoly of the use of force. But this too is being usurped because 'force' is redefined or broadened to *limiting the rights of people*. Community policing is also redefined; police *and* the community - however defined- create conditions of public safety and the minimization of risks.

Peter Manning also redefines police and policing in terms of boundaries, scope and authority. Traditionally we view police as a national enforcement organization which is mandated to control crime *within* the State's borders. The army is the State organ responsible for defending the borders and if necessary to operate beyond them. In addition, the analytic concept of 'policing', which consists of all of the regulative and enforcement agencies, both public and private, are traditionally local-national bounded.

Due to the globalization of politics, economics and crime, the concept of 'police' and 'policing' changed. They have broadened out and have entered into the cross-national or transnational arena. In the not too distant past, colonial policing included the army and the police for imposing and maintaining public order. Subsequently both armies and navies were engaged in *peace-keeping operations* internationally which became known as 'gunboat diplomacy'.

In our contemporary globalizing world traditional crimes are increasingly becoming transnational (especially various types of organized crime enterprises). This is especially so with regard to those crimes which involve the creation, transferring, security and validity of information. We are now confronted by

- new types of national interests which police must protect;
- new rights which must be defended and
- by new types of policing methods (of surveillance and enforcement) which are possible because of new information technologies.

'Policing' is what the US Army and the US Drug Enforcement Agency (DEA) are doing in South America; what the UN forces are doing in Africa and in Kosovo. These new developments make the relationships between territory and authority fluid and enabled the broader legitimation for the use of force (including lethal force), of violating State rights (sovereignty) as well as personal rights across State frontiers.

Focusing on 'information crimes', Manning also redefines 'force'. For example, within the sphere of information, the use of cybernetic actions which limit peoples' actions, enforcing situations and conditions on them. New targets are arising for policing. 'Policing information' is a mandate for preventing and controlling cyber-crimes. National police enter into the international arena in order to protect the interests of private but multi-national corporations. The 'locus of control' has also changed. The traditional direct encounter between police, suspects or criminals need no longer be necessary given the availability and increasing use of remote control surveillance of people or spaces. These developments, which are increasing, create new aspects of control, accountability and the protection of rights with associated dilemmas and paradoxes which are created.

1 Consent of the Governed: Police, Democracy, and Diversity*

Lawrence W. Sherman

Abstract

Democratic policing is founded on the consent of the governed. That consent requires four principles of policing that culminate in the need for empirical evidence about how best to achieve democratic values through police practice. The first principle is that the mission of policing is to achieve compliance with the law, rather than to dispense coercion: to achieve ends rather than to employ any specific means. The second principle is that diverse democracies require diverse means to achieve compliance among diverse peoples. The third principle is that police can build the master identity of all citizens in democracies as citizens. The fourth principle is that empirical evidence on how to obtain compliance through persuasion and good manners ("polite policing") will help police minimize the use of coercion, and increase the legitimacy of the democratic nation-state.

Key Words: Consent, diversity, diverse democracies, legitimacy, master identity, restorative justice

We hold these truths to be self-evident,
that all men are created equal,
that they are endowed by their creator with certain unalienable rights,
that among these are life, liberty, and the pursuit of happiness.
That to secure these rights, governments are instituted among men
deriving their just powers from the consent of the governed.

—United States Congress, July 4, 1776

Introduction

These words were written by a homogenous group of Anglo-Saxon, Protestant Christian, highly educated, wealthy, land owning, English speaking males. The date was July 4, 1776. The place was Philadelphia, the city of Brotherly Love. Six months later, my great-great-great grandfather was marched through the streets of Philadelphia in chains. He was a slave. He spoke no English. His father had sold him to a barbaric ruler, who had paid a "cattle tax" to ship him through another ruler's lands so he could be indentured to King George III and shipped to America (Griffith, 1976: 468). Yet like the rich men who wrote the Declaration of Independence, my ancestor spent his life devoted to the central task of the police in a democracy: persuading people to obey the law because it is the morally right thing to do. In other words, he helped to create and maintain the consent of the governed so when Professor Amir asked me to address the topic of police and democracy, I readily gave my own consent. I knew that in both practical and theoretical terms, addressing this topic was the right thing to do—especially if I added one more ingredient: *diversity.*

There are no greater challenges police face in democracies than the Latin motto printed on every US dollar: *E Pluribus Unum* (out of the many, one). The more diverse the society, the more important it becomes for police to say that *"nation-building is our most important product."* But that is far easier said than done.

This challenge is so great that police deserve all the help we can give. The good news is that social science has paid increasing attention to this question in recent years. The less good news is that we still have a long way to go. But if police and social science work together, a great deal more can be learned. We can use that knowledge to build the consent of the governed, in all their splendid diversity, to obey the one law of the land. My central thesis is that in diverse democracies, the fairness and effectiveness of policing are much the same thing. For there is increasing evidence that fair policing—especially polite and respectful policing—is the most effective way for police to reduce offending and to build a democratic nation The more diverse the society, the greater the effect of fair and polite policing.

This thesis has four building blocks:

- The first thesis is to view policing as a process designed and implemented for achieving compliance, rather than for dispensing coercion—a definition based on ends rather than means.

- The second thesis relates to the enormous complexity of achieving compliance to common laws in culturally diverse democracies.

- The third block uses the story of my great-great-great grandfather to show how police can use the concept of *'master identity."* labels to promote good citizenship.

- The fourth and largest block is the empirical evidence for my central thesis that police obtain the greatest compliance with the law through persuasion by example that the law is both procedurally fair and morally right.

The empirical evidence for this thesis is not, by any means, conclusive. But it is promising enough to warrant far more investigation. Persuasion is not the only way that police achieve compliance with the law, I suggest, but it is probably the most pervasive and widespread. Thus the conclusion we shall reach is that greater collaboration between police and criminologists in research on this thesis can help strengthen both policing and democracy.

Policing for Compliance

Many scholars have defined policing by its means of production, the technology which police employ, and the raw material which they process. Bittner (1970) and Klockars (1985), for example, define police by the use of force. Reiss (1992), Shearing (1995) and Manning (1992) stress the processing of information. But this approach is limited in time by the technology and materials of each era. It is comparable to defining capitalism as the ownership of factories.

The enduring characteristic of policing in all times and places is the result it attempts to achieve. The defining characteristic of capitalism is the goal of profit. The defining characteristic of policing is the goal of *compliance with the law*. No matter how the technology and raw materials may change over time, the goal remains the same

In a democracy, police face strict requirements on the technologies which they employ. They are prohibited from using many efficient methods to reduce crime, such as summary execution or torture of offenders. Less obvious is the method which they are required to use in everything they do. That method is persuasion—also known as marketing, selling, or evangelism—that we should all obey the law. Not only because crime will be punished. Not only because crime is shameful to your family. Not only because crime is sinful under most religions. But because democracy is the best form of government, and it is morally right to obey democratic laws.

Democracy, by definition, must create and maintain the consent of the governed in an equitable fashion. This task falls more heavily on the police than on any branch of government, for very good reasons. No other branch of government has more face to face contacts with citizens. No other branch of government has such intrusive powers. No other branch of government can deprive citizens of life and liberty in the blink of an eye. No other branch of government can do as much to justify the very form of government, nor has as much to justify.

Social scientists have given a technical term to maintaining the *consent of the governed*. That term is *legitimacy*, which Max Weber (1919 trans. Gerth and Mills, 1948:78) defined as the "inner justification" for men to obey the *"authority claimed by the powers that be."* Gerth and Mills (1953) call legitimacy the essential element of authority, as distinct from power in general. *"Power,"* they said, *"is simply the probability that men will act as another man wishes."* Authority, in contrast, is a special kind of power: *"legitimated power,"* which creates *"voluntary obedience."* The basis for that obedience is an idea: *"the idea which the obedient holds of the powerful or of his position"* (Coser and Rosenberg 1969: 169).

Viewed from this perspective, the most powerful weapon a police officer employs is not his or her gun. It is his or her mouth. For the mouth is a source of persuasion, the tool for creating an idea of the police as fair and morally just. That idea, as Weber pointed out, is the necessary condition for maintaining a nation-State, which he defined as a *"human community that (*successfully*) claims the monopoly of the legitimate use of physical force within a given territory"* (1919, Gerth and Mills, 1948: 78). Because they are delegated the power to dispense legitimate force as the need arises (Bittner, 1970), the police are the most important agency of any government. It is for just this reason that the words police speak outweigh bullets they shoot.

Words create symbols. Symbols create ideas. Ideas create the consent of the governed. Animals exercise power with brute coercion, perhaps accompanied by grunts and growls, but men control each other by setting up what Suzanne Langer called *"symbols of power.* [T]*he mere idea that words or Images convey stands there to hold our fellows in subjection even when we cannot lay our hands on them. Men oppress each other by symbols of might"* (Coser and Rosenberg, 1969: 169).

Dictatorships clearly realize the power of words and symbols to create consent with their emphasis on the cult of the charismatic leader (Weber, 1919, trans. Gerth and Mills, 1948: 79). Both Hitler and Mao, for example, took a page from Rosseau's (1762, as quoted in Coser and Rosenberg, 1969: 169) *Social Contract* which observed that *"The strongest is never strong enough to be always master, unless he transforms his strength into right, and obedience into duty.*" In other words, even in dictatorships, police cannot watch everyone every minute. While fear of punishment may go a long way to shaping behavior, it can never go far enough. Compliance with the law, in Rousseau's theory, must depend upon voluntary belief in the idea that the law is right, and that the government has the moral right to make the laws.

In this respect, the only difference between policing a dictatorship and policing a democracy is the content of the idea that gives the government the moral right to govern. In Weber's terms, the difference is the basis of legitimacy, the justification for a monopoly on the use of violence exercised by the police. A democracy dominates its' citizens not with symbols of the traditional authority of a hereditary or religious ruler, nor with the charismatic authority of a great dictator, but with the symbol of legality: the idea that we should obey the law because:

- it is the law
- democratic law is the fairest and best rule for all the people
- the law rules all persons equally, — even the head of State or government — and, most especially, the police

There is no better illustration of this point than in the contrast between the founding of the police in London and New York. As historian Wilbur Miller (1977) has shown, the London police were created almost on a trial basis. Their primary task was to persuade the public that police were servants of the people, and not their masters. They were recruited, trained and supervised with the goal of persuading all the people to accept the right of police to enforce the Law. They used their powers lightly, stressing compliance over punishment.

In New York, by contrast, the first police were manifestly biased, created by native-born Americans to control recent immigrants. They made little attempt at persuasion, but made massive use of coercion, effecting astonishing numbers of arrests each day for public intoxication. New York police worked openly for one political party, and were fired if another party won the next election, so police worked very hard to manipulate elections.

As Miller summarizes the contrast between London and New York, the London police set out to create legitimacy; the New York police set out to demand it. The arguable result, until very recently, has been far lower rates of crime in London than in New York. Anthropologist Geoffrey Gorer (1955) has suggested that the decline of violence throughout 19th century England resulted in part from the cultural influence of the British police officer as a role model for obedience to the law. The U.S., in contrast, often saw the police as a role model for violence: violence against immigrants, against labor unions, against Jews and Negroes and Chinese, or any of the other "un-American" groups officially blacklisted by the federal government as threats to social stability, ineligible for federally insured mortgages (Jackson, 1985).

What the New York-London contrast reveals, of course, is the powerful challenge that diversity poses to any democracy. The history of police and crime in those cities might have been very different had New York been homogeneous and London been a multinational melting pot.

But as we look at the modern world, we must realize that homogeneity is dying out and human migration is on the rise. The concepts of police and democracy mean little without confronting diversity.

Policing Diverse Democracies

Around the world, the most advanced industrial democracies have generally become the most diverse. As measured by percentage of resident population born outside the country, most of the European Community is in the same range as the United States, with 5-10% of residents foreign-born. France exceeds ten percent, and 1 of every two children born in Brussels is a Muslim. Most of the Arab world exceeds 20 percent of residents foreign-born. Israel and Australia may top all the democracies, with Israel at approximately 50 percent and Australia at 23 percent foreign-born (National Geographic Society, 1998).

There are, of course, many different kinds of democracies. Theorists often classify them according to their guarantees of human rights, such as freedom of speech. Yet in practical terms the most significant difference among democracies is their treatment of diversity, or the rights they guarantee to citizens of different identity groups whether religious, racial, ethnic, economic, sexual or cultural in character. A pure democracy can, in theory, create a law that harms 49% of the population. But a democracy that protects the legal equality of groups, as well as the numerical equality of individual voters, is a diverse democracy, one as committed to the Constitutional tolerance of nonharmful differences among its people as it is to the democratically determined intolerance of harmful conduct

We may define a diverse democracy as distinct from a merely multicultural democracy. Many democracies have multiple cultures, but exclude minority cultures from participation in the democracy. My own country did that to African-Americans from 1776 until the abolition of slavery in 1863. Japan denied citizenship to resident Koreans for over a century, and Germany is only beginning to embrace Turkish immigrants as full citizens. A diversely democratic nation is openly committed, at least in theory, to full participation by all subcultural groups. Examples of diverse democracies that I know best are Australia, the U.S. and Israel (My emphasis on the words "in theory" is illustrated by the fact that I am denied the right to vote for a Senator or Congressman because I reside in a predominantly African-American city called Washington D.C.).

The commitment to diversity, at least in theory, greatly increases the challenge of policing a democracy. That is true for at least three reasons:

- the complexity of legitimating symbols,
- the constant suspicion of group inequality before the law, and
- the challenge of democratic diversity within the police institution itself.

Complexity of legitimating symbols.

In a diverse democracy, the central task of the police remains the same: persuading people to obey the law because it is the morally right thing to do. But that task relies upon the manipulation of symbols. In a homogeneous society, those symbols are widely shared between the police and the public. Those symbols include language, humor, honor, and values. The more diverse a society becomes, the more complexity there is in the symbols that police must manipulate to legitimate the law.

Merely communicating to a Russian-speaking immigrant, for example, poses a great challenge to police in New York, Sydney or Jerusalem. Communicating to a Russian-speaker with such primary police weapons as subtlety, respect, and even humor is almost impossible to imagine. In the absence of rich verbal symbols to legitimate domination, police inevitably fall back on brute force to achieve compliance.

Police in diverse societies also lose the power of patriotic pride to make people want to obey the law. This symbol is illustrated by David Bayley's (1976: 48) observation in Japan two decades ago:

> *Three policemen were called to a home where an estranged brother had come to pester his working class family for drinking money. The policemen led the man, boisterously drunk, up the street. Patting him on the shoulder, they gave him a mock lecture: "Are you a Japanese man? You don't act very manly. You should act manly or maybe we should cut off your penis..." The man smiled groggily, wanting to play up to the humor, and finally managed to stagger to the koban.*

This story shows both an appeal to a shared national identity and a common cultural basis for humor. Both tools of persuasion help police to legitimate their conduct and their government. But both become difficult, if not impossible, to use in a nation or community of recent immigrants, racial diversity, or other stark dividing lines.

Suspicion of Inequality.

The most important symbol which police manipulate in a diverse democracy is equality before the law. Even democracies most committed to this principle, however, have long and tragic histories of its denial. Famous martyrs of unequal law enforcement become symbols of inequality before the law, from (as in the U.S.) Dred Scott to Rodney King.[1] These martyrs may serve to deter the legal system from other acts of inequality. But they also help to unify cultural identity groups in the role of victims of immoral aggression by the larger society. A group's identity as law's victim de-legitimates compliance with the law, and legitimates vigilantism in its place (Weisburd, 1988; Black, 1983), becoming yet another cause of crime.

The minority role as victim casts the police in the reflected role of an "occupying army," in the words of the African-American writer James Baldwin.

It is just this attempt to de-legitimate the democratic police role as invasive and oppressive that led the Royal Ulster Constabulary to extraordinary lengths in Belfast. At the height of the "troubles," the British Army was present in great numbers to combat terrorism. But regular police business still went on. The high risk of assassination of the civilian police made it inadvisable for them to work alone, or even in pairs. So the British Army served as bodyguards for the civilian police, driving them in armored cars to answer domestic disturbance and burglary calls. The army protected the police while they mediated disputes and made civilian police arrest decisions. But the soldiers always stood by silently; they did no police work themselves. While it may have been more efficient to turn police work over to the army, it would have been immeasurably less effective. The Royal Ulster Constabulary enforced the law on behalf of all the people of Northern Ireland, Protestant and Catholic alike, while the British Army was literally just an occupying force from another country (May, 1998).

In contrast to such "divided" societies, multicultural societies have the added complexity of minority groups hostile to both the police and each other. Each group may accuse the legal system of favoring the others by failing to punish them with equal enforcement of the law. Democratic societies with no majority identity group may be increasingly exposed to this problem, in which the police are labeled as unfair to all. During the summer of 1992, for example, the Mayor of Philadelphia and his police force investigated three separate shooting deaths, which led to simultaneous accusations of favoring whites over Hispanics, Hispanics over blacks, and blacks over whites (Bissinger, 1997)

The suspicion of inequality is most manifest in charges of purely group-targeted harassment. African-American groups have documented cases in which black drivers have been stopped not for reckless driving, nor for driving while intoxicated, but for "*driving while black*" (Cole 1998). The American Civil Liberties Union has now won three lawsuits against police discrimination in traffic enforcement. This followed a famous videotape showing police stopping two blacks driving 24 miles per hour in a 25 mile zone; within 60 seconds the officer smashed the verbally defiant black passenger into a shattering storefront glass window (NBC News, 1989). (The idea of such unfairly targeted enforcement helps explain the strong African-American opposition to President Clinton's impeachment, with the view that prosecutor Kenneth Starr and the news media have illegitimately targeted certain politicians for charges of "*adultery while elected.*")

Diversity in the Police Institution.

The classic response to the suspicion of inequality, at least in diverse democracies, is to recruit police officers from all cultural identity groups. But this solution creates problems of its own. Diverse police institutions can suffer internal conflicts that mirror those in the larger society. In organizations dominated by a single ethnic group, newcomers are treated with contempt and suspicion. A Jewish officer in the Irish-dominated New York police of the 1940s fought this contempt by proving himself worthy through repeated feats of heroism. His reward for this was two nicknames. The first was "medals," for all the medals he earned for his bravery. The second was a well-meant, if insulting, mark of acceptance by the "real" police, who gave this Jewish cop the nickname of "Reilly" (Neiderhoffer, 1967).

Multicultural democracies can de-legitimate police very easily by using police appointments as a form of redistributed wealth. In recent memory, a newly elected Mayor of New Haven (Connecticut) demoted all the Irish-American police commanders who had served the previous Mayor, who was himself of Irish descent. The new Mayor, an Italian-American, promoted all Italians to top command positions. The promotions and demotions all happened on the same day, later called "The St. Patrick's Day Massacre."

As diversity increases in a police department, all systems of rewards and punishments become hot spots of alleged inequality. The Baltimore Police, for example, doubled the proportion of African- American officers in that majority African-American City over the period 1994-98, from 18 to 36% of its officers. This success was followed in 1998 by federal civil rights charges of discriminating against black officers in disciplinary decisions (Janofsky, 1998).

Even worse problems for legitimating legal equality arise when minority police are mistaken for criminal suspects and beaten or shot by majority police. In one recent Boston case, for example, a plainclothes African-American officer was first to arrive at a restaurant after a shooting incident. As the black officer chased the shooting suspect, he was grabbed by uniformed white officers who mistook him for the suspect. Because they thought he had shot a police officer, they kicked and beat him, only to discover that he was a police officer himself (Associated Press, 1998). The success of the black officer's federal lawsuit against his colleages legitimates black and white equality before the law of the national government. But it clearly undermines the legitimacy of the local police force.

As a police officer observed in the homogeneous West Germany of the 1960s, "*Democracy is always hard on the police*" (Berkley, 1969:1) He recalled how much simpler police work had been under Hitler. But if democracy makes police work hard, a diverse democracy makes police work geometrically harder. Perhaps the hardest thing that diversity creates is the challenge to the concept of master identity, the shorthand labels by which police, prosecutors and others quickly process information about people in a complex world (Sudnow, 1966). My ancestor provides a hypothetical case in point.

Diversity and Master Identities

My great-great-great grandfather arrived in America as a slave. From that fact, you might infer his "*master identity.*" My colleague John Braithwaite defines a *master identity* as that status which "*overrides all other statuses in determining how people will respond*" to someone (Braithwaite, 1989: 18).

The idea of "*master identity*" is part of two different theories of crime. One theory says that a *master identity* "labels" a person in the eyes of police. A *master identity* of "criminal" increases the odds that police will accuse someone of crimes in the future. As Claude Rains said to protect Humphrey Bogart at the close of the film classic Casablanca, "*Round up the usual suspects.*" Even as democratic a society as Holland assigns *master identity* in this way. Dutch police routinely check the computerized criminal history of automobile drivers stopped for traffic violations. If violators have no prior criminal records, they are usually not charged. If they do have prior records, they are routinely charged with the traffic violation (ASC, 1998).

This theory also suggests that the more people are labeled and treated as criminals, the more they take on that *master identity* and act like criminals. While the evidence for this theory is mixed, Braithwaite (1989: 19-21) attributes that to poor measurement of the key concepts. He argues that stigmatizing people as criminal pushes them away from mainstream society and into subcultures providing normative support for continued lawbreaking.

The second theory of crime to rely on the concept of "*master identity*" is subcultural. The theory claims that oppositional cultures support lawbreaking by people whose *master identity* is membership in that subculture. While the idea was first developed to describe lower-class culture, it may be even more important in multicultural and politically divided societies. Members of political minority groups may take on that membership as a *master identity*...transforming that identity to the role of 'victim of inequality' before the law legitimates attacks on the police as representatives of the State. It may also justify attacks on majority group citizens as unfairly benefiting from an unjust State.

For the police, there is a very important question about this theory. That question is whether they help create master identities that hinder police legitimacy. Conversely, the question is whether police can actively promote the *master identity* of "citizen" for all people, regardless of who they are or what they have done in the past. That is an arguably different question from whether police should keep close watch on serious repeat offenders, or from seeking suspects during criminal investigations. The question about *master identity* is whether police can manipulate it to foster compliance with the law, rather than disobedience—whether police can make anyone and everyone believe that they are the kind of person who wants to obey the law because it is morally right to do so.

Consider my ancestor, Henry Rossman. He was a slave. You might think his *Master identity* was African, or black. But he could have been labeled a miscengenator, someone guilty of the crime of interracial marriage. According to the U.S. Census of 1790, he was also a polygamist, with two wives living in his cabin in central Pennsylvania. Thus he was at least technically a criminal on two counts, although he was never charged or prosecuted. His *master identity* might have been a schoolteacher, which he was, or a Protestant Minister, which he later became. He had also been a prisoner of war, held in a concentration camp for 7 years. By which of these roles would we stereotype him? What label should he wear?

In modern America, that question would be answered very clearly. His *master identity* today is based on a social stigma that has lasted over two centuries. That identity is not the stigma of slave, which he was or of African, which he was not. It is the identity of a Hessian mercenary soldier. A member of an occupying army that stole and plundered from Revolutionaries and Royalists alike (Griffith: 1976:450). Hated and reviled even today as amoral coercive instruments of a de-legitimated ruler, King George III.

In modern Israel, my ancestor's *master identity* might be German, genetically linked to the mass murderers of the Holocaust. In the enormity of such crimes, a mere two centuries of separation does little to erase the stain of collective responsibility for the harm done. That is certainly how my Native-American relatives view white men in the U.S. today, a century after U.S. Army General Philip Sheridan's policy that the "*only good Indian is a dead Indian*" almost eliminated the entire race.

Against the power of such master identities, the idea of uniting diverse societies may seem like folly. Some say that the best fate that diverse democracies may hope for is peaceful coexistence of hostile identity groups. *E Pluribus unum*, they argue, or the creation of overriding master identities, is impossible. That argument, fortunately, is falsified by substantial evidence.

In the early U.S., for example, my ancestor eventually blended in with mainstream society and became a community leader. His master identity was good citizen, not "war criminal." In the days before computers, of course, it was much easier to escape one's past.

The best modern evidence for overriding divisive group identities comes most powerfully from the police themselves. Perhaps no *master identity* overwhelms ethnic group membership more powerfully than a police uniform. This is in part due to powerful stereotypes and prejudices against police, which unites officers as victims of such bias. For all their internal conflicts in the US, police of different racial groups have worked together remarkably well. Unlike the U.S. Military in World War ll, there are no separate police units for each race, no separate chains of command. The most important color in American policing is blue, the predominant color of the police uniform.

The diversity of the Israeli police is an even more powerful example. The range of religious, ethnic, cultural and language groups represented in that organization rivals the United Nations. The fact that many Muslims serve in the Israeli police is virtually unknown outside Israel, but it provides a clarion call to democracies less committed to diversity, where religious minorities need not apply to the police.

The power of organizational membership identity is also found outside the police. The late Chief Executive of Coca-Cola, Robert Goizueta, was once the subject of a news story. The reporter asked an associate whether Mr. Goizueta thought of himself more as being from Cuba, where he was raised, or from the U.S., where he had spent his adult life. The answer was that he thought of himself as being from Coca-Cola. He could also have said that he thought of himself as a Yale graduate. Universities, schools, sports teams, professions, trade associations, and other institutions of civil society can create other "master identities", leading to the nation-building identity of citizen.

These identities are all potential tools in the hands of the police, levers for the task of persuasion to obey the law. The family, in particular, provides powerful identities for police to build upon. The roles of parent, child, or sibling can all create a sense of responsibility to uphold the law. In the name of your family, in the name of God, or in the name of the law, the result can be the same: the belief that no matter who you are, or what you may have done in the past, you have a moral obligation to obey the law in the future. And you know you truly want to meet that obligation, because that is consistent with your *master identity* as a good citizen.

Recent theories of crime suggest that *master identity* is one of the most powerful symbols police can manipulate to build legitimacy, to persuade people to obey the law. Tyler (1990, 1998) suggests that the process, rather than the result, of police contact with citizens sends a message about the social value of the citizen's master identity. If that message is *"you and your kind are not welcome here,"* or *"you are not one of us,"* the effect is to reduce the citizen's future compliance with the law. Braithwaite (1989, 1998) suggests that if police treat criminal defendants and convicts with the *master identity* of "criminal," rather than "citizen," it will increase their odds of repeat offending. Sherman (1993) theorizes that if the *"master identity"* of the police themselves becomes de-legitimated by historical associations, even their legitimate actions can provoke collective defiance by stigmatized identity groups.

Evidence for Persuasive Policing

So much for the theories. What is the evidence? The best evidence comes from interviews with arrested offenders in Milwaukee who were tracked for repeat offending over six months or more (Paternoster, et al, 1997). Good evidence also comes from a controlled experiment in Australia (Barnes, 1999) which compares a more persuasive form of policing to traditional methods. Survey evidence from Chicago and Los Angeles suggests that minorities are particularly sensitive to the message that police communicate about their identity (Tyler, 1990, 1998). Finally, an intrusive program to reduce gun violence in Maryland, done politely, led to both less violence and fewer complaints about police misconduct (Carr-Friday, 1998).

Listening in Mllwaukee.

The Milwaukee police provide strong scientific evidence that polite policing reduces crime. The research is all the more impressive because Milwaukee is one of the most racially divided cities in America. In their analysis of American Apartheid, Massey and Denton (1993) rate Milwaukee's population of 600,000 at the top of the index of racial segregation. Vast tracts of the city are populated entirely by African-Americans, where 70 percent or more of the adults are unemployed Other areas of the city are lily-white, predominantly working class, with little unemployment. Those areas are home to most of the police, who in the late 1980s were mostly white, in a city that was one-third black

The effect of those neighborhood differences on police work and crime is staggering. In a controlled experiment on arrest for domestic violence, the effects of arrest were completely opposite in the two kinds of neighborhoods. Marciniak (1994) found that in the high-employment areas, arrest reduced repeat domestic violence. But in the high un-employment neighborhoods, arrest strongly increased domestic violence. There may be many reasons for that difference.

Paternoster and his colleagues (1997) thought that the legitimacy of police intervention may have a lot to do with it. So they put Tyler's theory of procedural justice to the test.

Paternoster examined two kinds of data. One was the interviews conducted by University of Maryland criminologists in Milwaukee police headquarters. Almost 800 offenders were interviewed immediately after being arrested and charged for battering their girlfriends or wives. The interviewers asked the defendants many questions, including the manner in which the police had treated them. Perhaps most important was the question of whether the police had taken the time to listen to the defendant's side of the story.

The other kind of data was the defendant's criminal history. The analysis examined both prior and future domestic violence by the defendants in the sample. This allowed them to control for the strong effect of prior offending on the "risk" of future crime.

Taking all these factors into account, Paternoster asked whether the way the police conducted the arrest would affect repeat offending. The result was clear and strong. Offenders who thought police had treated them fairly and politely had 40% less repeat offending than offenders who did not. Put another way, treating an offender like a "criminal" rather than like a "citizen" increased the repeat offending rate by some 60%. *Master identity* symbols matter. Listening to criminal suspects is a symbolic statement that they have value as citizens, no matter what they have done. Not listening is a statement that they do not matter, that they have been categorized in role of criminal and forfeited their rights as citizens. It seems that if police in a democracy would prevent violence against women, they must first prevent impoliteness by police.

Talking in Canberra.

The Australian Federal Police provide even stronger evidence about how police can create legitimacy. The jury is still out on whether more legitimacy produces less crime in Australia's national capital, a moderately diverse city of 300,000.

The Canberra experiment tests the premise that there is not enough talking, nor enough listening, in the legal responses to crime. In John Braithwaite's (1989) critique, the assembly-line justice of bureaucratic courts stifles the emotions, and especially the shame, that morality requires to be expressed. Neither the victim, the offender, nor the community have sufficient opportunity to confront the full scope of the harm that the offense caused. Victims get no apologies. Offenders get no chance to repair the harm.

To redress these problems, Australian police developed a program in 1995-1997 for diverting youthful offenders and drunk drivers from criminal prosecution (Sherman, 1998). Instead of going to court, these offenders go to a conference. The conference includes the victims, the victims' friends and family, the offenders' friends and family, and possibly a community representative. The conference is led by a specially trained officer, whose job is to make sure that everyone talks.

Most important, the officer's job is to manipulate the symbols of the offenders' *master identity*. If anyone tries to describe the offender as a bad person, the officer is supposed to intervene. *"We are here,"* he should say, *"to discuss the bad thing the offender has done and how to repair the harm. We are not here to call the offender a bad person."* The officer's message is clear: hate the sin, but don't hate the sinner.

The conference begins when the officer asks the offender to describe how, but not why, the crime happened. The officer then asks the victim to describe the consequences. Victim supporters can say more about the harm. Offender supporters are then asked how they feel about hearing of the harm the victim suffered. They often present the strongest condemnation of the crime, and may start to condemn the offender as well. But the officer leads the discussion away from the *master identity* of "criminal," and towards the *master identity* of "good citizen." The premise is that good citizens repair the harm that they have caused. The question for a group consensus is how the offender should repair that harm. In the "deliberative democracy" of the community justice conference, the group must reach an agreement that both victim and offender will accept.

Once the agreement is reached, it is carried out under the supervision of the police. If no agreement is reached, the case can (in theory) be sent to court for prosecution. But an agreement is almost always reached. In most cases, the offender keeps the promise made, and the charges are dropped without creating a criminal record. This further affects the offenders' *master identity*, preserving their right to travel overseas on an Australian passport, and to enlist in the Australian armed forces, which is a privilege, not a duty. This approach has been used in almost 1,000 conferences in Canberra during its first five years. Drinking drivers who complete the agreement are saved from having their name published in the newspaper, which would stigmatize their *"master identity"* and limit their opportunities for employment.

This innovative program is being evaluated with the strongest research design in human science, the randomized controlled trial. There are actually four separate trials, divided by offense types:

- youthful violence (under age 30),
- juvenile arrests by store security guards,
- juvenile arrests for property offenses against personal victims, and
- driving while over the blood alcohol limit.

Extensive preliminary analyses of the data so far are posted on the internet (www.aic.gov.au, click on "restorative justice," look for RISE reports). Here are some highlights:

Conferences Differed From Court In Many Ways

Based on systematic observations by independent observers of both court and conferences, the conferences greatly exceeded the court on most important dimensions. These include time and effort, participants present, and the emotional intensity of the proceedings, Conferences had more statements than court about the offenders' *master identity*, both supportive and critical. Offender behavior was also more often defiant in conference than in court. But offender apologies to victims were ten times more likely in conferences. So were statements of forgiveness of the offender by the group. Overall, offenders and victims spent far more time talking about the offense in conferences than in court (Barnes, 1998).

Most Victims Said Conferences Were Fairer Than Court

Belief that both the practical and emotional harm of the crime was being repaired was higher among victims whose cases went to a conference. Reconciliation of the victim and the offender was far greater in conference cases than in court for both property and violence experiments. Victims were less likely to fear repeat victimization by the offender after conference cases than after court cases. Victim respect for the police, however, was mixed between the two juvenile property crime experiments. Property victims reported higher respect for police after conference cases than after court cases, although victims of violence did not. Satisfaction with the way their case was handled was somewhat greater for conference than court cases among property victims, but there was no difference among violence victims. What about offenders?

Conferences Fairer Than Court

Offenders said conferences were fairer than the courts in both procedures and results. Offenders in conferences were far more likely to say that people listened to them, that they could correct any factual errors, and that they had the opportunity to shape the discussion. Drunk drivers sent to court were more likely to say that the penalty was too hard than drivers sent to conference. They were more often angry and bitter after court than after conference. Offenders sent to conferences reported much higher levels of restorative justice, or the opportunity to repair the harm they had caused by their crimes. They also reported a greater sense of forgiveness.

Perhaps the best evidence of persuasion is this: offenders sent to conferences reported far more respect for the police and for the law than offenders sent to court. At the same time, the threat of punishment appeared to have a greater deterrent effect among offenders sent to a conference than those sent to court. Overall, the program has clearly increased the capacity of the police in that diverse democracy to build legitimacy, respect for law, and a sense of citizenship in a just nation-State.

Race and Sensitivity in Chicago and Los Angeles.

The value of the Canberra program is made clearer by Tyler's (1990, 1998) survey research in Chicago and Los Angeles. The Chicago research polled a sample of the population to ask about their recent contacts with government, from a traffic stop to getting a license. It also asked about how likely people were to obey the law themselves. Across the population, when people felt police treated them unfairly or rudely, they said they became less likely to obey the law themselves. Most striking, these results were largely independent of the result of the encounter— whether or not, for example, police actually wrote them a speeding ticket Even people who thought they got off lightly lost respect for the law if they thought they had not been treated with respect.

Tyler's (1998) subsequent research in Los Angeles focused more narrowly on people who had been prosecuted in the criminal justice system. Here again, he found that fair process mattered more than fair outcomes. And fair process mattered even more to blacks and Hispanics than to whites. The minorities seemed much more vulnerable to disillusion with the law if they heard a message that they were "unwanted." While this can happen to whites as well, whites have less historical reason for sensitivity than minorities.

Tyler's work suggests that police must work even harder in diverse democracies to earn the consent of the governed. Believing that the law is fair and right is hard to do when you are a minority group member raised on stories of police brutality and oppression. While police may understandably resent the stigmatic "*master identity*" that minorities impose on all police, such resentment only makes matters worse. The Canberra experiment documents that prejudices against police can be changed, and in the context of far more intrusive methods of policing, so does the Prince George's County TAG (Take Away Guns) project.

Consent of the Governed in Maryland.

Homicide by handgun is the leading crime problem across the US. The local police agency serves a diverse county of almost one million people, of whom over half are African-American, with income levels ranging from nothing to millions per year. Historically a white police agency serving an increasingly black population, the Prince George's County (PGC) police had an historical reputation for insensitivity to minorities. In the early 1990's the agency hired more African-American police and mitigated its bad reputation. At the same time, however, the level of handgun violence rose dramatically, just as in the rest of the nation.

In late 1996, the police planned a major new strategy against gun violence. Using computerized crime maps of shooting events, the University of Maryland identified 9 major highways around which gun violence was concentrated. These highways were major corridors from high-crime areas of Washington DC into the suburban Maryland county. These corridors carried cars, and the cars carried guns. Based on a program developed in Kansas City (Sherman and Rogan, 1995), the PGC police decided to use traffic enforcement to take away guns.

The theory of the plan was clear: drastic increases in traffic stops and moving violations, searches of the car where legally possible, requests for the driver's consent to search the car where compulsory search was not possible. Given Maryland's strict laws against carrying concealed handguns, the strategy could lead to arrests for a felony. More important, it could discourage people from carrying guns in their cars (or in their clothing), and reduce the number of crimes resulting in shootings.

But there was one problem: "*driving while black*." The high proportions of black drivers on the highways meant that the major increases in traffic enforcement could spark accusations of unfairness. To avoid that charge, the program had to be as persuasive as possible. First, the officers had to persuade the drivers that being stopped was in the best interest of the public, including the drivers. Second, the officers had to persuade the driver to consent to a search of the car—time consuming at best, and humiliating at worst. Third, police had to persuade the drivers that they had ample grounds for appeal if they thought the procedure was unfair.

The training for the program addressed all of these concerns. The officers were given a script to explain the program. Almost apologizing, the officers said that the reason for the traffic stop was not just the broken taillight, but the serious problem of gun violence. The officers appealed to the driver's "good citizen" identity to help them to fight gun crime. To show the driver that the consent to search was truly voluntary, the officers gave each driver an official letter signed by the district police commander. The letter contained the commander's telephone number, inviting any complaints or comments.

The results? Traffic stops rose by over 400 percent and gun crimes declined by 49 percent. But most remarkable was this: complaints about police misconduct declined 30 percent. The emphasis on polite policing not only prevented any complaints about the Take Away Guns Program, it also spilled over into other encounters between police and citizens. The emphasis on explaining the reasons for police action, persuading citizens to cooperate, and apologizing for having to be so intrusive—all of this was a new way to do police work, and all of it may have helped persuade citizens to give more consent to be governed.

Policing by Consent

Social science is only beginning to understand the policing of diverse democracies. The evidence just reviewed is a mere starting point. Many more experiments are needed to find out what works to build support for the law. Such experiments are likely to have mixed results, revealing as much complexity as clarification. But the method of trial and error holds more promise than any other.

As Reiss (1992) points out, research and development is the core technology for police solutions to crime problems. Police cannot do what works without first learning what works, Collaboration between police and social scientists opens the door to learning by doing, testing and comparing, seeking cause and effect. Police control the test tube, social scientists control the microscope. If we try to put more persuasion into the test tube, we can measure consent with the microscope.

What is striking about the research so far is how much effect police can have on legitimacy in such a short time. Images of the police—both positive and negative—are shaped from a very early age (Berkley, 1969). Yet in the space of a short encounter with the law, a substantial modification in those attitudes can take place (Barnes, 1999). Such findings offer hope for diverse democracies—hope that the police can reduce alienation, create legitimacy, and help build a nation-State.

All of this assumes, of course, that the basic de-legitimating problems of police abuses are under control. That premise is clearly relative. Every nation has problems of police integrity, corruption and brutality. Such complaints have led Amnesty International to investigate police torture in the U.S. Meanwhile, police in Mexico and Russia have been accused of organizing syndicates for robbery, kidnapping and murder. The weak and nascent democracies have far more basic police problems than the advanced, diverse democracies.

But in any democracy. it is in the nature of the police institution to be volatile (Sherman, 1998). That is why it must earn its legitimacy every day, in every citizen encounter, through persuasion, by word, and by deed. For as the evidence suggests, there is no other way to create and maintain the consent of the governed.

Lawrence W. Sherman, Ph.D., is the Albert M. Greenfield Professor of Human Relations in the Department of Sociology and Director of the Fels Center of Government at the University of Pennsylvania. The author of many experiments and books on the causes and effects of police practices, he is also the scientific director of the Reintegrative Shaming Experiments (RISE) at the Centre for Restorative Justice of the Australian National University, Research School of Social Sciences. He is currently the President of the International Society of Criminology and the President-elect of the American Society of Criminology.

References

Barnes, Geoffrey C. (1999). "Diversionary Conferences, Procedural Justice, and Young Offenders: An Analysis From the RISE Experiments" Paper Presented to the American Society of Criminology, Toronto, November 19.

Bayley, David (1976). FORCES OF ORDER. Berkeley: University of California Press.

Berkley, George (1969). THE DEMOCRATIC POLICEMAN. Boston: Beacon.

Bissinger, Buzz (1997). A PRAYER FOR THE CITY. NY: Random House.

Bittner, Egon (1979). THE FUNCTIONS OF THE POLICE IN MODERN SOCIETY. Bethesda: National Institute of Mental Health.

Black, Donald (1983). "Crime as Social Control." AMERICAN SOCIOLOGICAL REVIEW 48: 34-45.

Braithwaite, John (1989). CRIME, SHAME AND REINTEGRATION. Cambridge: Cambridge University Press.

Braithwaite, John (1998). "Restorative Justice." ." In Michael Tonry, Editor, THE HANDBOOK OF CRIME AND PUNISHMENT. N.Y.: Oxford University Press.

Carr-Friday, Sophia (1998). Unpublished evaluation of the TAG (Take-Away Guns) Program, Prince George's County (MD) Police Department.

Coser, Lewis and Berndard Rosenberg (1969). SOCIOLOGICAL THEORY: A BOOK OF READINGS. N.Y.: MacMillan.

Gerth, Hans and C. Wright Mills (1953). CHARACTER AND SOCIAL STRUC-TURE. N.Y.: Harcourt, Brace & Co.

Gorer, Geoffrey (1955). EXPLORING ENGLISH CHARACTER . London: Creset.

Griffith, Samuel B. II (1976). IN DEFENSE OF THE PUBLIC LIBERTY. N.Y.: Doubleday.

Jackson, Kenneth T. (1985). THE CRABGRASS FRONTIER: SUBURBANIZATION OF THE UNITED STATES. N.Y.: Oxford University Press.

Klockars, Carl B. (1985). THE IDEA OF POLICE. Beverly Hills: Sage.

Manning, Peter K. (1992) "Information Technologies and the Police." In Michael Tonry and Norval Morris, eds., MODERN POLICING CRIME AND JUSTICE: A REVIEW OF RESEARCH, VOL. 15. Chicago: University of Chicago Press.

Marciniak, Elizabeth (1994). "Community Policing of Domestic Violence: Neighborhood Differences in the Effect s of Arrest." Ph.D. Dissertation, University of Maryland, College Park.

Massey, Douglas and Patricia Denton (1993). AMERICAN APARTHEID: Segregation and the Making of the Underclass. Cambridge, Mass.: Harvard University Press.

Miller, Wilbur (1977). COPS AND BOBBIES. Chicago: University of Chicago Press.

National Geographic Society. IMMIGRATION AROUND THE WORLD. Washington, D.C.: National Geographic Society.

Niederhoffer, Arthur (1967). BEHIND THE SHIELD. N.Y.: Anchor Books.

Paternoster, Raymond, Bobby Brame, Ronet Bachman, and Lawrence W. Sherman (1997). "Do Fair Procedures Matter? Procedural Justice in the Milwaukee Dometic Violence Experiment. " LAW AND SOCIETY 31: 163-204.

Reiss, Albert J., Jr. (1992). "Police Organization in the Twentieth Century." In Michael Tonry and Norval Morris, eds., MODERN POLICING CRIME AND JUSTICE: A REVIEW OF RESEARCH, VOL. 15. Chicago: University of Chicago Press.

Rosseau, Jean-Jacques (1762). THE SOCIAL CONTRACT. Rev. ed., trans. By Charles Frankel (N.Y.: Hafner, 1947).

Shearing, Clifford (1992). "The Relation Between Public and Private Policing." In Michael Tonry and Norval Morris, eds., MODERN POLICING CRIME AND JUSTICE: A REVIEW OF RESEARCH, VOL. 15. Chicago: University of Chicago Press.

Sherman, Lawrence W. (1993). "Defiance, Deterrence and Irrelevance: A Theory of the Criminal Sanction." JOURNAL OF RESEARCH IN CRIME AND DELINQUENCY. 30:445-473.

Sherman, Lawrence W. and Dennis P. Rogan (1995). "Effects of Gun Seizures on Gun Violence: 'Hot Spots' Patrol in Kansas City." JUSTICE QUARTERLY 12: 672-693.

Sherman, Lawrence W. (1998). "American Policing." In Michael Tonry, Editor, THE HANDBOOK OF CRIME AND PUNISHMENT. N.Y.: Oxford University Press.

Sudnow, David (1965) "Normal Crimes" SOCIAL PROBLEMS, winter, pp. 255-276.

Tyler, Tom (1990). WHY PEOPLE OBEY THE LAW. New Haven: Yale University Press.

Tyler, Tom (1998). "Trust and Democratic Governance" in Valerie Braithwaite and Margaret Levi, eds., TRUST AND GOVERNANCE. N.Y.: Russell Sage Foundation.

Weber, Max (1919) Translated by Hans Gerth and C. Wright Mills (1948). FROM MAX WEBER: ESSAYS IN SOCIOLOGY. London.

Weisburd, David (1988). JEWISH SETTLER VIOLENCE. University Park: Pennsylvania State University Press.

Notes

1 Dred Scott was the slave in a famous test case of the rights of slave owners before the U.S. Civil War. Rodney King was a black man beaten by Los Angeles Police Officers who were videotaped by a private citizen during the beating.

* Keynote Address, Conference in Honor of Professor Menachem Amir, Institute of Criminology, Hebrew University of Jerusalem January 7, 1999

2 Police and Democracy*
Gary T. Marx

Abstract

This article considers some varieties, and supports for, a democratic police and briefly contrasts policing in the United States, United Kingdom and France. Democratic policing should be viewed as a process and not an outcome. Societies experience a continual tension between the desire for order and liberty. There is a paradox in the fact that a democratic society needs protection both by police and from police. Given the power of new surveillance technologies, democratic societies must continually ask "how efficient do we want police to be and under what conditions is the use of these technologies appropriate?"

Key Words: Democratic policing, accountability, community police, democratic police, 'neutral' police, democratic society, police system, structure, rule of law, undemocratic police

Introduction

Democracy, whether viewed as a process or an end condition, is defined by broad values involving participation and formal rules about procedures such as elections. But for most persons most of the time these are removed from daily life. That is not true for the police, the agency of government that citizens are most likely to see and have contact with.

All industrial societies use police to control crime and to contribute to public order (e.g., mediating and arbitrating disputes, regulating traffic and helping in emergencies). But the organizational conditions under which police operate, the means they use and the ends they seek vary greatly between democratic and non-democratic societies, even as there are overlapping areas involving the control function of policing.

One element in defining a democratic society is a police force that:

- is subject to the rule of law embodying values respectful of human dignity, rather than the wishes of a powerful leader or party
- can intervene in the life of citizens only under limited and carefully controlled circumstances and
- is publicly accountable.

These conditions are inherent to police in a democracy. As inherent are ongoing myths. For example, it is a myth that all that stands between total chaos and social order is the police. Social order has multiple sources. These include socialization to norms, a desire to have others think well of us, reciprocity, self-defense and the design of the physical environment. Yet police are an important factor. Their importance increases with the heterogeneity and size of a society as well as with the more recent globalization of the world.

A defining characteristic of police is their mandate to legally use force and to deprive citizens of their liberty. This power is bound to generate opposition from those who are subject to it. It also offers great temptations for police abuse and abuse on behalf of the authorities controlling them. Law enforcement requires a delicate balancing act. The conflicts between liberty and order receive their purest expression in considerations of democratic policing, which is not necessarily equivalent to 'policing in a democracy.' For example, until recently South Africa had many of the trappings of a democratic society for white citizens, but its policing was highly undemocratic. One can also imagine a monarchy rather than a republic, in which the police are none-the-less broadly accountable to law and the public and police power is limited and consistent with value such as those in the U.N.'s Universal Declaration of Human Rights. The general political framework of a country involving the means of choosing leaders and establishing rules may show a degree of independence from the organization and activities of police even though there is some link between them.

It is ironic that police are both a major support and a major threat to a democratic society. When police operate under the rule of law they may protect democracy by their example of respect for the law and by suppressing crime. Police are moral, as well as legal actors.

But apart from the rule of law and public accountability, the police power to use force, engage in summary punishment, use covert surveillance, and to stop, search, and arrest citizens, can be used to support dictatorial regimes, powerful vested interest groups and practices. When non-democratic regimes are toppled, a prominent demand is always for the elimination of the secret police. The term "police state" as represented by Germany under National Socialism and the former Soviet Union under communism suggests the opposite of a democratic state. Police are subservient to a single party, not a legislature or judiciary. The policing of crime and politics merge and political dissent becomes a crime. Here the police function may not be clearly differentiated from and may overlap that of the security services (e.g., as with the military or national intelligence agencies). This may also involve cooperation with citizen vigilante groups or they themselves becoming vigilante groups.

The meaning of the term "*police*" has changed over the last 5 centuries. The word police comes from "*polity,*" meaning the form of government of a political body. In Europe in the 15th century it referred broadly to matters involving life, health and property. There was no distinct police force. Policing was done intermittently by the military and society was largely "un-policed." With the formation of modern states with clear national borders beginning in the 18th century, policing became concerned with internal security and the prevention of public dangers. With the expansion of the law over the next several centuries, police came to be increasingly concerned with internal security, the prevention of public dangers such as crime and disorder, and the prevention or redress of breaches of law. They also came to be more controlled by the law. (Fogelson (1977), Lane (1967), Critchley 1972).

There is no simple or widely agreed upon definition of a democratic police. Indeed it is easier to define a non-democratic police and non-democratic police behavior than their opposites. But viewed abstractly all democratic police systems share the ideal that police powers are to be used according to the rule of law and not according to the whims of the ruler or the police agent. The police, as the arm of the state's power, must be used in a restrained fashion and proportional to the problem. In the original British model there was to be policing by consent and hence an unarmed police. Ideally citizens would accept police authority out of respect, rather than out of intimidation (Melville-Lee 1901;Colquon 1969).

A democratic police is defined by both its means and its ends. Some means are simply too aborhant and are prohibited under any circumstances: torture and summary execution, kidnapping, and harming the family members of a suspect. However there may be a transfer (or what sociologists call a "functional equivalent") of dirty policing away from police to other agencies such as those concerned with national security or to private police. Other means involving the use of force, the denial of liberty and interrogation must only occur with due process of law. Due process does not refer to questions of guilt or innocence, but with the way in which guilt is determined.

In most Western democratic countries stringent actions such as wiretapping or holding a suspect in custody for more than a short period of time must be sanctioned by independent judicial or executive authorities. Should force be required it should be the minimal amount necessary for self-defense or to insure an arrest. Punishment (if called for) should only occur *after* a judicial process. The laws that police enforce, their resources and the way they use their power in enforcing laws is determined by a democratic process involving varying degrees of openness, oversight, and accountability to the public, however indirectly.

The idea of a democratic police includes content as well as procedure. Thus for police to enforce laws that support racial discrimination, even if passed by a legislature, is hardly democratic according to contemporary standards. It is easier to specify democratic procedures than democratic content. But at the most general level such content involves respect for the dignity of the person and the ideas associated with universal citizenship, limits on the power of the state to intrude into private lives and public accountability.

In a democratic society police must not be a law unto themselves. In spite of strong pressures and temptations to the contrary, they are not to act in an explicitly political fashion, such as by spying on or disrupting groups they disagree with or failing to enforce the law against groups they support or to enforce laws they personally disagree with. Nor are they to serve the partisan interests of the party in power, or the party they would like to see in power. Their purpose must not be to enforce political conformity. Holding unpopular beliefs or behaving in unconventional, yet legal, ways are not adequate grounds for interfering with citizen's liberty. When opponents of democracy operate within the law police have an obligation to protect their rights, as well as the rights of others.

In an important sense a democratic police is a politically neutral police. For example, in a racial or labor disturbance police are not to take sides, nor should they spy on, or disrupt the legal actions of an opposition political party.

Democratic societies strive for equal law enforcement. Citizens are to be treated in equivalent ways. Police are trained to behave in a universalistic fashion. Should their personal attitude depart from the demands of the role they are playing, this must not effect their behavior. Police show neutrality if they simply enforce the rules in equivalent contexts regardless of the characteristics of the persons or groups involved (e.g., race, gender, age, ability-disability status or social class).

But apart from this ideal, there is a second sense in which police are not neutral–they are agents of a particular state and enforce the laws of that state. To those who disagree with those laws, police behavior will not appear neutral since it is on behalf of the regime in power. This is one reason why even in a democratic society police are likely to be much more controversial than other agencies of government.

Varieties of and Supports for a Democratic Police

There are social, scientific and moral debates over what practices are most conducive to a democratic police (e.g., centralization vs. decentralization, specialists vs. generalists, internal vs. external controls, closeness or distance from those policed, maximum or minimum discretion, single vs. lateral entry). But it is clear that a democratic police can take many forms.

Democratic societies show wide variation in their police systems. For example, in the United States there is a quasi-military, rather decentralized, non-standardized, fragmented system, although one which mixes local and national police agencies. There is a single entry system. Those who supervise come from the rank and file. There is a Bill of Rights and other laws, which significantly circumscribe the behavior of public police. Private police and citizen initiatives are permitted. In many western countries, particularly with globalization and the weakening of national borders, there has been an increase in private policing and some blurring of the borders between the public and private police. Police have relatively little to do with the judicial system until they actually make an arrest. The adversarial system gives the accused opportunities to challenge the government's case. Police have powers denied to the citizen. There are clear procedures for citizens to file complaints against police and police are subject to a greater degree of direct political control such as by a mayor or city council, appointment of the police chief and control of the budget and specification of priorities than in many countries in Europe. There is also reliance on technology and preventive and anticipatory policing. The export of this (e.g., sophisticated stings and surveillance technology) to Europe has caused some to see an "Americanization of policing" (e.g., Nadelmann, Van Outrive and Cappelle, 1995).

In Britain policing is explicitly non-military and local, although more standardized than in the U.S. Responsibility for controlling it is shared among the Home Office of the national government, a local police authority and the head of the local force. There is no formal Bill of Rights, yet in principal police have no power beyond that of the ordinary citizen and police are unarmed. In a society where the populace has limited access to weapons it is easier to imagine an unarmed police. However, even in Great Britain there are some armed units, there are procedures for regular police to gain access to firearms and some police may carry private weapons. Citizens are seen to have a responsibility for contributing to the policing of their own communities. Internal organization and self-control are emphasized. The symbolic meaning of police as representatives of the nation is stressed and police are trained to see themselves as exemplars of moral behavior. The development of the British police has involved a continual public debate about how to protect democratic liberties while maintaining effectiveness against crime and disorder.

In France policing is highly centralized and less service and community oriented. There is a single national legal system. There are rival national police systems (one, the

Gendarme, is a part of the military and the other, the National Police, is a part of the Ministry of Interior). They serve the national, not local, government and are subject to civilian control at the higher levels. Private policing and citizen involvement play a much smaller role and are not valued to the extent that they are in the Anglo-American tradition. Through a system of lateral entry, police leaders are recruited directly into supervisory ranks. The prosecution plays an important role in criminal investigations. The judicial system is non-adversarial and it is relatively difficult for citizens to file complaints against police. Given its turbulent political history, the French believe that if democracy is to be protected, the rights of society must take precedence over those of the individual. Police are given greater leeway in the collection of political intelligence.

The democratic police ideal is generally supported by a variety of organizational means including:

- a division of labor between these who investigate, arrest, try, and punish;
- a quasi-military bureaucratic structure which limits discretion and tries to create audit trails;
- the separation of police from the military and the creation of competing police agencies rather than a monolith;
- external agencies (or compartmentalized parts of the organization) that monitor its behavior and that must give permission for certain highly intrusive actions;
- police who can be readily identified as such (e.g., in uniforms with names or identification numbers and clearly marked cars), or in the case of undercover police whose identity is hidden;
- a courtroom trial in which police actions are deception is publicly revealed and judged; and
- adequate compensation and working conditions comparable to at least the average level of the society.

These efforts involve the belief that liberty is more likely to be protected if power is diffused, if competing agencies watch each other and if police identities and actions are visible.

Police Control and Accountability

Given the potential for abuse, police face numerous external and internal controls. In the United States police are in principle bound by federal and state constitutions, statutes, and the common law. Courts through the exclusionary rule attempt to control police behavior by excluding illegally gathered evidence. Underlying this is a belief that it is less evil for some criminals to escape than for the government to play an ignoble part. Courts may also issue injunctions against particular police actions and may offer citizens compensation for violations. Prosecutors may play a role in police supervision (this has become more important in the USA but is still generally less important than in Europe). Prosecutors may refuse to accept cases which the police present and may prosecute police for criminal violations. Legislative bodies, through the passage of laws, control of appropriations, the ratification of appointments, and through holding oversight hearings may also exercise some control. Executive branch authorities, such as governors, mayors and city managers, agency heads, police commissioners, citizen review boards, auditors (and in several European countries, "ombudsmen") also exercise some control. Internally, control of police is sought through selection, training, defined procedures, policy guidelines, and supervision. In defining a given system it is necessary to look beyond formal documents and expressed ideals to actual behavior. For example, in the former USSR citizens, in principle, were granted many of the same political rights as in the United States, but in practice these were denied by the KGB, particularly when it was concerned with political conformity.

On the other hand, even systems that are democratic will have examples of undemocratic police behavior. Police organizations in the United States and Western Europe are not without occasional 'lapses,' particularly when this involves issues of ethnicity and class (e.g. unlawful stops and searches and political surveillance, inappropriate use of force, the use of police power for personal gain and discrimination in law enforcement, corruption), but these are hidden and contrary to the official policy.

Community Policing

A community-policing model has become more prominent in recent decades. In some ways this represents a break with the professional-bureaucratic, technical, law enforcement model of policing which sought to keep police from the community in the presumed interest of neutrality and efficiency. This model focused on arrest after a crime occurred.

In contrast, community policing seeks to immerse police into a local community (e.g., by a walking assignment to a particular neighborhood rather than by a patrol assignment by car to a large area). Police are encouraged to view themselves as community advocates and to be problem-solving partners with a local community. They should anticipate community needs and problems and intervene to solve them (e.g., helping potential criminals find jobs or lobbying for lights in a city park). Police should be generalists, rather than specialists, in a decentralized organization. Community policing is an explicit effort to create a more democratic force. It is based on the assumption that policing will be more effective if it has the support of, and input from, the community and if it recognizes the social service and order maintenance aspects of the police role. Of course this can involve sticky issues such as:

- what constitutes a community (is it based on geography or shared values and life style which may transcend location at a fixed physical setting)?

- there is always the danger of powerful groups pursuing their own agendas and labeling this for the "community" ignoring the legitimate needs and interests of minorities.

- how to resolve tensions between professionalism/expertise and democratic participation and the danger of police being captured by a given segment of a diverse community.

A related development here is the spread of private police. (Shearing and Stenning 1987); Johnston 1992). In the United States there are far more private than public police and their number has significantly increased in recent years. This raises important questions for democracy. On the one hand such police can serve as a check on public police and can enhance democracy through their independence. They (as with an independent press) can monitor and investigate police behavior and they can conduct parallel investigations. By offering competition they may spur police to improve. They may also contribute to a more orderly society. Yet they may also undermine democracy. When a basic need such as security is treated as a commodity, the poor are clearly at a disadvantage. The effort to restrict the right to use coercion to agents of the state under law, can be a means of increased societal equity. The first goal of private police is to serve their employer rather than justice, or the public at large. Much of the activity of private police involves informal action and is not subject to judicial review. The law has simply overlooked it. Private forces are generally subject to far less stringent controls than the public police. They may also enter into questionable alliances, carrying out illegal or unethical actions for public police. With their greater resources, there is also a danger of their being co-opted by public police.

New Threats to a Democratic Police

In 1835 Alexis de Tocqueville (1998), a French visitor to the United States, who was a great student of American democracy, felt that the state was acquiring more and more direct control over its citizens. He did not specifically have police in mind. But 20th century developments in policing support his observation.

To do their job effectively many police believe that they cannot know too much about the community, and they dare not know too little. With their special powers, police (along with the military) are a much greater potential threat to democratic regimes and practices than is the case for other government agencies such as those concerned with education or welfare. The special powers to detain, arrest, interrogate, search, and use force come with special responsibilities and the need for continuous vigilance on the part of supervisors, the executive branch of government, courts, the public, police organizations and, of course, the officers themselves, relate to their own behavior and that of their co-workers as well as the schools and programs mandated to train 'rookies' as well as veteran police. The potential for abuse is ever present. Democratic policing should be viewed as a process and not an outcome.

An important task of a democratic society is to guard against the misuse of physical , psychological, and moral coercion by police as well as to uphold human, civil and social rights and dignity in an equitable manner. A related task is to guard against the 'softer' forms of unwarranted secret and manipulative control made possible by new technologies. Because these are often subtle, indirect, and invisible, this is clearly the more difficult task.

In his novel *1984* (1998), George Orwell described a society with both violent and nonviolent forms of social control (a boot stomping on a face and Big Brother watching on the video). In linking these two Orwell offered a model based on his experiences during the Spanish Civil War and his observations of the former USSR, Germany, and Italy. Yet in contemporary democratic societies these two forms are increasingly uncoupled, and the latter is in ascendance. Aldous Huxley (1990) in his novel *Brave New World* emphasized 'softer' forms of control. He may be a better guide to the future than George Orwell (1998).

To judge current democratic societies only by traditional standards focusing on overt and direct police behavior can result in a vision which is too narrow and an optimism which may be unwarranted. Given powerful new technologies that can silently and invisibly pierce boundaries of distance, darkness, time, and economic and physical barriers that traditionally protected liberty (if also violations), police may become less democratic in their behavior. New information extractive technologies are making it possible to have a society in which significant inroads are made on liberty, privacy and autonomy, even in a relatively nonviolent environment with democratic structures in place.

In recent decades subtle, seemingly less coercive forms of control have emerged such as video surveillance, computer dossiers, and various forms of biological and electronic monitoring and behavioral and environmental manipulations. (Marx 1988, Lyon 1999 Crime, Law, Social Change 1999)

Technology may make police more efficient. Powerful computer data bases that analyze crime patterns may help solve crimes and locate perpetrators. New forms of identification involving DNA or computerized fingerprinting may help convict the guilty and protect the innocent. New technologies may help control police. For example, police accountability might be enhanced by the video-taping of all police encounters with citizens. This could serve as a deterrent to misbehavior and offer a new form of evidence in disputed accounts (although it might also mean a more passive police hesitant to innovate or take risks).

However there is no necessary guarantee that the enhancements of police power offered by new technologies will be used to protect, rather than to undermine democracy, particularly when this can happen so silently and effortlessly. A democratic society must ask the question, *"how efficient do we want police to be?"* Democratic societies have traditionally been willing to sacrifice a degree of order for increased liberty. Similarly, citizens must seriously ask themselves: *"What am I willing to give up*, or '*suffer'* in order to become and remain reasonably protected?"

Democratic societies experience a continual tension between the desire for order and the desire for liberty. Both are essential. As the case of the police state suggests, one can have the former without the latter, it is not possible to have a society with liberty which does not also have a minimum degree of order. The balance between these will vary depending on the context and time period. Democratic policing seeks to avoid the extremes of either anarchy or repression.

In an open democratic society which respects the dignity of the individual and values voluntary and consensual behavior and the non-violent resolution of conflicts, police, with their secrecy and use of violence, are an anomaly. They are charged with using undemocratic means to obtain democratic ends. Police offer an ethical and moral paradox that will forever make democratic citizens uncomfortable.

A Caveat

Restrictions on police are not a sufficient guarantee of freedom. Taken too far, they may even guarantee its opposite, as private interests reign unchecked and/or citizens take the law into their own hands. Yet a police whose power is too great is also a danger. President Abraham Lincoln posed the dilemma well when asked, *"Must a government, of necessity, be too strong for the liberties of its' own people, or too weak to maintain its' existence?"*

There is a paradox in the fact that a democratic society needs protection both by police and from police. On a broader scale, this is one of the major challenges of democratic government. President James Madison argued that *"you must first enable the government to control the governed; and in the next place, oblige it to control itself."*

Gary T. Marx is Professor Emeritus of sociology at M.I.T. He has taught at the University of California at Berkeley, Harvard University, M.I.T. and the University of Colorado. He is currently affiliated with the Bainbridge Island Bike and Kayak Club. He has pursued his interest in social control through studies of police and civil disorders, community police patrols, agents provocateurs, provocateurs and informants, undercover policing and new surveillance technologies. His book on undercover police has been well received by scholars and practitioners and a double issue in the journal Crime, Law and Social Change (Sept. 1992) is devoted to the issues raised in that book.Additional personal information along with many of his articles are available on his web page: mit.edu: mit.edu/gtmarx/www/garyhome.html garyhome.html E-mail: "gtmarx" <gtmarx@bainbridgeisland.net>

References

Bayley, D.H. Patterns of Policing: A Comparative International Analysis. New Brunswick, N.J.:Rutgers Univ. Press, 1985.

Berkeley, G. The Democratic Policeman. Boston:Beacon Press, 1969.

Bittner, E. The Functions of Police in Modern Society.New York: Oelgeschlager, Gunn and Hain, 1980.

Chapman, B. Police State. London: Macmillan, 1970.

Colquon, P. , A Treatise on Police in the Metropolis. Montclair, N.J.: Patterson Smith 1969

Critchley, T.A. A History of Police in England and Wales, 2d ed.. Montclair, N.J.: Patterson Smith 1972.

De Tocquiville, A. Democracy in America.. New York: Harper Collins, 1998.

Donner, F. The Age of Surveillance. New York:Knopf, 1980.

Fijnaut, C. and Marx, G. Undercover: Police Surveillance in Comparative Perspective. The Hague: Kluwer Law International, 1995.

Fogelson, R. Big City Police. Cambridge: Harvard Univ. Press, 1977.

Huxley, A. Brave New World. New York: New American Library Classics, 1990.

Kleinig,J. The Ethics of Policing. New York: Cambridge University Press, 1997.

Johnson, L. The Rebirth of Private Policing. London: Routledge, 1992.

Lane, R. Policing the City. Cambridge: Harvard Univ. Press, 1967.

Lee, W.L. A History of Police in England. London: Metheuen, 1901.

Marx, G.T. Undercover: Police Surveillance in America. Univ. of California Press, 1988.

Marx, G.T. "Civil Disorder and the Agents of Social Control," Journal of Social Issues, Winter, 1971.

"Thoughts on a Neglected Category of Social Movement Participants: Agents Provocateurs and Informants," American Journal of Sociology, September, 1974.

"Ironies of Social Control," Social Problems, February, 1981.

"Routinizing the Discovery of Secrets: Computers as Informants," with N. Reichman, American Behavioral Scientist, April, 1984.

"The Interdependence of Private and Public Police as Illustrated by Undercover Investigations," Crime and Justice Systems Annual, Vol. 21, 1987.

Undercover: Police Surveillance in America. Berkeley: Univ. of California Press, 1988.

"No Soul in the New Machine: Techno-Fallacies in the Electronic Monitoring Movement" with Ron Corbett, Justice Quarterly, September 1991.

"When the Guards Guard Themselves: Undercover Tactics Turned Inward," Policing and Society, Vol. 2, 1992 (a).

"Under-the Covers-Undercover Investigations: Some Reflections on the State's Use of Deception in Intimate Relations," Criminal Justice Ethics, Spring 1992 (b).

"The Engineering of Social Control: The Search for the Silver Bullet" in J. Hagan, Crime and Inequality, Stanford University Press, 1995.

"The Declining Significance of Traditional Borders and the Appearance of New Borders in an Age of High Technology" in P. Droege (ed) Intelligent Environments, Elsevier Science: Amsterdam, 1997.

"Social Control Across Borders" in W. McDonald Crime and Law Enforcement in the Global Village, Anderson, 1997.

"The Policing of Protest as a Developing Area of Social Research," in Donna Della Porta and Herbert Reiter, The Policing of Protest in Contemporary Democracies, University of Minnesota Press, 1998 (a).

"An Ethics for the New Surveillance", The Information Society, vol. 14, no. 3. 1998 (b).

Muir, W.K. Police: Streetcorner Politicians. Chicago: Univ. of Chicago Press, 1977.

Nadelmann, E. "The DEA In Europe" in Fijnaut, C. and Marx, G Undercover: Police Surveillance in Comparative Perspective. The Hague: Kluwer International, 1995

Orwell, G 1984. New York: Harper Perennial Library, 1998.

Shearing, C. and Stenning, P.C. (eds.) Private Policing. Beverly Hills, Ca.: Sage, 1987.

Shelley, L. Policing Soviet Society. New York: Routledge, 1994.

Silver, A. "The Demand for Order in Civil Society: A Review of Some Themes in the History of Urban Crime, Police, and Riots." In The Police, edited by D. Bordua. New York: Wiley, 1969.

Skolnik, J. and J. Fyfe, Above the Law: Police and the Excessive Use of Force. New York: Free Press, 1993.

Van Outrive, L. and Cappelle, "Twenty Years of Undercover Policing in Belgium: The Regulation of a Risky Police Practice" in Fijnaut, C. and Marx, G Undercover: Police Surveillance in Comparative Perspective. The Hague: Kluwer International, 1995.

Glossary

Democratic Police A publicly accountable police force subject to the rule of law and embodying respect for human dignity which can intervene in citizen's lives only under limited and carefully controlled conditions in an equitable fashion. What about equity?

Police Neutrality Equal enforcement of the law focusing on the behavior of the suspect, regardless of irrelevant characteristics such as ethnicity, gender, class and life style, or the personal attitudes of the enforcer. However, since the laws themselves (even if universally enforced) do not equally reflect the interests of all social groups, to those not favored by, or disagreeing with, the laws, police behavior will not appear neutral.

The New Surveillance New technological means of social control such as computer dossiers, video surveillance, electronic location monitoring, drug testing, and DNA analysis which vastly expand the human senses in their ability to covertly cross barriers of space, distance, darkness, and time that have traditionally protected liberty as well as rule violation.

* Revision of paper originally appearing in The Encyclopedia of Democracy 1995.

3 William Bratton's Perspective on Democratic Policing*

Eli B. Silverman

Abstract

Nations that are emerging from military dictatorships and communist regimes intentionally created structurally dysfunctional justice systems. It may take years of rising crime rates in order to make the necessary changes in their policing systems. The media plays multiple roles in opening up police organizations and making them more transparent. Although training has improved during the last 30 years, training is the Achilles heel of democratic policing in America.

Key Words: Accountability, police responsiveness, transparency

Democratic Policing—Its Meaning

As a consultant who frequently travels abroad to Latin America, Asia, Europe and South Africa, the phrase "democratic policing" has become increasingly interesting and meaningful to me. I have found a marked contrast between the *effectiveness* and *competency* of the police of these emerging democracies and the police in the United States, where we have a more mature constitutional democracy. Nations that are emerging from military dictatorships and communist regimes have often intentionally created constitutional and structurally dysfunctional criminal justice systems to ensure that the power of the police and prosecutors is limited. Now that these nations are emerging, it may take years of rising crime rates to justify and bring about necessary changes in their policing practices and policies to make them more effective systems. These nations see the United States as a potential role model for policing practices that are effectively confronting difficult issues such as police corruption, racial tension and crime.

This interest in the components and merits of the democratic policing philosophy has recently become a staple of international conversation, competing with the "community policing" philosophy which has received the bulk of professional attention during the last several years. There may be an interesting tug-of-war as to which of these two terms emerge as the most fashionable, but in any event, they both represent policing rooted in democracy, in which government is "of, by and for the people" and in which power is constitutionally invested in the government and the police through an election. We should be striving for policing that reflects the idealism of democracy but at the same time ensures that democracy will survive. Democratic policing exists to enforce the rules and laws that effectively control the activities of all citizens who cede some of their freedom for the common good.

Transparent Policing

Democratic policing is really *transparent policing*. This is in stark contrast to traditional patterns of policing closed to the outside world and internally compartmentalized, impeding the sharing of vital information. But in the 21st century, the true embodiment of democratic policing will be organizations whose transparency ensures a minimum of secrecy and a maximum of accountability, responsiveness and openness. During the last ten years I have seen more transparency and openness on the part of many police organizations than at any other time in history. During my twenty six years in law enforcement, and as head of five major police organizations, it was a policy that I embraced and encouraged. It not only improved the effectiveness of those organizations but improved community and media trust and support.

Police Accountability

The very essence of democratic policing is *accountability* to the public. As public and media demand more accountability from policing, openness and transparency will grow throughout the United States. There continues to be a growing debate about the need for, and the effectiveness of, the multitude of systems and mechanisms currently employed in order to hold police accountable to the public for their actions (or inactions).

Over the last several years in New York City, for example, the issue has taken on an added dimension in light of the controversial police shooting of two unarmed black men (Amadou Diallo and Patrick Dorismond) and the brutal beating of another black man (Abner Louima).[1] In the minds of a large segment of the minority community in New York City, and many in the media, these tragic incidents have raised unresolved doubts as to the responsiveness and accountability of the NYPD. In an effort to address these concerns a vast array of investigations have been initiated by the U. S. Department of Justice, the New York State's Attorney General, local District Attorneys, the City Council, and others. Earlier incidents had resulted in the creation of an ineffective Civilian Compliance Review Board (CCRB) and a Mayor's Committee to Combat Police Corruption.

In the United States, with its over 14,000 separate police agencies and its tradition of decentralized policing, the debate is intensifying. A consensus on the most appropriate way to organize and operate monitoring agencies is unlikely to quickly emerge given the diversity and multiplicity of police agencies and oversight mechanisms, but there is growing public and political consensus and impetus about the need for outside monitoring – which most law enforcement agencies and their leaders still resist.

Whatever their effectiveness, the efforts of many outside monitoring agencies to hold police organizations accountable for performance, abuse, brutality and corruption is a perfectly healthy example of democratic and transparent policing. In contrast, the absence of internal police monitoring subject to outside monitoring can be seen as emblematic of non-transparent police organizations that concomitantly lack public trust. We should be encouraged by recent trends such as national accreditation standards for police agencies as well as the growth of media and public demands for accountability, usually in the form of review boards. The challenge is to make them as effective as possible to address and resolve the identified deficiencies that created their need in the first place.

There is no rosetta stone for the perfect oversight mechanism, nor is there any panacea for the problems which they are meant to address. The nature of the monitoring apparatus will often depend on the level of trust between the public and police at any particular period. In a democratic society, the public ultimately has to decide the level and nature of outside monitoring which is necessary to satisfy their concerns about police responsiveness and accountability. Police leaders, however, can go a long way toward addressing and minimizing those concerns by the transparency of their own policies and actions.

Role of the Media

As previously mentioned, the media are a significant ingredient in the mix of ingredients necessary to bring about and ensure democratic policing. The media actually plays multiple roles (investigative and informational) in opening up police organizations and making them more transparent. The reality is that most people gain their impressions of crime and the police through the media. Recent events in New York City illustrate the crucial role of the media in shaping public perceptions. Despite the Mayor's and Police Commissioner's repeated recounting of the significant decline in the use of police force and citizen complaints, there is widespread community and media reluctance to accept these seemingly indisputable statistics. The Mayor and Commissioner are frustrated by the public's failure to grasp this reality. But it is my belief that it is the City's and the police department's failure to open up the police department to the media, watchdogs, and various public officials that engenders mistrust and a feeling that there may well be something to hide.

Training and Democratic Policing

Although training has improved during the last 30 years, training is still the Achilles heel of democratic policing in America. No police department provides sufficient training either for recruits or officers. Most recruit training spans a 4-6 month period. In-service training primarily focuses on re-certification of firearms and CPR skills or specialized topics. But training rarely reflects the enormous strides in modern policing's ability to prevent, detect, and solve crime. The technological advances in crime mapping, compstat systems and DNA are frequently not adequately addressed in most police training and skills development. The ultimate irony is that even as American policing has finally accepted responsibility for crime control and has begun to learn how to prevent and control it, most police departments, and certainly colleges and schools of criminal justice, do not teach crime prevention skills.

As important, in the 21st century there will be the need for more public investment in upgrading police technology and technology-related training to serve a multi-cultural society. Technological training needs to be viewed as essential productivity-enhancing and performance shaping tools in the police officer's toolbox. Technology can advance democratic policing by restraining and deterring improper police-citizen interaction through more extensive use of video and audio equipment. Furthermore, in an era when racial profiling is of great concern, racial tensions and incidents can be reduced and controlled by more extensive use of 'swipe card' technology on drivers licenses and in police cars that automatically indicate the driver's race, thereby negating an officer's ability to either intentionally or erroneously record that information. These are just a few examples. Additional improvements in these critical areas will increase trust and respect on the part of the public as police continually strive through training and technology to improve their practices and procedures.

Recruitment

Recruitment is another key factor in fostering democratic policing. More and more police agencies are requiring a college education. In New York City for example, two years of college or its equivalency is helping to promote a more diverse and educated pool of recruits with the appropriate skills and sensitivities critical for service in a multicultural society. But in a time of tight labor markets where there are literally millions more job opportunities than there are candidates in certain age groups from which the police must recruit, new efforts are necessary. Those efforts must focus on attracting more candidates from minority communities, as well as women and gays. Candidates with multi-language skills must also be aggressively recruited.

William Bratton, President of the New York City based consulting firm, The Bratton Group LLC.*, is a consultant, public speaker, columnist, and commentator on issues of public safety, security, and criminal justice throughout the United States and abroad. He served as Police Commissioner for the New York City and Boston Police Departments and re-engineered five major police agencies. His experiences are described in his autobiography* Turnaround, *published by Random House.*

Bratton

Eli B. Silverman, Ph.D, is a Professor in the Department of Law, Police Science and Criminal Justice Administration at John Jay College of Criminal Justice, City University of New York. He has

previously served with the U.S. Department of Justice and the National Academy of Public Administration in Washington D. C. and was a Visiting Exchange Professor at the Police Staff College in Bramshill, England. He was head of the Section on Public Budgeting and Finance of the American Society for Public Administration. He has served as consultant to numerous criminal justice agencies. The author of many articles, his most recent book is NYPD Battles Crime: Innovative Strategies in Policing, *Boston: Northeastern*

Silverman   *University Press, 1999.*

References

Bratton, William and Knobler Peter, (1998), Turnaround: How America's Top Cop Reversed the Crime Epidemic, New York: Random House.

Segel Frederick F., (1997), The Future Once Happened Here, New York: Free Press.

Silverman Eli B.,(1999), NYPD Battles Crime: Innovative Strategies in Policing, Boston: Northeastern University Press.

Notes

1   Controversy erupted in August 1997 when four NYPD officers were charged with torturing, sodomizing and brutalizing Abner Louima, a Haitian immigrant, inside a police precinct where a wooden stick was shoved in his rectum and then his mouth. In the first of at least two trials, one officer pleaded guilty and was sen-

tenced to 30 years while a second officer was convicted of assisting the first officer. Passions were further inflamed after the February 1999 killing of an unarmed West African street peddler in the foyer of his Bronx New York apartment building. Four members of the New York City Police Department's elite Street Crime Unit (SCU) fired 41 bullets, with 19 striking Amadou Diallo who arrived from Guinea almost three years ago and had no criminal record.

* Based on an interview done by Prof. Eli Silverman with former Police Commissioner William Bratton, August 10, 2000, at the request of the editors.

4 Police, Policing, State and Society: Some Basic Problems in Protecting Human and Civil Rights

Menachem Amir

Abstract

The relationship between police, policing and democracy is full of conflicts and paradoxes. This stems from the involvement of police in politics. Police and policing are not a-political. Police at times serve political interests. Police are said to be the defenders of democracy, but at times the police collaborate in attacking and even in destroying the democratic system of society and government. This paper discusses the social and normative aspects and kinds of democracy which the police often conceive as restraining "efficient" police work. The tension between police and the democratic process becomes most distinct when the totalitarian social and political regimes are in the process of transformation towards a democracy. The situation of the police and policing under these conditions and processes are discussed. The belief is also noted that"democratic policing" and "democratic police" will optimally be attained.

Key Words: Accountability, democratic rules, democratic policing, democratic police, police in a democracy, equity, ethics, types of democracy

Introduction

The framework and contexts within which discussions concerning the police and their policing takes place are related to various aspects of the relationship between the Police and the State, (specifically, the standing and role of the police) as well as its responsibility and the control of its actions. This article will not focus on the normative, legal and philosophic facets of this relationship, notwithstanding the importance of these considerations. Rather it is posited that accountability of, and the control over, the police continues to be the most important aspects of this issue. In simplistic terms: to whom and with respect to what is the police responsible and accountable for its actions?

A healthy, functioning, democratic State is a centralized, flexible and strong entity which possesses a variety of resources. The most important resource being the budget. Max Weber already remarked that whoever controls the budget controls the State. The State also maintains the symbolic status of *exclusivity*, especially concerning the use of coercion, including physical force, vis à vis other organizations and individuals which function in society. While the State (the political society) is the primary source of coercive control, it nevertheless operates within the frameworks of civil society, which are the primary sources of consensual hegemony between various groups in the public arena. On the one hand there is the State. It has an organizational function with respect to governing systems, represents the will and the need for central control, constitutes a system of rule enforcement, and is responsible for providing the conditions for the legitimacy of the government. On the other hand, there is "society," especially democratic society, which acknowledges the existence of special ideologies and interests of various groups and of individuals. These groups may even compete with the interests of the State, question and warn of the power concentrated in the hands of the State, and may even attempt, under certain conditions, to undermine, weaken and control this State power. Political terrorist groups are an example of this.

Civil society, in contrast to the coercive power of the State, seeks *consensual control* of its members based on tolerance of different and often conflicting interests of various groups within society. While the police serves the State, in a democratic society it is not expected to serve the State's specific institutions (such as the government or political parties). The police are expected only to protect them. Thus, there exist autonomies (and social arrangements) which are inter-related:

- society, which strives for relative independence from the central control of the State, and
- the State, which demands independence from society.

This independence is necessary to enable the State to exert, under certain conditions, its exclusive ability to use force both internally (primarily through the police) in order to maintain the interests and continuity of the State, as well as externally, to defend its borders (through the army). The State exerts this force in order to protect social structures and to enable them to achieve their goals. At the cultural-symbolic level, the State defends and validates the definition of membership in the State (citizen subjects, non-citizens and "undesirables") and also maintains and protects its symbols (flag) and the symbols of civil society (memorial days, etc.). Thus, the police functions in the arena where society and the State converge, and as such it reflects the relations between them. Subsequently, research about the police constitutes one of the sources for understanding state-society relations (Bayley, 1990; Jones at al, 1994)

The above analysis describes a complex, dynamic reality: the police in a democratic, modern society must contend with a difficult situation owing to the fact that, in effect, it serves two masters. On the one hand, the police is employed as an operational branch of the State and is responsible for maintaining public order and the law. On the other hand, the police constitutes an entity which is also required to protect and serve the needs of individuals and the demands of the organized public (community and civil society). The police face an inherent potential conflict, which may occasionally emerge between the State and society, due to the multiplicity of social groups, and their different (and often conflicting) interests which make it difficult, if not impossible, to equitably enforce the law.

The scope and level of police activities depend on:

- the relative power of the State and society, and
- the character and the outcome of the discourse between society (at the community level) and the police as an organization.

Underlying these various tensions is the conflict between the supremacy of the rule of law, equitable enforcement of the law and the unavoidable acquiescence to sectarian political demands. Under the European system the State "wins", while under the British and American systems, society and the community prevail (Bayley, 1990; Mawby, 1990). The police is undoubtedly an agent of the State. Some even claim that it represents and attempts to protect and promote the interests of the upper classes and their desire to control the other classes (for a discussion of this Marxist outlook see Grimshaw and Jefferson 1992).

Another perspective, seemingly neutral but functional, views the police (via law enforcement and maintenance of the social order) as a means of institutionalizing the central values of society which are considered to be vital (Parsons, 1961). Yet another approach, which constitutes the ideological foundation of community police claims that the police solely or mainly represent, or should represent, the interests of society (community), and those of the various groups within it.

Police and Politics

The discussion of the relationship between the institutions of government (not the State as a whole), society, and police, raises the question concerning existing and possible political[1] involvement of the police. This issue, hinted at earlier, will be further elaborated.

All research pertaining to this issue indicates that *all policing is political*, with varying degrees of police political involvement in the political system and in political processes. The nature of government and of the State does not enable the police to remain politically neutral (see for example Bayley, 1982; Brewer, 1994; Brodeur, 1983, 1977; Gamson and Yuchtman, 1977; Reiner, 1983). Research documents the shattered illusion of liberal police and policing in a democratic and liberal State (Grimshaw and Jefferson, 1987; Huggins, 1988). Moreover, processes of police centralization and militarization (Waddington, 1991; Jefferson, 1993, 1994) were observed in England and in other Western countries (Uglow, 1992; Fielding, 1984; Reiner, 1983, 1992a, 1992b). Policing was found to be political; i.e., it was neither detached nor was it independent of specific government institutions such as political parties. Expressions of a political disposition and a tendency towards biases, even racism, towards minority groups were found among police officers and police units (Lee, 1981).

Various aspects of the contentions that a relationship exists between police, policing and politics or the involvement of police in politics are summarized below in increasing order of severity:

- Police officers hold political opinions and beliefs which affect their behavior
- Policing is in itself related to the political discourse - it is an issue in political party debates and manipulations. According to a more extreme outlook the police is viewed as taking a side in the political debate: of a certain political party, usually the ruling party. In other words, the police is directly involved in party politics.
- The relationship between police and politics is also expressed in the debate concerning the national budget and its allocation. The police not only receives a share of the budget, which is both determined by and reflects politi-

cal as well as additional priorities, its ability to receive a suitable budget which will meet its needs may also depend on its willingness to serve, unequivocally, the needs of a certain political party (Reiner 1922). The police may also accumulate a relatively large degree of power, even to the point where it can maneuver and influence the debate concerning budgetary priorities.

- The relationship between police and government policy. The police not only enforces government policy by enforcing laws about which public consensus does not always exist, it sometimes actively supports certain policies and laws, displaying a bias against the ideological and organizational-political party opposition to official government policy (Findlay and Zvekic, eds. 1993). The police may thus support the solution of certain social "problems" as they are defined by the government, and the means which the latter views as appropriate for their solution (drugs, gambling, immigration policy, etc.).

- Finally, police behavior, mainly in situations which are visible to the public such as political gatherings and demonstrations (Marshall 1992;15), influence the public's perception of the government and its institutions and as a result indirectly affects party politics. In most cases such police behavior is not only intended to receive a larger share of the budget, but also to create a positive image of the police as an organization and to cover up inappropriate police behavior.

In summary, the police is neither apolitical nor independent of government institutions. Rather it is a part of them. The police is influenced by these institutions and often actively influences them. As such, it is one more institution in the political system which is, at times, involved in advancing the struggle *against* the policy of various governmental institutions (economic, political, religious, etc. (Fijnaut and Marx, 1995)).

The conditions which determine the political dependence or independence of the police and its degree of political involvement (either forced, or initiated by its commanders) are:

- The *State's and society's characteristics* (the government's degree of centralization, the stability and continuity of political power, social and political influences, and the degree of government involvement in social conflicts and rifts).

- *Situational factors* such as the state of crime and social disorder, which in instances of mass behavior, may get out of control and determine the degree of the use of coercion and force intervention and the control rendered to the police under such conditions.

- *Accountability, monitoring and control mechanisms*, and the role and meaning of accountability (personal and systemic) which exist in the State and in society with respect to the behavior of the police and police officers.

It is evident that every police organization in a liberal and democratic State must create a balance between total dependence on the government and its independence. This is critical if it is to be able-to provide equitable and efficient policing, which will be unbiased, non-discriminating, non-violent and free of corruption. The following section will discuss the issue of police and policing in a democratic form of government and society whose mandated essence is the protection of human, civil and social rights..

Police and Democracy: Some Basic Problems Critical Issues

A review of the theoretical and empirical literature concerning the relationship between "Police and Democracy" can easily stir up a sense of pessimism and cynicism. The literature presents conflicts and paradoxes in the attempts to create democratic police and policing, especially in crisis situations such as mass riots or in instances where police officers attempt to be "efficient" in fighting crime (Waddington, 1994). An in depth examination of the literature reveals several assumptions, some explicit and others implicit, concerning this relationship.

- The first assumption is that the police organization, as perceived by civilians, is an anomaly in a democratic-liberal society. For this reason it is also labeled "*the ambivalent force*" (see Neiderhoffer and Blumberg 1979). The police, according to this approach, views democracy as an "*interfering mechanism*" in its efforts to maintain public order and to fight crime. It is however not as the liberal stance proclaims that the State and its organs, including the police, is just a "*night watch,*" given its ongoing mandate in a democracy to fight crime and to maintain public order. Moreover, the police perceives the democratic values upheld and governed by the law, as well as the regulations of the police organization itself, as " *technical-bureaucratic matters*" or as too "soft," permissive and impractical, hindering efficient and adequate law enforcement. This approach maintains that line officers often create "*dramas of legality*" in order to explain the use of force or the violation of rights, and/or to deceive the public and the police command (Manning 1997). Such a portrayal of the police underscores its ambivalent and even cynical attitude which often ignores equitable law enforcement aimed at protecting civil rights (Goldstein, 1977). Such an approach does not , however, negate the legitimacy of the democratic regime. But in its name police officers protect the citizens by violating laws.

- Another aspect of the relationship between police and democracy relates to the fact that democratic values require *transparency*, control of society over all government and public agencies, including the police, and of course accountability to the legal institutions, the State, the legislature, and the public. The argument in favor of a "democratic policing" calls for a police organization which is subject to the law that defines and protects values of civil and individual rights which often conflict with values of pragmatism and efficiency as well as with budget limitations. Those who receive a service in lieu of taxes paid, not only have the right to investigate and monitor the efficiency, quality and effectiveness of the service, but also to examine whether it adheres to the law and whether or not the service which is provided is based on principles of equity, equality, justice, personal honesty and integrity.

It should be noted that a democratic regime does not necessarily mean "democratic policing" nor does "service oriented policing" necessarily mean that this is a "democratic police". These kinds of policing can be deployed by a quasi-military police as is the case in Israel or in many police departments in the USA. Police organization, as a service-provider, is not exempt from these noted demands.

Police ambivalence towards democracy also stems from the fact that this organization received the mandate and responsibility to perform tasks and activities which are almost impossible to execute consistently and simultaneously, and often conflict with or contradict each other (Manning, 1977). For example, the police is required to protect and promote a democratic social order consistent with the democratic structure and outlook of the government. This includes democratic and móral values of both individual and group human and civil rights and the means to protect these rights in a fair and honest manner and may therefore create a tension between these values and the rights and interests of the public in general and some sections of the public as well as the government in particular. But then another conflict arises. This can occur when the police are retained by the State and civil society to protect them, are used as an arm of the government to execute its governing duties while also using the police to enforce illegitimate, corrupt, corrupting, and even anti-democratic policies. Police is called upon to defend democracy but it can also be considered a threat to the democratic system by serving a particular interest of social and political powers. For example in totalitarian regimes the police are called upon to police political dissent as a "crime" without having to be accountable to the public. In addition they may even become partners to certain "publics" and carry out "vigilante policing."

- The second approach claims that occasionally the police may even constitute a threat to democracy (Marx, 1988). This approach bases its argument on the fact that the police organization is very similar to the army, with the authority to use force against individuals and groups, Thus, it can potentially serve the government and political forces by the mere fact that it is subject to the edicts of the government and the influence of powerful groups in society (Reiss, 1971), and may take a side (and use force) in political and party struggles.

It is important to remember that it is inherently difficult for the police to function according to democratic norms given that it must maintain a level of control over individuals and organizations, using physical force if necessary, (as is often defined by the police), to ensure the maintenance of a liberal-democratic state and society. However, the public, or certain public sectors, are not willing to submit to the "use of power" in the broad sense of the term, especially unnecessary and unreasonable physical force. This, in turn, creates fear, suspicion and mistrust in police officers and in the police as an organization, and undermines the police legitimacy, as well as that of the regime, which the police often symbolize (Ulrick, 1991).

The secrecy and biases involved in policing, as well as the skepticism itself, as to whether police officers can make informed decisions (in light of their background and training), also raise such misgivings and fears. These fears are heightened by failure to apply internal and external controls to police behavior.

Another approach, especially predominant in established democracies, assumes that democracy and its processes have, as it were a, "guaranteed existence" and as such that they are not fragile. They therefore are not in need of protection (Sherman, 1993). There is a sense of having reached the ultimate state - a governmental "Nirvana". However, such an outlook does not take into account that democracy must not only be protected from the forces which received the mandate to protect it - the controlling political system which include the police, the judicial system, but also from private police and security enterprises and the "defense industry," including the armed services. Some of these may even threaten the police monopoly to use force.

In this context, varying definitions of *"policing,"* which go beyond mere official police control of behavior or situations, are required. Moreover, while the police is part of the law enforcement and judicial system, supposedly controlled by democratic norms, laws and democratic political arrangements, it is "atypical" within this system. It is the largest, most expensive, most prominent and most professionally diverse organization, with the widest sphere of discretion-making compared to other parts of the law enforcement and judicial system. (Wilson, 1968). The police can and do even constitute a force which creates "street justice" (Sykes, 1977; Muir, 1986).

An examination of the history of the first modern police force in England, in 1829, indicates that the police organization was established and was expected to be an a-political and value-neutral, even sterile, entity, except for the democratic values which it serves by virtue of the fact that it is mandated to uphold the law (and the constitution if it exists).

The police, as previously noted, often view these values as constraining, even interfering, with the achievement of its goals which it perceives as being the essence of its mission. These include, for example, law enforcement and maintaining public order as values unto themselves (Goldstein 1977;112).

Whereas the police organization is obligated and required to enforce all laws equitably, society or some sections of the population are not always interested in this stance (e.g. gambling or drug related crimes). Moreover, the police itself does not want to act equitably and can not always do so. This could imply, in effect, their being indifferent to political considerations and to a social reality characterized by a multiplicity of groups, some culturally and politically opposed to each other. Therefore, police officers in the field, police commanders and police as an organization, need to compromise. Occasionally this means deceiving citizens with which it comes in contact (e.g. offenders or witnesses), and even to cooperate with offenders, and to resort, occasionally, to other actions which are neither democratic nor professional (Delattre, 1989; Marx, 1988). The police ,of course, invests efforts to act professionally and properly and also to "look good" in terms of democratic values. This may be done at times for the sake of receiving resources, legitimacy and cooperation from the public. However, even under 'community policing', police can and do demand their right to carry out aggressive-based, 'zero tolerance' policing which paradoxically undermines the police wish and need for broader legitimacy (Crank, 1994; Dennis, ed. 1997).

Definitions and Distinctions

The recurring use of the term "democracy" must be defined for the purpose of our discussion. The discourse spans from Plato to Lenin with various societies with different forms of government claiming that they are "democratic." The term usually refers to:

- 'democracy' as *a form of government*, in other words a representative parliamentary system with institutionalized procedures for the change of government (elections, etc.); but also of *accountability* of the government services (including the police) to the legislature (the "people"), the judiciary and to the law.

- 'democracy' as *a value system* within which the government exists and functions. In other words, a framework of democratic values which are linked to a network of individual and group human, civil and social rights, dignity, justice, and which guarantee the freedom of expression, and the right to organize and to act within group frameworks which determine -based on consensual agreement - government policies and that of its institutions (including the police); These value systems are constantly evolving and being enlarged given that democracy is a dynamic process.

- 'democracy' as *a way of life*, characterized by tolerance of, and compromise between, demands of individuals and groups (Grimshaw & Jefferson, 1987: 22-20; Reiss, 1970; Shadmi, 1994; Waterman & Burfiend, 1991, 19; Souryal, 1992, 296-298); and

- democracy as *a process*, including monitoring and accountability, the right for redress of one of the State's machinery (i.e. the police organization).

Some scholars differentiate between two pure and analytically distinct "basic" approaches to "democratic values": the liberal, secular, parliamentary approach which emphasizes individual rights, and the Community approach. The former has received more attention and constitutes the core of, and a model for, the democratic outlook (Gray 1995; Xii).

The liberal-individualistic political approach emphasizes the following values and principles:

- *Universal human dignity* and *civil political rights* and *a social democratic* approach which are not to be denied, barring emergency situations. These rights are anchored in the concept and the status of citizenship, and constitute a barrier and a haven from government arbitrariness and oppression. Each citizen has equal rights and duties, the most important of which are personal freedom which is a basic and just condition, as well as other freedoms such as freedom of speech and freedom of gathering and organization (Gray, 1995: 55). They are not to be denied except under special conditions specified by the law and the constitution (Rawls, 1971).

- *Maximum equality, justice and equity*, in light of the differences (social, economic and other) between people and groups, while taking into consideration budgetary and other limitations (Henkin. 1978).

- *Recognition of inherent variation and differences* between people and groups (the right to be different) and acknowledges social and cultural pluralism, alongside the supremacy and unqualified rights of the individual and his/her uniqueness, which take precedent over any particularistic value (e.g. religious). There exists, as a result, a policy of minority representation and protection against arbitrariness and tyranny of the majority, as well as different but equitable policies of government agencies towards people and groups within the framework of the law (Bent, 1974), which is coupled with the central democratic principle of the majority rule through representation arrangements (or the parliamentary system). This approach also acknowledges the need, under conditions specified by the law (or the constitution), to restrict or curtail democracy under certain conditions. These legally-based restrictions are to be applied to *all* individuals and systems, including limited temporary infringement on their freedom;

- *Restraints imposed on the government* based on consensus, free choice and control of the majority, which may even apply to the legislator and to government representatives, agencies and civil servants, as defined by the law and/ or constitution. Hence, *democracy is the rule of law and not the rule of the people.* It is government by the people and for the people *through the law* (and other democratically agreed upon control arrangements). While the statement is accepted as a truism, it should be remembered that people are enacting and enforcing laws and this does not automatically guarantee democratic laws and their enforcement.

A new and different approach (although its roots are time-honored) is that of "Community democracy," (Bell, 1993; Shadmi, 1994; Wallach, 1989; Waltzer, 1994) which represents the next stage following the emphasis on the rights of groups and minorities within the community.

"No man is an island," said the poet, as the individual is not only the product and a member of the group to which he or she belongs, but also of the community within which he lives. Therefore, not only governing arrangements, but also each and every individual and group must care and be responsible for the *"general good"* (Wallach 1988). According to this viewpoint, the liberal approach is "too individualistic." Alongside the supremacy of basic individual and civil rights, the continued emergence of individual "rights", to the point where they are trivialized (allowing, for example, burning the national flag, total prohibition on smoking, etc.), engenders disregard of community welfare and of the public interest. There are those, among the advocates of the individualistic approach, who ignore conflicts between groups with "rights," thus separating the "private" and the "public" domain of the public. Supporters of the "community democracy" also claim that justice and equality are values which are dependent on historic and social contexts as well as on "culture" (values, morality and practices). Such values have ascendancy over, or correspond to, the law and to other control arrangements pertaining to the behavior of individuals and groups. These are the 'informal control mechanisms' which are often more efficient than that of the rule of law and its mechanisms (Bell, 1993). Additionally, each community shares common values such as the security of the group and of the government itself. It is useful to remember that in certain democratic regimes there are some groups which do not share the mainstream social norms and may actually opt to challenge or even to topple the rulers, even using undemocratic means (i.e. the USA during the Vietnam war; the anti-nuclear protestors in England; the "drug culture").

An additional claim is that under extreme democratic pressure towards individual and social rights, society and the State in effect weaken and undermine their power, because these "rights" entail elements which defy and challenge their authority. Extremists of the community approach who, upholding the "protection of society and the State," create tendencies towards the status quo, even to the point of hostility towards the forces of "disorder" which are built into the democratic-liberal structure. The democratic pressure for equitable law enforcement conflicts with the commitment and policy from which it stems - to cater to the differing needs of various "publics." This, *ipso facto,* implies different policing policies towards theses publics.

The *community democracy* approach, its interpretation of democracy and its derived ramifications emphasize:

- A distinction - as in the liberal approach - between State and civil society. The police is one of the "brokering" institutions and linking arrangements between them remains. It is understood that the police serve *both* State and civil society as defined within the framework of the law.

- The right of the governed to know about the actions of government, its policies and underlying assumptions. In other words, 'transparency' of government actions and public knowledge and acknowledgement of these actions.

- Controls on government are a right and even an obligation of the governed. All government agencies and civil servants are accountable to the citizens (and towards the law). The responsibility vis à vis the public is even larger in the case of those who have the power to enforce behavior and punish individuals in the name of the law. The most important or primary entity representing the official enforcement system is the police. The police must operate under the rule of law and must be subordinate to the justice system. The police is required to serve the law as a goal unto itself, and to refrain from "flexible", self-defined use of the law for the personal benefit of police officers or for the purpose of achieving organizational goals.

Control by the law, the justice system, public organizations and the media is also aimed at reducing potential inherent risks of "community democracy":

- that of "vigilante" justice and "morality" actions of groups within the community,

- political involvement (which may lead to political corruption of the agencies of government, including the police), and

- invasion of the privacy of community members (see for example Manning, 1995).

There is a danger that undemocratic groups will take advantage of democratic openness to influence government policies and actions, or will even to attempt to overthrow the government.

The extreme analytic depicting of these two differing approaches to democracy, in the value-moral sense, can achieve an equilibrium and support each other through what Walzer (1994) called "*social democracy*". This is basically a set of norms and arrangements which answers, at least at the local level, the needs and rights of the individual, while addressing the more general problems of the community. Individuals and groups in this case are referred to as "*customers*" rather than "*policed*" persons. *Community policing* is one type of police adopting "social democracy" approaches.

The police - as well as every other government agency- in a democracy, is expected to act based on the principles of a democratic, social-moral order, regardless of the specific "order," which we choose to believe in, and the feasibility of its full implementation, in all cases. However, research indicates that in a democratic State there is a clash between the "moral order", which is founded on virtually absolute values and the social order which is based on practical and pragmatic considerations. For example, special situations, special community needs and conditions, and bureaucratic, budgetary and other demands which require differentiated law enforcement. The fact that the police employs its authority and power to infringe on the various freedoms of individuals and groups creates conflicts which in turn raise dilemmas for police officers and the police as an organization, for example with respect to "equality" in the quality of policing both as a value and as a type of concrete policing.

Aristotle in his *Ethics* defined "*equality*" as similar treatment of, and attitudes towards, similar people. However, people are neither similar nor equal, and the democratic principle therefore establishes the principle of "*equity*." Research has indicated that individual police officers, police units, and sometimes even the policy of the police organization, are biased and inequitable. Police officers create and maintain an exclusionary stance regarding which people and groups are more "desirable" or "less desirable", based on their perception of and attitude towards them as posing an actual or potential threat to police (officers and organization). This can and does result in inequitable police behavior which challenges the law (Goldstein, 1977; Lee, 1981; Van Mastright, Uldriks, 1991). A "pure" universal or standard form of policing is not feasible and is neither desirable to police officers in the field nor to the police organization for several reasons:

- Unrelated to the law, and which are rather based on the characteristics and conditions of the 'policing' environments as well as on considerations of efficiency and the interests of police officers in the field and on the police organization (Manning and Van Maanen, 1978; Walker 1989);

- Because police activities are serving different and special individuals and groups in the community, which produces non-uniform policing or

- Because differential policing treatment is exercised in order to prevent the deterioration of certain situations into violence and disorder (Skolnick, 1966:6; Muir 1977).

- Because private police and security services are expanding and challenge the State monopoly of curtailing liberty (South, 1988).

These situations are characterized by a basic, inherent conflict which exists between law and order. The challenge remains to maintain social order as a general principle, but within the bounds of the law and of democratic values. The ideology of liberal democracy emphasizes initiative and "flexibility" rather than blind obedience to rules, while the "rule of law" emphasizes civil duties (alongside civil rights), and limitations on both the initiatives and "flexibility" of law enforcement personnel. Such a situation, by definition, is unstable given the actual and potential conflicts associated with the various interest groups whose existence is guaranteed in a democracy. The need to handle differing situations and to react to varying expectations of different groups requires that police officers:

- behave differently in different situations based on their judgement as to which values should be emphasized and which arise from the very basic choice or maintaining the balance between the need

- to obey the law in full, (personal rights versus "the public good", equity versus necessity; conscience versus convenience, unqualified law enforcement versus due process).

These considerations are based on the police officer's sufficient, sensitive understanding of the concepts "*liberty*," "*justice*," "*equality*," *social order*, *individual's rights* and *security* or *public order and safety*. These concepts are, for many, obfuscated. This makes it easy to explain and justify law and value violations which are carried out in their name, as well as types of interpretations provided by police officers as to what action should be taken. On occasion these may even involve circumventing the law (Davis Braswell at al, 1991; Klockars, 1979, 1980). Questions pertaining to the definition of "order," who defines "order," and how much "order" is imperative, and for how long, as well as the nature of "law and order enforcement" (strict, permissive, immediate, gradual, etc.), remains. Given that the conception of "law and order" varies in different public sectors and at different times, only serves to stress the importance of the questions asked and the aspects discussed above.

Another problem relates to the perceptions of law enforcement and control being associated with "oppression," or with frequent violations of due process and civil rights (Braithwaite, 1989:151-158; Packer, 1968). However, it is important to remember that law enforcement and maintaining the 'social order' are a social service, and that both include elements of crime prevention (Cohen & Sampson, 1988; Sherman, 1992, 1993) or minimizing the harm resulting from crime (Wilson, 1988). Moreover, "social order" is not determined by a clear and fixed list of rules, but rather it is a product of processes, political decisions, negotiations and compromises, and policies which are experience-tested. When the latter concepts are not clear and/or are not agreed upon, then the police often formulates its own definition of what it expects with respect to public order (and other areas). This is a paradoxical situation, because it reinforces behaviors which the police make an effort to prevent and to control when manifested by the public. The police may even request legal-judicial approval to temporarily violate a law for the purpose of maintaining law and order (for example granting permission to delinquents to commit offences within a police constructed informant network , e.g. Marx, 1988).

Line police officers and their commanders can and do view democratic principles as "ideals," as a statement of intent, as an available ritual of consensual agreement for placating public demands due to the following empirically-based considerations:

- the work conditions of police officers,
- the effect of the bureaucratic, almost military model of the police organization,
- the professional culture of the police organization and of police persons,
- as well as the limited national budget allocated to the police.

Consequently, it is claimed that the police have failed to integrate democratic values into policing, despite the lip service it pays to democratic values and its obligation to support and protect them.

Disregard of behavior norms dictated by democratic values may also stem from the social, ethnic-class, gender-biased backgrounds of many police. These effects, under certain conditions, do not constitute a suitable foundation for the development and/or maintenance of democratic-liberal attitudes. In many cases, police officers are not trained, intellectually and emotionally, to a commitment to democratic norms and their implementation. Moreover, the working conditions[2] of police officers can and do also contribute to this problem. As a result, police officers often assume the need for immediate control of people and situations, as well as for the use of force against people in order to compel them to surrender to police authority. The media reflects this state of affairs when it glorifies tough, strict and efficient police officers representing the "Sheriff

John Wayne", the "Dirty Harry Policeman" syndrome and most recently the "zero tolerance" policing (Klockars, 1980).

The relationship between police, democracy and social change are highlighted in situations of social change. Increased frequency and severity of crime have always been considered to be a by-product of social change. This is a known sociological truth related to Durkheim and Merton's theory of *Anomie,* whose manifestations can be witnessed in societies and countries undergoing social and political change. This is especially 'visible' in countries changing from political and economic centralization and political oppression to democracy and liberalism. East European countries, the states of the former USSR, or South American countries are examples of such (Shelley, 1994; Shelley and Vigh, 1995; National Institute of Justice, 1995;Findlay and Zvekic, 1993). Such a change creates a faulty impression among many, including law enforcement agencies. Democracy and its norms, especially various freedoms, tolerance and protection of individual rights, are posited as being the reason for, or at least as, creating the conditions leading to, increased crime, which up until then may have been unexposed. From this perspective democracy makes pro-crime-conditions possible where as non-democracy (authoritarian or totalitarian systems) does not. The reality that in the latter political systems police have to relinquish their former "ends" of their policies and the "means" of policing. This often is blurred. One should free police from a co-existence with the security-military forces while being subjected to the rules of democratic laws. Economic change characterized by increased prosperity, a free market, and abundant consumer products, is also considered to be a factor which increases the frequency of new types of crimes and crime in general. Democracy is then blamed for the disrespect of authority, including that of the police, and for disregard of the law which up until then was the law of the privileged and the corrupt and was exercised in a discriminating and arbitrary manner (See, for example Shelley and Vigh, 1995, for the former eastern bloc). The economic change described above creates more opportunities and targets for criminal activity (Shelley and Vigh, 1995). Under these circumstance, the police is the first organization to be attacked by those who demand change (democracy), by virtue of the fact that it was the political tool of the previous government which ruled without the constraints of the law and human rights. The police loses its legitimacy and credibility, and continues to suffer from this image as long as most of those who served in the former regime continue to fill its ranks. One of the ongoing dilemmas during transitions to democracy is having to rely on experienced police from the former non-democratic system since there aren't enough 'untainted' new ones or a sufficient number of new police candidates to carry out the needed "democratic policing." In these countries, and especially in western States (National Institute of Justice, 1995), the belief exists that "importing" European (especially American) police technology will naturally create 'democratization' of the police and of policing. (Nadelmann, 1993). It is also assumed in the West that everyone wants a democratic police and policing and therefore relations with police organizations in the west that will help clarify the meaning and essence of this concept. These social-political cases failed to distinguish between:

- a 'democratic police' in terms of structure and methods and a professional police organization which is not necessarily democratic,
- a democratic police organization and "democratic policing", and

- a democratic society and a 'democratic police.'

  Moreover, the missionary zeal of the west to establish a multi-party form of government, and as quickly as possible, is a prescription, at least in the first stages of social change, for a sense as well as at times for a condition of anarchy (e.g. for the eastern bloc see Shelley and Vigh, 1995; for South America see Huggins, 1998) for the following reasons:

- It brings to the surface the ethnic, class, religious and geographic divisions which were suppressed under the totalitarian regime.

- During its initial stages, democracy weakens the existing control agencies and arrangements, including the police. These agencies, which lacked legitimacy in the past, lose their deterrence ability, and as a result have difficulties exercising their role.

- It is easier for criminals, both veterans and novices alike, to operate in a democracy because this type of government also requires the police to make "*ineffective compromises* [3]" in enforcing 'law and order' where it was previously supported by both internal security agencies and the army (for example political and police intelligence).

- Hostility towards the police persists, despite the change, especially if many of those who served the past regime (especially at the command level) remain in the force. Even if these individuals are willing to change, their ability to change the system is limited and slow. At the same time, dismissal or voluntary resignation, often of professional police persons and commanders, decreases police efficiency and effectiveness (See Shelley and Vigh 1995 for the eastern bloc).

- The diminishing of police authority, and reduced fear of the police, as well as economic and social changes, increase street crime and previously unknown types of offences. Offences such as drug-related ones, organized crime, prostitution, new types of white-collar crimes, as well as police corruption and violence, previously concealed due to suppressed freedom of the press, are now conspicuous and penetrate public awareness.

- However, legislation of democratic laws is not sufficient to change the police, although such actions set a goal for the new regulatory services, including the police. These actions however fill the symbolic role of the law.

During the initial phases of the democratic change the quality of police work decreases. This is not only because of the lack of trust in the police, a decline in its authority and continued lack of cooperation with it. This also happens because, in many instances, professional police officers and the command are discharged or resign as a result of the democratization processes within the police organization, and some even join the world of organized crime (For Russia see Lombardo, 1995). Police officers who replace them are likely to be insufficiently trained, are not fully inculcated in the inherent 'demands' of democratic values and processes and the police organization can and often does encounter many budget problems which hinder the acquisition of new technologies needed to deal with the quantity and types of new crimes. Moreover, the veterans who remain in the organization find it difficult (if they are at all interested) to change. They believe in professionalism in the sense of skills, not in its moral-value significance.

Hence, the phenomenon of the social change 'paradox' which while generating "more democracy" is challenged, and perhaps threatened, by more crime and a perceptible lack of social order. This paradox also raises the claim that law enforcement, even if it involves violation of rights (for example use of force and violence) may be efficient in maintaining law and order and low crime rates. But it is also a short-lived achievement following reduced fear of the government and the police. On the other hand, the effects of compromise, legitimacy and a tradition of consensual arrangements have long-term consequences in that they engender increased legitimacy and trust in the government and its representatives. Democracies develop slowly, but in order to sustain them, swift and abrupt action must be taken in certain areas. For example, a concentrated campaign against corruption to promote a civil service state administration.

These conditions - in which "civil society" and the demand for its supremacy develop - also highlight another dilemma: what is more important or adverse to society - crime or social disorder? Society is concerned with the problem of crime. The State is troubled by the issue of public order. The police is worried by both. Society demands and the State requires, the police to address *both* crime and the danger of social disorder, especially situations of riots (Shapland and Hobbs, 1989). It is a particularly difficult task for the police in societies undergoing a change from political totalitarianism to democracy to address this task within the framework of democratic values and arrangements. In this context the longing for the old order/regime among a large part of the public as well as the law enforcement agencies, is understandable. The belief that democracy always connotes "good" is not accepted as a truth. As noted above, in a totalitarian regime the police had increased ability to act and to maintain the social order, and as a result the level of street crime was very low. This gives rise to the argument that due to the increased level of crime and social disorder during the transition period, there should be more police and it should be more efficient. However, as Abraham Lincoln already said in the past, "*whoever is willing to lose his freedom for the sake of security will ultimately lose both!*"

We described the potential conflict between a democratic form of government and the police, especially in situations in which the police organization appears to control the law and to employ it for its purposes. We also discussed how the commitment of police officers to the norms of the organization, to the professional group and to personal values may override their commitment to democratic values. Situations exist where disregard of these values is accepted and even institutionalized. In extreme cases, disagreement may involve opposition individuals and police units to government and police policy that are viewed as obstacles hindering efficient and effective policing. 'Death squads' may evolve or groups practicing "street justice" (Huggins, 1991; Steytler, 1993).

Three additional issues need to be noted in this analysis concerning the potential or real problematic relationship between police, government and democratic society:

- democratization of the police organization,

- arrangements defining the relations between the police and the democratic government, and

- finally "democratic policing" in a democratic framework of police organization...

We will briefly address each of these issues:

- There have been several attempts to change the quasi-army structure of the police. In effect these attempts failed (de-centralization of power, etc.), except for instances which have not yet been proven, where a policy of community police and policing has been implemented (see attempts to conceptualize and to democratize the police in Angell (1971). It should be obvious to both leaders and ordinary citizens that creating and maintaining democratic policing requires trust, education and leadership different from those which exist today, as well as openness to a society which maintains democratic values and processes which include police monitoring and control mechanisms.

- Arrangements pertaining to the relations between the police and a democratic regime, aimed at introducing democratic values as guidelines for police policy, and ensuring democratic monitoring of the police have been manifested at three levels (in decreasing order of extremity). These include:

  - enabling community groups to influence police policy (Shadmi, 1994);

  - openness of the police to increased public criticism of its actions and its treatment of deviant behavior of police officers and units, (for example, civilian committees which address programs or complaints against police officers within the framework of police-community relations), and finally

  - full, continuous and comprehensive cooperation between the police and the community, as reflected in the philosophy and practice of community police and policing. (Oliver, 1998)

  - The third question is whether effective policing (which reduces crime rates and the fear of crime, maintains social order and is sensitive to public demands) is at all possible in a democratic society. The experience in the West is not encouraging. (e.g. Manning, 1997)

However, formulators of the idea of "community police" believe that this is not only possible, but also necessary (Trojanowic and Buqueroux, 1994). It is necessary because the police, as an organization, can not ignore democratic values if it strives to receive legitimacy for its existence, its overall policy, and the policing techniques which it claims to be effective. It is also imperative if it aspires to gain public support and cooperation, which are a necessary condition for effective and efficient policing.

A pessimistic and problematic picture has been drawn. However, the discussions and arguments concerning the complex relationship between police and democratic government may be mistaken in presenting the conflicts between them as extreme and abstract differences. Instead, there is a need to recognize that reality poses the need to choose - and accumulate experience in doing so - between a range of options in order to address complex and varying situations which require different types of actions. Awareness and sensitivity to nuances are imperative because it is impossible to define a "pure" principle, or several principles as guidelines for general solutions to different and varying situations. Rather, there is a need for compromises, flexibility and implementing creative decisions. The concept of, and the need for, personal, group and organizational judiciousness and sensitivity to human, civil and social rights of those who are 'policed' is vital. Equally vital and critical is that the law, court decisions, professional ethics and of course democracy (in the sense of values and arrangements) prevail, serving as a guiding and controlling framework.

Supporters of the "community policing" approach, at the local level and as a general and national policy, claim that it embodies an organizational system comprised of both ideas and strategies for action which combine and address, and as such also bridge the presumed conflicts and clashes between police and democracy. These ideas address the need to protect and develop the public good and its welfare while maintaining individual rights. These rights also include the individual's rights as an independent entity and as a member of the community, to influence the definition of the "social good" and the ways in which to maintain and promote it. Policing is not only defined in terms of *control of criminality* but also as being one of the methods and mechanisms for the effective, efficient and equitable solutions of social wrongs and injustice, which is one of the principles of democracy.

We expect that in spite of the imperfections of democracy that "democratic policing," including "community policing", will exist if police personnel, leaders and communities will be replaced; unless the democratic system as a whole will disappear.

---

*Prof. **Menachem Amir** received his Ph. D. at the University of Pennsylvania. He is a member of the permanent faculty of The Institute of Criminology, at the Hebrew University, Jerusalem, Israel, and has served as its director. He specializes in, and writes about, the mafia, juvenile delinquency and victimology, and is currently concentrat-*

ing his work on organized crime (national and international), police and police issues. He conducts research for the Israeli government in the areas of police violence, community policing and undercover police work. He has been a consultant for various Israeli government Ministerial Committees; has published widely, and has served as a member of the editorial boards of: Violence, Aggression and Terrorism and The International Journal of the Addictions (Substance Use and Misuse). *His most recent books are* Force and Control: Police Violence Patterns and Issues *and co-editor of* Organized Crime: Uncertainties and Dilemmas,

Amir   *Volume 1 of The Uncertainty Series. Prof. Amir has lectured at various universities throughout the world (Sweden, Finland, Australia, Canada, USA, South Africa, and The Netherlands). He is married to a feminist and women's studies medical sociologist and Prof. of Social Work, father to two daughters and a grandfather to two.*

References

Angel, T. (1971). Toward an alternative to the classic police organizational arrangement, Criminology 9:195-206.

Bayley, D. (1990). Patterns of Policing: A Comparative International Analysis. Rutgers University Press.

Bell, D. (1993). Communitarism and its Critics. Calerbron Press.

Bent, P. (1974). The Police and the Law Enforcement. D.C. Heath.

Braithwaite, T. (1989). Crime, Shame and Reintegration. Cambridge University Press.

Brodeur, J.(1983) High Policing and Low Policing: Remarks about the policing of political activities. Social Problems 30(5).

Crank, J. (1994). of Policing and responses to crime. Law and Society Review 8:305-51.

Culberson, W.C. (1990). Vigilantism: Political History of Private Power in America. New York: Praeger, Ch. 1:1-47.

Delattrer, E. (1977). Character and the Cops: Ethics in Policing. University Press of America.

Dennis, N. (1997) (ed.) Zero Tolerance: Policing Free Society. London, IEA, Choice no. 5.

Findlay, M. and Zvekic, V. (eds.), (1993). Alternative Policing Styles. Boston: Kluwer.

Fijnaut C. and Marx, G. ((1995) Undercover: Police Surveillance In Comparative Perspective. Hague: Kluwer.

Gamson, W. and Yuchtman, E. (1977). Police and Society in Israel. In: D. Bayley (ed.), Police and Society. Sage, pp. 195-219.

Goldstein, H. (1977). Policing a Free Society. Ballinger Publications.

Gray, T. (1995). Liberalism. University of Minnesota Press.

Grimshaw, R. and Jefferson, T. (1987). Interpreting Police Work. Unwin Press.

Hebenton, B. and Thomas, T. Policing Europe: Co-operation, Conflict and Control. St. Martin's Press.

Henkin, L. (1978). The Rights of Man Today. Boulder, Colorado.

Huggins, M. (1998). Political Policing: The United States and Latin America. London: Duke University Press.

Jefferson, T. (1993) Pondering para-military. British Journal of Criminology. 33(3: 374-381)

Johnson, L. (1992). The Rebirth of Private Policing. Routledge.

Jones, T. et al. (1994). Democracy and Policing. London: Policy Study Institute Press.

Klockars, K. (1968). Thinking About Police. McGraw-Hill.

Klockars, K. (1980) "The Dirty Harry Problems". The Annals 452:37-47.

Lee, J. (1981). Some structural aspects of police deviance in its relations with minority groups. In: C. Shearing (ed.), Organizational Police Deviance. Butterworth.

Locke, T. (1965). Two treatise of Government. In: P. Laslett (ed.). New York: Mentor Books.

Manning, P. (1997). Police Work (3rd ed.). MIT Press.

Manning, P. and Van Mannen, J. (eds.), (1978). Policing: A View from the Street. Goodyear Publisher.

Marx, G. (1988). Undercover. Berkeley: University of California Press.

Mawby, R.I. (1990), Comparative Policing Issues. Unwin Hyman.

Muir, W.K. (1997). Police: Street Corner Politician. Chicago: University of Chicago Press.

Neiderhoffer, A. and Blumberg. A. (eds.), (1979). The Ambivalent Force. Dryden Press.

Oliver, W. Community Oriented Policing: A Systematic Approach to Policing. New Jersey: Prentice-Hall.

Packer, H. (1968). The Limits of Criminal Sanctions. Stanford University Press.

Rawls, J. (1971). A Theory of Justice. Harvard University Press.

Reiner, R. (1992). The Politics of the Police. (2nd ed.). University of Toronto Press.

Reiss, A.J. (1971). The Police and the Public. Yale University Press.

Shadmi, E. (1994). Controlling the Police: A Public and Integrative Approach. Police and Society 4, pp. 119-129.

Shapland, J. and Vagg, T. (1989). Policing by the Public. Routledge.

Shearing, C. and Stenning, P. (eds.), 1987). Private Policing. Sage Publishers.

Sherman, L. (1993). Why Crime Control is not Reactionary. In: D. Weisburd and C. Uchida (eds.), Police Innovations and Control of the Police. Springer Verlag, pp. 171-180.

Skolnick, J. (1966). Justice Without Trial. John Wiley Publishers.

Souryal, S. (1992). Ethics in Criminal Justice. Anderson Publishers.

Steytler, N. (1993). Policing Political opponents: Death Squads in South Africa. In : M.Findlay and V. Zvekic (eds.), Alternative Policing Styles. Kluwer, pp. 157-171.

Sykes, G. (1946). Street Justice: A moral defence of order maintenance Justice Quarterly 3, pp. 497-516.

Troajanowic, R. and Bucqueroux, B. (1994). Community Policing: How to Get Started. Cincinnati : Anderson Publishing Company.

Uildriks, N. and Van Mastrigt (1991). Policing Police Violence. Kluwer.

Waddington, P.A.J. (1994). Liberty and Order: Public Order Policing in a Capital City. UCL Press.

Wallach, J. (1989). Liberal Communitarism and the task of Political Theory. Political Theory 15, pp. 581-611.

Wilson, J. Q., (1968), Varieties of Police Behavior. Cambridge: Harvard University Press.

Walker, S. (1999). Police in America. (3rd ed.). New York: McGraw-Hill.

Waltzer, M. (1994). Multi-culturalism and Individualism. Dissent, pp. 181-191.

Notes

1 By *political* is meant police involvement and bias toward specific political and social vested interest groups. As an outcome of this then police can become an "interest group" itself.

2 For example, shifts, job pressures, community misunderstandings which may turn to hostility, etc.

3 Policing, democratically, has in a sense, a built-in contradiction since being effective may challenge what the law permits and that which is constitutionally guaranteed (i.e. rights and human dignity).

5 The Police:
Social Control, the State and Democracy
*Nigel Fielding**

Abstract

Three broad models may be identified for the organization of the police and the delivery of policing services in contemporary societies: the law enforcement model, the service model, and the community model. Each model is examined by reference to its philosophy, organizational structure, output, management policy, and its operational strategy and tactics. The merits and drawbacks of each model are considered, and an assessment made of the fit between the models and different forms of political organization. A glossary of key terms is included.

Keywords: Models of police organization, Police and the State, Evaluating Community policing

Introduction

Throughout the world the police are increasingly subject to persistent and critical public scrutiny, vigorous government pressure to change and modernize, and a squeeze on resources (Bottoms and Wiles 1996). These pressures can cause lower morale amongst police, a feeling that clarity of mission is being lost, and bewilderment at the contradictory implications arising from the new agenda of external bodies which were once seen to value and support the police (Skogan 1996).

Of course, these pressures manifest themselves differently according to the particulars of local context; the problems of policing are different in the transitional period of the new eastern European states to those faced by the LAPD (Los Angeles Police Department). But there is sufficient in common for us to identify a set of universal models for the organization of the police institution and for us to use this heuristic model to consider the potential and constraints of each model to deliver policing in the future (Manning 1977).

We may consider three broad models of policing: the *enforcement* model, the *service* model, and the *community* (or geographic responsibility) model. Each will be examined by reference to its *philosophy*, its *organizational structure*, its *output*, its *management policy*, and its *operational strategy and tactics*. However, in comparing and assessing these models we must remember that they are analytic constructions and one would not expect to encounter policing systems in the real world that were pure examples of any single model. In practice there is always some overlap in respect of particular elements, whichever model predominates. With this caveat in mind we might go on to note that the models can be analyzed in respect of their relationship to a given society's political form as well. Figure 1 attempts to capture the way each model relates to three broad types of political system.

Figure 5.1

	Enforcement Model				
	Philosophy	Organizational structure	Output	Management Policy	Operational structure/ tactics
Representative democracy	Crime control, legal authority	Quasi-military bureaucracy Centralized, Little public access	Reactive	Command-orientated Closed Rank-based	Patrol-based Specialist functions eg detection Load-shedding
Authoritarian (Corporate state, command)	Crime control Ideological authority	Military bureaucracy No public access	Proactive Severe and inflexible	Politically directed Closed Rank-based	Street patrol Use of informers Political cadres with police functions
Totalitarian (dictatorship, police state)	Repression of opposition Force and monopoly of violence	Military bureaucracy No public access	Arbitrary	Maintain control of resistant elements	Politicized Personal loyalty-based

	Service Model				
	Philosophy	Organizational structure	Output	Management Policy	Operational structure/ tactics
Representative democracy	Public service, community-based authority	Locally-based bureaucracy Maximal public access	Highly reactive to public priorities	Maximum consultation mechanisms Liaison functions	Non tradi-tional performance measures Limited specialisation Load-sharing Constant change of priorities

Figure 5.1 continued

	Service Model Continued				
	Philosophy	Organizational structure	Output	Management Policy	Operational structure/ tactics
Authoritarian (Corporate state, command)	Elimination of resistant political elements	Local commit-tees of dominant political groups	Elimination of non-conformity	Loyalty to regime	Community members Informal social control Police as agency of last resort to political repression
Totalitarian (dictatorship, police state)	Support for demagogue	Military bureaucracy with access for dictator's placement in community	Violent repression order at stage-managed rallies	Control subords Eliminate dissidents	Political 'education' Identification of dissidents

	Community Model				
	Philosophy	Organizational structure	Output	Management Policy	Operational structure/ tactics
Representative democracy	Order & security Community-based authority	Flexible 'Flat' internal relations not structured by rank Moderate public access	Proactive Preventative	Up and downward communication Informal and knowledge - based Advancement performance-based	Problem-solving approach Community input in setting priorities and providing info. for crime control Call-analysis Inter-agency Patrol role in detection

Figure 5.1 continued

	Community Model Continued				
	Philosophy	Organizational structure	Output	Management Policy	Operational structure/ tactics
Authoritarian (Corporate state, command)	Express 'will of people'	Military bureaucracy includes community elites	Pol uniformity	Provide channels to pol elite to warn of community demands and discontents	Black committees and other informal pol bodies used to gather info and feed to police
Totalitarian (dictatorship, police state)	Maintain adherence to leader(s)	Political cells linked to police	Pol control Elimination of dissidents aided by local police cadres	Identify and enlist new adherents, repress	Op stat Maintain powerful force and repressive control in all comm'y sectors using informers and informal agencies such as school-based pol education

Philosophy

An organization's 'mandate' is what society expects of the organization, on the basis of which it is granted 'license' to act within the social domain established by that mandate. The mandate exercises compelling influence: organization members take it to heart in their understanding of what they should do, the priorities they should pursue and the ways they should validate their work. The police mandate is commonly understood to be one of law enforcement. Legally it can be argued that this is a misconception, at least in the policing systems based on the example of the Metropolitan Police in nineteenth century England (which would include the United States of America along with many former British colonies). The founders of London's 'new police' were clear that order maintenance was the precedent condition for the exercise of law enforcement and was therefore pre-eminent. The community's consent, and indeed support, was needed before enforcement could effectively proceed (Reiner 1985). But this emphasis is more familiar to constitutional lawyers than to the police and what matters most in understanding everyday police work is that the lower ranks believe that their sacred mission is law enforcement. This leads to a preoccupation with issues relating to response (the speed of response, the number responding), with deterrence (the effectiveness in terms of crime control of a uniformed presence on the streets), and with apprehension (with effectiveness perceived in terms of detection and clear-up rates). These preoccupations prompt a 'crisis response' approach, the idea that law enforcement-style policing is reactive, depending on citizens to invoke an emergency response orientated to a short-term solution to crises.

In the law enforcement approach the police gain their authority from the law. The law is the best guide to good and bad practice. The brief of the police can be read off from the law: the police apply the law in the statute books, as interpreted by the courts. There is little justification for action outside this brief. The police are an agency of the criminal justice system. Work outside the narrow brief provided by the law is the domain of other agencies (e.g., social welfare services, probation, voluntary agencies). This approach offers clarity of purpose. It gives a ready means of identifying extraneous concerns, a way of bringing consistency to the work of the agency and a clear focus for training. It also constrains the institution in its relations with other institutions. For example, it limits the political voice of the police. By and large, the authority of the police under the law enforcement model is firm, fair and limited. By 'fair' I mean that police take their place as dispassionate evidence-gatherers feeding an adversarially-based justice system.

Such considerations affect the police role. As noted, the role is legally defined and also limited by law. The institution and its officers are distinct and separate from other institutions (the constitutional division of responsibility for the police between executive and judicial branches reflects the doctrine that power should not be concentrated in any single branch of government). In this model the police are law enforcement officers, their professional expertise is crime fighting and their sole concern is crime. It should be acknowledged that the authority, role and functions of the police do differ according to the political form characteristic of a particular society (i.e., democratic, authoritarian, totalitarian; see Figure 1 above). As noted above, the law enforcement model is particularly characteristic of those Western democracies associated with the common law, many of which had their origin as colonies of Great Britain.

The police institution is granted effective monopoly of the use of physical force in civil society. In the law enforcement model this power is controlled by two doctrines which must be finely balanced. The first is that the police are the exclusive source of law enforcement action. The community has only a passive role, volunteering information when required to, bearing witness, paying the police levy through taxes. The community support the police and grant them autonomy within their field of professional expertise, provided it is assiduously and narrowly defined as the enforcement of law without fear or favor. This approach has become stronger over historical time, as resistance to the police as a social institution has declined amongst all social classes, the form of crime has become more organized, and political terrorism has become a more widespread challenge.

The second balancing doctrine in the police monopoly of the use of physical force in everyday, civil society, is that the police are, and must be, apolitical. At an [1] individual level officers may not hold political office, are in many countries denied membership of employees' organizations, and must eschew involvement in all but the most mainstream community organizations. At an institutional level, the political system in many countries offers a constrained accountability designed to keep both community and central government distant from all significant ('operational') policing decisions (in some countries, such as the United States, senior officers are elected, but changes at the top do not affect specific police operations). From the perspective of the political institutions of society, the police must not engage in politics if their mandate is to be preserved. Stick to the letter of law enforcement and there is no need for political interference, is the message for the police. It must be noted that this is in respect of electoral or party politics. The negotiation of budgets, operational styles and policies, and personnel matters, are, of course, intrinsically 'political' in the sense that they represent exchange relationships between the political institution and the institution of social control. But these are not acknowledged to be 'political' matters in the same sense as electoral politics. In the law enforcement model, no police act is political. The Nuremberg defense is not only available but sacred: the police follow the orders codified in law. Advocates of this model suggest that if one wishes to change policing, one must change the law.

Organizational structure in the law enforcement model

The law enforcement model adopts a quasi-military form of bureaucratic organization, the pyramid shape of the classic organization chart. Policing organized for law enforcement favors an institution which is formalized, paper-based, rule-oriented and standardized. The drawbacks of military-style hierarchies in terms of motivation, productivity and ethics are well-known. Each tier of separate ranks can be a barrier to communication and an encouragement to job demarcation and inflexibility (Manning 1979; Chatterton 1979; Baxter and Koffman 1985).

It is a curious fact of the police organization that the ranks lowest in the hierarchy enjoy the greatest discretion. They largely patrol alone or in pairs and supervision is distant and inconsistent. Decisions are personal and largely non-reviewable, since each patrol officer controls the means by which superiors hear of his/her actions, whereas chief officers are constrained by accountability to government. Against the backdrop of militaristic hierarchy, this is indeed paradoxical. But, located in a hierarchy, the low-level discretion exists in great tension with the centralizing elements of the organization. Powerful discipline codes apply to subordinates whose occupational deviance happens to become visible to supervisors. There is a dramatic centralization of management, with all roads leading to force headquarters. Administrative support and authority over personnel is gathered to the center. At station level, the pyramid is replicated. Operational initiatives from the lower ranks are passed up the chain of command. By the time they come back down with approval granted, circumstances have often changed. The law enforcement approach offers a finely-tuned reactive machine but with a limited capacity for proactive intervention.

Output

While the organization is most comfortable delivering fast response to public demands for action, the requirements of criminal investigation and crime prevention are less well-addressed by the enforcement model (Manning 1980). Since an effective response to such demands cannot be provided by reactive patrol units, the organization specializes such functions. Unfortunately, the hierarchical structure offers a poor environment for specialist units. Its inhibition of communication across ranks and functions obstructs the pooling of information, teamwork and planning. Because information is a valuable resource conferring personal advantage, individuals both in specialist units and in routine patrol sections may keep it to themselves (Hobbs 1988). Problems of poor working relations interfere with crime investigation. The kind of planning which is the hallmark of proactive work is inhibited by a number of factors.

The key to crime pattern analysis is good information. The reactive posture leads the police to prioritize short-term information with a direct payoff. This inhibits local crime pattern analysis (Morris and Heal 1981). While patrol officers may hold local knowledge offering a good basis for pattern analysis, their isolation within the hierarchy means that maximizing the use of such information falls foul of internal divisions of rank and status. There are problems in coordinating this information and making it available to managers whom can form an overview. Further, while crime collators draw information together, the reactive posture makes for haphazard use of the information (Clarke and Hough 1984). Some officers regularly visit the collators but others do not. Some groups are briefed by collators every shift, others are not. Much information stays with those who have collected it. There are worries about other units appropriating a case upon which one has expended effort. Detectives look down on patrol officers and may disparage information from them. Patrol officers resent the status of detectives and will not pass on what they know. Another problem is that, despite the advent of information technology, crime information may not be kept in a form enabling crime pattern analysis. The law enforcement organization is content to tabulate data for official statistics, but the form in which this information is held is seldom adequate to support pattern analysis for operational planning.

Impaired crime pattern analysis inevitably affects deployment. Without a grasp of the pattern of demand, and with a primary orientation to meeting reactive demand, operational deployment is dominated by servicing emergency calls (Manning 1988). There is little accommodation to the geographical or temporal distribution of demand. Ideally, local crime statistics would support a strategy in which crime problems were identified and deployment was attuned to it. This would involve teamwork across the divisions of rank and function, with senior patrol and detective officers determining the strategy and deployment being set in collaboration with mid-ranking operational officers. Instead, deployment in the law enforcement model is often done by working through an established list of duties until one runs out of officers to deploy (Fielding 1995).

The notoriously separate world of the detective is an obvious obstacle to teamwork. It is a closed elite (Laurie 1970). One consequence is that it becomes somewhat divorced from public priorities. For instance, detectives seldom attend the public meetings which are an important source of information about the priorities seen by local people in many forces (Fielding 1995). Determining the priority between the investigation, say, of burglary relative to racial attacks, is done on criteria unresponsive to public concerns and fears. Links between detectives and community groups (e.g. neighborhood watch) are even more remote than between detectives and patrol officers.

Crime prevention poses a real challenge to a reactive, law enforcement organization. Compared to crisis response, crime prevention activity is somewhat intangible. The more time that crime prevention officers spend spreading their message to businesses, local authorities and homeowners the more distant they become from the core units of the organization. There is, of course, an argument that uniformed patrol has a

crime prevention role, providing a deterrent effect. Against evidence that patrol officers were statistically unlikely to encounter a crime in progress and be in a position to
intervene more than occasionally in their career (e.g., Manning 1977) it was argued that
uniformed patrol did have the benefit of providing a visible deterrent to crime and
reassuring the public (Kelling 1974; Hough 1995). But, where patrol officers feel subject to sustained pressure from dispatchers dealing with emergency calls, there will be
little incentive to deploy officers merely to deter crime by walking the beat.

Management policy

The law enforcement model bespeaks a closed organization, somewhat detached
from its environment, resistant to influence from the community, and operating to an
internally-defined agenda. Communication tends to be top down and command-ori-
ented; orders are issued, but by the time they reach their destination managerial intention may have changed. Because orders must be issued before things happen, response may be delayed. Paradoxically, managers must rely on subordinates for information about the nature of demand, the types of problem to which the organization must respond and so on. Managers are liable to be led by subordinates because
they control information about the interface with the public. There is little flexibility and there is also the opportunity for the stickler to do only what is specified in
orders rather than what is needed.

Authority under such a management system is distributed by rank (Manning
1977). Much effort is expended in job demarcation, for example, determining what
level of rank should take responsibility for supervising special initiatives such as
the management of child protection. The trappings of office necessary to make
each rank distinctive divide the organization, a problem which has preoccupied
recent efforts at police reform, including the official Sheehy Inquiry into the future
of the British police (Home Office 1994). As people move up the hierarchy the skills
they have developed may be lost if those skills are tied to the functional responsibility of a particular rank. Police researchers often hear from officers that a particular incumbent has been promoted beyond his or her competence, or 'kicked up-
stairs' to reduce their destructive influence on operational policing. Promotion in
the law enforcement model is by longevity and contacts (e.g., the New York Police
Department's notorious 'hook') as well as merit, creating logjams at a particular
grade. Personnel control is rule-oriented and punishment-centered (Manning 1977).
Procedure is by-the-book rather than attuned to cases. Standard responses are
preferred whether appropriate or not, simply because their use is established and
less likely to be questioned. Again, the rank structure insulates supervisors, so
that the application of discipline may seem capricious.

Leadership resides in the office rather than its incumbent. Incumbents may in-
terpret their role flexibly and be anxious to take soundings from the ranks, but in the
end decisions are reviewable only by those of higher rank (Lustgarten 1986). At the
most senior levels, such a leadership style may lead to quirky variations in policy. At
intermediate and lower levels, incumbents adopt a reactive posture. There is little
incentive to plan; initiative is reduced to what is permissible for a particular rank
(Young 1991). Decision-making is diluted, with responsibility to deal with a problem disappearing up the hierarchy. In this circumstance it is most sensible to deal

with the work as it comes, as there is little to be gained by innovation or anticipation. As to the assessment of productivity and effectiveness, management prefers quantitative measures, such as arrest figures. While readily counted, these may not give a good reflection of the quality of service. They are 'internal' measures which may not take account of performance criteria which strongly affect the public's regard for what the police do (Weatheritt 1993).

Operational strategies and tactics

Not all the characteristics associated with prioritizing law enforcement are dysfunctional. Police organizations oriented mainly to crime control have the great advantage of providing what is widely perceived as the *raison d'etre* of the police institution. Yet it must be recalled that there is another branch to the phrase 'law and order'; as well as law enforcement the police institution should promote order maintenance.

Order maintenance policing is concerned with the production and maintenance of 'public order' (or 'civil order'). Public order offences include breach of the peace, being 'drunk and disorderly', trespass, obstructing the police in the course of their duty, making an affray, and, *in extremis*, participating in a riot. As this partial list suggests, the less serious offences against public order are among the most common offences overall and in many jurisdictions the police spend more time dealing with order maintenance than with crime control. In doing so the police have to use their judgment and discretion to achieve a level of regulation which is deemed to be the 'normal state (or condition)' in a particular locale (a neighborhood, borough or region). This normal state varies by the social geography of the locale in question. Behaviors which are tolerated and even normal in an inner urban area may not be acceptable in a prosperous suburb. Norms of public order vary by 'time' as well as by 'space' or 'place'. A behavior, such as singing loudly and shouting in public, may be tolerated at bar closing time in a town center but not be acceptable in the same place an hour later when most revelers have dispersed. The norms of tolerance can be hard to establish or may be contested, and this presents police with a considerable challenge when seeking to determine whether a behavior should be excused or an arrest should be made. For example, citizens with different moral values may dispute what should be tolerated and what should be censured. In the case of communities with significant political, religious or cultural schisms this can be a major and continual problem. As well as dealing with troublesome citizens the police may have to deal with partisan bystanders and with pressure from groups seeking official endorsement of their particular values and point-of-view. These latter considerations are more likely in respect of major public order events, such as political or religious protests, marches, demonstrations and riots than they are in respect of what is sometimes called 'local public order'. Thus, the order maintenance category includes the regulation of a wide range of behaviors from the mundane and routine to the serious and exceptional (Waddington 1995). Order maintenance interventions are therefore a trying test for the police.

Several of the more notorious problems which have prompted a general disenchantment with contemporary policing, and allegations of corruption, bias and incompetence, have in fact related to public order issues. It may be no coincidence that public concern in countries as disparate as South Korea, Germany, the USA, India and South Africa has been raised by cases involving suspected terrorists, large-scale industrial and political disorder, and conflict with ethnic minorities. Public order represents a trying test for the police institution. While the public may happily accede to the prioritization of crime control by the law enforcement-oriented organization, the consensus begins to break down as the focus shifts to public order. This presents the law enforcement-oriented organization with obvious difficulty and it is in this respect that over-emphasizing law enforcement may problematic the relations of police and public. Such an organization may be less able to respond to public order issues than one with a different organizational structure, managerial posture and operational approach.

The operational posture of the law enforcement model is well-known, since this is the traditional orientation of police forces in large metropolitan areas. Organizational routines and procedures are set by the crime orientation. Over the years the functional units which are designated, the proportion of personnel in each particular unit, their training and competencies, the paper-based procedures and the relations with other agencies, all come to be modeled on how criminal cases are processed. Other sorts of demand, such as terrorism, labor unrest and other forms of civil unrest, have to be channeled into an apparatus set up to handle the criminal case. Indeed, the crime-based approach is informed largely by individual crime and may not even be appropriate for other types of crime such as organized crime or corporate crime, such as price-fixing conspiracies. In the law enforcement model the organizational posture is reactive. It 'waits' for a crime to occur and then proceeds with well-rehearsed routines. It is not suggested that such routines are in themselves inappropriate. The organization has had many years to perfect them. The problem is that the routines are more appropriate for some types of demand than others. Even within the 'crime' type of demand, the routines are more effective with major crime than with high volume local crime. The form of a burglary investigation differs little from that of a murder investigation, but in the former it is less effective because the scale of resource needed to make the standard response work cannot realistically be made available. Yet the organization presses on with the standard response because it 'knows' nothing else.

In a literal sense the organization which adopts a reactive stance is 'controlled' by the public, for it is the public which activates demand for service. The organization waits for a crime to be notified by someone with an interest in its prosecution. In this posture there is no need to diagnose the nature of crime in general. The organization works with what it is given by the public. It 'understands' crime only in these terms. In this sense, crime to the police is incident-specific. Repeated incidents of a similar *modus operandi* will prompt efforts to detect a pattern, but the organization is not set up to take its gaze off the streets to consider more broadly the shifts in patterns of crime across a jurisdiction or indeed at a more macro level across a society. In this respect it is difficult to think in terms of operational *strategies*. The organization has an array of tactics, but a strategy requires the long and the broad view. A capacity to take the long view is not a strength of the law enforcement model.

Thus, while we can identify certain tactics which make for effectiveness in regard to particular types of demand, we must recognize that the different models of policing vary in the support which they offer to these tactics and the priority that they place on the different kinds of demand. At the level of on-street interventions against individual suspects effectiveness is contingent on sensitive observation and a capacity to impute motives on the basis of local knowledge, the ability to convey power in a tangible but generally understated way, and a refined capacity for negotiation. At the level of interventions against more sophisticated, organized crime operations the key effectiveness criteria are high quality information and closely-coordinated operational response, which may involve tactical alliances with other agencies. These factors influencing the effectiveness of police interventions are not in themselves contingent on the particular model which a police organization adopts. However, the three models have different capacities and abilities to support the tactics which are necessary to successful interventions.

Thus, it is no surprise that in recent years the police have been criticized in many countries as a result of unanticipated public sensitivity in at least two areas: the control of crimes against women, particularly the handling of rape investigations and domestic violence (recent examples include Belgium, Pakistan and Canada), and the control of racially-motivated assaults (recent examples include the U.S.A., Turkey and France). Since the posture is response-based, as public expectations in these areas have changed the police have begun to adapt, but it has been at the cost of a number of notorious instances where the traditional approach has failed, with negative effects on police/public relations and at the cost of many victims whose suffering has been aggravated by secondary victimization inflicted by the system. Secondary victimization refers to harm caused by the response to the victim by the criminal justice system itself. For example, a rape victim may experience secondary victimization as a result of insensitive police interrogation to establish the facts of the case, or due to inappropriate medical examination. The 'victims movement' has faced considerable opposition in securing more say for victims in court and in sentencing decisions (Rock 1986). The law enforcement model only places the public at the center of its approach in activating police service. Once that has happened, the response is police-based. There is little subsequent role for the public, even victims.

Looking at routine patrol, the response to calls for service emphasizes rapid response, leading logically enough to the issuing by political authorities in some jurisdictions of precise time limits for response to various types of call, regardless of the characteristics of the area policed, the resources available or the nature of demand. The stopwatch approach to performance measurement is consistent with the use of quantitative performance measures noted above. It is precise, readily-monitored from above, easily-tabulated for external consumption but provides only a limited index of quality of service. Another trait of the reactive, rapid response tactic is that it is indiscriminate. Studies of the information provided to patrols by dispatchers indicate that the information given is so scanty that it is very difficult to anticipate what will meet the officers on arrival at the scene. Now it is true that a high proportion of calls from the public are in fact trivial. But it is hard to judge which of the calls will prove trivial. Since any call may be genuinely serious, it seems safest to offer a full patrol response to each. In short, there is little call screening.

What of response at the scene? This is characterized as 'load-shedding'. Patrols working on the reactive model have, after all, to be ready to respond instantly to the next demand. The call described as burglar-on-premises over the radio may turn out to be the husband returning unexpectedly and raiding no more than the larder, but the next call could be a murder. Thus, the patrol response is dominated by time pressure. The preoccupation of patrol officers is first to determine what exactly is happening, second to determine if it is arrestable, and third to clear the scene as rapidly as possible if it is not arrestable. The 'load' is then shed onto whatever other avenue presents itself. If it is a domestic dispute, then 'there is nothing the police can do'. If someone involved seems not to be fully in control of their mental faculties, it is a matter for social services. It should be added that such terminations are no more than those offered by patrol officers in order to disengage; there is no monitoring of outcomes, and seldom would officers actually initiate the referral to another agency.

In law enforcement models, patrol is organized on a shift system, in which groups of officers work together serially across the twenty four hour clock, with a spell on one time shift being followed by a change to the next time shift and so on. This system has effects on officers' metabolism and outlook. It means it is most likely that they will share their social life with those who occupy their working life, a strong base for the development of an occupational culture. The system is only loosely calibrated with the incidence of demand. It is obvious that demands for police service vary in volume and type over the twenty four hour cycle, but the strongest influence on numbers available is the numbers absent for training, sick leave and so on. Officers are assigned to particular duties not on the basis of possessing particular skills but simply because they are there that day. Further, despite experiments in many forces with 'directed patrol', where officers are assigned to deal with a particular problem on a given shift, patrol is largely random. Directed patrol relies on sufficient officers being available to 'borrow' some from the rapid response units required by reactive policing. Since this condition seldom obtains, patrol is generally reactive.

What of criminal investigation? We have already seen that detectives inhabit a closed world (Hobbs 1988). Detective units carry large caseloads (Manning 1980). The criminal justice system is subject to tight budgetary pressures in many countries, including Western democracies such as the US, Britain and Australia, and relies on a high volume of guilty pleas to function. In London each extra contested plea involves detectives in two weeks extra work on the case. It would not take a large increase in suspects claiming innocence to break the system (Laurie 1970; Murray 1996). It would be surprising if the pressures experienced by detectives for efficient case-handling were not transmitted to suspects, by whatever means. A law enforcement approach is, of course, particularly consistent with the prosecutorial emphasis of the common law system of justice (Cotterrell 1989). This is a system of contest where, once a suspect has been identified, police have a heavy stake in proving that their suspect did it. Of course recent years have seen legislation to regulate the conduct of investigation more closely (Waddington 1994), and a different approach prevails outside common law jurisdictions. The evidence here is mixed, but it is well-known that the effect of more tightly controlling the station process has often been to drive the application of pressure to the pre-station and pre-charge stages of the process (McConville et al 1991). Another effect of the detective section keeping to itself is that there is little patrol involvement in the investigation of cases. The detective effort is centralized and not only aloof from other functions but from the broader public. The most significant figures in the detective's world are other detectives, known criminals, and informers (Hobbs 1995).

In sum, the enforcement model of policing offers an organization oriented to the control of crime and the enforcement of law. It enjoys the clarity of purpose which comes from a narrow role and requires little from the public other than consent and tax revenue. Its organizational form does not satisfy demands other than those of law enforcement and, further, it is not especially successful in addressing the goals it sees as primary.

The Service Model Philosophy

In most countries the best representation of a service model of policing is probably offered historically in the practice of rural constabularies (Young 1993). A service model plan was not adopted fully, but evolved in response to the nature of demand. Where volumes of crime were low, and, importantly, where the resources available to the police were limited by a restricted tax base, the service model grew up. While it accommodates crime control, its daily routine is dominated by service-type relations with the public (ibid). Major crime being a rare occurrence, when it does happen the demand may prove too much for the force, siphoning officers from established roles and requiring assistance from metropolitan forces more experienced in investigating major crime (Shapland and Vagg 1988). Order maintenance remains part of the brief but here too, if there is a major incident help will be sought from other sources (historically, the militia and other forms of armed citizenry). The forms of service reflected the pace and calendar of the rural year. Officers played traditional roles in community life, spent much time on patrol, and responded more positively to minor demands than officers under a law enforcement model.

Organizational structure of the service model

Organizationally there is little to distinguish the traditional service model from the law enforcement model. The bureaucratic foci of the organization remain the force headquarters and the divisional/station hierarchy. The divisional (or regional) tier of police administration may be more marginal than in the enforcement model; there are really two points on the horizon, the entirely local (station) and the summit of local power (force HQ). Thus, 'centralization' works somewhat differently to the enforcement model. The rhythm of local stations is seldom disturbed but, when it is, the line of authority more quickly leads to headquarters. Headquarters itself is embedded in close relationships with other local institutions. It is highly responsive to established interests, such as major landowners, and is a major purchaser of goods and services from local businesses. Its purchasing policy is a source of potential inefficiency, if not actual graft. Specialization is affected both by the constraint on resources and the more restricted opportunities for circulation of officers between different roles. Thus, specialist functions involve smaller numbers of officers who stay longer in the specialist role. Thus, what is gained in expertise may be lost in boredom.

Output

Where the service model features a close responsiveness to what the community (especially local elites) wants then we again see a largely reactive organization. Priorities are set by a form of consultation. The mechanism will largely be through existing social occasions and a host of informal contacts with interested parties, largely established interests such as landowners and the business community. In the abstract, public concerns could be built into the priority-setting process via some type of community forum. There would be meetings whose membership reflected an effort to identify all those with an interest in the provision of police services. Initial meetings would not involve the police doing any more than recording demands. Police would then examine how such demands might be met and sketch in conflicts between different demands and between these and the resources available. There would be further meetings at which police thinking was explained. Community interests would have further occasion to lobby for their demand and this would be followed by a negotiation resulting in the publication of an annual plan for priorities to be followed by the police. It is worth describing such an abstract process so that it may be contrasted with what we have now.

Management policy

If there were a force which took so seriously the public role in priority-setting, it would require not only an organizational structure set up to support planning and to change plans on short time scales, but a managerial style quite different to the traditional hierarchies found in provincial forces. This is because once priorities had been set in the consultative way mentioned above, the organization would have to respond to the lobbying it had stimulated long after the policy formation process had passed its peak. There would be a need for liaison officers at the divisional/area level (for example, to cope with lobbying about traffic enforcement on routes taking in several local areas) and at the station level (for example, to cope with vociferous local interests whose case had not been accepted in the regional-level negotiation). But this would also be a force that was more open to the public, and which could consequently expect the public to help it. One would not need, for instance, to orchestrate neighborhood watch schemes, because the higher level of contact with the force would open channels for routine reporting of suspicious circumstances.

Nevertheless, these additional consultative mechanisms would not come free. Time would have to be devoted to running the process, time when officers would not be in operational roles, and having stimulated the consultative process, ongoing effort would be required to maintain it. Liaison roles would have to be created. There would also be changes in 'employee relations'. There could not be such complete reliance on hierarchical relations, because each officer in direct contact with the public would have distinctive local interests to represent. These might lead him or her into contact with superior officers which would have to be accepted as a basis for a greater measure of independence so long as responsiveness to local interests remained the priority.

Operational strategy and tactics

Assuming no change in resources, a service-oriented force would have to rethink the balance of effort between crime control, order maintenance and general services. If, for instance, the community required police to expend effort teaching children the rudiments of lawful conduct and 'citizenship', there would be a considerable demand which would inevitably deplete officers available for general patrol. Even in urban areas the concerns of local people are chiefly low-level. Serious crime seldom touches them. Crime problems are most likely to be car crime and residential burglary. Police would have to deal with complaints about parking, noisy neighbors and stray dogs. Under the enforcement model these issues would all be dealt with by other agencies.

The service model takes the police a long way from their ingrained priorities. It is not that police are unfamiliar with these problems. But they can turn them away, in the way described in discussing the enforcement model. They are also used to mediating demands. For example, elderly residents and businesspeople may complain about groups of youths congregating on street corners. Presently, officers may be aware that there is nothing else for teenagers to do and turn a blind eye while agreeing with complainants that it is a nuisance. Under the service model, officers would have to do something about the teenagers.

An organization working on the service model could not rely on current quantitative performance measures. The shift in priorities would soon indicate a significant decline in traditional indicators such as arrests. Further, there would be large fluctuations from one year to the next, as priorities were changed. One can imagine a cyclical process in which, as priorities rotated between, say, car crime, injuries to livestock and playing football with local teenagers, different police responsibilities were under-resourced so that a new problem would emerge, new effort would be applied to it so that another responsibility ran into trouble and so on. Meanwhile, with new responsibilities being prioritized, reflecting lower-level concerns, qualitative indicators would have to be adopted. For example, if priority was given to educating schoolchildren as mentioned above, an indicator would be required of how effective the lessons in responsible citizenship had been. Such things are not readily measured. The service model thus moves police some way from traditional measures of performance.

Regarding patrol and specialist response, specialist sections would be pared back, because patrol sections would have the direct contact with a now-more-demanding public. This would insulate specialists such as detectives, but this could be addressed by involving detectives in the priority-setting public meetings. Patrol sections would also face a new demand. They would have to explain to members of the public why their particular demand could not be met. It might be that it was not one of the agreed priorities, or that dealing with these left too little time to take on another issue, or that a traditional demand such as a crime investigation could not be dealt with as quickly as the member of the public wanted. Service organizations have to explain why service cannot be provided or why things have gone wrong when there is a complaint. These are pressures from which the enforcement model is free.

The Community/Geographic Model Philosophy

The enforcement and service models are at opposite ends of the spectrum. We now turn to a mixed model. First we must note that the community policing model takes a different inspiration at the level of the *police mandate*. Here community order, peace and security are prioritized over crime control. Crime control is a means to enhance the community's peace and security. The model also endorses a preventative as well as reactive form of police response (remember that it is a mixed model; reactive policing still has a place here).

In this conception of the mandate, the police derive their authority from society or, in common law jurisdictions, from the community as it grants that authority through law. In the enforcement model we saw the police as an agency of the criminal justice system. In the community model the police are an agency of local government and the community. A major part of the bill for police services is still derived from local taxation. The role of central government would be less in a community model. There would be scope for the sort of adjustment to local norms and standards which is intrinsic to the common law approach (and in which the service model represents an extreme). The distinction between common law and Roman law jurisdictions can be over-stated. While the police reap their authority more directly from the State in the latter, all modern polities expect the police to respond to local concerns and reflect local norms and standards. In both types of legal system the police role under the community model would be socially-defined. The question is in what areas and to what degree.

It is necessary to differentiate between community policing as the more responsive provision of conventional police services such as order maintenance and crime control, and the pursuit of 'outreach' functions. This is an established tension in community policing (Fielding 1995). Should community policing entail community work, such as efforts at community-building, promoting community spirit? Or should it involve making the provision of traditional police services more accessible, for instance, by setting up police offices on high-crime estates? Since we have discussed the service approach as a separate model, our discussion here will focus on the core of the community-policing model: the provision of patrol officers who have long-term assignments to a particular beat. To this may be added the institution of public consultation mechanisms (as in the service model), but with a brief to focus on problems of crime and order. In short, the community model we will examine is not preoccupied with 'outreach' but with public order and law enforcement. It is, however, committed to delivering those traditional ends by new means.

One of these means is that the police take their role alongside other legal and social agencies. Neither order nor crime are seen as problems exclusively to be handled by the police. Local government, architects, the business community, social services, voluntary agencies, probation, and the courts are among the other agencies with a role. This is a broad brief and multi-agency approaches demand much effort in servicing inter-agency relationships. The model imposes a heavy round of meetings and requires officers to adopt a more forthcoming posture than may be usual. Consequently, this model requires officers to be granted more autonomy and responsibility than the hierarchical approach offers. The community model has not discarded crime control but broadens its diagnosis; officers have to seek ways of responding to social problems that have criminogenic influence but which may carry them a long way from the sorts of service they have customarily provided. A good contemporary example is that of drug law enforcement. Police in liaison with 'street agencies' must turn a blind eye to offending (drug consumption by street addicts) as partners in a joint effort which, among other things, provides sterile drug taking equipment as a response to AIDS.

So far we have put this in terms of new relationships with partner agencies (and these may be agencies with whom police customarily have a poor relationship). The community model also offers the community itself a more active role. The means are similar to the consultative mechanism in the service approach, but the agenda is more circumscribed because the focus is on crime and order. The idea is that the police and community share responsibility for crime and order. Thus, while there is attention to priority-setting, the range of priorities is more limited than in service models. Further, rather than the community having a major say in setting priorities but leaving it to police to operationalize these interests, in the community model the public have a role in controlling crime and achieving order. Examples are neighborhood and business watch schemes. The community is also client of policing services. Thus there is a role for surveys of levels of satisfaction with policing.

The difficulties that the police face in pursuing a community-based response to crime and order problems arise from the problems of community associated with contemporary social bonds. Industrialized societies have for some time been marked by a change from 'community' to what Tonnies (1950) called 'association', where bonds are not geo-local but revolve around particular interests shared with a network of people who may be widely separated spatially and have little in common except for the particular interest which brings them into association from time to time. Individuals may participate in several associative networks, none based in their local area. This weakens the tie of purely local bonds. There is also a class effect. The pursuit of non-geo-local bonds is for the socially mobile and the relatively well-off. Those still relying on the community for their social network are the poor, the disabled and the elderly.

All of this suggests that the police pursuit of 'community spirit' may be a lost cause. As a mechanism of controlling crime, promoting community integration where it does not already exist is pointless. There is doubt whether any agency can achieve it, and of all agencies the police are the least likely to do so. This is another reason for focusing on those parts of the police mission with which local people are most likely to identify, namely, the direct control of crime. Neighbourhood Watch, which benefits from a degree of self-interest, can contribute, but the core effort remains with the police and their provision of a high level of foot patrol on the beat. While much has been made of the public role by advocates of the community approach, the greater contribution is likely to be made by partner agencies than by the public. The main role of the public is as client and as consultee in the priority-setting process.

It was noted that the police maintained an apolitical posture in the enforcement model. In the community model the police acknowledge a 'political' role, not in the sense of electoral politics but in that of mediating interests. We have already noted the varying role of the police during the process of negotiating priorities in the service model. The police are long used to mediating industrial conflict, racial conflict, religious conflict, sports-related conflict (e.g., football hooliganism) and indeed social conflict of all sorts (Fielding 1991). By their particular handling of public order events, their construction of the range of action their mandate permits in respect of these, and their responsiveness to sectional community interests, party politics, local and central government, the police play a role that is inescapably and fundamentally political. The community model removes the need for the police to maintain the claim to apoliticality. They may be more open in their mediation of competing interests. Where this seeks to address some elements of the interests of all parties to a conflict, it will give all parties an incentive to continue to invest legitimacy in a process at the heart of which stand the police. It is likely, though, that this more explicitly political role would excite controversy from time to time.

Thus, instead of a separation of police and politics, the community model supposes that police are engaged in a relationship of mutual responsibility with community and political representatives. While police must respond to priorities and demands from such bodies and individuals, these groups must themselves respond to operational practicalities upon which the police are the experts. This often will mean that police will be in the position of explaining what will be neglected if some particular interest is emphasized. Implicitly this means abandoning the claim to an exclusive say over 'operational matters'. But it is more than just doing what 'the community' wants, because any thoughtful approach to community must begin by seeing that there is not one community but many. It goes without saying that, if operational matters are open to discussion the same must apply to broader matters of policy.

Organizational structure of the community model

The *organizational structure* of the police under a community model would differ from that associated with an enforcement model. One cannot imagine a police institution able to abandon the core characteristics of bureaucracy, any more than any other large organization could survive without rational decision-making, meritocratic criteria for career advancement, auditing systems and so on. However, the community model would reward structures which offered greater flexibility in some of these respects. In particular, the model requires the adaptation of 'rules' to fit the situation, since service delivery would vary by the nature of the community policed, its agreed priorities and so on. Further, since officers' responsibilities would be more externally-directed, taking account of community expectations, they would be less closely informed by the rank structure and more by their effectiveness as seen by external audiences. This would subtly undermine the structuring of working relationships based solely on rank. The result could be a more collegial atmosphere, where divisions of rank were weaker and where temporary working relationships in response to various demands would expose officers to a greater range of intra-organizational contacts. But this could also make for uncertainty and occupational deviance; new criteria for the exercise of discretion would be required, along with changes to training and staff appraisal.

If the organization is to be driven by 'front end' and community-based demands, then its effectiveness hinges on decentralization of authority and management function to meet such operational requirements. Local police commanders will need more autonomy, including budgetary control. It follows that, to protect the interests of taxpayers, they would also have to bear greater responsibility if things go wrong in terms of, e.g., excessive overtime payments expended on some local priority. The community model presses for a flatter rank structure. It also imposes new demands on frontline officers, many of which would be unfamiliar and for which training would be hard to devise. Such a model requires fewer intermediate managerial grades and more frontline grades to signal different measures of skill and experience. The moves towards greater functional specialization seen in the enforcement model are inhibited. The community model rewards those who become generalists, drawing on skills relevant not only to crime control but to negotiation of demand, consultation and information-gathering.

In sum, the community model tends towards a more open organization than in the enforcement model. It interacts more with its environment, is more sensitive to its environment at a political level, and is more open to change. This responsiveness also makes it orientate more strongly to product-oriented criteria of effectiveness, rather than relying on fiscal criteria. To achieve these ends, considerable change is required in organizational structure as well as occupational roles. Further, the organization would find itself more open to charges of political bias, and matters previously seen as 'internal' would be subject to outside pressure.

Management policy

We have already anticipated some of the *managerial policy* which would be associated with the model. Greater interaction between ranks would be expected and necessary. Internal communication would involve 'downwards' consultation. Mechanisms would be needed to gather and evaluate feedback from frontline officers. As information flowed up the organization for decision, interim statements of likely decisions would need to be offered back for assessment by frontline officers. A monitoring function would be necessary in respect of programs. This approach to communication would work against formality and rank-based deference. Managerial authority would not come from rank but from knowledge and contribution; already in some specializations some rank officers enjoy a better grasp of the function than those who manage them (a UK example is child protection). Changes to managerial training would be necessary. Promotion would be performance-based, with an assessment of the officer's value to the organization rather than criteria such as longevity.

A flatter hierarchy and a more flexible approach to functional responsibility (assignment by expertise not rank) calls for new means of creating incentives and rewarding achievement. Personnel control would have to shift, from being punishment-centered (as in the enforcement model) to being reward-oriented. Supervisory control would be by direct involvement working alongside those supervised. This does not mean creating an environment in which junior ranks can get away with anything. Peer pressure to pull your weight can be a most effective means of controlling conduct. More open and flexible structures also mean that managers get better information about what is happening. This model requires leadership to be participatory rather than accorded by rank. More responsibility is delegated but there is better frontline knowledge on the basis of which to assess whether individuals are measuring up to the responsibility. There is also more the manager can do to regulate conduct. The manager can be more proactive because s/he has more routine contact with lower ranks, rather than relying on annual appraisal or the promotion process. For this to work, change would be required in established management style, policy and practice.

A broader range of information would have to be available to managers so that they could assess productivity and efficiency. As well as things that can be quantified, the supervisor would need to draw on assessments of the quality of interventions in, for example, public consultation meetings. Performance measurement would also be more product-oriented than under the enforcement model, which relies more strongly on internal measures. It would not matter so much how many arrests an officer has effected, and would matter more whether the officer had solved problems s/he set out to tackle.

Operational strategy and tactics

The community model emphasizes a problem-solving approach relative to the generally reactive stance of the enforcement model. Like the service model, it grants the community an input to operational matters. But it limits the expectations of all parties to those matters relating to order and the control of crime. Because there is a role for reactive, fast response service delivery, but a place for proactive efforts too, effort must be devoted to differentiating the response to calls for service, with greater effort to sift between units for that which is best suited to the demand. Call screening and call analysis become greater obligations. Unless more resources are directed to call screening, there would be a consequent worsening of response time. This approach also requires considerable input from other agencies. Recall that the enforcement model displayed a 'load shedding' trait. In the community model, too, those first on scene may well terminate by referral to some other agency. But the community model expects that this will be both better-informed (because of more extensive inter-agency relations) and more closely monitored, with follow-ups which can be initiated both by the police and other agencies. In the community model, the approach is one of 'load sharing'. To ensure that 'sharing' did not become 'shedding', liaison roles would have to be created.

In the enforcement model, criminal investigation was a specialist function. It suffered from heavy caseloads and relative isolation from other functions. In the community model several features would limit the caseload. There would be case screening to filter cases purely for the detectives. The role of uniformed officers in preliminary investigations would be enhanced. Giving patrol officers more ownership of cases that came up on their beats would promote communication across the divide. Training of patrol officers would have to be extended. Frontline officers may well be able to identify reasons behind fluctuations in crime rates. But there would be a danger that, if many individuals were involved, the effort could become diffuse and there could be problems in controlling the giving out of information which could, at worst, work its way back to the offender. It is not so much a system of increasing the numbers involved, then, as a matter of involving a representative of a different function, usually the local patrol officer, at the early stage of an investigation.

The community model, as described here, emphasizes patrol and a territorial basis of responsibility. This is a system based on beats, where the patrol officer gains a sense of beat 'ownership' and responsibility. But the model does not presume that the effort is solitary. Urban beats may be local but they still represent large numbers of residents, more than any single officer could hope to know. Thus, the community model requires adoption of a team perspective, drawing on the functional links and multi-agency partnerships indicated above. Where there is teamwork there is an incentive to plan interventions, pursuing a proactive, problem-oriented brief. Crime prevention becomes a basic patrol strategy by the regular, predictable availability of a known officer to whom information can be given. Long term beat assignment encourages the growth of trust, so that residents know the information will be acted on in a way that is sensitive to their interests. They may want, for example, an individual to be warned rather than arrested. A new relationship would be required between beat sections and the smaller number of reactive patrols which would still be needed to cope with emergencies and unpredicted demands.

The community model aims to provide police services to support a safe and secure environment and, while its structure is informed by elements of the service model, it can maintain the emphasis on the control of crime which is characteristic of the enforcement model. But to do so it requires considerable change on the part of the organization and its personnel. Further, it is necessary to determine the balance between 'outreach' and other elements of the community policing brief. It has been suggested here that the best prospects for community policing lie in focusing the police effort on crime control. But it must be recalled that the research evidence is incomplete and also that, where members of the public have wished to see the police adopt a more 'human face' through efforts at outreach, there would be concern at the police concentrating on crime control.

Evaluating models of policing

As we have reviewed these models, we have noted various problems associated with each model and its elements. There is no perfect model, nor any policing system which is a perfect instance of a single model. Nevertheless, we can assess some difficulties which arise from an overemphasis on each ideal-typical model. The enforcement model offers a forceful reactive machine but proceeds by its own dictates once activated by the public. It is primarily a crisis response model. Its emphasis on crime control leads to the neglect of other demands. The community has a passive role. The model denies the political nature of the police mission. It favors a quasi-military organizational model with strong centralizing tendencies, both of which militate against cooperation and communication across the organizational structure. Specific demands calling on particular skills are handled by the creation of specializations. It measures its success quantitatively. Its routine interventions are superficial, legalistic, and may amplify the hurt felt by victims. In many ways, its demerits are the reason so many people are currently spending so much time looking at alternative ways of delivering police service.

The service model offers an approach which is even more reactive than the enforcement model. While the public invokes police response in the enforcement model, in the service approach their involvement extends to re-thinking the balance between crime control and the provision of social services. This would lead to a more open organization but one in deep and continual crisis about its purposes. The services provided may be benign but would continually provoke concern at the neglect of what police officers customarily see as their essential and distinctive mission. The model also gives the political process a higher profile, with the potential to impose frequent changes of priority. Resources for crime control would be squeezed in favor of community services. Such services may subtly have an impact upon crime and order, but these effects would be diffuse and hard to measure.

The community model is construed here as a mixed model. While 'outreach' has certainly been a part of liberal constructions of community policing, these cannot be the essential feature of a community model which embraces the enduring concern of the police with order and crime control. The community model represents the inversion of the traditional enforcement model's balance between 'law and order'. It puts order first and law enforcement second. The idea is that order must be achieved if the consent and cooperation of the community is to be gained so that enforcement can proceed efficiently. Thus, the mixed model seeks to enhance the community's role, not because it wishes to promote neighborliness and social integration but because it wants to maximize the information available as a means of facilitating the pursuit and prosecution of those who create problems of crime and disorder. The principal difficulties of the community model lie in the organizational environment, internal relationships, the status of patrol work, and the belief that the public can play a *direct* role in policing.

In large part the roles and obligations of police officers working under the three models will already have been apparent in the profile of each model. Officers under the enforcement model play a role orientated to law enforcement and their rights and obligations are dictated in a standardized way by the quasi-military hierarchical form of the organization. Officers working under the service model play a role orientated to public service and they grant the public (and seek from the public) a strong input to determining the organization's priorities. Thus, their rights are greater than those granted by the enforcement model, since they must have the latitude to seek public input and respond to it. However, there are additional obligations to the public, rather than solely to the organization as in the enforcement model. Officers working under the community model play a complex role whereby they seek community contact primarily to get crime-relevant information which is then used to bring about crime control. Like officers working under the service model they have obligations to the public as well as to the police organization and these obligations may involve collusive or manipulative relationships with citizens whose loyalties are suspect or divided.

In terms of *training*, the enforcement model presents the fewest challenges and complexities. The principal requirement, apart from physical fitness, is that the officer knows the law - it is sometimes said that this approach to policing requires a recruit with the qualities of an 'athletic lawyer'. Training to support the service model would require special attention to procedures for cultivating and maintaining a strong public input into the priority-setting process, and attention to negotiating and bargaining skills. These are particularly difficult to train for, and require a sophisticated grasp of consultation procedures which would be expected in both frontline and supervisory officers (Fielding 1988). The training requirement of the community model would pay some attention to negotiation skills but would emphasize effective interpersonal means of getting information, as well as training in techniques of crime pattern analysis. Operational competence would share core skills with the enforcement model.

Thus, both alternatives to the dominant model, that of law enforcement, require a more demanding training and may also necessitate changes to recruitment and selection criteria. Prevailing systems of police training have been characterized as *collective, sequential, fixed, serial, closed* and involving *investiture* (Van Mannen and Schein 1979). Batches of novices are trained at the same time, and the process follows a series of identifiable stages, e.g., recruit school, probation, and first posting. The closed socialization mode binds together the batch in a process which is orientated to investiture into the new status and 'stripping away' of the old; desocialization precedes socialization. Trainers seek to reduce any diversity among recruits. It could be argued that neither the service nor the community model would be well-served by this approach. The human relations and interpersonal skills necessary to the success of these models may call for a more individualized approach to training, where the training offered is more closely attuned to the personality and capacities of each recruit. The greater degree of involvement with the public would argue against the elements of prevailing systems of training which focus on creating a group identity and occupational culture. Diversity among recruits may be treated as a boon, not a problem.

All three models are, of course, vulnerable to organized or random corruption and police deviance, and all three could be abused so as to create violations of citizens' civil rights. This is inescapable in any model which operates on the basis of a monopoly of the application of politically-legitimated force and is the price that society pays to avoid the greater evils of vigilantism, vendetta and mob rule. Nevertheless we may identify particular weaknesses of the three models. The enforcement model is particularly susceptible to occupational deviance, due to the rigidity and draconian nature of its disciplinary system. The service model is especially vulnerable to graft and corruption, since very close and broad-based relations with the public are sought. The community model is especially subject to what has been called 'noble cause corruption', where officers 'bend the rules' to catch and prosecute suspects by any means. While this can also happen in the enforcement model it is especially likely in the community model because the officers cultivate informers and other public contacts who may give unreliable information in order to serve their own interests.

Such problems are only one reason that any given society is unlikely to adopt the pure form of any one of the three models in its entirety. Many factors determine the models of policing which are displayed in different societies, not least the fact that social institutions tend to emerge and to evolve rather than to be installed in a single act of constitutional law-making. We should expect to see as many interpretations of the basic models as there are different interpretations of 'democracy' itself. Thus, we probably need to borrow elements from each model rather than endorse one model in its entirety. We are in the realm of balancing factors, which implies that exaggerating any one approach will prove dysfunctional.

When, finally, we look to the future of research in this field we must recognize that, while empirical research has been a major strength of police studies, and this is true of studies of policing systems right across the world, not only in the Western liberal democracies, there is now a need for conceptual and theoretical synthesis. We need a systematic analysis of the benefits and advantages of the police as an institution. We need to compare the effects of the different models and see what mixture of elements best fits the requirements of our communities, recognizing that, as we enter the twenty-first century, human societies are converging on a set of similar concerns and problems in respect of the control of crime and the achievement of public tranquillity.

Nigel G Fielding, Ph.D., is Professor of Sociology and Deputy Dean of Human Studies at the University of Surrey, Guildford, England. His research interests are in policing, especially community policing and police training, and in qualitative research methods, specifically software for qualitative data analysis. He has been Editor of the Howard Journal of Criminal Justice since 1985 and is co-editor of the Sage Series on Social Science Computing. He has published twelve books (four of them on policing), fifty journal articles and over 150 other publications.

Fielding

References

J. Baxter and L. Koffman (1985) Police: the constitution and the community, Abingdon: Professional Books

Bottoms and P. Wiles (1996) 'Crime and policing in a changing social context' in W. Saulsbury, J. Mott and T. Newburn, eds., Themes in contemporary policing, London: Policy Studies Institute

M. Chatterton (1979) 'The supervision of patrol work under the Fixed Points System' in S. Holdaway, ed., The British Police, London: Edward Arnold

R. Clarke and M. Hough (1984) Crime and police effectiveness, London: HMSO

R. Cotterrell (1989) The politics of jurisprudence, London: Butterworth

N. Fielding (1988) Joining forces: police training, socialization and occupational competence, London: Routledge

N. Fielding (1991), The police and social conflict, London: Athlone

N. Fielding (1995), Community policing, Oxford: Clarendon

D. Hobbs (1988) Doing the business, Oxford: Oxford University Press

D. Hobbs (1995) Bad business, Oxford: Clarendon

Home Office (1994) Report of the Sheehy Inquiry into the Role and Responsibilities of the Police, London: HMSO

P. Laurie (1970) Scotland Yard, Harmondsworth: Penguin

L. Lustgarten (1986) The governance of police, London: Sweet and Maxwell

P. Manning (1977) Police work, Boston: MIT Press

P. Manning (1979) 'The social control of police work' in S. Holdaway, ed., The British Police, London: Edward Arnold

P. Manning (1980) Narcs' Game, Cambridge, MA: MIT Press

P. Manning (1988) Symbolic communication: signifying calls and the police response, Cambridge, MA: MIT Press

M. McConville et al (1991), The case for the prosecution, London: Routledge

P. Morris and K. Heal (1981), Crime control and the police, London: HMSO

A. Murray (1996), 'Sentenced to a crime wave', Sunday Times News Review, London, 5 January.

R. Reiner (1985) The politics of the police, Brighton: Harvester Wheatsheaf

P. Rock (1986) A view from the shadows, Oxford: Clarendon Press

J. Shapland and J. Vagg (1988), Policing by the public, London: Routledge

W. Skogan (1996) 'Public opinion and the police' in W. Saulsbury, J. Mott and T. Newburn, eds., Themes in contemporary policing, London: Policy Studies Institute

F. Tonnies (1950), Community and association, London: Routledge & Kegan Paul

J. Van Maanen and E. Schein (1979) 'Towards a theory of organizational socialization' in B. Staw, ed., Researching organizational behaviour, New York: JAI Press

P. Waddington (1994), Liberty and order, London: UCL Press

P. Waddington (1995) Public order policing, London: UCL Press

M. Weatheritt (1993) 'Measuring police performance: accounting or accountability' in R. Reiner and S. Spencer, eds., Accountable policing: effectiveness, empowerment and equity, London: Institute for Public Policy Research

M. Young (1991) An inside job: policing and police culture, Oxford: Oxford University Press

M. Young (1993) In the sticks: cultural identity in a rural police force, Oxford: Clarendon

Additional resources

There are now a number of specialist e-mail discussion groups on the Internet for those interested in scholarly discussion of matters relating to policing and criminal justice. There is also at least one e-mail listserv for serving police officers. Most of these discussion groups are US-dominated and pay little or no attention to policing/ criminal justice in countries outside North America. The most internationally-oriented e-mail discussion group is 'UNCJIN' (United Nations Criminal Justice International). To subscribe, send an e-mail message with 'subscribe UNCJIN' in the subject line and blank space in the main message area to UNCJIN-L@LSERV.UN.OR.AT

Glossary

accountability: political arrangements by which the police are made responsible to government and/or electorate

child protection: a specialist police function involving the investigation of child abuse and child sexual abuse. Often involves close cooperation with social welfare services/social workers.

crime collators: specialist police officers who compile statistics and other information about crime and criminals in a local police area

crime pattern analysis: the identification and analysis of regularities in the occurrence of particular crime problems

discipline code: the intra-organizational means by which police officers' actions are controlled

discretion: the range of flexibility that officers are granted in interpreting the law

frontline officers: police in daily contact with the public, especially patrol ('beat') officers the 'hook': an informal system of promotion operating in some police departments, notably that of New York City, where advantage was conferred on applicants known to senior officers from their early service and/or contacts made in training

license: the realm of activities sanctioned or legitimated by an organization's mandate

load-sharing: taking responsibility for solving a policing problem jointly with another agency

load-shedding: diverting a demand for police service onto a non-police agency or another police unit

mandate: an organization's mission, its reason for being maintained by the State and/or accepted by society

neighborhood watch: locally-based crime prevention schemes where citizens are encouraged to report suspicious circumstances in the locale, coordinated by a police officer or member of the public

operational: as in 'operational tactics'. Refers to the level of specific police activities or interventions. Contrast to 'policy' level

'outreach': attempts by the police to foster community spirit and improve police/ public relations in local community

police: social institution granted a monopoly of the legitimate application of force in civil society

proactive: police action which precedes or anticipates public perception that a particular problem requires a police response

reactive: police action which responds to public demand for service

* Department of Sociology, University of Surrey, Guilford, Surry, GU25XH, England;
  E-mail: n.fielding@soc.surrey.ac.uk

Figure 5.2

	Enforcement Model	Service Model	Community Model
Balance of reactive/proactive	Reactive	Highly reactive	Proactive
Operations accountable to public	No	Yes, highly	Moderately
Emphasis	Crime control	Community service, responsiveness to public priorities	Order maintenance as a means to achieve law enforcement
Community role	Passive	Active	Information-providers
Performance measures	Quantitative =arrest response times	Citizens surveys Public participation rates in priority-setting forums	Qualitative and quantitative

6 The Changing Face of the Governance of Security and Justice

*Clifford Shearing**

Abstract

This chapter explores the implication of shifts in the way that security and justice are being promoted for the place and role of governmental violence in the maintenance of order. It argues that the emergence of a logic of risk as well as challenges to the established denunciatory and expiatory conception of justice is refiguring the way in which violence is being used as a tactic of governance.

Key Words: Governance, Security, Policing, Justice, Restorative Justice, Risk-logic

Introduction

This chapter will consider the implications of shifts in the governance of security for the use of violence as a regulatory strategy. By the governance of security I mean simply what is done intentionally to promote secure places within which people live, work and play.

In using the phrase - *the governance of security* - rather than more established terms like *policing* and *justice,* I am deliberately distancing myself from conventional ways of thinking about security. I do so in order to bring into view features and developments within the regulation of security that the language of "criminal justice" tends to elude. In the analysis to follow I will attempt in the words of Ulrich Beck (1996:9) to *move the future which is just beginning to take shape into view against a still dominant past.* I will do this by reciting three emblematic stories that illustrate contrasting ways of thinking about the regulation of security. The first parable expresses a"backward–looking" (Packer 1968) approach to security that focuses attention on violent punishment as a device for expiating the harm and pain that violations of security have created. The second parable expresses a "forward–looking" orientation that directs attention away from the past and toward the promotion of security in the future. The third, which will be presented later in the paper, will be used to present a the preoccupation with the past presented within the first story

Parables

My first parable is a wonderful tale by a great story–teller, and a fellow southern African, Doris Leasing (1986:9–10).

There was once a highly respected and prosperous farmer ... in the old Southern Rhodesia, now Zimbabwe, where [Lessing] grew up. ... The farmer decided to import a very special bull from Scotland. He cost £ 10,000, ... [I] t was a very large sum for the farmer. A special home was made for him. He had his own keeper, a black boy of about twelve. All went well; it was clear the bull would soon become the father of a satisfactory number of calves. Then he suddenly and quite inexplicably killed his keeper, the black boy. Something like a court of justice was held. The boy's relatives demanded, and got, compensation. But that was not the end of it. The farmer decided that the bull must be killed. When this became known, a great many people went to him and pleaded for the magnificent beast's life. After all, it was in the nature of bulls to suddenly go berserk, everyone new that. The herd boy had been warned, and he must have been careless. Obviously, it would never happen again ... to waste all that power, potential and not to mention money — what for?

"The bull has killed, the bull is a murderer, and he must be punished. An eye for an eye, a tooth for a tooth," said the inexorable farmer, and the bull was duly executed by a firing squad and buried. In commenting on this series of events, Lessing notes, that what the farmer had done — this act of condemning an animal to death for wrong doing — went back into the far past of mankind, so far back we don't know where it began, but certainly it was when man hardly knew how to differentiate between humans and beasts.

Lessing goes on to note how tactful suggestions along these lines from friends or from other farmers were simply dismissed with: *"I know how to tell right from wrong, thank you very much."*

My second story expresses a very different way of thinking about the governance of security, one in which the moral concerns that dominated the first story are replaced with more instrumental and pragmatic ones.

A large steel company in Canada was losing portable power tools – drills, saws, sanders, and the like — as a result of employee theft. The Chief Executive Officer (CEO) was concerned about the size of the loss and what it was doing to the company's profits. So he called in his Director of Security, and asked him to come up with a solution to this problem. Like many directors of security in the mid–1980s, this person was an ex–police officer who had taken up work in private security as a second career. He had changed his institutional location but had not changed his way of thinking — he still thought and acted like a police officer. This mind–set was reflected in his response to the CEO?'s request. At their next appointment he presented a plan to the CEO. He proposed that the company hire undercover officers who would spy on the workers and discover who was stealing power tools. On an appointed day workers would be searched as they were leaving the plant and the evidence collected here in conjunction with the evidence collected during the undercover work would be used to provide direction and justification for searching workers' homes. On the basis of the evidence collected, charges would be laid and the offending workers would appear in court and be sentenced and then punished for their thefts. After presenting his proposal the Director sat back to bask in the glow of his CEO's praise for his proposals. To his surprise and then horror, he found that the CEO was not happy with the plan at all. Instead he looked at the Director and asked him if he was crazy. From the plan he said it was clear to him that the Director had no understanding of the community within which he worked and what its values were. To make his point the CEO drew out the implications of the proposal for the company. What the Director was suggesting, the CEO noted, was that he should agree to hire undercover agents and then pay for the Director and others in the security department to use the evidence the new agents had collected to help the police lay charges. At the conclusion of the court process the company would lose the workers charged either because they would be imprisoned or he would have to fire them. These workers, the CEO pointed out, were people who the company had spent a lot of money training. As the company would now be short staffed he would have to spend money advertising for new employees and then train the ones he hired. These new employees, he pointed out, were undoubtedly going to be just as likely to steal from the company as the ones who had left. The whole process, he pointed out, would likely reduce morale within the company and this would probably have an effect on productivity. He pointed out that this would likely also harden attitudes within the union and that this would make the forthcoming salary negotiations more difficult than they would otherwise have been. The net result of the Director's "solution" was that the company would lose a lot more money. Whatever the tool–loss this was likely to be doubled or tripled. After reciting all of this, the CEO turned to the Director and said he did know how he could save a lot of money — he could fire the Director, as he was useless to him. Before deciding to do so, however, he said he was prepared to give the Director a week to re-think matters and to appreciate the nature of the community within which he worked. In doing so he said that he might start with the premise that the company was in the business of making, not losing money. Well, this shook the Director up and the prospect of unemployment concentrated his mind. As he reflected on the situation he began to think that perhaps the employees who were removing tools from the plant were not bad people after all, that they were just parents, wives and husbands who had repairs to do on their homes, toys to build, and so on. They needed tools and the company had tools. The problem is that they did not know how to ask the company to borrow them so they just took them. And once they had taken them they did not know how to bring them back. This line of thinking radically changed the way he saw things, and as he saw the situation differently, new solutions came to mind. By the time his appointment with the CEO came around he had a new proposal. He proposed that the company do nothing whatsoever about the tools that had been taken — what was gone — was gone. However, the company should do something about what happened from then onwards. What they should do, he suggested, is open a tool library that would enable employees to take tools home in the evenings and on the weekends and bring them back. This time the CEO smiled a big broad smile and he found that his next paycheck was a little bigger than his last one. Our Director had imagined an alternative to the established way of doing security.

Justice and Security

Both these stories are concerned with the governance of security. However, each story gives expression to a different mentality. The first, while it takes place on a farm rather than in a court room, illustrates a denunciatory, retributive mode of thought that has been central to criminal justice within Anglo–American societies — a way of thinking that, as Lessing suggests in her own analysis, has proved to be remarkably resilient. Lessing's farmer was very concerned about the past and what might be done to undo the harm that had taken place. He felt that while the material things that had taken place might possibly go some way to compensate the family of the boy for their loss, there was a social and moral dimension to what had happened that extended beyond this relationship between offender and victim.

More was required. A symbolic, societal order had been violated that needed to be put right. A *"mystical balance"*— a moral equilibrium symbolized by the scales of justice —had been upset that had to be corrected (Zehr 1990:74). Until this correction was accomplished, neither he, nor the others would be able to "go on" with their lives in a normal way. Something extraordinary had happened that needed an extraordinary symbolic response before the ordinary state of affairs could be recovered and ordinary life continued. Justice had to be done. This required a sacrifice that would expiate the wrong — the bull had to be killed. The scales upset by the extraordinary had to be leveled before things could be normalized. All this had to be done, as the farmer made clear, quite independently of the future and what might be done about it.

This way of conceiving the relationship between the regulation of the past and the future — in which denunciation and expiation reestablish the normality that the managing of future risks requires — captures the essential arguments that take place regarding the objectives that courts should pursue. Within this way of thinking utilitarian purposes are admissible only to the extent that they can be integrated with denunciatory and expiatory ones

Herein lies a source, and perhaps even the source, of the centrality of violence to criminal justice. The tight coupling of symbolic and instrumental concerns that underlies Lessing's farmer's motivations is possible in practice because violence can be utilized to provide for both the regulation of the past and of the future. Violence has been central to criminal justice because it can be used symbolically to expiate the past and to provide a basis for preventing future wrongdoing. Punishment, and the pain it produces, provides for the simultaneous accomplishment of the goals of symbolic and instrumental ordering.

The mentality that infuses the second story is quite different. In this story punishment is not accorded any special privilege. Our CEO is deeply skeptical of the claim that the wrongs of the past must be symbolically corrected before one can go on. For him the past should be left to take care of itself. It needs no rectifying. There is no problem of "going on." One simply turns one's back on the past and goes forward. It is the future, and the future exclusively, that concerns him. Efforts devoted to symbolically reordering the past makes no sense to him. Indeed, he views a concern with expiation and denunciation as counter–productive. Rather than allowing one to go on by providing for closure, they keep the past alive and maintain its grip on the present, and thus, on the future. Accordingly, his response to the logic of retribution that pervades criminal justice would be not to improve it but to abandon it.

In summary, what distinguishes the mentalities that infuse each of our stories is the *priority* they give to the problems of the past and to the future. For Lessing's farmer, it is the past and its symbolic order that must, in the final analysis, be determinant. For our CEO, it is "*colonization of the future*" (Giddens 1991:111) that must carry the day.

Although our farmer's views about which ordering problem should have priority have dominated the governance of security within Anglo-American societies, this hegemony is increasingly being questioned and contested. It is to this challenge and the search for alternatives that I now turn.

Actuarial Security

Recently, Ulrich Beck (1992) has argued that our contemporary social context is fundamentally different from the one that was dominant only a few decades ago he termed this context the *risk society*. Beck (1992:10), in developing this argument, observes that *just as modernization dissolved the structure of feudal society in the nineteenth century and produced the industrial society, modernization today is dissolving industrial society and another modernity is coming into being.*

An implication that I draw from Beck's argument, although it is not one he identifies directly, is that an essential difference between yesterday's world and today's risk society is that while in yesterday's we could, and did, act on the assumption that if things went wrong we would be able to remedy them. If we did not have the knowledge, or the capacity, to do so at the moment this was something that future generations would be able to resolve. This way of being is not longer viable. Modernization has created conditions that have put our collective future indeed the possibility that we will have a future, at risk. We are creating problems that neither us, or our offspring, may be able to solve. We can, and increasingly do not, assume that the problems humanity is creating will be ones it can resolve. We can no longer assume that the future will be "OK". Whether one wants to take the argument this far, or not, the point of Beck's argument is nicely captured by Giddens (11991:123-4) when he writes that it *is not that day-to-day life is inherently more risky than was the case in prior eras. It is rather that, in conditions of modernity... thinking in terms of risk and risk assessment is a more or less ever-present exercise....*

This concern with risk is giving rise to a new mode of living. Instead of going ahead and doing things and then coping with the problems this might create if and when they arise, we now seek to anticipate problems and to avoid them. An obvious example of this risk based way of thinking is the way in which we seek to anticipate and avoid the possibility of a nuclear accident occurring. With such an accident and other similar potential problems, we do not adopt an attitude in which we are willing to risk the problem occurring knowing that we will be able to cope with it when and if it does.

As a consequence, while it is certainly true that a concern with risk is as old as humanity itself, we are today organizing our lives around risk and the development of risk reduction strategies to an unprecedented extent, and so a *qualitative* rather than a simply quantitative shift has occurred. We live in a risk society in which risk technologies have acquired a new priority. Associated with this is a new risk mentality. This new actuarial mentality promotes a concern with the discovery and application of new and innovative ways of coping with the present in ways that will hopefully ensure that we will be able to enjoy a future. Beck (1992), in developing his arguments for the emergence of a risk society develops somewhat different, but compatible arguments. He argues that there has been a fundamental shift in the central problem of modern society from one of wealth production to risk management. As human beings have sought to respond to the *"dictatorship of scarcity"* they have created a new set of problems — *Are "the sources of wealth are 'polluted' by growing ' hazardous side effects'"* ?(1992:20). While these problems are not new their nature and extent makes them qualitatively different. Beck (1992:21) summarizes his argument in his definition of 'risk':

> *Risk may be defined as a systematic way of dealing with hazards and insecurities induced and introduced by modernization itself. Risks, as opposed to old dangers, are consequences which relate to the threatening forces of modernization and to its globalization of doubt.*

Whether one accepts either Giddens' or Beck's account of the reasons for the contemporary concern with risk, their contention that we live in a society in which risk and its management occupies a central place in human affairs is persuasive. This concern with risk, and the emergence of strategies and associated institutions for coping with them, is being felt across the many and varied arenas of governance. One of these is security, where, as I have noted, an actuarial mode of governing is emerging.

Seen from the perspective of the above analysis, what our CEO was advocating was a risk–based approach to security that argues that his company can no longer afford the luxury of a mode of management that focuses attention on the past. The message of our CEO to his Security Director was: "*Hey, your insistence that we fix the past is going to put us out of business, and thereby deny us a future so get going and make sure we as a community do what is required to secure a future for ourselves.*"

There is nothing "soft" about this actuarial approach to the governance of security. It is not designed to make things easier or better for people who cause problems. Neither is it "hard." Rather, it seeks to move away from this way of thinking about security entirely. Its concern is not what risk reduction will mean for individual offenders or victims. Instead, the whole victim–offender dichotomy is eclipsed. Its focus is on populations and opportunities.

At this point it is useful to shift gears and turn to Foucault's thoughts on the "art of government." Foucault, working from very different premises, and within a very different theoretical framework from Giddens and Beck, draws attention to a similar shift in governance. He identifies a shift to an art of governance which he refers to as *governmentality* (which he uses to refer both the idea of mentalities of governance generally and a particular way of thinking about governance). He describes this particular mentality of governance as a way of governing that seeks "*the right disposition of things arranged so as to lead to a convenient end*" (1991:93). He elaborates on this idea of the governing things as follows:

> *The things which in this sense government is to be concerned are in fact men, but men in their relations, their links, their imbrication with those other things which are wealth, resources, means of subsistence, the territory with its specific qualities, climate, irrigation, fertility, etc.; men in their relation to that other kind of things, customs, habits, ways of acting and thinking, etc.; lastly, men in their relation to that other kind of things accidents and misfortunes such as famine, epidemics, death, etc. (1991:93)*

Law within this governmentality promotes a disposition of things.

> *[I]t is a question not of imposing law on men, but of disposing things; that is to say, of employing tactics rather than laws, and even laws themselves as tactics — to arrange things in such a way that, through a certain number of means such and such ends may be achieved (1991:95).*

If the business of law is the business of moral ordering – of creating moral balances then the business of instrumental ordering is the tactical arrangement of things with law and moral ordering regarded as one possible thing to be used in this way. Law, like other things, becomes a device or procedure for accomplishing a way of doing things that will promote security.

Our CEO sought to respond to risk as Beck has outlined it by employing a governmentality that sought to provide for a distribution of things that would minimize hazards and insecurities. Seen in this light what our CEO was insisting upon was a government of things. The logic he encouraged his Security Director to embrace was one that looks to the most appropriate way of arranging things so that the end of security, understood as loss prevention, will be realized. In recognition of this focus on "things" Ronald Clarke (1995) has termed this way of governing security a situational approach. This situational focus is not simply a future oriented strategy. The focus within this approach is not on persons per se but on modifying the situations within which they act to encourage behavior that is consistent with the end of security. The world is conceived as an assemblage of sites to be modified so as to encourage more appropriate action from people whose natures are accepted as given. Persons and their propensities are accepted as they stand. Attention is not only directed away from a concern with the past but from future–oriented strate-gies that seek to rehabilitate people.

As Malley (1997) notes, this way of governing security is not: concerned with the meaningful activities of individuals, involving intentions, motivations, under-standings, guilt, fault, etc. Instead, its focus is on the distribution and effects of behaviors –in the sense of "external" physical dispositions rather than, "internal" states. ...[I]t seeks to develop ways of manipulating risk-bearing behaviors in order to increase security.

Within this actuarial *logic* (Feeley and Simon 1994), violence no longer has the privileged status it has hitherto enjoyed as a device that can be employed to simultaneously remedy the past and colonize a future. What makes violence a useful governing strategy is not the pain it causes but its utility as a way of compelling a particular distribution of things. It has no special priority. It is simply one possible device among many for disposing of things so as to promote the realization of security. Within this logic, violence, as a source of risk reduction, is attractive only to the extent that it incapacitates (or deters). Its attractiveness as a source of denunciation and expiation disappears.

As deterrence (both specific and general) is now viewed within increasing suspi-cion because of the difficulty of ensuring certainty of detection, what remains is the value violence holds as a source of incapacitation, particularly through its use as imprisonment. However, within this mentality imprisonment ceases to be viewed as punishment and becomes instead a vehicle for keeping dangerous people in a situation in which their potential to harm to others is minimized. One does not imprison to be just — one imprisons because prisons provide an existing, and hence convenient, space within which to keep dangerous people out of harm's way.

Prison, as Feeley and Simon (1994:174–175) suggest, becomes a place for ware-housing troublesome things. To the extent that this requires prison reform the focus of this is to reshape prisons so that they can cost–effectively meet an incapacitative objective. In Ontario, Canada for example, the government has decided that the best way to do this is to close down small prisons designed to promote rehabilitation and replace them with mega–prisons whose sole purpose will be to warehouse potentially dangerous bodies.

While this shift in thinking and language is now beginning to become more and more evident within the political and policy arenas of state governments, it has long been established within private governance. Here, the terms policing and police have been replaced by security (both as a noun and a verb) and crime has been replaced by a variety of context specific terms, the most common of which is *loss*. This, as the argument to this point suggests, is not just a matter of semantics. It denotes a different way of constructing and thinking about people as things and in relation to things.

This difference in location is critical in identifying and understanding shifts in the use of violence as an ordering mechanism. What was critical about our CEO was that he was not operating within a state context. His milieu was what one might think of as a *corporate community*. He did not take his point of reference to be society as a whole. He acted within a community context. He saw the world as fractured rather than as one piece. There are several implications of this that are worth noting.

The first is the comfort our CEO quite obviously felt with the mentality of governing through a logic of risk. This resonated with the culture of management and the logic of the market place with which he was already familiar. He simply brought his normal problem–solving repertoire to bear on the problem of security. His security problem was, for him, simply another economic problem to be addressed by identifying the appropriate mobilization of resources. He was through his training as a business person, already familiar with the idea of promoting *"the proper distribution of things"* to achieve a desired end. His complaint about his Director of Security was that he was operating within a logic of criminal justice with its emphasis on denunciation, a logic that he felt had no place within his business world. What he required of him was that he stop thinking like a police person and start thinking like a businessperson. He should stop thinking as an agent of *society* and start thinking in terms of *community*.

A second implication is that our CEO was not constrained by a whole set of existing strategies, institutions and practices for doing security that had an affinity with a different mentality. He was not constrained by a series of "social technologies." He was thus in a very different position to someone wishing to promote an actuarial logic within criminal justice. Consequently, he had relatively little cultural or institutional resistance to overcome. He was able to work from a comparatively clean slate. His situation was thus very different to that of most police managers who typically work within cultural and institutional contexts oriented to the goal of moral ordering and the primacy of force as a device for its accomplishment.

Third, our CEO, unlike those who operate within other non–state communities (for example, volunteer organizations), had access to something akin to a tax base that he could draw on to govern security. He had resources to deploy.

It is these and related factors that have enabled persons operating in a wide variety of corporate communities to govern in the manner advocated by our CEO. A central feature of governance within these communities is a mentality of risk reduction. While corporate communities are central to the complex network of governance that has emerged alongside state governments, these *"private governments"* and the *"bubbles of governance"* that they create are not limited to business communities narrowly conceived. There are a wide range of what might be called *"contractual communities*" that now pervade Anglo–American societies. These include such spaces as communities of library users, the residential communities that North American's term *gated communities*, communities of shoppers at malls as well virtual communities such as the communities of credit card holders and internet users. Together, these communities, or arenas of governance, form a complex and expanding archipelago of private governments that together establish what we might term an emerging "*neo–feudalism.*"

One of the features of this new feudalism is that the contracts that establish these arenas of governance are, in part, contracts that set out such things as the proper expectations (rights) and responsibilities (duties) of community members. A ubiquitous example is the contract that persons enter into as library user. Most libraries today require, as part of this contract, that members agree to submit themselves to electronic scanning as they enter and leave the book collection. Similar contracts are required if one wishes to fly. At the Toronto airport this contract is quite explicit. As one enters the area restricted to passengers, one faces a sign that reads:

> *You are not required to submit either your bags or your person to a search if you do not wish to board an aircraft.*

In our contemporary world we move around this feudal–like archipelago of governance by moving from one contractual community to another. As we do we move from one bubble of governance to another. Each of these bubbles has its own mode of governance and its own rules that set out the conditions of "citizenship" or, perhaps more accurately, "*denizenship*" in these new spaces of governance.[1]

The logic of 'risk-governance' dominates these contractual spaces. Within them the governance of security tends to take place in the manner advocated by our CEO. Here, the traditional view of punishment as a source of the pain that denunciation and deterrence require has increasingly given way to risk–based strategies. The strategies of governance within this archipelago are very different from those advocated by Lessing's farmer. They are worlds apart. Within the world of our CEO, the established notions of justice have little meaning. Here punishment is not a central practice of governance.

These contractual spaces are, of course, not the only spaces in which people live their lives. While some people spend more time within these spaces than others do, everyone spends part of their time there, and if they are poor probably most of their time is spent outside these bubbles. An actuarial logic has developed both inside and outside these neo–feudal bubbles of governance. What differentiates them is the extent to which this logic has taken hold of thinking and the way in which it has done so.

Actuarialism Within the State

The logic of risk has, over the last decade or two, begun to penetrate the spaces and institutions of the state in ways that are fundamentally refiguring criminal justice. Two features of these developments are significant for the argument being developed here. First, it is important to recognize that the emergence of an actuarial mentality within criminal justice has not led to a wholesale abandonment of existing ways of thinking about and regulating security. Rather, these ways of being have been, and are being, molded and adapted to fit within a risk–focused mentality. Habits of mind and action that were developed within the context of a logic of denunciation and deterrence are acquiring new meanings and functions under the influence of a logic of risk — the use of prisons as warehouses to incapacitate people, noted above, provides one example. As Feeley and Simon (1994:174) note:

> *Possibly the clearest indication of actuarial justice is found in the new theory of incapacitation, which has become the predominant model of punishment. Incapacitation promises to reduce the effects of crime in society not by altering either offender or social context, but by rearranging the distribution of offenders in society. If the prison can do nothing else, incapacitation theory holds, it can detain offenders for a time and thus delay their resumption of criminal activity in society.*

The second point to note is how the re–birth of private governments that has accompanied the emergence of a risk logic has enabled the development of elaborate networks of security institutions that include both state and non–state resources. This possibility has permitted agencies within the state to graft risk strategies located within non—state spheres of governance onto their own endeavors. As Bayley and I have argued (1996:588), the central feature of community policing is the attempt by the police to build partnerships and networks that position the police and non–state entities as *co–producers of public safety*. In exploring this development, Ericson and Haggerty (1997) have recently identified the many ways in which state police have organized themselves as brokers who operate the knowledge conduits that networked policing requires

In developing these partnerships, states typically seek to take advantage of the logic and institutions of non–state sites of governance and to direct their operations in a manner that enables them to *rule at a distance* (Rose and Miller 1992). In the networks of security that these partnerships have established— in which the state seeks to maintain control of the *steering* of governance while encouraging others to accept responsibility for the *rowing* (Osborne and Gaebler 1994)—the pattern that has emerged is one in which state agents seek to coordinate the available regulatory resources while preserving states claims to a monopoly of violence. There are now many examples of this strategy within the policing arena. Perhaps the most ubiquitous are neighborhood watch and safe house schemes in which citizens are encouraged to become the eyes and ears of the police and to call upon them when a coercive response is required to preserve order.

What is being encouraged through these developments is a division of labor in which the state remains a key source of security through its access to violence while non–state resources are mobilized to establish security networks that operates according to risk management principles. Among the clearest indications of this is the difference between the security strategies employed within the new feudal domains that the emergence of *mass private property* has established — for instance the security practices within places like Disney World — and they way in which poor neighborhoods are policed through the use of target-hardening strategies by police agencies.

One possible consequence of this emerging risk framework one would expect to find is changes in the legal framework within which security operates to permit the application of risk strategies by the state and its partners. Some evidence of this exists within the United States in recent court decisions that permit the use of coercive resources within a risk framework. Simon and Feeley (1994:185) draw attention to this when they write that:

> [g]overnment action against criminal activity, even when mixed with traditional punitive functions, is increasingly subject to a different constitutional standard because instead of emphasizing the goals of public justice, it emphasizes the goals of risk management. It is preventative rather than responsive. It seeks not to punish but to exclude those with criminal proclivities. It is directed not at a general public norm but at security within a specialized and functionally defined area (1994:185).

Of course, states and their agents must frequently contend with the fact that other participants of the networks that they are part of and seek to manage may, and often do, view things differently. These others frequently seek to mobilize networks, including state agents, to do their bidding. The result is that security networks have become sites of contest as participants with different aims seek to mobilize the resources available to promote their objectives. Thus, for example, one finds a host of private governments calling the police only when it suits them and doing so in ways that will fit them into an actuarial framework of risk reduction even though the police themselves might be operating within a punitive stance of moral ordering. This is evident, for instance, in the ordering of financial markets by private regulators where although the objective is very clearly the instrumental ordering of the future the law is often invoked to initiate prosecutions when this is viewed as beneficial from the perspective of risk reduction (Addario, et al. 1990).

Justice and Risk

Where states remain either exclusive participants in providing security or are able to shape security networks in accord with their ends, the problem of ordering the past tends to be given greater weight than is the case in non–state spheres of governance. Where police have taken charge of a case, they remain likely, if the evidence permits, to follow a retributive logic and to set in motion processes that will give this logic concrete expression. Accordingly, while our CEO might have little difficulty insisting that attention be focused exclusively on the future this proves to be more difficult within the context of state institutions, where, as the term *criminal justice* reminds us, a concern with *doing justice* (where justice is understood in expiatory and retributive terms) remains a priority. To the extent that this is true, and participants are operating within what Zehr (1990) calls the retributive *paradigm* a tension arises between the dictates of the actuarial logic, as it gains influence, and the requirements of justice. Although corporate victims, like the shareholders our CEO represents, may have little interest in seeing *justice* done because they have not been directly involved in the harm that took place, this is less true of individual victims. These victims, who continue to mobilize the criminal justice processes through reports to the police of wrongdoing, are more emotionally involved and less sanguine about the idea of leaving the past to take care of itself. For them, the problem of remedying the past is more pressing. Their concerns and feelings tend to be closer to those of Lessing's farmer than they are to those of our CEO. To the extent that victims' concerns dominate criminal justice and this has tended to be more, rather than less the case, the pursuit of justice continues to play a critical role within state governance of security. To the extent that justice is understood within the framework of the retributive paradigm, this sets up a tension that limits the extent to which a risk logic can be pursued within state processes.

In recognition of this, a significant movement has emerged under the rubric of *restorative justice* which is seeking to establish a way of doing justice that will challenge, and it is hoped eventually replace, the conception of justice that lies at the heart of the retributive paradigm. This shift has its roots, like the actuarial shift within the world of business in the institutions and practices of tort law and the development of mediation as a mechanism for dispute resolution (Auerbach 1983:95–97). Restorative justice seeks to extend the logic that has informed mediation beyond the settlement of business disputes to the resolution of individual conflicts that have traditionally been addressed within a retributive paradigm. It seeks to find ways of responding to the anger and hurt of victims in a manner that does not lead to the punishment, stigmatization and exclusion that have characterized the operations of criminal justice. The concern expressed by advocates of restorative justice is similar to that of our CEO. The difference is that they propose a response that acknowledges the importance of symbolically reordering the past.

Once again, a story, this time from John Braithwaite, can be used to capture the essential features of the nature of, and the argument for, restorative justice.

Imagine that a teenager is arrested for robbery. Braithwaite calls him Sam. Instead of sending him to court the arresting officer refers Sam to a facilitator who convenes a restorative justice conference. When the facilitator asks about his parents, Sam says he is homeless. His parents abused him and he hates them. Sam refuses to cooperate with a conference if they attend. After going through various obvious possibilities the facilitator concludes that there is enough of a positive connection between Sam, his Uncle George, his older sister and his hockey coach to have them attend a conference. So, they and the robbery victim and her daughter are invited to a conference. [They all attend and] sit on chairs in a circle. The facilitator starts by introducing everyone and reminding Sam that while he has admitted to the robbery, he can change his plea at any time during the conference and have the matter heard by a court. Sam is asked to explain what happened in his own words. He mumbles that he needed money to survive, saw the [workman] knocked her over and ran off with her purse. Uncle George is asked what he things of this. He says that Sam used to be a good kid. But that Sam had gone off the rails. He had let his parents down so badly that they would not even come today. *And now you have done this to this poor lady. I never thought you would stoop to violence*, continues Uncle George, building into an angry tirade against the boy. The hockey coach also says he is surprised that Sam could do something as terrible as this. Sam was always a troublemaker at school. But he could see a kinder side in Sam that left him shocked about the violence. The sister is invited to speak, but the facilitator moves to the victim when Sam's sister seem too emotional to speak.

The victim explains how much trouble she had to cancel the credit cards in the purse, how she had no money for the shopping she needed to do that day. Her daughter explains that the most important consequence of the crime was that her mother was now afraid to go out on her own. In particular, she is afraid that Sam is stalking her, waiting to rob her again. Sam sneers at this and seems callous throughout. His sister starts to sob. Concerned about how distressed she is, the facilitator calls a brief adjournment so she can comfort her, with help from Uncle George. During the break, the sister reveals that she understands what Sam has been through. She says she was abused by their parents as well. Uncle George has never heard of this, is shocked, and not sure that he believes it.

When the conference convenes, Sam's sister speaks to him with love and strength. Looking straight into his eyes, the first gaze he could not avoid in the conference, she says that she knows exactly what he has been through with their parents. No details are spoken. But the victim seems to understand what is spoken of by the knowing communication between sister and brother. Tears rush down the old woman's cheeks and over a trembling mouth.

It is the sister's love that penetrates Sam's callous exterior. From then on he is emotionally engaged with the conference. He says he is sorry about what the victim has lost. He would like to pay it back, but he has no money or job. He assures the victim he is not stalking her. She readily accepts this now and when questioned by the facilitator says now she thinks she will feel safe walking out alone. She wants her money back but says it will help her if they can talk about what to do to help Sam find a home and a job. Sam's sister says he can come and live in her house for a while. The hockey coach says he has some casual work that needs to be done, enough to pay Sam's debt to the victim and a bit more. If Sam does a good job, he will write him a reference for applications for permanent jobs. When the conference breaks us, the victim hugs Sam and tearfully wishes him good luck. He apologizes again. Uncle George quietly slips a hundred dollars to Sam's sister to defray the extra costs of having Sam in the house, says he will be there for both of them if they need him.

Sam has a rocky life punctuated with several periods of unemployment. A year later he has to go through another conference after he steals a bicycle. But he finds work when he can, mostly stays out of trouble and lives to mourn at the funerals of Uncle George and his sister. The victim gets her money back and enjoys taking long walks alone. Both she and her daughter say that they feel enriched as a result of the conference, [they] have a little more grace in their lives (1996:3–4).

Restorative justice, as Braithwaite's story exemplifies, promotes a conception of justice that seeks to restore relationships without a resort to exclusion and the other costs that our CEO found so problematic. While the advocates of restorative justice do not tend to draw attention to its compatibility with the use of an actuarial logic in colonizing the future, this is one of its consequences. The logic of restorative justice fits easily with that of actuarialism.

Restorative justice seeks to refigure the ordering of security through processes that shift the meaning of events from one of contesting and disputing *selves* to one in which the contestants are restored to the status of *non–disputing selves* who are once again in a position to get on with the business of living together (Pavlich 1996). What is significant about this approach to justice is that, unlike the conception constructed within the retributive paradigm, it does not call into being consequences that conflict with the aims of an actuarial approach to security.

What the emerging techniques of restorative justice provides is a moral logic that fits with, and reinforces, the instrumental logic of actuarial security. It provides the symbolic, past oriented side of the instrumental, future–oriented logic of risk management. This link between the instrumental and the symbolic, although central to many of the programs of restorative justice that have emerged, is often overshadowed by the attention given, by their advocates, to shaming as a device for doing justice. However, what is evident in most of these programs is that in practice the outcomes that result typically include the development of community based surveillance networks that mobilize local resources to monitor and control the future behavior of the wrongdoer. This is particularly evident in the variety of forms of *community services* that wrongdoers contract to undertake as part of the mediation process. A central feature of such service is often that it places the risky person under the surveillance of both state and non-state persons who contract to assist in preventing a reoccurrence of wrongdoing.

Conclusion

I have argued that a 'risk-logic' has emerged that is re–shaping the governance of security within both state and non–state terrains. This actuarial logic is being shaped by existing institutions and habitual practices. This is particularly apparent within the state sphere where the institutional forms and practices that developed in association with a retributive logic have operated to shape the manner in which an actuarial logic is realized.

In examining this shift in governance I have explored its relationship to established concepts and practices of justice. I argued that justice, understood within the context of the re–ordering of the past, was much less of a concern within non-state arenas, where corporate victims are central, than it was within the state sphere where individual victimization is more significant. Within non-state governance of security, an instrumental rather than a moral approach tends to predominate. This instrumental focus has meant that the question of justice, understood as a symbolic response to wrongdoing, tends to remain on the sidelines. This contrasts with the situation within the public realm. Within this sphere not only is justice a central question in the ordering of security, but the retributive paradigm that tends to predominate does not fit well with the way of thinking advocated by a risk mentality. This tension is being lessened where the mentality and practice of restorative justice is taking hold within criminal justice.Each of these developments has implications for the use of violence within the governance of security. In both a risk–oriented mentality of security and a restorative conception of justice, violence loses its privileged status as a strategy to be deployed in the ordering of security. This does not mean that it has been eclipsed as a strategy, but rather that it is considered as one means among others to be used in the governance of security. Further, in both these emerging mentalities, the mechanisms of coercion within criminal justice come to be seen less as a device for inflicting pain and more as a set of resources to be considered in reducing risk.

If the mentalities identified in this chapter continue to gain ground, this will have very significant implications for the way in which violence is used and justified within the governance of security. Just how the tensions between different paradigms for thinking about and doing security and justice will be worked out will depend on the outcomes of the many experiments that are taking place around the world in both public and private arenas. The patterns of ordering that we will live with in the future will be shaped through practice rather than philosophical discourses which will, like Hegel's "*owl of Minerva*" take flight only after the new practices are themselves beginning to shift yet again.

My hope is that as we engage in these experiments that we will do so in ways that give voice to the knowledge of and concerns of the poor and the marginalized as well as the rich and the powerful. It is taking action to encourage and facilitate these experiments that we as social thinkers remind ourselves that "*the owl of Minerva takes its flight only when the shades of night are gathering*" (Hegel 1836) and do more than simply identify and make sense of the shifts that are reshaping the governance of security.

Clifford Shearing, Ph. D., is Director of the Centre of Criminology at the University of Toronto. He also coordinates a Community Peace Programme at the School of Government, University of the Western Cape. He studies shifts in governance through the window of policing and regulation. His most recent book (with Mike Brogden) is Policing for a New South Africa *(Routledge, 1994). He is presently working with poor and disadvantaged communities in South Africa to develop processes of policing and dispute resolution that express their experience and knowledge.*

Shearing

References

Susan Addario, Mary Condon, Clifford Shearing and Philip Stenning, "Controlling interests: Two conceptions of ordering financial markets." Pp. 88-119 in Martin L Friedland (ed.), Securing Compliance: Seven Case Studies, Toronto: University of Toronto Press, 1990

David Bayley and Clifford Shearing, The Future of Policing. Law and Society Review. 1996, 30(4): 585–606.

Ulrich Beck, Risk Society: Toward a New Modernity. London: Sage, 1992

John Braithwaite, "Restorative Justice and a Better Future." Dorothy J. Killam Memorial Lecture, Dalhousie University, October, 1996.

Richard Ericson and Kevin Haggerty, Policing the Risk Society. Toronto: University of Toronto Press, 1997

Malcolm Feeley and Jonathan Simon, ?"Actuarial Justice: the Emerging New Criminal Law" Pp. 173–200 in David Nelken (ed.) The Future of Criminology London: Sage, 1994

Anthony Giddens, Modernity and Self–Identiy: Self and Society in the Late Modern Age. Oxford: Polity, 1991.

Georg Hegel, Philosophy of Right. London: George Bell and Sons, 1836.

Doris Lessing, Prisons We Choose To Live Inside. Concord, Canada: Anansi, 1991.

Pat O'Malley, "Introduction", in Pat O'Malley (ed.) Crime and the Risk Society. . Aldershot: Ashgate Publishing, 1998 (forthcoming)

David Osborne and Ted Gaebler, Reinventing Government. New York: Plume, 1993.

Herbert Packer, The Limits of the Criminal Sanction. Stanford: Stanford University Press, 1968

George Pavlich, "The Power of Community Mediation: Government and the Formation of Self–Identity." Law and Society Review, 1996, 30(4): 707–733 *

Howard Zehr, Changing Lenses. Waterloo, Ontario: Herlad Press, 1990

*   Center of Criminology, University of Toronto School of Government, 130 St. George
    Street, TORONTO, Ontario M5S 3H1, CANADA; E-mail: c.shearing@ utoronto.ca
    University of the Western Cape.

I am grateful to Sebastian Scheerer for drawing to my attention the ' significance of distinguishing between citizens and denizens'.

7 Policing In The Information Age[*]

Peter K. Manning

Abstract

The paper argues that changes in social structure are reflected in patterns of policing that are no longer national, but are transnational. In the past, it has been useful to focus on policing in industrialized democratic states and examine their histories, structure, and emergent properties (cf. David Bayley 1976 1979). The definition of policing, drawing on Weber and Bittner, relies on the duty of citizens in a legitimate order to comply with even implicit commands, while force is held out to ensure compliance. This family of definitions implies the existence of a bounded designated and named territory within which a mandate obtains (Sheptyki 1995a). The monopoly of legitimate force, a trait of the state according to Weber, is problematic (Rheinstein, 1967: 5-10). Global or transnational policing (Sheptycki, 1995) means application of force in quasi-legitimate fashion when war has not been declared. "Policing" is no longer easily defined or restricted to national forces with national mandates, restricted territorial duties and narrow legal limitations. New national interests and international patterns of control change the relationships between democracy and security. Changes in international relations and the economy, as well as those in information technology, transportation and communications, are now reflected in policing. The mandate is being shaped by concerns not only for personal security, but for the security of information as property as well as information as a symbol or an expressive matter. Many traditional policing issues, not discussed in detail here, such as restraint, information control, both concealing and revealing, respect of citizens' privacy, and compliance are being changed and these changes affect both police and citizens in democratic nations.

Key Words: Policing, information age, legitimate force, social control, transnational policing

Introduction

In the past, it has been useful to focus on policing in industrialized democratic States and examine their histories, structure, and emergent properties (cf. David Bayley 1976 1979). Even the definition of policing, drawing on Weber and Bittner, relies on the duty of citizens in a legitimate order to comply with even implicit commands, while force is held out to ensure compliance. This family of definitions implies the existence of a bounded, designated and named territory within which a mandate obtains (Sheptyki 1995a). The monopoly of legitimate force, a trait of the State according to Weber, is problematic (Rheinstein, 1967: 5-10). Global or transnational policing (Sheptycki, 1995) means application of force in quasi-legitimate fashion when war has not been declared. "Policing" is no longer easily defined or restricted to national forces with national mandates, restricted territorial duties and narrow legal limitations. New national interests and international patterns of control change the relationships between democracy and security.

Policing What?

Policing is formal social control, an official response to a grievance (Black, 1993:5). It is third party intervention in the name of authority into social relations. Although the distinction between public and private policing has a long history, it is perhaps more useful at present to see "policing" as an analytic term or ideal type and identify its central features (Forst and Manning, 1999). Based upon the control of territories and people, Anglo-American policing's (and other European systems) origins are militaristic. The divided system of a domestic and benign front combined with a reserve of cavalry or armed and mounted troops was devised in the colonial settings of the Indian sub-continent and Ireland, and then modified by Robert Peel.

The relationships between national policing, which reflects in some sense on the sacred aspects of the State, and the growing trend toward transnational policing, are not well understood. An analysis of policing, "security," and democracy must synthesize the literature on the state and policing (Bayley, 1979) as well as that on national and transnational policing (Benyon, et.al. 1993, Nadelmann, 1993, Fijnaut, 1993 Harding, et.al. 1993 Sheptycki, 1995, 1996, 1996a). The growth of transnational policing, with changes in the world economy,[1] requires re-thinking of the assumed connection between authority, territory and policing. A new conception of policing in an information age is required, a conception of policing in which:

- national boundaries are less marked and clear,
- where information is a commodity, and
- secrecy and security concerns arise from global information networks that are both public and private.

Following are some evident changes in policing:

- Policing, which now crosses borders, is done cooperatively among nations or groups of nations. Conversely, nation-states possess less control over the definitions and punishment of crimes within their borders.

- Territory and official control are not always correlated. Setting aside that police may not indeed control their nominal national territories (as in periods of rebellion or upheaval), or differentially control segments of the territory, the level of control and source of control via policing are now more problematic in international relations. Individual powerful nations can redefine the need for "peace-keeping" or police action in other nations, as the United States and allies did in Kuwait and Iraq and Kosovo; the United Nations has "peace-keeping" forces that have been active in several countries for long periods of time, and ad hoc forays by American troops, a heady mixture of economic power and legal justification, are seen in American invasions of Panama, Grenada, Haiti, Somalia, undeclared war in Nicaragua and Guatemala and the enforcement of American drug laws in Columbia, Bolivia, and Mexico. REFS if possible

- The use of policing as force internationally has always arisen from many sources, but now the analytic task is to explain the conditions under which and frequency with which force is applied under the label of "policing." Policing has typically been restricted to domestic, low politics, non-rebellious regulation within States, not across them (Manning, 1997: 98-100). "Military action" within the borders of another country without permission was regarded as an act of war.

- The nature of "violence" itself is changing, becoming more symbolic and yet more present visually via the world wide web and international satellite networks. Violence is less significant than the threat of such, and symbolic force, threats and words, are as central to much policing as is physical or weapons-based force. Bourdieu (1977) argues violence is changing: it now includes symbolic violence, the destruction of meanings, connections, continuity through invisible domination, and this destructive force can rapidly cross borders via mass media, especially television.consoder briefly distinguishing between 'violence', violating and being violated.

- The growth of internationalist enforcement, policing the world, is paralleled by the rise of networks of chaos and terror, that compete with State-based and transnational groups of organized and official police. Consider the growth of sea and air piracy; terrorism; a huge network of private policing, with transnational dimensions (Pinkerton, Wells-Fargo, Wackenhut); and pan-national liberation groups e.g., Hez'aballah. These compete for the monopoly of force within and between nation states. Rapid and cheap transportation, miniature explosive devices, easy movement within the EEU, and transnational corporate movements of information, especially electronic fund transfers, constrain enforcement (and create opportunities for new forms of crime note some examples), whether based on "national interests" or redefined as international threats.

- The application of force within and across borders now is in part based on cybernetic actions and reactions mediated by very sophisticated information technologies rather than human observation. The first fully televised war as spectacle, the "Gulf War" (Kellner, 1992) was a prelude to the computer-imagery and guidance used in bombing of Kosovo. This bombing as peace-keeping relied on virtual command and control, satellite pictures rather than on-site observations (Ignatieff, 1999).

While national police in the Anglo-American appear to be more "militaristic" in their weapons, legal rhetoric, use of SWAT teams and warrant-serving units, dress, strategies and tactics (Haggerty and Ericson, 1998; Kraska and Kappeler, 1998), American army personnel are now training police for domestic "democratic policing" in Eastern Europe, mounting service projects in developing nations and arguing for a service dimension to their international mandate.

The police in nation States are grappling with new functions: policing information, its use, sale, and synthesis. Modern technology permits social relations across vast spaces instantaneously- mediated communication by sound, pictures, texts, film links the world in a continuous web of stimuli and imagery made possible because all forms of information (sound, pictures, texts, graphics, and numbers for example) can be digitalized and transmitted.

These changes in policing are the result of other changes. Changes in social relations, information systems, and property rights now exist. Historically, policing in industrialized societies combines protection of the States' interests with the security of citizens' property and well-being. The concept of property and its protection are changing. It is widely acknowledged that information is property, a commodity to be bought and sold, a source of conflict, secrecy and competition between corporations, States and individuals.[2] But in addition, whereas a trait of totalitarian policing was information control, and the linking of loyalty and politically correct thinking, reading and speech, democratic policing is now confronted with a new challenge arising from the commodification of information: it now has economic and political value. Collective and individual rights with respect to information-as-property are being identified and adjudicated.

The rise of transnational policing parallels the growth of information policing functions, including regulating the flow of information nationally and internationally. Transnational policing is regulation of a new, growing and resonant kind of social space. The police role in formatting information exchange, monitoring the content, and identifying types of "cybercrime," is now emergent. The rapid growth of an infrastructure of information technology and of skills in policing is notable.[3]

Changes In National Interests

A number of factors have changed the definition of national interests, matters for which the State is responsible to its citizens. These include information, its transport, security and validity; and the integrity of the "core" information that is the basis for the profitiability of often global megacorporations. This shifting view of information leads to competition between the State and corporations over possession of, and the right to, trade in valued information.

Information has always been assumed to be a criteria for rational choice. The notion market-patterned rational choice as "human" and the base line for judging wise and just decisions, once only the conceit of economists, has now become the new conventional wisdom. The popularity of the new rationalism is based on re-imagining the role of information in markets. In traditional liberal and Keynesian economic thought, information was considered slippery and often unavailable. Unlike a market in commodities, or services, information could not be easily valued; it could only be symbolically named, tracked, sold and bought. Von Mises, Von Hayek and the Austrian School of economics argued for the important role of interrelations of uncertainty and subjective assessments in (often unintended) shaping market stability. They argued that useful information is embedded in ignorance and endogenous forces and unpredictable contingencies. Regulators cannot predict such activities accurately. The subjective side of market function means that disruptions and changes are enstructured by routines, rules and procedures that unintentionally stabilize complex markets. Ironically, regulation of uncertain information markets will increasingly be both a cause and consequence of market dynamics. Like "readings" of market behaviour, enforcement procedure shapes markets. The rules of thumb that enable "best estimates" of targeted behaviour create conditions under which information markets change. As the information monitoring infrastructure increases, the markets become reflexively tied into conceptions of the market, in turn based on modeling, simulation and computer-based controls on trading. Rather than ignorance being error variance, it was an essential component in deciding; it would be irrational to be too rational under such circumstances.

It is not clear whether the market in information, seen as a commodity which reflects itself, will follow the same patterning as other goods and services. While information acts as a variable in economic models, this new role of information as commodity is contingent upon the creation of scarcity. The modes of control on the Internet, in the market of high tech stocks which are about information and its processing, and in the information trades (media, publishing, academic research) are emerging, as discussed below.

In the United States, the notion of the "national interest" once based on patriotism (a contrast conception with other nations' freedoms) and "anti-communism" reified in the guise of the Soviet Union, is being redefined. The United States government, in cooperation with large corporations, many in the former defense industry, has broadened its definition of the national interest to include "information." Although its denotations are debated, this information connotes industrial secrets and ideas with research and development potential. Protected by linking military actions as deterrence, domestic and international intelligence and counter-intelligence, the national interest now includes the *security of information*. While this includes the traditional classified and secret materials central to governing, it is now expanded to include strategic information useful for opening and maintaining markets, and for sustaining American economic suzerainty. Information held secure in the national interest entails both State-held and proprietary corporate information. This linguistic transformation of information as a basis for national strength and survival in the context of economic competition implies the obligation to use strategic means to protect and enhance it. Extensions of strategy to assure the protection of information- waging a "war," an "information war,"[4] and guarding diligently against external threats- are underway. Domestic security and the national interest now include diligent protection of information, intelligence gathering and counter-intelligence designed to prevent industrial espionage.[5]

Competition exists within and between private industries and private industry and the federal government. In addition to the anti-trust suit (1999-2000 still under negotiation) facing Microsoft, other attempts to crack the State-industrial monopoly on information exchange are present. These include illegal "hacking" and computer piracy (Shimamura and Markoff, 1996). GAO in 1996 reported that 250,000 hackers had penetrated DOD and were 60 per cent successful (GAO report, May 1996). Not all penetrations of computer security systems are motived by gain.[6] Some, apparently, merely risky gaming, statements of identity, or efforts intended to dramatize the struggle for democratic control of information. They are part of the emerging patterns of deviance and control in cyberspace. The fantasy of complete information control, or conversely, the fear of being penetrated, drives governmental concern for security. Yet, information is different: it can be stolen, copied, shifted about, and used without leaving any obvious traces. The controversy in the United States (which lead to a Supreme Court decision) about Napster, a net-based company that allows people to down load copyrighted music, is in part representative of the question of what rights exist concerning ownership of something that has been copied and exists in electronic form. As is often the case, no true "original" exists.

Corporations are now concerned to protect secrets that constitute their competitive advantage in world markets. Economic espionage is perceived as a major threat some 54 nations have been identified as engaged in economic espionage (DeGenaro, 1996). Global corporations operate in many legal contexts, and are governed completely by none. Some nations, such as The People's Republic of China, do not respect international copyright agreements. What is commercially acceptable to sell and trade internationally may be, and usually is, inconsistent with U.S. governmental designations of classified information. A corporation, while seeking to have its core secrets protected by government actions, including efforts by the FBI in the U.S., may at the same time wish to trade abroad without governmental approval. Computer software as airplane guidance systems can be adopted to warfare; sales may be profitable but may finance warfare against the selling nation or its allies. The interests of corporations and governments are frequently inconsistent, the trade with China is perhaps the most salient example of mixed motives in trade and its promotion.

Changes In The Locus of Control

The growth of information policing as an orchestrated practice is not unrelated to the decline in other modes of social control, and so a review these with reference to the United States is relevant. These trends are occurring to a lessor degree in all industrialized nations. Consider social interaction between persons, once face to face, that is now mediated by an information-processing monitor.

Traditionally, self-control, whether provided by the super-ego, ego, or the significant other, based on primary group processes, has been considered the foundation-source of social control. Mead (1936) and fellow pragmatists assume face to face interaction, co-presence, where the myriad of cues given and given off are assessed directly as the basis for the growth of selves and of community. Increasingly, interpersonal processes are mediated and produced by the mass media and aspects of modern experience are derived from electronically represented images rather than exclusively from direct, sensate personal experience. The interposition of the visual media alters the relationship between an audience, performance and self, and a performance once bound by mutually shared expressive burdens is less constrained. Media frames new social realities (definitions of the real and the significant), and shown on screens which create erstwhile social realities. As bizarre as the new 'reality" shows are- "Survivor;" "Big brother," and others, they indicate the flexibility of "real." Artificially created, edited, scripted, introduced, hosted, commercialized and broadcast for money on television, these are called "real" and "reality shows."

Extensive and powerful *mediated* interactions now may shape organizational as well as personal life, and compete with face-to-face experiences for salience. The invention or systematization of the World Wide Web gave the network of computers a new range, flexibility and presence. There are now almost 78 million users in the U.S. and 128.2 world-wide (April 2000); 1 billion web pages; 150 million searches done daily; and 3,200 search engines available. Estimates of time spent at computer screens vary, but more than 2 hours a month are spent in searches, and e-mail for those who use it runs to almost 2 hours a day. (NYT, 29 June,2000).

Computers with screens enabling various forms of visual interaction, whether in the form of "surfing" the WWW, playing video games, or participating in bulletin Boards, FACs, MUDs, or other interactive sites, permit interactions to exist "stripped," free of specific settings, times, people or places (Meyrowitz 1985; Gergen 1991). Furthermore, this interaction can be carried out with code words, passwords, false or notional identities, or with no direct connection to a social role (identified by a work, family, or personal attribute). Skilled users can masquerade via false names, codes, the origins of their messages, and use deceptive programs (Shimamura and Markoff, 1996). The Internet is a visual text, and displays and distributes dreams, fantasies, fears and passions as well as information narrowly conceived. It is increasingly difficult to distinguish and mark the limits of these electronic realities or predict how they will shape interactional vicissitudes.

New artificial selves are created by means of "bots" or software that profiles types of consumers and typifies individual users. Amazon.com, for example, has a program that will watch out for books, records, or other consumables that fit your tastes as profiled by your queries. "Cookies," caches of sites or files one has viewed, can be monitored and used for market research. It is now possible for parents to buy software to block access of users (their children) to certain sites or sites with key words (e.g. sexual in nature), thus providing a techno-mechanical surrogate for actual monitoring and control (Lansing State Journal, 24 August 1999). Similar mechanisms are being marketed for encrypting messages on the Internet and for increasing governmental controls in security-sensitive information. Within the Internet, new forms of control are emerging which substitute mechanical-electronic means for interpersonal social controls- these include site access fees, licensing fees for use of certain software and fees for access to analogous to pay-for-view cable channels. What is clear is that "hits" on websites, and associated indications of "success" are an emerging criteria for e-commerce and controls on investments in sites.[7]

Changes In Policing

These developments are the pre-conditions for the rise of information policing, information-based policing, and the use of information by third parties to control grievances. Formal modes of control are inversely related to informal modes, but the dance of control is one of expansion and contraction rather than ever-escalating formal powers (Black, 1996).

Legal controls have thus far been unevenly applied to the Internet. Although police officers posing as child molesters to try to lure child porn dealers into illegalities such as using the mail or telephones to dispense goods, and occasionally an arrest is made as a result of internet transactions, most conventional computer crimes such as fraud, embezzlement, and money laundering committed with or via computers are not well-monitored by police forces. In general, but not entirely, they lack the knowledge and expertise to investigate such crimes. The publicity and dramaturgy occasioned by the rare capture of "hackers" indicates the paucity of actual surveillance and sanctioning (Shimomura and Markoff, 1996). The computer industry and universities have combined to develop alert Centers, such as one at Carnegie-Mellon in Pittsburgh, that monitor and spread information to users about "hackers," breaks in security, threatening viruses and offer new protections against penetration.

Policing of new modes of information exchange are emerging. Several new modes of gathering information exist internationally. Private corporations have vast capacity to monitor many transactions, aggregate them, and create lists for marketing purposes, internal surveillance, or evaluation. While the police have long had the cooperation of credit card companies in pursuing fraud and criminals using credit cards, the security system now has devised ways to profile those at risk by "credit card abuse." The notion of profiling and typifying, as the 1999 controversy in the United States about race profiling has surfaced, uses simulation of characteristics to produce likely violators of drug, immigration, or traffic laws (New York Times, 20 June, 1999). Once large networks of information are linked, profiles can be created of offenders and applied to the public. Everyday surveillance, such as use of parking lots, supermarket purchases, catalog shopping and using a credit card, generate data that can in turn be used to profile, model and anticipate behaviour. Satellite pictures of great clarity and resolution, able to detect objects as small as one meter, can now be purchased by corporations or individuals. These images are limited by license or by ad hoc "shutter control" over certain satellites (New York Times 5 September, 1999).

Symbolic space is now as open to policing as is physically defined space. The Justice Department is proposing legislation that would allow agents to enter homes and disable any encrpytion devices the residents own, and/or install devices that would allow them to "read" or de-code an encrypted text (New York Times, September 4, 1999). The FCC, at the urging of the Justice Department, has adopted new rules concerning monitoring cellular phone calls and callers (92 million plus subscribers in the U.S.). This legislation would allowing tracking of movements of users (by call location on the basis of a warrant) through phone companies. A literature on computer crime is growing and the FBI is recruiting agents with computer skills. The FBI monitored Internet transactions carried by the "Freemen" from inside their isolated ranch during the "Siege of Montana" in 1997. The FBI now has a specialized unit for "economic espionage" and actively seeks industry cooperation in identifying information loss and other economic crimes. The CIA intends to monitor international economic crimes and to protect information, if the Director's congressional testimony in 1996 is an indication. Software firms are also entering the battle.

Policing Security

I hope that it is clear from this outline that "security" is a word with changing meaning and policing's attention to it differs among the industrialized nations. It is not possible to make easy predictions because cooperation is emergent; information sharing quite guarded and primitive in practice; the other that is a threat is variously represented; "computer crime" is largely undefined and the approach by police unrefined and quite crude; and the rise of transnational crimes of terrorism and nationalism is a striking counterpoint to the declared new global order of the post-cold war period.

Law may not be the source of guidance in future policing. The laws of Western nations, and recent law in the rest of the based on European law, reflect nineteenth century ideas concerning privacy, institutional insulation from public law, deterrence, the "rational man," and property. Cyberspace is a new social space that must be defined analogously and metaphorically - what it is like and why? Information networks are altering these 19th century ideas as we approach the next century. Information-based policing moves away from the founding notions of policing based on the idea of benign reaction to public nuisance and crime, harsh treatment of riots and large-scale disorders. Based on surveillance and simulation (modeling of the future based on present data), and abetted by means to monitor information networks, policing will increasingly encompass notions of intervention and prevention, intelligence-gathering and analysis, counter-intelligence and disinformation, largely based on electronically gathered stored, processed and transmitted information. We are as yet unable to predict the direction and consequences of "the net"[8] (Rochlin, 1998). Because the processes of control work analogically and metaphorically rather than literally, the representations of transnational crimes are increasingly important.

While evidence exists of some formal international cooperation among nations, there is also evidence that much conflict and competition also exists. Competition between agencies is apparent within the United States and Europe. While something is known of the form of these relationships, little is known of the actual content of information exchanged between agencies and consequences, if any, of such exchanges. This remains difficult to determine for any given force, let alone international exchanges. An increase in the frequency and number of queries to NCIC or Interpol, for example, replicates the police concern with the means of policing, rather than the ends. In 1994, the FBI purchased a new, vast, computer system (GAO,1994) because the validity of the data the NCIC computer contained was dubious, and few controls had been exercised in accepting or erasing warrant information.

"Computer crime" is seen as both a national threat in the form of computer users who pirate credit card numbers, songs, disrupt service by jamming sites or send out viruses. It has a moral tone, as fears of children's' access to pornography, illegal sexual liaisons precipitated via the Internet, and the destruction of family values via media-based entertainment, are discussed in the national press. It is also seen as global, part of a potential threat by criminals, such as terrorists and revolutionaries, to international peace. "Computer crime" remains an undefined sink from which many conflicting ideas are drawn. The most urgent threats, targets of control, and dangerous enemies, are unclear. Many are symbolic such as the threat to family values in the United States, or the "crimes" exist solely in cyberspace. While trying to use the model of national·law to define the procedures by which the crime is attacked and controlled, the same computer experts see it as global, sinister, and complexly configured somewhere in cyberspace. The contradictions in this formulation have not yet been addressed.

Attempts to regulate Internet communication using the wedge of seeking to control of "pornography," and the commercial v-chip and other software that blocks access and usage, suggest that regulation and control of the WWW may emerge not on the model of "free speech," or freedom of the press, but on the model of commerce, as a form of U.S. interstate commerce. More importantly, there is an attempt to control the means by which information is processed, hardware and software or metainformation. These include codes, software, and encryption devices which reorganize *data* (mere fact) into *information* (data with social meaning). The first signs of the computer revolution brought forth counter-efforts to control the distribution of software. The invention of the PC, its successful refinement and marketing by Apple, were driven initially by a democratic vision of spreading and diffusing mundane and technical (programs) knowledge. Microsoft, by controlling and marketing the DOS system adopted by IBM, changed that dramatically. The present movement to gain control of information via the Internet reproduces the successful attempt to control sales of software and restrict free access to large main frame computers.

The growth of the fears and risks of cybercrime are a product of several non-independent forces. The "watchdogs," heads of security at computer and telephone corporations (a misleading distinction), are themselves working the emerging edges of legality and ethics, breaking into corporate records, demonizing a few targets, stripping them of moral credibility, and exaggerating the costs and risks of "hacking" through inflated statements of the costs of "losses" elevate their own status while breaking the law themselves (Goodell, 1996). This enterprise, a form of moral entrepreneurship, is driven also by the complicity and active involvement of media figures in the investigations, publicity, alerts and panics surrounding computer "break-ins" (Shimomura with Markoff, 1996). The language of cybercrime refers to physical, not virtual realities, treats information as property that can be "secure," "violated," "compromised," or stolen and valued in comparable, monetary terms, introduces trust and contractual obligations as a basis for electronic transactions, and personalizes data files.

Comment

Changes in the international relations and the economy, as well as those in information technology, transportation and communications are now reflected in policing. The mandate is being shaped by concerns not only for personal security, but for the security of information as property as well as information as a symbol or an expressive matter. Many traditional policing issues are not dealt with here, such as restraint, information control, both concealing and revealing, respect of citizens' privacy, and compliance, are being changed and these changes affect both police and citizens in democratic nations.

Markets are exploding and imploding. China is now the world's third largest economy and hosts some 10,00 named "joint ventures," while Japan is "downsizing" its indigenous manufacture of vehicles and shifting a larger proportion of its production to the United States (Detroit Free Press, June 23, 1996). Local practices and myriad trade rules exist in Eastern Europe and the former Soviet Union, and economic development within and without the United States is uneven. Local control of markets by Provinces and cities exists in China, and in economic development zones within the United States.

At the same time, unification of international trade practices and regulations exist in the form of NAFTA, EEU, GATT, The Maastricht Treaty, and the United States' designation of "Preferred Nation" status periodically to specific nations. These signal a movement toward centralization and homogenization of laws and practices and the growth of politico-economic unions. Counter to these trends is the creeping internationalization of the ecological crisis and concepts of managed "risk" rather than market forces sustaining relationships. Witness the now world-wide "Green-Movement" and anti-nuclear protesting and power movements in Europe. These changes in markets are complemented by the rise of contests over emerging "market(s) in information" (Castels, 1996).

Peter K. Manning (Ph.D. Duke, 1966), is Professor of Sociology and Criminal Justice at Michigan State University. His interests are in organizations and occupations, fieldwork methods, social theory and policing. He has taught at Duke University, MIT, Oxford, the University at Albany, and York University (Toronto). Formerly a fellow of Wolfson and Balliol Colleges Oxford, and the Oxford Centre for Socio-legal Studies, he has been awarded grants from NIMH, NSF, NIJ and ESRC (England), and was a fellow of the Rockefeller Foundation at the Bellagio Villa in March, 2000. He is the author of 12 books, many articles and chapters, and recently published Police Work *(2nd.ed.Waveland, 1997) and (with Brian Forst)* Privatization of Policing: Two Views *(Georgetown University Press, 1999). His book,* Picturing Policing: The Illusion of Control, *is forthcoming. He is named in* Who's Who in America *and* Who's Who in the World *and was given the Bruce Smith Sr. Award in 1993, and the O.W. Wilson Award in 1997, both by The Academy of Criminal Justice Sciences. His current research includes fieldwork on community policing in several sites in Michigan, the rationalization of policing, with emphasis on the role of information technology in the U.S. and U.K., and legal decision-making. Recently his research has focused on the impact of information technology (crime mapping, CAD, crime-intelligence) on policing practice.*

Notes

1   The growth of multinational corporations whose interests and subunits extend globally, and whose loyalties are only nominal national, have obviated identification of economic interests and State interests. The movement of cash and resources within these corporations has, according to some, "emptied the State" because States can little control, tax, and monitor monetary movements. This concomitant decentralization of State power and control is dramatized by the decline and collapse of the Soviet Union as a coherent economic-political force, and the dedifferentiation of several sovereign States the former Yugoslavia and States within the Soviet federation.

2   Information as property is reflected in the grow of "intellectual property" offices in universities in the U.S.; a growing body of socio-legal works on the topic (Coombe, 1999, Boyle, 1998, Lessig, 1999) and is illustrated in a striking fashion by efforts to control access and use of the Internet. Commercialization of exchanges on the Internet (USA Today June 25 1996) is underway in spite of resistance by those who use it. Developed as a secure national defense network that would permit multiple links between computers in the event of war or other national crisis, it was then hived off to the National Science Foundation for support and development (Rheingold, 1993:7), and privatized in due course.

3   This capacity is indicated by the number of police forces using computer-assisted dispatch. It has great potential and is being refined rapidly in the Anglo-American world. This geo-coding and crime intelligence, mobile digital terminals and Internet connections, as well as the growth national databanks, dedicated computer networks, and information sharing capacities. The UK has a national crime faculty with links to the Home Office, and a national intelligence model; some constabularies such as Kent, Lancastershire, and others, are developing crime-mapping and crime intelligence units for strategic analysis of crime and disorder.

4   This new definition of information as the bases for war was foreshadowed in 1992 by the Industrial Security Initiative of the Bush Administration, and indicated by congressional testimony. The Director of the Central Intelligence Agency, John Deutsh, a former MIT Professor, testified before a Senate Subcommittee about the potential for disruptions in communications, threats to national interest due to potential loss of secrets, and for information wars. These will be wars over information and wars about information. He said an information war could become a 21st century national security threat second only to nuclear, biological and chemical weapons. The New York Times (June 26th 1996), labeled these future contests "cyberwars." Mr Deutsh proposed creating a "cyberwar center" in the National Security Agency. The FBI now has an information security unit within the counter terrorism division of the Bureau. This placement suggests that along with purity of food and water, electrical power and transportation, that the networks for transmitting information are to be protected up to and including by military means. A 1996 conference, "Vision 2021," hosted by the Defense Security Research Center (formerly PERSEREC), proceedings of which were published (Sarbin, 1997), considered the future of security including information security.

5   Since June, 1996, five bills have been introduced in Congress intending to provide coherent protection of the economic secrets of the United States. Two of the five contain provisions for the enforcement of American commercial law abroad to protect information.

6   An ironic twist to this is that corporations who use encrpytion (passwords based on the factoring of prime numbers) as protection against random penetration and industrial espionage, are being courted by software corporations who announce in the media that they have been able to break into "secure systems." They do this to emonstrate that corporations are vulnerable and should purchase the protection they are selling (New York Times, 6 September 1999)!

7   While emphasis has been on the negative aspects of computer based access to the WWW, such as loneliness, "addiction," and virtual violence visited on co-participants, electronically mediated relations, organized around e-mail, the World Wide Web, pagers, cellular phones, and FAX machines, also create, enhance, sustain, and make possible relationships. They forge links between otherwise distant and unconnected people (Gergen, 1991, Rheingold, 1993). These relations range from quite intimate relations, such as courtship, Internet sex via chatrooms, trading of erotic pictures, sounds and texts, to business transactions and play, "surfing," following one's curiosity across sites, hearing messages, watching videos, reading texts, or seeing amazing graphic displays. The daily newspapers are full stories of people who find love, are raped, compromised, defrauded, and even die as a result of Internet-based interactions. Informal modes of control have arisen as well in listservs, chatrooms, and other virtual communities "beating people up" (verbally), "flaming" them, banning them from use and gossip, all appear to play a role. These changes in interpersonal relations, partially shaped by the media and all forms of screened interactions, affect selves, manners, customs, and etiquette as well as security.

8   During the last year, a number of developments in policing e-communications were publicized. The British government announced new powers for police to monitor

e-mail and other e-communications (NYT 19 July, 1999), as did the White House in a policy statement (NYT 18 July, 1999); the FBI established a "National Stolen Art File" (www.fbi.gov/majcases/arttheft/art.htm) as did Interpol's at its "Cultural property site" (www.usdoj.gov/uscb/culturehome.htm). The FBI (Washington Times, 25 July, 2000) announced the use of a new surveillance device for the internet, an "ISP surveillance software" called "carnivore," that allows an agent to connect a laptop to an ISP and monitor its transactions including the address of every e-mail message that passes through it. They are required to obtain a warrant prior to this surveillance. The aim is to increase trust in the Internet and protect e-commerce (quote from a federal DA ibid). Meanwhile, when the U.S. National Drug Control Policy Office was discovered to be tracking those who viewed its anti-drug advertising on the Internet, it ceased. It was using "Double-Click," a firm that sells the software to monitor visits to sites and determine which ads were most effective in sending viewers to the Policy Office's sites (NYT 22 June, 2000). The interweaving of profit, commerce and national security is becoming increasingly banal, but the infrastructure for policing the Internet is slowly emerging, program by program.

* 19 Sept.2000. Some of these points were developed initially in a chapter forthcoming in James Scheptyki (ed..), Transnational Policing. London: Routledge. I presented a preliminary version to the meetings of the Law and Society Association, Strathcylde University, Glasgow, Scotland, July 10-13, 1996.

Section II
Introduction
Stable Democracies

Stable Democracies

We wanted to present a description of what may be seen as being the routine relationships between police and democracy in stable democratic States. From the articles which we have received we chose one 'welfare State' (Finland), one State which has to deal with 'natives' ("Aboriginals") and waves of immigrants (Australia), and one 'special' democracy (although each case is special) Japan. What is 'special' about Japan is that Japan was transformed from a totalitarian State into a stable democracy without the crises which befalls other States in transformation towards democracy, as will be examined in the next section.

According to Andrew Goldsmith, Australian police maintain the basic principles of democracy: *political accountability, transparency,* and *accessibility.*

Australian police operate in a very heterogeneous society which absorbs new immigrants and natives -Aboriginals who demand their social-economic representation and civil rights within the social-economic-political system.

With the rising rates of crime, especially organized crime (drugs, illegal immigrants, etc.) the police is called upon to "wage war" on these new crimes, adopting the American models of policing organized crime. The police also has to compete with the increase in private security and policing services.

Challenged by and facing new types of crimes and rising crime rates Australian police commanders enter into politics. They appear in the media, emphasizing that they *"sell public safety and security against petty street crimes."*

Community policing was introduced to Australia and adapted from the USA model. Thus also in Australia 'problem-oriented policing' sometimes became a 'zero-tolerance' campaign, mainly in the drug scene. The equity and civil rights principles of democratic policing is often violated. Australian police are accountable to the political system but there is weak accountability to the community.

Ahti Laitinen provides a general description of an almost non-problematic policing in a stable democratic welfare State. We learn about Finland's demography and society with an interesting history of local community police and policing since the Middle ages. It is interesting to note that a special 'class' of policemen existed much before the establishment of the, supposedly, first modern police in 1829 in England. What is also interesting is that the successions in police reform in Finland center around the protection and advancement of human and civil rights, as well as mechanism of control over the police. For these purposes, on the national as well as local levels, various agencies, advisory boards and ombudsmen were established. Their mandate was to guarantee that the police will behave according to the general law. There are also special rules which govern the police who are mandated to abide by the police ethical code.

Finland is facing new social problems which demand attention from the police. These include, among others, immigration (some of it being illegal) and minorities who have problems of absorption even in this welfare State. Finnish police is supervised with regard to its 'engagement' with these groups. The emphasis is again upon the protection of their human and civil rights.

According to Laitinen, the main functions of the Finnish police is to prevent crime as well as to investigate and prosecute white collar crimes. Finnish 'security police' are engaged in the investigation of organized crime. We know from other sources that Finnish community policing programs are designed mainly to prevent youth deviance and crime (alcohol and drug-related, etc.).

Minoru Yokoyama's Japan is a special case in the relationship between police and democracy. First, Japan was forced by the American conquerors, at the end of World War II, to change from a totalitarian State to a democracy. This meant having a constitution which upholds and protects democratic principles. Japanese police were separated from the security and army forces apparatus. Japan's police is controlled by the political level mainly through the allocation of the budget; the public (the media and civil groups); political parties in the cabinet and the parliament. This is especially so in cases of the violation of civil rights in the course of police activities against organized crime or in crowd control events.

Japan does not have special community policing programs. A special type of contact with the community, in the form of the *koban*, has existed in Japan since prior to World War II. Small police stations consisting of 3-5 policemen were in continuous contact with the public as a control mechanism on the life and movement of the people.

This institution is one among others which explains the efficiency of Japanese police in their crime prevention as well as in maintaining low rates of street crime, which currently is on the rise. The police were able, until recently, to control organized crime groups (the *Yakuza*) as well as to supervise and control street crimes.

In spite of Japan's military defeat and the enforced democratization, its past basic social institutions and personal and group behaviors, such as compliance to the authorities (family, employers), the cultural heritage of respect as well as fear for the law and the police have remained. Japanese police are continually exposed to training as well as towards democratic and service-oriented policing. But the police culture and police commanders are resistant, or at least ambivalent, to extend democratic principles within their organization and activities.

Japan's police is ready to listen to suggestions from below - from the public - but remains reluctant to accept them. Policemen and commanders - just as in many Western police forces - protect their deviant comrades who are accused of corruption and violations of human and civil rights.

What also remains from the former American rule, is the non-neutral political stance of the police - the ongoing harassment of labor unions and left wing groups and political parties

8 Police Power and Democracy in Australia[1]

Andrew Goldsmith*

Abstract

This paper asks how is police power in Australia changing and why, and is it becoming more or less accountable in the process? The specific issues considered are police powers and law and order politics, drug law enforcement, police manage-ment philosophies, and global integration. Some conflicting objectives evident in such areas of police work as illicit drugs and police-community relations that make policing more uncer-tain are examined. It also probes the implications for greater accountability and transparency in new managerial approaches, and asks whether the citizen in a democracy can be equated with a customer in the marketplace?

Key Words: Police powers; accountability; transparency; drug law enforcement; globalization; Australia

Introduction

"*Policing by consent*" has been the hallmark of police legitimacy in liberal-demo-cratic societies such as Australia for the best part of two hundred years. The "consent" in question is that of the "governed," i.e., the citizens of the nation-state. However modern-day Australia is a very different place from nineteenth century English society, where this idea was developed. It is indeed now far removed from the Australia of the 1950s, in which there was far less social and cultural diversity. What does such a notion imply now for policing in our increasingly divided, insecure, and heteroge-neous society? What also does it mean in the light of recent changes to government and public administration, as concepts of *privatization* and *corporate management* have influenced the organization and practices of public police forces? In such a time of rapid social change and flux, it becomes even more important to ask whether the police are, as the "consent" idea implies, the servants of all, or whether, as "customers" rather than "citizens", the new corporate police philosophies and practices have rendered policing less, rather than more, responsive to the community-at-large (David and Hancock, 1997: Palmer, 1999). Changes to police powers and the grow-ing access to surveillance, DNA and other technologies also pose important ques-tions about how the police relate to the citizenry. Issues such as these, I shall argue, cannot be detached from wider cultural and other factors, for example, con-cerns about police effectiveness, and public perceptions about a deterioration in public order and crime (Lupton, 1999).

These are big questions that cannot possibly be answered fully here. However I propose to examine a number of themes which, in my view, serve to mark some impor-tant defining and/or emerging themes of contemporary policing in Australia. In this analysis of some present practices and possible trends, I propose looking at:

- current law and order politics, including changes to police powers;
- policing illicit drugs;
- the spread of corporate 'managerialism' to policing, and its consequences for police/community relationships; and finally
- changes to police functions, methods and structures occasioned by global-ization of crime.

Each of these themes is important in and of itself. However, I propose to link their analysis here in part by considering how they affect the transparency, accessibility and responsiveness of police policies, procedures and practice to ordinary citizens. *Transparency* implies the potential for citizens to have knowledge about police work that provides the basis for feedback and indeed criticism. Without knowledge of this kind, police forces cannot be held properly accountable to the societies they serve. By *accessibility*, I refer both to the existence of opportunities for citizens to make them-selves heard on matters pertaining to policing, and to the ability to be able to call upon police services in times of need. Situations of "under-policing", as well as "over-policing", can emerge that raise questions about equality of access to police services in addition to question about oppressive or discriminatory policing (Cunneen, 1992). *Responsiveness* refers to the extent to which police actions are reflective of the de-mands for service of the community at large, not just of particular sectors of any given community. Ensuring transparency, accessibility and responsiveness for citizens means providing some means whereby imbalances in the distribution and kind of police ser-vices provided can be redressed. The pervasive and potentially coercive nature of police power, even in societies widely recognized as "democratic", makes their ac-countability highly important.

A preliminary point that needs to be made is that public policing in Australia is highly centralized by comparison with the United Kingdom, Canada or the United States of America. Australian policing is organized according to the jurisdictional bound-aries of the six Australian states as well as the Northern Territory. In other words, each of these jurisdictions has its own police force. In addition, there is the Australian Federal Police, which provides local policing in the Australian Capital Territory. How-ever, the AFP is mainly engaged in national police tasks as defined by federal laws.[2] Australia, with a population approaching twenty million, thus has only eight public police forces, with the vast majority of its citizens being served by one or other of seven police forces.[3] State and territory police forces vary in size (as measured by number of sworn police officers) between 13,471 in New South Wales to 876 in the Northern Territory (Australian Bureau of Statistics, 2000).

Scholars familiar with policing in Canada, the United Kingdom or the USA would be struck by another feature of Australian policing. There are no local level police commissions, boards or police authorities with at least limited jurisdiction over police matters (c.f. Loader, 1996), nor do municipal authorities exercise any direct power over, or have responsibility for, how police services are provided for or held accountable at the local level (for Canada, see Stenning, 1981). While each state and territory has at least an ombudsman or Police Complaints Authority to deal with individual citizen complaints (Lewis, 1999), the chief police officer (known usually as the Commissioner) is directly accountable to the Minister of state government with policing responsibilities (often called the Minister for Police), and ultimately to state (or Territory) Parliament. All these organs of government in other words operate at state, rather than local, level. While centralized policing of this nature finds its justification and origins in the (then, and still) sparsely settled nature of vast tracts of Australia, the desire of colonial governors (the colonies which preceeded the development of states) to rule from the centre, and the desire of political leaders and senior police to ensure the growth of more professionalized police forces (Finnane, 1994), it nevertheless means that Australian citizens have no modern experience of making input at the local government level on policing questions. This pattern has been compounded in recent years by the largely separate development of regionalization of state police services within a number of states *and* the municipal state boundaries within those states.[4] From an accountability perspective therefore, it can be said that Australians have lacked, for all their limitations, the kinds of local-level decision-making bodies in the policing area that are familiar to citizens living in most other First World English-speaking countries (Stenning, 1981; Lustgarten, 1986).

Law and Order Politics

Policing is a deeply political activity, even where its execution is not always according to democratic principles. The police are implicated, directly or indirectly, in most law and order campaigns in Australian politics. This may occur at the instigation of the police themselves (though police tend to tread relatively carefully in most instances), or more commonly, when political pressure from particular quarters in the political arena or civil society for a change is brought to bear upon the legislative bodies. The implications of the changes often have direct repercussions for how policing is done. Reform proposals in relation to such issues as child abuse, drug consumption, organised crime, possession of firearms, and women's safety usually logically entail a new, and generally more interventionist, role for the police in the affairs of citizens. Particularly as social definitions of public problems change, police are exposed to conflicting public expectations and a variety of normative perspectives.

Domestic violence is just such a case. In the 1970s and early 1980s heightened consciousness of women's vulnerability to violence in the home led to new domestic violence legislation which defined new tasks and responsibilities for police in this area (Finnane, 1994). This did not of course mean that a law enforcement response to domestic assaults was immediately seen by all affected as appropriate, including by many police officers required to implement the new laws. In the area of illicit drugs, there remains a lack of public unanimity regarding the status of some drugs, and whether law enforcement is an appropriate response in all cases of users of 'hard' drugs (Maher and Dixon, 1999). When pressure for changes to certain laws comes from outside the police, the police may find the legislative changes that follow more or less congenial, in terms of what is implied for their relationships with the public. When there is little broad community consultation prior to such changes, this can negatively affect police/public relations by involving the police in often unpopular tasks. Police can also suffer when a moral panic (e.g., home invasions) fails to produce any or significant legislative change, leaving them open to the perception that they are not dealing firmly enough with offenders under the existing law. Police, in other words, cannot always be counted among the beneficiaries of law and order politics.

Police powers

Politics around police powers draw heavily from statements and perceptions about the levels of crime and disorder in particular societies. "Fear of crime" is now discussed quite openly, and indeed measured, as perceptions of growing lawlessness play a significant role in debates on public safety issues (Lupton, 1999). The underlying basis for these concerns is not purely chimerical. In the past twenty five years, the official crime data points to dramatic increases in serious assault (more than 600%), but to a lesser rise in property crimes, such as burglary, motor vehicle theft, and stealing (less than 130%). In the late 1990s, while the trajectory in violent crime rates continued in an upwards direction, there were clear signs of leveling off in relation to property crimes (Mukherjee, 2000:55-56). The oxygen of publicity has also played its part in bringing about changes. New anti-stalking legislation has responded to publicity given to particular cases and concerns that existing domestic violence laws are not broad enough to deal with the problem. Changes to firearms control legislation from 1996, spurred in particular by a widely-reported mass shooting of more than thirty persons by one armed man at Port Arthur, Tasmania, have meant that police have become more involved in the management and enforcement of stricter gun licensing regulations.

Apart from firearms, law and order agendas have also been concerned with other kinds of arms, and in particular, the possession and use of knives. In New South Wales, the *Crimes Legislation (Police and Public Safety) Act 1998*, extends the range of offences in relation to custody of knives in public places or schools, and empowers police to conduct electronic or frisk searches of persons, their bags or other personal effects where they reasonably suspect the person has unlawful custody of a knife, firearm or prohibited weapon. Similar concerns have led to legislative provisions of a similar kind in other states.

The political exploitation of public fear of crime has proven useful in a number of contexts for the promotion of the case for an expansion of police powers. One area in which the police appear to have a more direct influence in promoting change is in relation to powers connected to organized and other serious crime. In recent times, Australian police and other law enforcement agencies have been empowered to undertake undercover operations in relation to a broader spectrum of serious criminal behaviour than previously (Bronitt and Kinley, 1995). However, improving the effectiveness of policing is another argument used by police to advance the case for certain changes. Rising levels of fear regarding the state of our public environment ("quality of life" issues) continue to drive extended police powers for dealing with 'troublesome' users of public space, such as young people and the homeless. In NSW, the granting of power to police to detain a person after arrest for the purposes of investigation, and new police powers to give reasonable directions to persons in public places, and to request a person's name and address, in certain circumstances, have formally strengthened the hands of police to deal with order maintenance as well as criminal investigation matters. The subject of DNA databases is now very much on the law enforcement agenda, with State and Federal governments taking active steps to establish such databases, and empowering police to take samples from suspects as well as from arrestees and those with criminal records (New South Wales, 2000).

Zero-tolerance policing in Australia

The prominence given to this issue in Australia in recent years (though it appears now to be waning) is a clear example of how law and order concepts and ideas can get rapidly transmitted or even transplanted from one nation, most commonly the United States, to another. The US debate on this issue came to Australia in the late 1990s as a result of visits by James Q. Wilson and William Bratton and an enthusiastic reception for the idea from some Australian media, politicians and senior police officers (see Dixon, 1998).

A precise definition of this concept in relation to police work is difficult, but the strategy is a street-level one, focusing on common offences of disorder with a view to improving the "quality of life" of ordinary citizens, and eventually to bring about a reduction in the incidence of serious crime (Dixon, 1998). Philosophically, it derives its essence (though not the descriptor) from the "Broken Windows" thesis of James Q. Wilson and George Kelling in their 1982 article of that name in the *Atlantic Monthly*, a US magazine. Kelling, by the way, also became a familiar face on late night public television in Australia around the time of the visit by Wilson. Many aspects of the thesis remain contentious, not least being the potential sanction it gives for discriminatory law enforcement targeted against some of the least well-off sectors of society. Among police chiefs, academics, and politicians, another area of debate has been whether zero-tolerance policies could rightfully take credit for a significant crime reduction in New York City. In Australia, its relevance for this country has generated some academic interest (Dixon, 1998). Australian homicide and other serious crime rates, generally speaking, have been no match for the likes of a New York City, nor does Australia have yet the kinds of inner-city problems faced in many US cities. In the area of homicide, the gap between Australia and the US has narrowed over the last 25 years. However, in 1998, the Australian homicide rate was 1.7 per 100,000, whereas the US rate was 3 to 4 times higher (Mukherjee, 2000:53)

Nonetheless, messages of the "zero-tolerance" kind seem to have a timeless appeal, resorting as they do to images of firm action and reclaiming the public domain from forces of disorder and contagion. This appeal is not lost on ambitious politicians or sensation-seeking media workers. Nor does it lack resonance for those frightened by changes in their living environments and personal circumstances, or those directly concerned about crime patterns and rising levels of incivility. The commodification of personal safety has managed to capitalize upon these wider social trends. The consequence is the increasing ranks of middle-class and elderly persons bunkered down behind their high walls, screened windows and deadlocked doors. In the 'society of strangers' in which many urban dwellers now live,[5] there are signs of declining strength of institutions of civil society, and of increased public apathy towards mainstream politics. "Fear of crime" further individuates the citizenry, sapping the capacity of citizens for collective action and participation in political affairs, including matters of policing. At a time when members of the public need to be drawn more into mainstream public life, the opposite seems to be occurring. In the area of public safety, we look more and more for impersonal guarantees of our safety and reassurance for our galloping distrust of others around us (Giddens, 1990).[6]

"Zero tolerance policing" also raises serious questions about the equitable distribution of police resources, and in particular, the potential to discriminate against more marginal members of society. The real danger is that the privileged "two-thirds" of society will define what "quality of life" means (and hence what actions police will take), while the disadvantaged "one third" will bear the brunt of what will inevitably be pretty repressive policing (Hogg and Brown, 1998).[7] In a democratic society, policing should not compound social divisions of this kind, but must work to find ways of being sensitive to the needs of different, and therefore all, social groupings. Governments, corporations, and those constituting the advantaged two-thirds must also assume responsibility for these issues, and not simply let it become an issue for law and order fads such as "zero-tolerance".

Senior police involvement in the media

One conspicuous change in the last fifteen years or so has been the greater acceptance of senior police participation in these debates. The civil service model of senior police behaviour, whereby police commissioners and their deputies adopted a self-consciously independent and apolitical style, has been eclipsed in the past two decades by a more managerial-style police command. According to this new model, senior officers are trained, as well as appear more inclined, to participate in public debates on various policing issues. This shift has coincided with the decline of the idea of constabulary independence, a doctrine associated with British policing, under which police officers were deemed to be responsive to the law exclusively, and thus insulated from direct political influence or direction (Lustgarten, 1986). In the increased limelight cast upon Australian police forces in the Vietnam War protest era and since, the credence previously accorded this doctrine by senior police officers largely disappeared by the early 1980s.

Police participation in public discussions can be evaluated in terms of whether the contribution takes the form of a monologue or instead forms part of a genuine dialogue. The latter is more consistent with a democratic sensibility towards policing, while the former approach concedes little in this regard. Dialogue also implies an openness to receive criticism from outsiders. While the media-friendliness of senior police has greatly improved, it remains moot whether this change of communicative style has led to greater dialogue, better understanding between police and public, or significant operational changes on many issues. Concerned by embarrassing "leaks" to the media, several Australian police commissioners have recently moved to prohibit or greatly restrict conversations between serving police officers and members of the public on matters unrelated to immediate operational needs without the approval of senior police (Bearup, 2000). Any assessment therefore about improved transparency in Australian policing must contend with some disparate tendencies, and recognize the difficulties police have in changing their organizational attitudes towards openness, especially when senior police are acting to close down communication channels in some directions. On a more positive note, however, in the new climate of public relations and institutional self promotion, senior police participants inevitably run the risk of rejoinder from their mobilized articulate critics. Senior police now find it more difficult to ignore the claims by women, gays, indigenous persons and other minority groups on matters central to policing, as their public pronouncements are starting to show.[8] The role of the media in empowering at least some groups critical of the police, though much less those in society's bottom third, cannot be denied or ignored.

Policing Drugs

This area of law enforcement has become a significant policy priority in recent years. This focus is undoubtedly linked to concerns about Australia becoming a marketplace for imported heroin and cocaine as well as for cannabis and amphetamines. Despite a longstanding policy of prohibition, there is clear evidence that the percentage of the population who has ever used illicit drugs has increased since the 1980s. This is particularly true for marijuana and amphetamines (Makkai, 2000:67). Australia-wide in the year 1997-98, there were 61,152 drug arrests of 'consumers', while 23,494 'providers' were arrested (Makkai, 2000:75).Public health issues around needle use and HIV/AIDs infection have served to challenge to some degree the reliance upon traditional law enforcement methods for tackling this social problem. Drug law enforcement has made its presence felt in the field of police corruption, especially in the light of the findings of the New South Wales Royal Commission into the NSW Police, chaired by Justice James Wood, which reported in 1997 (New South Wales, 1997).

In terms of overall policy, there is less unanimity today that the prohibitionist perspective, with all it implies for law enforcement, is the appropriate official strategy. While governments have largely held firm so far in terms of resisting overt decriminalization, the Federal government's adoption of a "harm minimization" approach to the illicit drugs issue has encouraged the development of new interagency arrangements between police, health and other welfare authorities, and the trial introduction of "shooting galleries" for known injecting users. Certainly, some senior public figures, including a couple of police commissioners, have admitted the shortcomings of traditional law enforcement methods and the need for a stronger public health response from government and other agencies.

The forging of new partnerships between police and health workers is a significant departure in terms of practical responses to this growing problem, but these relationships remain hostage to vestigial "get tough" politics and policies, and a shortfall of funds to provide adequate treatment facilities for addicts. In the meantime, needle-using addicts continue to use public toilets and alley ways for shooting galleries (Maher and Dixon, 1999).

The links between illicit drugs and the threat to police integrity was powerfully demonstrated in Australia in the mid-1990s. As the findings of the NSW Royal Commission into the NSW Police Service (known as the Wood Royal Commission, after its commissioner, Justice James Wood) showed us just three years ago (New South Wales, 1997), we urgently require a long-term amelioration of the illicit drug problem in Australia. Without it, we are faced with the prospect not just of continued drug use and related property and violent crime, but also of ongoing threats to the effectiveness and integrity of state police forces. Unjustified personal enrichment and questionable police practices also are linked to a grave risk to public confidence in the police institution once revealed by media or other sources. While a number of Australian police bodies now have external review bodies to try to tackle problems of police corruption (e.g., NSW's Police Integrity Commission), these bodies cannot neutralize all the potent corrupting effects associated with a prohibition-dominated drugs policy. In Australia as elsewhere, the connection between vice law enforcement (e.g., illicit drugs) and police corruption has been clearly established (James and Sutton, 1999); Weatherburn and Lynd, 1999). Unless the external environment is changed, internal changes to police policies, including integrity testing and training, will be no match for the corrupting influences associated with illicit drugs. Until this point is reached therefore, the perceived integrity of the police from the point of view of the public will remain precariously in the shadow of prohibition-based policy.

In terms of changes to policing practice, drug law enforcement has encouraged the use of aggregated data to identify patterns of street dealer sales, thus enabling "crackdowns" on particular "hot spots." It would seem there are clear risks arising from this approach. A recent study of street-level law enforcement in Sydney by Lisa Maher and David Dixon point to a range of undesirable, and presumably unanticipated, effects promoted by law enforcement strategies directed at disrupting street markets for drugs (Maher and Dixon, 1999). These include displacement of drug dealers into new areas, and the practice of unsafe methods of needle-use. While perhaps more focused than earlier law enforcement approaches to drug issues, these methods remain law enforcement approaches. The empirical picture suggests that police, instead of concentrating upon the major sources and purveyors of illicit drugs, primarily target the minor distributors, often who have serious addictions themselves (Makkai, 2000; Maher and Dixon, 1999). In relation to this second group, street-level law enforcement needs to take place in a way which actively minimizes, rather than exacerbates, the harm done to drug users. As Sutton and James, among others, have pointed out, there continues to be a real need to embed attempts at harm minimization into routine law enforcement practices (Sutton and James, 1996; Weatherburn and Lynd, 1999).

Finally, it needs to be recognized that persisting with traditional law enforcement methods, especially towards those suspected primarily of personal addiction or low level distribution, can have quite negative effects in terms of police-community relations (Scarman, 1993, Maher and Dixon, 1999). The consequences in terms of classifying people as "users" or "addicts" are compounded especially where the drugs being policed are not regarded by many normally law-abiding people as requiring criminalization. Drug law enforcement in its current form in Australia continues to dominate public policy responses to illicit drug issues, at the expense of exposing a large number of persons (mainly youth and young adults) to the criminal justice system. The apparently unchecked willingness of many younger people to experiment with various illicit drugs, and the public health risks associated with street-level "crackdowns" by police, suggests that the police are at danger of worsening relations with many young people, and of adding to the health risks faced by drug addicts. Maintaining heavy-handed police responses to illicit drugs threatens the social isolation and disorder problems witnessed in a number of British inner city areas in the early 1980s (Scarman, 1983), as well as alienating certain groups (including many young people) further from the police (Maher and Dixon, 1999). If police are to establish more positive relations with these groups, more resources for diversion and treatment programs, amongst other things, must become a part of a coordinated police-health response, allowing police to deal more selectively and effectively under the law with higher level dealers and traffickers. Police performance indicators, supervisory practices, and internal auditing procedures must serve to reinforce a shift in priorities in this area.

Changing Organizational and Policing Styles: The Corporate Managerial Shift

Australia's police forces, once quasi-militaristic and bureaucratic in nature, now seek to emulate the modern service corporation. This change has largely occurred since the late 1980s, since proponents of modern management methods turned their attentions to the public sector, including the police. Improved budgetary efficiencies, enhanced performance, and greater accountability have been the justifications proposed for these changes. Talk about "professionalization" in the early decades of the twentieth century was supplemented in the later decades by talk about problem-solving approaches and community partnerships. Now the rhetoric has embraced corporate managerialism, and particular the ideas of performance management and customer service. Kappeler and Kraska have referred to a "*corporatization of democratic ideals*," whereby police now provide a "product" to their "customers", "clients" and "consumers" (Kappeler and Kraska, 1998:294-295). Australian police forces now have mission statements vision statements, and business plans, often made available through their websites on the Internet, to complement, and at times replace, the older-style administrative guidelines, rule-books, disciplinary codes, legislation and the common law. A highly simplified scheme of some of the major conceptual shifts evident in Australian policing in the past eighty years appears below:[9]

Table 8.1: Australian Policing: Two Management Ideologies

Selected Foci	Traditional	Corporate
Organisational philosophy/ies	civil service, military-bureaucratic	private sector, market-based
Key official norms	laws, internal rules	vision, mission statements, business plans
Key values	order maintenance, stability, loyalty	adaptability, efficiency, performance
Style of interaction	exclusive	inclusive/exclusive
Status of individual recipient of police service	citizen	Customer
Form of accountability	legalistic	managerial, public relations
Source of legitimacy	"consent of the governed"	"customer satisfaction"
Measure of accountability	largely subjective	highly quantitative

The reference to style of interaction in the above table is intended to point out an important difference between traditional and corporate police management practices. The traditional police organization conducts itself principally in an autonomous, and hence self-sufficient, way. This serves to distance the police from those they purportedly serve. They are "exclusive" then in two senses. On the other hand, the corporate police department is "inclusive" in that it is more inclined to invest in consultants (i.e. outside expertise), to talk about "partnerships", and to outsource certain functions (e.g., prisoner transport, vehicle maintenance). There is then a greater degree of interdependence in some senses. How inclusive these organizations now are in terms of their relations with members of the public has become a key question for those concerned to preserve policing as a democratically constituted activity.

In view of the longstanding centralized nature of Australian policing and an absence of meaningful local mechanisms to permit fine-tuning of policing to local needs and priorities, changes of this nature immediately suggest the continuation of hands-off type policing. If the corporatist analogy is to carry any weight in terms of improved accountability or effectiveness, then "minority shareholders" must have the collective ability to challenge the direction and approach of the corporation. This can prove elusive enough in the private sphere. Why it should be more likely to deliver greater accountability to individual citizens in the public sphere is by no means apparent. From a community relations perspective, it is arguable that the new police mission statements, vision statements and organizational plans promise little that is concrete or recognizable by many police "clients," particularly those for whom police services are imposed rather than freely solicited.

A "market" for public safety?

The market place implies an element of consumer choice, made possible by a range of competing service providers. Consumerism of this kind in relation to public safety is not characteristic, at least yet, of policing generally in democratic societies.[10] For many people at the margins of society, the police officer-citizen relationship is rarely one of choice as to initiation or negotiation as to substance. To try to render these frequently unequal and coercive contacts in terms of the language of contractualism and consumerism is not just reductive of the complexity of the formal relationship under law and the lived experience of those directly involved. It is also to engage in transmogrification of a kind that threatens to efface the collective dimension of "policing by consent." Public safety needs to be considered to be a larger question than simply meeting the security needs, perhaps even tastes, of individual "customers" or "purchasers." It has been, at least since the time of Thomas Hobbes, and remains, though unfashionably perhaps now, a public good. The collective security sought in return for the citizen's "consent" was premised upon some notion of shared public responsibility for the common good, not upon "consumer choice" or "customer satisfaction."

The poverty of the market analogy for police work is most evident at the level of officer-citizen interaction. When a police officer intervenes in a scuffle outside a night-club between security staff and an evicted patron, who exactly is her "customer" or "client"? Does the police *customer-service strategy* apply to the bouncer (who called for police assistance), to the patron (who didn't), or to both? What exactly does it mean in this context to pursue *"customer satisfaction"*? And what if none of the parties to the fight wishes to press charges, despite evidence of physical injury? Are the "customers" right? Should the absence of individual desires to proceed formally with charges alone dictate the outcome? Upholding the law and protecting life in areas such as domestic violence surely shows us that, whatever the limitations of particular strategies, good police work will often present cases for official action in the absence of willing victims or witnesses.[11]

More accountability and transparency?

Some implications of the shifts described offer a potential for the improvement of police services and greater accountability. Enhanced police managerial powers to remove officers under suspicion of wrongdoing, at least temporarily, and to terminate their services based upon findings of culpability at the civil rather than criminal standard have been advocated increasingly, and implemented to some extent, in Australian police forces (see New South Wales, 1997). There is also more rhetoric about the improved responsibility of police supervisors and managers for those under their command. Unfortunately, few senior "heads" have rolled publicly in recent times to give real substance to changes of this kind (Goldsmith, 2000a). If these things are occurring, there is a case for giving them greater publicity, even in aggregate form, so as demonstrate positive moves away from previous practices. There is also a case for publicizing the police organizational learning outcomes of citizen complaints and successful civil actions for damages against police (Freckelton, 2000; Chevigny, 1995). Again, this information is difficult or impossible to locate by the ordinary person, and is rarely if ever revealed by the media. Increased public understanding of the use internally by police of modern auditing practices, and of improvements in data collection and analysis in problem-oriented policing type, would provide greater transparency and reason for confidence to the general public.

Corporate managerialism is not necessarily inconsistent with improved accountability, responsiveness or transparency. It just needs to be established, and here, given the questionable nature of the corporate analogy, the burden should be upon those introducing changes of this kind. Whether or not these self-adopted organizational styles are of substantive significance in terms of positively structuring police-citizen and police-community relationships is ultimately an empirical question. For anyone interested in improving police-community relations or indeed police effectiveness in matters of public safety, such questions might be explored by reference to the changes in the ways in which the police deal with the community. Firstly, one should look at these changes *positively*, in the context of the extent and meaning of changes in levels of community consultation and police involvement in community policing, and secondly, *negatively*, in terms of how police handle criticism. It may arise in confrontations with members of the public,[12] and when officers have become the subject of formal public complaints. In relation to the former, an important performance indicator would be to examine the improvements, if any, in police services provided to those groups and individuals whose relationships with the police have been most vexed and unsatisfactory (young people, indigenous people, the homeless etc). Measures of this kind are sorely needed, though rarely encountered to date. Again, if they exist and are being used, they should be more effectively publicized.

Inadequate public participation

Too much community influence in the application of the law can result in bias and inconsistency in the administration of criminal justice. However too little responsiveness by police to community concerns can leave important sections of the community feeling alienated from the police. As noted earlier, formalized local level accountability mechanisms for policing have been conspicuously absent in Australia. In the last decade or so, police-community contact, other than in the course of operations or requests for assistance, has been formalized largely through Neighborhood Watch groups or "community consultative committees."[13] While these arrangements have often been dressed up in the language of "partnerships", they have been found frequently to lack clear mandates, to provide citizens with little or no influence over police policy, to be unrepresentative of the wider community, and to suffer from little or no ongoing commitment by police (CJC, 1997:chap. 5; James, Sutton, and Englehardt, 1993). There has been, until recently, little or no alignment between arrangements of this kind and local government structures. In a study of police and community in Brisbane, Queensland, the Criminal Justice Commission concluded:

> *Local government is undoubtedly a critical stakeholder in the identification and resolution of local policing problems. There has been a lack of appropriate structures for including local government, and other key community representatives, in the process of identifying and addressing local policing problems. (CJC, 1998:52)*

Apart from the lack of integration of policing with municipal governance and the other criticisms detailed above, a fundamental weakness of many of these arrangements has been their police-auspiced nature. In practical if not always exclusively formal terms, the police have had the running on how these bodies were constituted and conducted. Various surveys have found that the membership of these bodies tends often to be composed of middle-class, white professional people over the age of 40 years. In many instances, these bodies are established in areas without serious crime problems, so that youth noise and graffiti issues tend to dominate the agenda. Not surprisingly, such arrangements tend to have a short shelf life, especially if not supported by the police.

In the last two or three years, there have been some attempts to strengthen local police/community consultation arrangements. In Queensland, for example, in 1997, a program of Community Policing Partnerships started. One feature of these Partnerships is their alignment to local council areas; another is that their citizen membership can make recommendations to a state board (CJC, 1997). Similar moves have been announced in Victoria. It remains true of any such bodies of this kind that without clear mandates, a broadly representative membership, training and support for members to perform their role independently, and a degree of influence about how and what types of local policing services are delivered, these arrangements will remain largely window-dressing and public relations exercises. To date, many such police/community "partnerships" have been narrowly constituted, unequal, police-dominated relationships with few if any concrete outcomes in terms of establishing or restoring public confidence in, and identification with, local policing (James, Sutton, and Engelhardt, 1993; CJC, 1997). In particular, the young, the indigenous, the homeless, and others living on the margins of Australian cities, towns, and rural communities have tended to fall outside these arrangements, pointing to a serious lacuna in community policing arrangements. As David Bayley once noted, it makes little sense to hold a party and then for the host to do all the talking. Real partnership requires balanced police and community participation, genuine dialogue, and a real commitment to understanding each other (Bayley, 1989:75).

The trend to corporatization of police management arguably is yet to reverse the historical pattern of police-community relationships in Australia, despite the current talk of "clients" and "customer-service." There is no reason in principle however why certain features of police managerialism should not enhance accountability to all sectors of society. Regionalization, especially in large state police forces such as New South Wales, in association with greater responsibility at the regional commander level for the activities and achievements of policing, could result in better local-level understandings if sub-regional committees with broad community representation were established. If real community policing is to occur in the context of corporatist management, then the new tools of internal accountability and control should be adapted and applied to the field of evaluating progress in improving community involvement in police policies and practices. The importance of these undertakings might be demonstrated by a suitably expanded range of police performance indicators, to include for example measures of public willingness to report matters to the police across different sectors of society. There should also be measures of police responsiveness to the more socially vulnerable groups. While not unimportant in themselves, general public satisfaction surveys will tend not to reveal much about the more challenging areas of police-community relations.

Two areas of particular concern for police-indigenous relations in the last decade or so have been "over-policing" and "under-policing." In some rural towns and inner city districts populated by indigenous persons, there has been evidence of "over-policing", reflected in high police/citizen ratios (1:80), and unusually high arrest rates of indigenous persons for public order offences (Cunneen, 1992). In some more remote indigenous communities, there has been evidence of the converse situation, where "under-servicing" by police has occurred (Lincoln and Wilson, 1994). Rising levels of criminality in once traditional communities, often of serious crimes such as rape and aggravated assault, go un- or under-acknowledged by police (Lincoln and Wilson, 1994). A lack of broadly representative, empowered community consultation arrangements in these areas is sorely needed to ensure a better response by police. In addition, more than senior police management lip service is needed to improvements in anti-discrimination training and community policing.[14]

Handling criticism and complaints

Police, it seems, have rarely dealt with criticism well, whether its source lay in the community or within the rank and file police membership.[15] Public complaints against police officers have been an area of difficulty for the police for a long time (Goldsmith 1991; Lewis, 1999). This has a certain irony given recent enthusiasm for "customer satisfaction" among senior police managers. There is no doubt that the very idea of a public complaint about police service comes close to the kind of market concept of public services currently promoted by many public sector reformers. Only very recently, however, have the police begun to acknowledge publicly the potential value to be obtained from citizen complaints in terms of improving police performance and accountability (Goldsmith, 1991). Until the mid-late 1980s, Australians had few alternatives but to complain to police internal investigation units. The record of these units in meeting complainant needs and in persuading the general public of their efficacy was pretty woeful. If not corrupt, these bodies have been found repeatedly by official inquiries to be inefficient, biased, lazy, and generally uncommitted or incompetent in terms of undertaking thorough investigations of complaints against fellow officers (Queensland, 1989: New South Wales, 1997). While findings of this kind began to emerge publicly in the late 1980s, it seems that these problems continue to exist, as a recent inquiry into internal affairs within the NSW police has revealed (Police Integrity Commission, 2000).[16]

The emergence of oversight agencies (ombudsman offices, Criminal Justice Commission, Police Complaints Authorities) from the mid-1980s onwards has provided an alternative mechanism for people unhappy with police services (Goldsmith, 1991). While these agencies have not been without their critics and, as elsewhere, met with considerable police resistance (e.g., Freckelton, 1991), they continue to offer a symbolic as well as practical alternative to police internal complaint channels. Extending their effectiveness, accessibility, and credibility for indigenous persons and members of other marginal groups remains a challenge. An important recent development has been the move to extend the practice of informal resolution of complaints as a cheaper, quicker, and more effective way of resolving complaints (Goldsmith, 2000b). Informality however, can come at a cost in terms of diminished procedural entitlements of complainants. Socially vulnerable citizens are particularly at risk in these circumstances, especially where the informal resolution procedures are police-controlled, as they largely are in Australia, and where there are internal police pressures to "clear up" complaints by this method wherever possible (Goldsmith, 2000b). An ongoing need in this area is for the greater use of personal apologies by police officers in cases of admitted unsatisfactory conduct (many police remain reluctant to apologize face to face), and for greater commitment to the police departments to take on board the lessons to be derived from citizen grievances (feedback to complainants on any changes resulting from their complaints would be a positive move).

Private security and technology

Two other significant factors for the future of Australian policing are the privatization of policing, and the growing capacity of information and other technologies for surveillance and other law enforcement functions. Private security has grown significantly over the preceding two decades. Estimates of this growth vary, but sworn police/private security employee rates of in excess of 1:2 are common (Prenzler and Sarre, 1998) Government in Australia has become a significant client of the private security industry over the past decade or so, both in terms of preventive/guard tasks, and the deployment of technology. Court security and prisoner movement were tasks often delegated to police, which now have largely passed to private organizations. Local government has become a client of these organizations for the purposes of assisting with by-law enforcement and patrols of "hot-spots" characterized by underage drinking and graffiti. They have also become purchasers of surveillance technologies, in particular closed circuit television (CCTV) systems. Police however tend to be responsible for monitoring the screens, and responding to incidents observed by the cameras (Powell et al, 1998). Cost-consciousness seems likely to continue to drive economy measures of this kind, though public demand for a more visible "police presence"[17] is another factor that will determine the extent of private security involvement in the regulation of public and private space. Gated communities patrolled by private security firms now exist in Australia. Questions of competence and accountability will continue to arise as security is increasingly commodified and disarticulated more and more from the sight and immediate responsibility of the central state.

Police roles and methods have always adapted to the availability of new technologies. The passive monitoring of CCTV screens by police officers, noted above, is a shift in practice enabled by such technology. The motor car, and the portable radio, are two examples from earlier this century that enabled different staffing and patrol practices. Policing large public demonstrations has led to the application of new technologies of control to public order police work. Australian police have trailed and now use capsicum spray as a non-lethal alternative to firearms. There has been little, if any, open use of the stun gun/Taser device kinds of restraining devices used in the infamous Rodney King case. Undercover police work capacity has undoubtedly been strengthened by the use of microsize video recorders for gathering evidence in cases of organized crime and police corruption.[18] While little researched to date in Australia, the spread of networked computers has placed new information resources at the disposal of patrol officers, while police data bank capacities have facilitated their emergence as a primary source of information and intelligence for the private sector (Ericson and Haggerty, 1997).

New technologies can unquestionably contribute to making police work more effective and efficient. There is however the perennial civil liberties concern about excessive police intrusiveness into personal privacy, enabled by new listening and surveillance devices. As well, there is the inherent temptation for police to seek "technological fixes" for their intelligence and crime solving tasks, rather than relying upon their relations with the public and other investigative methods to provide information and solve crimes.[19] This tension within police work is likely to remain, and perhaps to increase, as technologies become further miniaturized and economical to operate, and as concerns about countering organized crime continue to influence law and justice policy.

As with most other forms of technology, much depends on how they are used rather than the intrinsic qualities of the technology itself. There can be little doubt however that new technologies can also contribute to greater accountability for police actions. Tape-recording of police interviews for all but very minor offences is now routine practice in Australia. In the public areas and detention cells of major police stations, the use of CCTV is increasingly common. Both uses of technology, while not eliminating the possibility of police abuses, render a larger proportion of police work more transparent than was previously the case. In principle at least, the proliferation of telephone technologies, most recently the mobile phone, has also greatly enabled members of the public to direct demands for service to police communications centres. This is a kind of "democratization" of policing, it might be suggested. In a society with relatively high individual access to telephones such as Australia, we are arguably also seeing a "virtualization" of police-citizen contact, as it becomes harder to walk or even drive to a local police station as they diminish in number, but easier to contact the police by electronic means. Ultimately, the impact of technologies on policing must be evaluated in terms of improved responsiveness to citizen requests and community needs, and the absence of evidence of their abuse. In the absence of more democratic local controls over policing in Australia, there is an even greater need for independent scrutiny and approval of requests by police for the use of many of the new technologies. While it remains commonplace for decisions about the use of surveillance and listening devices to be approved by judges, there is an upward trend in the number of applications of this kind made by law enforcement agencies, and it remains relatively unusual for judges to refuse to grant permission for their use.

Globalization and Transnational Law Enforcement

Until the early 1980s, policing in Australia was largely synonymous with state-level public police forces and domestic law and order issues. Since then, the growth in private security (referred to earlier) and the growing strategic significance of federal law enforcement agencies have been two of the most striking changes to the profile of policing. There has been a 'globalization of public problems' in the past two decades, requiring a reassessment of traditional police models and the development of new methods for dealing with national and cross-border issues. Transnational crime groups are now an integral feature of the global network society (Castells, 1998). Illicit drugs, mainly from the 'Golden Triangle', has been the primary influence upon changes to strategic thinking, in association with growing concerns about the organized crime element in Australia (Moffitt, 1885). Post-war immigration from southern Europe initially, but more recently from eastern Europe and South East Asia, is commonly linked to the development of organized crime groups in Australia. Ethnic and national identities feature in the analysis of many such groups by law enforcement experts (Australia, 1994).

More recently, people and arms smuggling (Mouzos, 1999) have become issues of concern for national government, together with illicit drugs. Once the poor relation of Australian policing, the Australian Federal Police (AFP)'s position and responsibilities as a national law enforcement body have been enhanced considerably. Their improvement in status has coincided largely with growing specialization of law enforcement agencies, with the creation of new bodies such as the National Crime Authority (NCA) in 1983. The NCA is a specialist law enforcement agency employing lawyers and accountants as well as police investigators, and is equipped with special investigative powers above and beyond those available to the state or federal police.[20] Other law enforcement responsibilities have also been delegated to specialized agencies such as the Australian Securities and Investments Commission (ASIC), which focuses upon compliance with corporations law, and the Australian Bureau of Criminal Intelligence (ACBI).

The AFP's future is closely linked to risk assessments concerning Australia's vulnerability to global crime patterns. Even with relatively large state police forces, the capacity of state governments and police forces to respond to transnational crime is limited. They will continue to depend upon the coordinating and other umbrella functions provided by national-level law enforcement bodies such as the AFP and the NCA. The AFP's links with INTERPOL and similar agencies will remain important and become better developed. The AFP is currently expanding its overseas liaison scheme mainly into Asia but also to include Latin America, in order to strengthen its network capacity to acquire and share criminal intelligence on various criminal activities. As risks become more dispersed and difficult to analyze at the domestic level, policing of necessity cannot any longer rely simply on local relationships and resources.

In response to new patterns of criminal enterprise (particularly illicit drugs, illegal arms, illegal immigration), less geographically-based, more intelligence-led police work is beginning to play a more obvious role in law enforcement (Gibbons, 1999).[21] Improving offshore intelligence is of growing importance. Advance warning systems of various kinds (over the horizon radar, ship movement detection, satellite surveillance etc.) mean inevitably an expanded reliance upon technologies in law enforcement in these areas. Recent calls by the leader of the Federal opposition and others for the establishment of an US-style Coast Guard service points to the difficulties traditional policing bodies face performing their duties off-shore. Greater cooperation between national law enforcement agencies and harmonization of regulatory instruments and procedures are also presaged by the globalization of crime risks (Nadelmann, 1997).

Restructuring law enforcement arrangements at the national, regional, and international levels has little obvious immediate nexus to the average citizen and his or her a local policing needs. However, there are features of these changes that will impact upon policing services more generally. These arrangements will inevitably need to be implemented locally, and thus will have an impact on citizens more directly. The sharing of risk assessments with other nation-states, for example in the area of illicit drugs, as well as sharing of new law enforcement technologies, powers and techniques, points to more policing issues being determined according to imperatives derived from sources outside the local, and indeed the national, community (Nadelmann, 1997). The perceived scale and urgency of the law enforcement problems raised may also serve to justify a less consultative, more intrusive, and potentially more repressive, response by the local law enforcement agencies.

Keeping national law enforcement bodies accountable to the nation-state polity is likely then to surface as an important policy issue in the future. The AFP is currently quite remote from local-level accountability, except in relation to its local policing responsibilities in the Australian Capital Territory, where it resembles State police forces. While this is hardly surprising given its range of tasks, it does mean that policy priorities of the AFP are effectively determined for the most part at the level of national ministerial/governmental input. Citizens may complain to the Commonwealth Ombudsman, but the complaints process tends to relate to local policing arrangements only (incivility, assault, failure to act etc). For the National Crime Authority, scrutiny comes in the form of Federal Parliamentary Joint Committee on the NCA, which looks at the operations of the NCA at least annually. However the scrutiny possible by such a mechanism is limited, as it does not have its own investigative branch or a permanent administrative wing to enable receipt of complaints from citizens in the way other accountability mechanisms tend to do (Goldsmith, 1991).

Conclusion

Police power in Australia is being challenged as well as extended. The changing composition of Australian society, new geo-political agendas, and new cultural attitudes towards political authority have made the idea of "consent" more elusive and contested. Conceptions of social order and law enforcement priorities have diverged in response to such challenges as transnational crime, the quest for personal identity, and generalized feelings of insecurity. However it remains doubtful whether police-community relations are deepening or are based upon improved understanding. Despite a new language of "partnerships", "customer service" and "responsibility", police/citizen contacts are being depersonalized, in part through the expanded use of new technologies of communication, but also as a consequence of the new managerialism. Technology is being used to centralize demands for police services, enabling the closure of local police stations. Managerialism in policing is highly focused upon regional police commands, often far removed from small communities with particular needs, and favours internal performance measurement and largely impotent and narrowly based "consultation" mechanisms over broader forms of citizen participation. Accountability is being redefined as a predominantly internal (and hence managerial) issue, rather than as one for broad public consultation and input. While police forces may be becoming more internally responsive in some ways due to mangerialism, their accessibility and transparency to ordinary citizens (ie externally) seems to have changed little or at all.

Australian police forces are also taking advantage of new opportunities, as well as being shaped by powerful external forces present in many other countries. Importantly, there are new configurations of external and internal risk (in particular, "fear of crime", "war on drugs") which are ideological as well as real in their significance. Crime is increasingly an issue of international relations, requiring a range of new structures and methods to combat its apparent octopus-like menace to societies around the globe (Sterling, 1994). New cooperative arrangements between national police forces are emerging, and new needs for extradition, asset tracing, and banking regulation are increasingly defining the reality of police work at one level. The bulk of policing will however continue to occur at the local level. Fragmentation of communities and increased economic uncertainty have had localized consequences in terms of renewed "fear of crime" and the commodification of personal safety. In part, this anxiety provides a political mandate for the expansion of police powers. Situational crime prevention and security hardware and services will continue to be promoted as first line responses to concerns about personal safety. The well-off, the elderly, and many women are likely to respond to, and demand, these new phantasms of security. For those however less able to pay for, or to participate in, the technologically mediated and more privatized forms of security provision, the old ghosts of personal insecurity will remain and the future of policing will be far more uncertain.

Andrew Goldsmith teaches in the Law School, Flinders University, Adelaide, South Australia. He teaches in the areas of criminology, criminal justice, and legal ethics. He has a longstanding interest in policing, and particularly in police misconduct and police accountability. He edited and contributed to "Complaints Against the Police: The Trend to External Review" (Oxford: Clarendon Press, 1991), and with Colleen Lewis has edited and contributed to "Civilian Oversight of Policing: Governance, Democracy and Human Rights" (Ox-

Goldsmith

ford: Hart Publishing, 2000). His current research projects include a study of policing, governance and public safety issues in Colombia. He is on the editorial board of several international refereed journals including "Policing and Society, International Criminal Justice Review, and Criminal Justice."

Notes and References

Australia (2000), *Report on Government Services: Volume 2: Justice, Emergency Management*, Steering Committee for the Review of Commonwealth/State Service Provision (Canberra: Commonwealth Government)

Australia (1999), *Linking Inputs and Outputs: Activity Measurement by Police Services*, Steering Committee for the Review of Commonwealth/State Service Provision, (Canberra: AusInfo)

Australia (1994), *Review of Commonwealth Law Enforcement Arrangements* (Canberra: Australian Government)

Australian Bureau of Statistics, (2000), *AusStats*, http://www.abs.gov.au/Ausstats/

Australian Institute of Criminology, (1999) *The Composition of Australia's Police Services 1999*, www.aic.gov.au/stats/pol99.html

Bayley, David (1989) "Community Policing in Australia" in Duncan Chappell and Paul Wilson (eds), *Australian Policing: Contemporary Issues* (Sydney: Butterworths)

Bearup, Gre.g (2000), "When the whistle blows" *The Age Good Weekend Magazine*, 10 June

Brogden, Michael, and Shearing, Clifford (1993), *Policing for a New South Africa* (London: Routledge)

Bronitt, Simon, and Kinley, David (1995) "Undercover Policing: Detection or Deception" in H Selby (ed), *Tomorrow's Law* (Sydney: Federation Press)

Chan, Janet (1996), *Changing Police Culture* (Melbourne: Cambridge University Press)

Chevigny, Paul (1995) *Edge of the Knife: Police Violence in the Americas* (New York: New Press)

Criminal Justice Commission (1998), *Policing and the Community in Brisbane* (Brisbane: CJC)

Criminal Justice Commission (1997), *Community Consultative Committees and the Queensland Police Service: An Evaluation* (Brisbane: CJC)

Cunneen, Chris (1992), "Policing and Aboriginal Communities: Is the concept of over-policing useful?" in Cunneen (ed.), *Aboriginal Perspectives on Criminal Justice*. Monograph series no. 1 (Sydney: Sydney University Institute of Criminology)

Davids, Cindy and Hancock, Linda (1998) "Policing, Accountability and Citizenship in the Market State" *Australian and New Zealand Journal of Criminology* 38

Davis, Mike (1990) *City of Quartz* (London: Vintage, 1990)

Dixon, David (1999), "Beyond Zero Tolerance", Australian Institute of Criminology, "Mapping the Boundaries of Australia's Criminal Justice System" conference, Canberra, 22-23 March 1999.

Dixon, David, (1998), "Broken Windows, Zero Tolerance, and the New York Miracle" *Current Issues in Criminal Justice* 10:96

Ericson, Richard, and Haggerty, Kevin (1997), *Policing the Risk Society* (Oxford: Clarendon Press)

Finnane, Mark, (1994) *Police and Government: Histories of Policing in Australia* (Melbourne: Oxford University Press)

Freckelton, Ian (2000), " in Tony Coady, Steve James and Seamus Miller, *Violence and Police Culture* (Melbourne: Melbourne University Press)

Freckelton, Ian (1991), "Shooting the Messenger: the Rise and Fall of the Victorian Police Complaints Authority" in Goldsmith (1991), *Complaints Against the Police: The Trend to External Review* (Oxford: Clarendon Press)

Gibbons, Sarah (1999) "Intelligence-led policing: 'The key to survival'" *Jane's International Police Review* 11:30-31

Giddens, Anthony (1990), *The Consequences of Modernity* (Stanford: Stanford University Press)

Goldsmith, Andrew (2000a) "An Impotent Conceit: Law, Culture and the Re.gulation of Police Violence" in T Coady and S James (eds), *Violence and Police Culture* (Melbourne: Melbourne University Press)

Goldsmith, Andrew (2000b), "Informal Resolution of Police Complaints in Australia: Better Understanding or Mere Bureaucratic Convenience?" *Law in Context*, 17 (forthcoming)

Goldsmith, Andrew (1999), "The Police We Need" *Alternative Law Journal* 24:127.

Goldsmith, Andrew (1991) "External Review v Self Re.gulation: The dialectic of police accountability procedures" in Goldsmith (ed), *Complaints Against the Police: The Trend to External Review* (Oxford: Clarendon Press)

Hogg, Russell and Brown, David (1998), *Rethinking Law and Order* (Sydney: Pluto Press)

Home Office (2000), *Feasibility of an Independent System for Investigating Complaints Against the Police* Police Research Serics Paper 124, (London: Home Office Research, Development and Statistics Directorate)

James, Steve and Sutton, Adam (1996), "Joining the War Against Drugs? Assessing Law Enforcement Approaches to Illicit Drug Control" in Duncan Chappell and Paul Wilson (eds.) *Australian Policing: Contemporary Issues* (Sydney: Butterworths, 1996)

James, S, Sutton A, and Englehardt, M (1993), *Review of the Barwon Police-Community Consultative Committee* (Melbourne: VICSAFE)

Kappeler, Victor and Kraska, Peter (1998) "A textual critique of community policing: police adaption to modernity" *Policing: An International Journal of Police Strate.gies and Management* 21:293

Lane, Bernard (1999), "Let police chiefs tell us how it is, Kirby urges", *The Weekend Australian*, 22-23 May 1999

Lewis, Colleen (1999) *Complaints Against Police* (Sydney: Federation Press).

Lincoln, Robyn, and Wilson, Paul (1994), "Aboriginal Offending: Patterns and Causes" in Duncan Chappell and Paul Wilson (eds), *The Australian Criminal Justice System: The Mid-1990s* (Sydney: Butterworths)

Loader, Ian (1996), *Youth, Policing, and Democracy* (Basingstoke: Macmillan)

Lupton, Deborah (1999), "Dangerous Places and the Unpredictable Stranger: Constructions of Fear of Crime" *Australian and New Zealand Journal of Criminology* 1

Lustgarten, Laurence (1986) *The Governance of Police* (London: Sweet and Maxwell)

Maher, Lisa and Dixon, David, (1999) "Policing and Public Health: Law Enforcement and Harm Minimisation in a Street-level Drug Market" *British Journal of Criminology* 39:488

Makkai, Toni, (2000), "Drug Trends and Policies" in Chappell and Wilson (eds), *Crime and the Criminal Justice System in Australia: 2000 and Beyond* (Sydney: Butterworths)

Marenin, Otwin (1998), "The goal of democracy in international police assistance programs" *Policing: An International Journal of Police Strate.gies and Management* 21:159

Moffitt, Athol (1985), *A Quarter to Midnight: Organized Crime and the Decline of the Institutions of State* (North Ryde: Angus and Robertson)

Mouzos, Jenny (1999), *International Traffic in Small Arms: An Australian Perspective*, Trends and Issues in Crime and Justice, No. 104, (Canberra: Australian Institute of Criminology)

Mukherjee, Satyanshu (2000), "Crime Trends: A National Perspective" in D Chappell and P Wilson (eds), *Crime and the Criminal Justice System in Australia: 2000 and Beyond* (Sydney: Butterworths)

Nadelmann, Ethan (1997), "The Americanization of Global Law Enforcement: The Diffusion of American Tactics and Personnel" in William F McDonald (ed.), *Crime and Law Enforcement in the Global Village* (Cincinnati, OH: Anderson Publishing).

New South Wales, Royal Commission (1997), *Final Report of the Royal Commission into the NSW Police Service, Volumes 1-4* (Sydney: RCNSWPS)

New South Wales (2000), *Crimes (Forensic Procedures) Bill 2000* (bill before the NSW Parliament, June 2000)

Palmer, Darren (1999), "'Confronting police culture' or 'the force is still with you'? Making sense of contemporary policing in Australia" *International Journal of Police Science and Management* 1:333

Police Inte.grity Commissions (2000), *Special Report to Parliament: Project Dresden - An Audit of the Quality of NSW Police Service Internal Investigations* (Sydney: Police Inte.grity Commission)

Powell, Kathryn, Sanderson, Matthew, and Foster, Rodney (1998), *Closed Circuit Television Surveillance: Application and Effectiveness in Inner Adelaide* (unpublished report for South Australian Police, Adelaide City Council and SA Attorney General's Department)

Prenzler, Tim and Sarre, Rick (1998), *Re.gulating Private Security in Australia* (Trends and Issues in Crime and Criminal Justice no. 98) (Canberra: Australian Institute of Criminology)

Queensland (1989), Report of a Commission of Inquiry into Possible Ille.gal Activities and Associated Police Misconduct (Brisbane: Government Printer)

Scarman, The Rt. Hon. Lord (1983), *The Scarman Report: The Brixton Disorders, 10-12 April 1981* (Harmondsworth: Penguin)

Stenning, Philip (1981), *Police Boards and Commissions in Canada* (Toronto: University of Toronto Centre of Criminology)

Sterling, Claire (1994), *Thieves' World: The Threat of the New Global Network of Organized Crime* (New York: Simon and Schuster)

Sutton, Adam, and James, Steve (1999), "Developments in Australian Drug Law Enforcement: Taking Stock", (unpublished paper, prepared for the Australasian Conference on Drug Strate.gy, Adelaide, 27-29 April 1999)

United Nations (1997), *World Drug Report* (New York: Oxford University Press)

Weatherburn, Don, and Lind, Bronwyn (1999), "Heroin harm minimisation: do we really have to choose between law enforcement and treatment?", *Crime and Justice Bulletin* no. 46, November 1999 (NSW Bureau of Crime Statistics and Research, Sydney)

1 This paper in part draws on some ideas sketched out in an earlier piece (Goldsmith, 1999), published in the *Alternative Law Journal*. I would like to thank Sally Burgess, former law student, Flinders University Law School, for her research assistance in preparing this paper. I have also benefited from discussions with a number of my Australian policing colleagues, but in particular I would like to thank David Dixon, Steve James, and Darren Palmer.

2 Apart from its local police services in the ACT, AFP police officers are known as 'federal agents'. Their work in many respects resembles that of the US Federal Bureau of Investigation (FBI).

3 I am excluding here the role of the AFP in policing the ACT, which has an area population of approximately 308,000 people. Source: Australian Bureau of Statistics (2000).

4 A policing colleague, Darren Palmer, informs me that the Australian state of Victoria has very recently (i.e. in 2000) moved to coincide the establishment 'local safety committees' involving police and community, with local government boundaries

5 Australia is one of the most urbanised nations in the world, despite its international reputation for wide open spaces. Recent patterns of rural decline have further contributed to the shift from the country and small towns to the major cities of Australia, especially along the eastern seabord.

6 Here I am mindful of Anthony Giddens' (1990) concept of "*ontological insecurity*", referring to the relative fracturing of personal relationships in modern social life and the consequent feelings of anxiety and distress experienced among many citizens.

7 While originally based upon work by Ralph Dahrendorf, I have taken the "two-thirds/ one thirds" notion of society from the recent work by Russell Hogg and David Brown (1998), especially 132-134, 204-210.

8 A recently reported speech by High Court justice Michael Kirby has added impetus to senior police participation in public debates. See Bernard Lane, "Let police chiefs tell us how it is, Kirby urges", *The Weekend Australian*, 22-23 May 1999, 13. Some recent examples of speeches of this kind by senior police officers are mentioned in this article.

9 I have based this scheme in part upon the discussion in Davids and Hancock (1998)

10 Some (e.g. Clifford Shearing) have argued for a more market-based system of public safety arrangements, though not one based upon the near or complete abdication of state responsibility. See Brogden and Shearing (1993). For a critique of the Shearing position, see Davids and Hancock (1998).

11 While other examples probably arise, the pursuit of mandatory arrest policies in some US jurisdictions is a clear example of the inapplicability of 'consumer sovereignty' to some such situations.

12 Otwen Marenin has suggested a very basic test of democratic policing: *When a person can yell, even offensively, at a police officer to her/his face and not get beaten up for it, for neither police culture, nor organizational norms, nor political preferences would sanction this exercise of force, then democratic policing exists"* Marenin (1998:172).

13 The terminology varies slightly. In Queensland, "community crime committees" were established around 1988, South Australia established "crime prevention committees" in 1989, and around the same time, the NSW police established "Re.gional Customer Councils".

14 Another example of the difficulty of changing police practice at the street level arises in the area of drug law enforcement, where a conflict between traditional law enforcement and 'harm minimization' policies embraced by police management introduces a tension for operational officers which can have the result of at best partial implementation of the policy initiative. See Chan (1996).

15 'Police whistleblowers' have tended to receive short shrift from police management and indeed many rank and file officers, while those outside the police who complain have often been termed 'troublemakers' and at times have been subjected to harassment and excessive or inappropriate charging practices. See generally Goldsmith (2000a).

16 The PIC was critical of the "lack of rigour by the investigating officers and their managers," and made a series of recommendations to Parliament to ensure new benchmarks of internal investigations including more thorough preparation of investigations and better supervision.

17 I include private security within this notion of "police," on the grounds that to the extent many citizens seek, and are reassured by, the presence of private security firms, in the absence of more frequent public police patrols, there is an element of common purpose or function between the two forms of security provision.

18 Most famously perhaps was its use by the NSW Wood Royal Commission investigative team to record an illicit exchange of money between an undercover police officer and another police officer under investigation for drug-related corruption. See NSW (1997).

19 The current interest in police circles in Australia and elsewhere in expanding the statutory powers of police to seek and obtain DNA samples from suspects and convicted persons, so as to establish a DNA database, points to this tendency. See NSW (2000).

20 In particular, the NCA can hold closed hearings in which persons under examination can be directed to answer questions, overriding any attempt to invoke the privilege against self-incrimination.

21 By "intelligence-led policing" I am referring to law enforcement strategies based upon the collection and assessment of data, often in large amounts, from a wide range of sources. This approach enables police to be more anticipatory in style, based upon predictions of future events and their location, derived from the analysis and assessment undertaken. This is in contrast to the individual incident-driven reactive inquiry characteristic of traditional crime investigation. Intelligence-led policing can be used in domestic as much as transnational or international contexts. See further, Gibbons (1999).

* Professor Andrew Goldsmith, School of Law, Flinders University, GPO Box 2100, Adelaide, SA, 5001, Australia. Telephone: +(61 88)201-3813, Fax: +(61 88)201-3630, E-mail: Andrew.Goldsmith @flinders.edu.au

9 Police and Democracy in Finland

Ahti Laitinen

ABSTRACT

Finnish citizens' trust in their police is higher than their trust in the Finnish courts, the administrative machinery or Finnish politicians. According to the polls, people see the police as an important organ for their security, and many people are ready to give the police more power, more money and other resources. The reputation of the Finnish police is currently high in Finland. At the same time, there continues to be an ongoing discussion in Finland about broadening police powers. Finnish police are under Parliamentary control. If somebody feels that he or she has been mistreated by the police, that person has a legal right to make an official complaint, and this will be responded to by an appropriate official. Opportunities to lodge a formal complaint exist both at the local and national level. Corruption among the Finnish police forces is extremely rare. According to international comparisons, the corruption of the Finnish authorities is the second smallest in the world, after Denmark. Appointments of Finnish police officers are not political. It might be that the appointments of only a few of Finland's most senior police officers - at the top of the administration - are at times political in nature. Contemporary Finnish police are, by and large, quite independent. Nowadays, individual police officers, as citizens, can and do have their own political opinions.

Key Words: Chancellor of Justice, Parliamentary Ombudsman, Council of State, Police advisory board, Limitations on police actions, Lodging a complaint

Introduction: The Finnish Context

Finland is one of the five Scandinavian countries, along with Denmark, Iceland, Norway, and Sweden. The social and political systems in these countries are very similar to each other. There is strong cooperation among the Nordic countries, although only Denmark, Finland and Sweden are members of the European Union. Finland and Sweden joined the EU in 1995.

The total area of Finland is 338,145 sq. kilometres; it is one of the largest countries in Europe. The population of Finland is approximately five million, and the population density of the country is low. Administratively, the country was divided into 4 provinces in 1996. Before that there were 12 provinces. This division affects police administration because the latter has been arranged on a provincial basis.

There are 461 municipalities, which have, since 1977, been of two different types: urban municipalities and rural municipalities. The majority of the inhabitants are nominal members of the Lutheran Church, which is an official State church.

Finland is a bilingual country. The official languages are Finnish and Swedish, but the Swedish-speaking people constitute only 6 percent of the entire population. Although the Swedish-speaking part of the population is a small minority, its economic and political position has traditionally been strong. Two other traditional ethnic groups are the Gypsies and Laps. These groups, however, are composed of only a few thousand persons. In addition, recently approximately one thousand refugees have come to the country, mostly from Africa and the former Soviet area.

The Historical Background of the Finnish Police Forces

In order to more fully understand the mandate and philosophy of the police in Finland it is necessary to consider the history and evolution of the Finnish police. The history of the Finnish police dates back to the Middle Ages when Finland was part of the Kingdom of Sweden. At that time, public order in towns was maintained in a different fashion from that in the countryside. In fact, it was not until new legislation was passed in the 1960s that these differences were done away with. The beginning of real police institutions is closely associated with industrialization during the nineteenth century. Certain types of police activities existed a long time before that period.

The towns in Sweden and Finland were at first allowed broad autonomy in keeping public order. According to a town law enacted in the 1350s, the maintenance of public order and safety was the responsibility of town councils, although the King's bailiff was supposed to keep watch over it. The administration began to be concentrated in the hands of the Crown during the seventeenth century. An indication of this development was that the administration of the towns was transferred from the town councils to royally-appointed provincial governors. Various classes of civil servants existed for maintaining order and public safety. A class called *"the Servants of the Town"* were closest to what we now call police officers. In 1776, an ordinance was passed for improving the deteriorating order and public safety of Stockholm, the capital of the State, and the position of Master of the Police was created (Jousimaa, 1986).

Police departments in Finnish towns, compared to other countries, were established early. Finland was joined to the Russian Empire in 1809, and the first Chamber of Police under the Czar was established in 1816 in Turku, the old capital of Finland. Though the famous London Metropolitan Police was established in 1829, the Chamber of Police in Helsinki, the capital of Finland, started functioning as early as 1826. The duty of these chambers was to keep order, prevent crime, maintain the peace, and to act as a court for minor offences. The Chamber of Police's judicial powers were not abolished until 1897. Since the State appointed the members of the Chambers of Police, there was considerable governmental authority over the police.

Following the example of Turku and Helsinki, the other large towns in Finland received their own Chamber of Police, and the policemen were given uniforms. In 1861, the expression "Police Department" was officially used for the first time. At the turn of the century, the town police were divided into the uniform and the detective (or plain-clothes) branches. During the years 1903 and 1904, the town police finally became part of the State administration. This, however, did not immediately result in any improvement in the handling of police affairs, as noted in a report of the Ministry of Justice in 1906, which referred to various shortcomings in the police. Politics, it was alleged, had interfered in police operations. Nonetheless, the town police continued to be administered under the system described above in the early years of independence from December 1917 to 1925 (Jousimaa, 1986).

The primary reason for the early establishment of the Finnish Police Chambers was not the increasing population of the cities as it was in many other countries. It was because the Russian authorities wanted to have a strict control over the citizens' movements. When the Russian Governor-General (the representative of the Czar in Finland) in the 1870s and 1880s demanded an increase in the number of policemen in Helsinki, the Helsinki city council resisted the proposal very strongly. This resulted in a fight for power between the wealthier Finnish citizens and the Russian State officials because the Helsinki city council regarded the police as the tool of the Russian emperors. At the end of the nineteenth century, the political situation began to change for the worse in Finland. The Imperial Russian authorities started to integrate Finland more closely with Russia. On the other hand, the nationalist forces in Finland considered it reasonable to develop the Finnish police as a bulwark *against* Imperial pressure. In addition, since a revolutionary working-class movement emerged in Finland, a strong police force also began to appear to the Finnish bourgeoisie as some kind of a safeguard for the protection of its own interests. Thus, the police, particularly in the towns, became the subject of many diverse political pressures in the period immediately before Finnish independence in December 1917.

Policing in the rural areas was different from policing in urban areas during the Swedish times (before 1809). Progress regarding the development of policing in the countryside was slow. Old provincial laws make mention of country sheriffs as some sort of keepers of the peace. In the sixteenth century, independent feudal lords became the King's bailiffs and it was their duty to oversee the state of law and order. The sheriffs had originally been the people's representatives to the king, and prosecution was one of the sheriff's many functions. After the sixteenth century, however, the sheriff was appointed by the King's bailiff, and he became the representative of the State entrusted with administrative duties, including the maintenance of law and order. Since the sheriff's office required a certain amount of personal expenditure in the carrying out of some duties, wealthy peasants were usually selected for the post.

During the years 1634 and 1635, the administrative system in the country was overhauled. The governors became the King's bailiffs and administrative districts became known as jurisdictional districts (*kihlakunta*). According to the Ordinance of 1688, the administration of the district was placed under the direct jurisdiction of the King's bailiff, who had many responsibilities, including the enforcement of law and order and prosecution. By the Royal Decree of 1675, provincial governors were required to appoint sheriffs. They were to be loyal peasants living in the area. The duties of King's bailiff were later transferred to the sheriff (Jousimaa, 1986).

The sheriffs' duties were delineated by a proclamation made in 1814 by the Governor-General when Finland became joined to the Russian Empire. It retained validity until 1898 when the rural police were given their own statutes and regulations. At the end of the last century, different alternatives were considered for improving policing in the countryside. It was decreed in 1891 that each sheriff's office should have a sufficient number of constables hired by the State. Constables were appointed by the provincial governor. Since then policing in the countryside has been the responsibility of the State and the role of the communes has been only nominal (Sinisalo, 1971). The town and rural police were brought under the same set of regulations by the Police Act of 1925. Towns, however, still had the responsibility of providing for one-third of the cost of the police department. This financial burden was removed in 1977.

There were other police reforms. With independence, the police became civil servants under the jurisdiction of the Ministry of the Interior. A special Police Affairs Department was created to direct, supervise and coordinate police operations in the country. Under the twelve provincial governors, there were police inspectors in the provinces for police affairs. Criminal investigation facilities improved in 1927, following the creation of additional positions for detectives in the provinces. These positions were transferred to provincial criminal investigation police units which began in 1938. In 1926, a Crime Research Centre was set up in Helsinki, which was also entrusted with the local Interpol responsibilities. In 1955, the Central Criminal Investigation Department was formed in the country's capital, Helsinki, by combining the Crime Research Centre and the Criminal Investigation Centre of the province of Uusimaa.

At the end of the 1920s and the early 1930s much, unrest and civil disturbance took place in Finland. One reason was the political situation of the time and another was the Alcohol Prohibition Law of the period. At this time, a Mobile Command Force was commissioned to deal with the situation. Over the years, this Command Force was given additional duties, its personnel were increased and in this way the present Mobile Police were formed. The Second World War interrupted the active development of the police. During the war, only the historical office of the King's bailiff was abolished and the bailiff's duties were transferred to the sheriff. The statute regulating inspectors of police in the provinces was amended and they were given the power of prosecutor in addition to administrative and law-enforcement duties.

Until the end of the Second World War, a police unit called the State Police existed in Finland, which was charged, in practice, with the task of preventing Communist activities in the country, though, formally speaking, their main task was to deal with activities against the State.

Finland was at war with the Soviet union between 1939-1940 and 1941-1944. After the Armistice with the Soviet Union in 1944, the State Police unit was controlled by Communists or left-wing officials until 1949, the very groups it had previously sought to control. During this immediate post-war period, the main duty of this branch of the police forces now became investigating and exposing Soviet Union activities. But the branch was abolished at the beginning of 1949. A unit of Security Police, with lesser authority than that of the ordinary police and without an *overt* political agenda, was established in its stead.

The Police Act (No. 84 /1966) came into operation in 1967. It was the first comprehensive law in Finland covering all police activities. It cancelled all separate regulations governing different branches of the police. In 1973, the Act was amended and provisions were made for units of advisory boards. This allowed members of the public limited opportunities to cooperate actively with the police (Jousimaa, 1986). In 1973, the Police Department of the Ministry of the Interior became the Supreme Command of the Police in Finland, while Police Bureaus were given the command of the police in the provinces. The new legislation did not change the field organization of the police. The Central Criminal Investigation Department was reinforced by putting the remaining provincial criminal police units within it.

A new Police Law was enacted in 1995 and the organization and the structure of the police changed. For example, certain international human rights demands were taken into account in the new legislation. These rights previously existed in Finland, but not in the police legislation.

The Government's Proposal for the Police Act of 1995

When the Government gave its proposal for a new Police act in 1994 (proposal No. 57), it listed several deficiencies. Basically, the Police Act of 1966 was inconsistent, and its norm structure was misleading. For example, some of the rules regulating the authority of the police were mentioned in a *decree*, and some in an *act* or in some *special acts*. The rules regulating the use of force were placed in the Penal Code, although they were comparable to other rules concerning the authority of the police. The most important weaknesses in the 1966 Police Act were the following:

- The general principles for police actions were diffusely set out in the Police Act, and then only in part.

- There were no norms for putting the duties of the police into a certain order of preference.

- There was no general provision covering the conduct of the police when arresting a wanted person.

- There was no general provision for police work in connection with domestic crises, when the actions were necessary for preventing crime or an otherwise dangerous situation.

- There were no rules in any law concerning the police for making a notification of the coercive measures used.

- The rule prohibiting molestation of one person by another - for example, harassment cases - were not included in the law (These norms came into force in the beginning of 1999 in a separate law).

- There were no rules for towing away vehicles other than cars or other vehicles used on the roads.

- The rules regulating the confiscation of property because of crime were inadequate.

- There were no rules regulating the control, supervising and receiving of information. Such activities were based on custom or 'laws of tradition'.

- There were no rules regulating police investigation procedures, especially in relation to the use of coercive means. Such investigation was still based partly on customary laws.

- There were no rules concerning the auxiliary police forces. This is a part of the police force into which honest, healthy and ordinary citizens have been recruited. They are intended for unusual situations, not for normal conditions, and their duty is to help the professional police. The first auxiliary policemen and policewomen were recruited at the end of 1998 and in the beginning of 1999.

- There was no rule on compensation for a foreigner who suffered as a result of the coercive measures of the police.

As can be seen, most defects in the earlier 1966 Police Act concerned the rights of citizens, and the coherence of the police legislation. By the 1990s, the observance of the provisions of the international agreements adopted by Finland had become important. The Finnish Government determined that the Police Act had to follow the rules of any international agreement. It should not be contradictory or in conflict with them. The following agreements were taken into account in drafting the legislative proposal on the police:

- International Covenant on Civil and Political Rights (No. 8/76 of Treaties of Finland).
- Vienna Convention on Diplomatic Relations (No. 4/70).
- Vienna Convention on Consular Relations (No.50/80).
- Convention on the Prevention and Punishment of Crimes against Internationally Protected Person, including Diplomatic Agents (No. 63/78).
- Procedure for Law Enforcement Officers adopted by the United Nations General Assembly, 1979.
- Recommendation of the United Nations General Assembly, 1980.
- Principles on the use of fire arms and coercive measures adopted by the Eighth United Nations Congress on Crime Prevention, 1990.
- European Convention on Human Rights (1953, Finland ratified it in 1990).
- Declaration on the police made by the European Council (1979).
- Convention for the Protection of Individuals with regard to Automatic Processing of Personal Data (No. 36/92).
- Recommendation No. R (87) 21 of the Committee of Ministers to Member States on Assistance to Victims and Prevention of Victimisation (The Committee of Ministers, under the terms of Article 15.b of the Statute of the Council of Europe).

Two of the agreements were seen as being of such importance that they were included in their entirety in the government's proposal in a form of appendices. These are the *Procedure for Law Enforcement Officers adopted by the United Nations General Assembly* in 1979 and *Principles on the use of fire arms and coercive measures adopted by the Eighth United Nations Congress on Crime Prevention.*

In the Government's Proposal for a Police Act, reference was made to many international agreements. The passing of the Police Act in itself was democratic, but the processing of these agreements was not democratic. The agreements were made by the government, and the only role which the Parliament had was to ratify the result.

Duties of the police[1]

The duties and organization of the Finnish police have been enacted in the Police Act of 1995 (493/1995). The main duties of the Finnish police are to maintain public order and security, to prevent and solve crimes and to forward investigated cases for prosecution. They also carry out other duties assigned to the police by law, such as different licence services, for example, driving licences and weapon permits.

The objective of police work is to ensure that people can enjoy the rights guaranteed to them by the judicial system and social order freely and without disturbance.

The powers of the police are based on the Police Act enacted of 1995. It covers the key principles to be respected by the police when carrying out their official duties. The Act also includes general provisions covering police work, provisions on police powers, the supply of information, and instructions governing police investigations.

The Supreme Police Command confirmed the existing modes of police action in 1995. Police work, in addition to legislation, is guided by the agreements on human rights, international police ethical norms, research data on people's expectations and the established police practice. The modes of action also include national long-term strategic goals.

Finnish police function in close cooperation with different authorities and sectors. The most important ones being the rescue services, the frontier guards, the customs, the social and health authorities, schools and traffic organizations.

Organization of the Police

The Finnish police are subordinate to the Ministry of the Interior. The police organization operates at three levels. Its activities are supervised and coordinated by the Police Department of the Ministry of the Interior, acting as the Supreme Police Command. The Ministry of the Interior's Police Department, acting as the Supreme Police Command, develops and supervises police work throughout Finland. It is also responsible for equal access to different services and for their quality. The Supreme Police Command develops the legislation, the administration, training and research for the police sector. A major part of the duties of the Supreme Police Command comprises the increased international contacts that have taken place since Finland's being part of the European Union.

At the regional level, there are provincial administration units of the police in 5 Provincial State Offices and the 90 Local Police Departments. The police district of the Åland Islands is an autonomous unit.

The Provincial Police Command is responsible for the planning, development and supervision of police affairs in the province and for promoting cooperation between the Local Police, the National Bureau of Investigation and the Mobile Police within the province. The Provincial Police Command allocates resources to the Local Police within the province and supervises and controls operations.

The Local Police maintain public order and security and seek to prevent crimes. The Local Police also investigate crimes and other actions endangering public order and security, control traffic, promote traffic safety and carry out other duties assigned to the police. The local police departments also serve as prosecution and restraining or control authorities.

In addition, there are separate National Police Units which are directly subordinate to the Ministry of the Interior: the National Bureau of Investigation, the Security Police, the Mobile Police, the Police School, the Police College of Finland and the Police Technical Centre. The Police Department of Helsinki Local District is also operationally subordinate to the Ministry of the Interior. The Police Department of Helsinki Local District is also responsible for some special national duties.

Advisory Boards

The Advisory Board of Police Affairs operates in conjunction with the Ministry of the Interior. It deals with matters related to maintaining public order and security and to the development of the police administration. The Government appoints the chairman, vice-chairman and members as well as their personal deputy members by open application with representatives of police affairs. The Advisory Board of Police Affairs is appointed for a maximum of three years at a time.

Each local police department has an advisory board to deal with police affairs, police operations and operations related to it.

All these advisory boards are required to monitor public order and security and the work carried out by the police. They also make proposals for improving law enforcement and submit statements on matters involving the police.

Municipal councils elect the members of the local advisory boards for the duration of their term of office. The Police Chief is also a member of the advisory board.

Personnel

At the end of June 1998, the entire police administration employed a total of 10,757 persons, of whom 8,378 were police officers. About 6 percent of them were women.

Table 9.1 Finnish Police Staff by Units

Local police	Mobile Police	National Bureau of Investigation	Security Police	Police Training Institutes	Police Technical Center
7,258	751	509	170	102	50

On the European scale, Finland has few police officers in relation to the population. In 1994, according to the study made by the University of Leicester, Finland had 594 inhabitants per one police officer, and in Sweden the corresponding figure was 520, in Great Britain 375, in Germany 284 and in Italy 237.

Budget

The police functions cover about 1.5 percent of the total State budget. In 1997, the costs incurred by police functions were almost 2.8 billion Finnish marks. Most of the costs, that is, 80 %, resulted from the personnel administration. Police operations represent an annual cost of 500 Finnish marks per inhabitant.

Police Organization is Based on Management by Results

The Ministry of the Interior sets the national objectives for police operations. The Supreme Police Command holds discussions on these objectives with every provincial command and national unit of the police and also with the Helsinki Police Department. In the discussions, the achievement of the objectives is assessed and new objectives and resources for the coming year are agreed upon. The Provincial Police Command conducts the corresponding negotiations with the local police units.

Each police unit can estimate the overall quality of its operations in accordance with the criteria developed by the Supreme Police Command. In accordance with these criteria, the Supreme Police Command grants an annual quality award to one police unit in recognition of the exceptionally good quality of the services. In 1996, the quality award was granted to the Laboratory in Criminal Technology of the National Bureau of Investigation.

National Police Units

The national police units are directly subordinate to the Ministry of the Interior and include the National Bureau of Investigation, the Security Police, the Mobile Police, the Police School, the Police Institute and the Police Technical Centre.

National Bureau of Investigation

The National Bureau of Investigation combats international, organized, professional, economic and other serious crime, carries out investigations, develops crime prevention, investigation methods and police information systems.

The National Bureau of Investigation also monitors trends in crime, carries out the technical investigations requested by prosecutors, pre-trial investigation, supervisory or law enforcement authorities and is responsible for any other prescribed tasks relating to the police information system and registers. It also serves as the national centre for the International Criminal Police Organization (I.C.P.O.-Interpol) and for the Europol Drugs Unit (EDU) and maintains contacts with authorities abroad.

Security Police

The Security Police are mandated to prevent schemes and crimes that may endanger the established social order or the internal or external security of the State and carries out investigations of such crimes. The Security Police also provides the authorities and corporations with the advice, instructions and information needed to maintain State security or to avert violations of this security according to the general principles confirmed by the Ministry of the Interior. In addition, the Security Police maintains contacts with authorities abroad.

Mobile Police

The Mobile Police maintain public order and security, control traffic and work to promote traffic safety. In addition, the Mobile Police endeavours to prevent crime, investigates offences and other events endangering public order and security and serves as a reserve police force.

Police Technical Centre

The Police Technical Centre supports police work by acquiring, maintaining and developing the equipment and material needed in police work. It also provides different expert services.

Police Training Institutions

The Police School situated in Tampere and the Police College of Finland situated in Espoo provide their students with vocational training. A special division of the Police School, the police dog training centre in Hämeenlinna, trains police dogs and their instructors.

The Police School selects students for basic police training. It provides basic police training and training for non-commissioned officers, as well as specialized professional training related to its field of activities.

The Police College provides studies at the polytechnic level. It also provides specialized professional studies in policing, and is responsible for commanding officers' training and other command-level training. The Police College is also responsible for research and development related to police work.

Only those who have completed the basic training can apply to the Police College. In the Police College, the teaching and degree requirements of a commanding officer's degree resemble those of the lower university degree. Students who graduate from the Police College have a chance to take a higher degree in a university cooperating with the Police College and to continue their studies even up to the level of the doctorate. An educational cooperation agreement has been made with the Universities of Turku and Tampere.

The Rights and Limitations on Police Actions under the Law

In making its proposal for the Police Act in 1994, the Finnish Government pointed out some of the defects in the old legislation. One or two of these directly concern the rights and protection of citizens; some are more indirect. Among other things, the new proposals were intended to improve the measures of police control.

The following fields of police actions are now regulated by law: Police Act 493/1995: sections 10-27. What the police can do and what not is mentioned in the sections. All sections are in accordance with the international agreements and EU legislation. Here, only the essential content of the sections has been mentioned. They all concern inter police - public relationships.

Establishing identity

In order to carry out a specific task, a policeman has the right to get information from everyone on his or her name, personal identification code, or when it is lacking, data on his or her date of birth, citizenship, as well as the place where he or she can be contacted. A policeman has the right to apprehend a person who refuses to give this data or who apparently gives false information on the matters referred to above. An apprehended person must be released as soon as the necessary data has been obtained, however, no later than 24 hours after the arrest (Section 10).

Arrest to protect a person

A policeman has the right to arrest a person to protect him or her from an immediate serious danger threatening life, bodily integrity or health, if the person is unable to take care of him- or herself or if the danger cannot be otherwise eliminated or the person cannot be otherwise looked after. The apprehended person shall be allowed to leave as soon as the need for apprehension ceases to exist, however, no later than 24 hours after the arrest. A person who has not been released by 8 o'clock p.m. may be kept under arrest until 8 o'clock in the following morning, if on the basis of a lack of accommodation or of a night's lodging or of some other special reason it is found to be justified (Section 11).

Arrest of a wanted person

A policeman has the right to apprehend a wanted person who is to be arrested or to be taken into custody in accord with a search warrant issued by a competent authority (Section 12).

Search for apprehending a person

In order to contact a person for purposes of an examination, on the basis of an order given by a commanding level policeman, a policeman has the right to carry out a search for this person in some other premises, room or vehicle in which he or she can, on very serious grounds, be suspected to be staying (Section 13.).

Protecting domestic peace

On the request by the possessor of an area protected by domestic peace or a place equivalent with it, or by his or her representative, a policeman has the right to remove a person who, without a legal right, trespasses there or neglects an order to leave. It is also possible to apprehend a person causing a disturbance, but he or she may be kept in custody only for the time it is likely that the disturbance will recur, however, at most for twelve hours after the apprehension. Provisions enacted by this Section shall be applied also to a business premises, an office, a hospital, a school and another similar institute including the courtyard (Section 14).

Search for a Person in danger and for a missing Person

In order to help a person, find a missing person or to investigate a death, a policeman has the right to enter a residence or another place and to conduct a necessary search there, if there are reasons to suspect that the life or health of a person is in danger or that he or she has become a victim of crime, an accident, or that he or she can be assumed on other grounds to be in the need of immediate help, or dead (Section 15).

Preventing a dangerous act and event

On the order of a commanding policeman and in urgent cases, even without such order, a policeman has the right to enter a building, some other place protected by domestic peace or a vehicle, if there are reasonable grounds to suspect that an act or event seriously threatening life, personal liberty or health or causing notable damage or loss to property or to the environment is taking place or threatening. In addition, another condition is that the measure is necessary to prevent an immediate danger or to search and to take explosives, weapons or other dangerous substances or objects into possession (Section 16).

Taking measures

In the case referred to in Sections 13, 15 and 16, a room or a place of storage may be entered by using forcible means. After the measure has been taken, the entered place shall be closed again in a suitable manner. A search shall not be conducted during the time between 9 o'clock p.m. and 6 o'clock a.m. without a special reason. Afterwards a report must be prepared or a note included in some other document (Section 17).

Cordoning off a place and area

A policeman has the right to cordon off, close or clear a place or an area in public use or prohibit or limit moving, if it is necessary in order to maintain public order and safety or to secure investigation or to protect measures to be taken at the scene of an accident, to protect the privacy of a person subjected to the measures or the property exposed to danger. A policeman has the right to prohibit or limit the moving of objects or to order an object to be moved in a place or area in public use, if it is necessary to ensure a police investigation. A policeman has the corresponding right even in an area protected by domestic peace, if the measure is necessary to prevent a danger threatening life or health or to protect property (Section 18).

Dispersal of a crowd

A policeman has the right to give an order to a crowd to disperse or to move, if the gathering is threatening public order and safety or is an obstruction to traffic. If an order to disperse or move is not obeyed, a policeman has the right to disperse the crowd with forcible means as well as to apprehend a refractory person. An apprehended person shall be released as soon as the purpose of the measure is served, however, after twelve hours after the arrest at the latest (Section 19).

Protecting from offences and disturbances

A policeman has the right to remove a person, if it can be concluded from his or her threats or other behaviour that he or she would likely commit an offence against life, health, liberty, domestic peace or property. A person may be removed also, if he or she causes a notable disturbance or an immediate danger to public order and safety. If a removal from a place is apparently an inadequate measure and a disturbance or danger cannot otherwise be eliminated, a person may be apprehended. The apprehended person may be kept in custody as long as it is likely that he or she will commit an offence or cause a disturbance or danger, however, at most 24 hours after the apprehension (Section 20).

Stopping and moving a vehicle

A policeman has the right to order a vehicle to be stopped if it is necessary for locating a wanted person or some other person to be apprehended, conducting control concerning vehicle use, maintaining public order and safety, or investigating or solving an offence. A policeman has the right to move a vehicle or to order it to be moved, if it is necessary for conducting control concerning vehicle use to maintain public order and safety or to prevent an offence (Section 21).

Security check

In the context of apprehension, arrest, remand and taking into custody as well as in the context of a measure of assistance targeted on personal liberty, a policeman has the right to search a person in order to ensure that he or she does not have objects or substances by which he or she could endanger the custody or cause danger to him- or herself or to others. In the situation referred to above, a person may also be searched in order to find a document required for identifying him or her. Dangerous objects or substances shall be taken away from the searched person. They shall be returned to him or her in the context of release, unless there is a legal impediment for doing so (Section 22).

Taking Dangerous Objects and Substances into the Possession (amendment to the law 1.3.1998/2)

In addition to provisions enacted by the Police Act or some other act, a policeman has the right to take explosives, weapons and other dangerous objects or substances into the temporary possession of the police from a person who is justifiably suspected of causing an immediate danger to public order and safety on account of his or her age, state of intoxication, state of mind or on the basis of other circumstances. Instead of a whole object, such part of an object or a part connected to it may be taken into the possession by removal of which a danger can be prevented. In regard to taking property into police possession, a protocol shall be prepared or a note included in some other document (Section 23).

Retention of Property Taken into Possession

Objects and substances taken into possession shall be returned to the possessor within fourteen days, unless there are legal obstacles for this. The above-mentioned object or substance taken into possession, which cannot be returned to its possessor or owner without danger, may be sold or surrendered to a person having a legal right for its possession with the consent of the owner. If this is not possible, the property may be sold at a public auction. If an object or substance cannot be returned, sold or surrendered without a danger, or if it is a question of property of little value, a commanding policeman has the right to order the object or substance to be destroyed. An opportunity shall be reserved for the owner and possessor to be heard prior to selling or destroying, unless it is a question of property of little value (Section 24).

Killing an animal

A policeman has the right to kill an animal causing a danger to the life or health of a human being. A policeman has the same right if an animal causes notable damage to property or seriously endangers traffic. An animal may be killed also when it is in such condition that keeping it alive would constitute apparent cruelty towards it (Section 25).

Authority of a policeman

When using the powers prescribed in the Police Act or some other Act, a policeman has in an individual case the right to give necessary orders and prohibitions obligating everyone (Section 26).

Use of forcible means

When conducting an official duty, a policeman has the right to use such necessary forcible means which can be considered justified in order to break a resistance, to conduct an arrest, to prevent an escape by a person who has lost his or her liberty, to remove an obstruction, or to prevent an offence or some other dangerous act or event posing an immediate threat. When estimating the justifiability of forcible means, the importance and urgency of the duty, the dangerous nature of resistance, resources available and other matters affecting the total estimate of the situation shall be taken into consideration. A person who, on the request of a policeman, or with his or her consent, temporarily assists a policeman in a situation in which it is necessary to resort to a foreigner in conducting a very important and urgent official duty of the police, has the right to use such forcible means in the assistance of the policeman to which the policeman, on the basis of his powers, authorizes him or her (Section 27).

All these regulations concern the *relationships between* the police and citizens. There are also norms in the Police Law which concern the technical means available to the police.

After prior notification, the police have the right to direct technical control at a public place or at a public road in order to maintain order and safety, to prevent an offence, to identify a person suspected of an offence, as well as to monitor special targets to be guarded.

A police officer, in addition, has the right to carry out surveillance of a person in a place other than his residence in order to prevent an offence, if it is suspected, on the basis of the person's behaviour or other evidence that s/he will commit an offence. Surveillance can also be carried out outside the area of domestic peace on a person who is suspected on reasonable grounds of co-operating in an offence for which the maximum punishment prescribed is more than six month imprisonment.

These kinds of operations are possible only if it can justifiably be assumed that with its help the information necessary for preventing a crime can be gathered. Similarly, technical surveillance may also be carried out against a person while she or he is staying in a hotel room or in a similar room. An intercepting or observing device shall not, however, be placed in a room or in a vehicle in which the person under surveillance is staying.

In addition, a prerequisite for intercepting is that it can be concluded on the basis of a person's behaviour or otherwise that he or she is likely to commit an offence for which the maximum punishment prescribed is at least imprisonment for four years or to commit a narcotics offence.

A prerequisite for technical observing and technical tracking is that it can be concluded, on the basis of a person's behaviour or otherwise, that he or she is likely to commit an offence for which the maximum punishment prescribed is more than six months imprisonment or the person is cooperating in committing this kind of an offence.

Immediately prior to and during a police measure, a policeman has the right to exercise technical surveillance on a person within the area of domestic peace, if this is necessary for undertaking the police measure in a safe manner and for preventing an immediate danger threatening the life and health of a person undertaking the measure or of a person to be apprehended or to be protected.

An order for technical surveillance is given by a commanding policeman or a policeman assigned as Investigator in Charge, and for surveillance lasting more than three days, a policeman acting as Chief of a police district, of a national police unit or as a Deputy Chief of such a unit can order such surveillance. On each occasion a notification is required for both surveillance and for the technical surveillance

A policeman who conducts a surveillance shall prepare a report without delay. The report shall be delivered to the Ministry of the Interior which prepares an annual report on the use of technical surveillance for the parliamentary Ombudsman.

Some Other Rules for Police Actions

A problematic new "right" was given to the police a few years ago. This is a right for wire-tapping which has been given to the police by the amendment of the *Coercive Criminal Investigation Means Act* (23.41995/402). This was strongly demanded by the police, but this was also publicly resisted, especially by people who were worried about the increase of police powers and the broader potential possibilities for controlling citizens thereby. When Parliament adopted the amendment, it set a number of preconditions for wire-tapping. The main preconditions were that the right could be used only in the investigation of serious crimes, such as murder, high treason, espionage, kidnapping, aggravated drug-related crime, aggravated counterfeiting, aggravated environmental crime, and an attempt at such crimes. Permission for wire-tapping has to be applied for and is given individually, in every case, by a decision of a lower court.

The number of permitted wire-taps has increased rapidly. In 1996, the courts allowed only three. In 1997, the number was 12 and in 1998 almost 150 permissions were given (up to the beginning of December). The court's position has not changed. Every year only very few applications have been turned down. The reason is that the police have recognized wire-tapping as an effective method of investigating crime. In spite of the increase in permitted wire-tapping, there has not been subsequent public discussion about the matter. Tele-communication surveillance is a technically different issue. Technical means now make it possible to know both the source and destination(s) of calls. Permission was given approximately 450 times for this type of operation in 1997.

There are also legal norms regulating the information collected by the police. A commanding policeman shall, without delay, review information collected in undertaking measures and records acquired with the help of technical surveillance. Information exclusively concerning a foreigner shall be destroyed after inspection without delay, unless it is needed for solving the offence.

Collected information and records which have not been entered into a data file or into pre-trial investigation material shall be destroyed after one year at the latest, since it is assumed that the information will no longer be needed for the purpose for which it was gathered.

There are, in addition, legal regulations, which, for example, are concerned with *the police investigation, assistance provided by the police, the obligation to observe secrecy, the right to remain silent*, and *an obligation to assist the police*. If a policeman breaks these regulations, s/he may be punished.

Finnish police, as can be seen from this review, have broad powers over Finland's citizens. On the other hand, all these rights have been regulated by the law. This is, however, not enough. In a democratic society citizens must have the right to safeguard how the police are following the legal norms.

Democratic Control of the Police

The Advisory Board of Police Affairs operates in conjunction with the Ministry of the Interior. It deals with the matters related to maintaining public order and security and the development of police administration. The Council of State appoints the chairman, vice-chairman and members as well as their personal deputy members by open application with representatives of police affairs. The Advisory Board of Police Affairs is appointed for a maximum of three years at a time.

Each local police department also has an Advisory Board mandated to deal with police affairs, police operations and operations related to it. Municipal Councils elect the members of the local advisory boards for the duration of their term of office. All advisory boards are required to *monitor* public order and security and the work carried out by the police. They also make proposals for improving law enforcement and submit statements on matters involving the police.

The Police are accountable to the Minister of Interior and the Minister is accountable to Parliament. *The Chancellor of Justice* of the Council of State has a constitutionally guaranteed position as an independent overseer of law in Finland. It is his duty to monitor the legality of the operations of the Council of State and other authorities, as well as other public agencies. The Chancellor of Justice is appointed by the President of the Republic. The Chancellor has access to information and accounts held by the authorities in so far as he needs them for the performance of his duties. He conducts inquiries, for example, on the basis of complaints made by members of the public. He can issue admonitions to the authorities and public officials for errors and lay down instructions for future conduct.

In addition to the Chancellor of Justice, the Finnish administrative machinery is also overseen by *the Parliamentary Ombudsman*. The duties of these senior authorities differ in practical terms only in that the overseeing of the legality of the activities of the Council of State is entrusted mainly to the Chancellor of Justice and that matters pertaining to conscripts and convicts are in the ambit of the Ombudsman.

The overseers of legality have no jurisdiction to alter the decisions of other authorities on the basis of complaints, nor to award damages. Their rulings are not subject to appeal. In addition to the senior overseers of legality, there are certain specialised authorities that have similar duties in more limited fields. These are the Equality Ombudsman, the Data Protection Ombudsman and the Immigration Ombudsman.

The appointment and dismissal of the National Police Commissioner, Deputy National Police Commissioner and Assistant National Police Commissioner, and the Chief of the National Bureau of Investigation as well as the Chief of the Security Police are made by the President of the Republic. Other police officers, for example, the Police Supreme Command, are appointed by the Ministry of the Interior.

The appointment and dismissal of a Provincial Police Commissioner also falls under the jurisdiction of the Ministry of the Interior. Other Police Officers of the Provincial Police Commands are appointed and dismissed by the Provincial Government in question. The Ministry of the Interior appoints and dismisses both the Director of the Police Academy (1998, the Police College) and the Director of the Police School, as well as the Police Chief and Deputy Police Chief of the Helsinki Police Department and the Head of the Police Technical Centre. Other Police Chiefs are appointed by the Provincial Governments (Wasastjerna 1998).

Sociological Aspects: The Public Image of the Police

Finnish citizens demonstrate a greater confidence in the police than in the courts, the administrative machinery or politicians. According to recent polls, people see the police as being an important organ of their security, and many people are ready to give more power, more money and other resources to the police. The police have made great efforts during recent years to improve their public image. For example, at the beginning of 1999, the police organized a country-wide exhibition called "The Police is Pop (= popular)". That event was a success.

In an international survey of 55 countries, the Finnish citizens noted an 80% satisfaction with Finland's with crime control. The figure was higher only in Scotland (84 %) and Sweden (82 %). In many countries, the share of satisfied citizens' was 20-30 % (Kangaspunta & Joutsen & Ollus 1998, 170-171).

An ongoing discussion exists about the broadening of Finnish police powers. For example, the right of the police in using and implementing wire-tapping was previously noted. At the end of 1999, the police demanded the right to set bugging devices in the homes of the people who were suspected of a serious crimes such as a drug related crimes, organized crime, etc. According to the proposal, this is to be allowed *only* by a decision of a court. Although the public image of the police is good, and although a great many Finnish citizens are ready to accept 'bugging' in connection with serious crimes, there have been resisting voices. This issue currently remains open.

The Possibility for Lodging a Complaint

Every Finnish citizen or person who lives in the country has a right to make a verbal or written complaint about a police action - or about an action committed by another State authority. A comparison will be made between the police and other authorities later in this chapter. Here, the focus is only about the complaints against the police. The system of complaint is organized in the same way as the police are organized in general. This means that it is possible to lodge a complaint firstly at the national level, secondly at the provincial level, and thirdly at the local level. The complaints, at each level, are dealt with by a civil servant or police officer higher than the person who is the subject of the complaint. Moreover, it is possible to lodge a complaint either with the Parliamentary Ombudsman or with the Chancellor of Justice. The members of Parliament have a right to make proposals concerning the police, and to raise a verbal or written question about the police (or any other matter) to the Minister responsible for the matter. Members of Parliament have frequently used this right.

All of these complaints were studied by the Ministry of the Interior in 1994 (Kanteluita , 1994). A new study is currently being undertaken, but it is not yet ready. Detailed information in this area is only available from the beginning of the 1990's.

Complaints at the National Level

The number of complaints at the national level are few compared to those at other levels. At the national level they totalled 135, of which 43 were decided in 1991. The rest were transferred to the lower levels. In 1992, the corresponding figures were 105 and 25, and in 1993 they were 143 and 37.

Many of the complaints are made by so-called "professional complainants". No remarkable and preliminary rulings have been made during recent years. The majority of complaints concern the preliminary investigations made by the police. Often complainants lodge an appeal for the starting of a preliminary investigation or for its redoing. If the decision happens to be negative for a complainant, s/he usually sends it either to the Parliamentary Ombudsman or to the Chancellor of Justice.

Complaints at the Provincial Level

The number of complaints at the provincial level at the beginning of the 1990s is presented in Table 2.

It is useful to explain the reactions to the complaints prior to commenting on these findings. There are different types of reactions. The weakest reaction is that the case does not give rise to any action. Secondly, it is possible to give instructions in regard to the future cases of a comparable kind. These usually concern the case in general. Then it is possible to caution a police officer and finally to bring a case to a court. Possible reactions made by the Parliamentary Ombudsman or the Chancellor of Justice are, in principle, the same.

Approximately, 50 per cent of the complaints concern the misbehaviour of a policeman or ' customer' service offered by the police.

Complaints concerning the misbehaviour of a policeman or 'customer' service offered by the police have given rise to very lenient reactions. In the years 1991 and 1992, 'instruction for future behaviour' were given twice. In 1993, a couple of 'cautions' or warnings were given to police officers. That is all! This is, however, understandable. Although a police officer may 'insult' some 'customer' by his or her behaviour, these acts do not cause any serious consequences. Besides, it is a truism that interpretation of 'misbehaviour' depends very much on the attitudes, tempers and personality of the person in question.

Table 9.2 Number of complaints at the provincial level

Reason for the complaint	Year		
	1991 (N=166)	1992 (N=216)	1993 (N=211)
Misbehaviour of a policeman, or inadequate customer service	48.0%	43.1%	56.4%
Preliminary investigations made by the police	33.1%	39.8%	27.5%
The use of coercive means	18.9%	17.1%	16.1%
In addition	100.0%	100.0%	100.0%
Source:(Kanteluita, valituksia ja kysymyksi poliisin toiminnasta vuosina 1991-1993).			

Consider the following typical case in this category: A police officer is investigating a crime and meets a person who *could be* a lawbreaker. According to the complainant, the police officer refuses to tell the reason for the investigation, resists telling his/her name or showing his/her badge (police officers usually have a uniform), or is otherwise arrogant.

According to those who make complaints, the usual arguments are that the preliminary investigation was imperfect, delayed, or not made at all. The consequences of these could be, in the worst case, quite serious for a complainant. If s/he is, for example, a victim of a complainant's offence, s/he cannot get the case into court because the case would be statute-barred. However, such complaints have resulted in only a few 'instructions' and/or 'cautions' to be given to police officers.

A police officer can even cause physical injuries when using coercive means. It has to be noted that in some cases a report about an offence is made directly and not as a complaint. That is why the figures in the table may present a somewhat misleading picture. The decisions regarding these types of complaints were, perhaps, more serious than in the previous two categories of complaints. Over a three-year period a report about an offence was made six times by the investigating authority, twice a 'caution' was given, and on nine occasions an 'instruction for the future' was given.

Consider the following typical cases in this category of complaints: The police use too much force in handling and arresting a drunken person. In some cases, a drunken person is placed under arrest for more than 12 hours, which is the maximum time allowed according to the *Coercive Criminal Investigation Means Act*. Some complaints have concerned a house search made by the police, and some the use of firearms when arresting a fleeing driver.

Complaints at the Local Level

The Ministry of the Interior did not study complaints at the local level. According to other information, there are few complaints at that level. This may be due to a lack of information about this option among Finnish citizens. An additional reason could be that a complainant does not trust the objectivity of the head of the police district. This why complaints are lodged with the Parliamentary Ombudsman or the Chancellor of Justice, or are lodged at the provincial level.

The Parliamentary Ombudsman and the Chancellor of Justice: Their Duties

In practice, the supervision of law is primarily carried out by ruling on a citizen's complaint which is lodged with the Chancellor of Justice against the actions of an authority or public official.

All citizens are entitled to turn to the Chancellor of Justice in a matter that directly concerns them, or in any other matter, should the complainant believe that an authority, public official, or public body has acted in a manner that violates their rights, or that a member of the Bar has neglected his or her responsibilities. All citizens may also turn to the Chancellor of Justice if they believe that a civil or human right guaranteed under the Constitution has not been observed.

The duty of the Parliamentary Ombudsman is to supervise the legality of officials' acts, including those of the police. The Ombudsman's authority covers all individuals who are engaged in public duties of some kind since the beginning of 1991. Members of the Council of State are also under the supervision of the Ombudsman. In contrast, neither the members of Finland's Parliament, and Chancellor of Justice, nor the President of the Republic are supervised by the Ombudsman..

There is a certain division of labour between the Ombudsman and the Chancellor of Justice, but complaints about the police can be given to both of them.. Every citizen has a right to lodge a complaint with the Ombudsman. Moreover, the Ombudsman is allowed to initiate an investigation and he has a right to aid from all public officials. In addition, the Ombudsman has a right to see and investigate all administrative documents.

Complaints to the Parliamentary Ombudsman

The history of complaints is presented in Table 3. It is impossible to divide the complaints into different categories as was done above. The number of complaints against Finnish State officials has increased significantly during the 1970's and the 80's. The 'natural' explanation is that the State administration has expanded widely during this period. Since 1980, the number of complaints has increased, but the polices' share of this has been quite stable. For example, both in 1991and 1992 the number of complaints were 207. In 1993, it declined to 128. However, the *number of decisions* each year was higher. In 1991 it was 207, 211 in 1992 and 241 in 1993. The reason is that some complaints were made more than a year previously. This indicates that the decision-making process is quite lengthy. This is a threat to the legal protection of the citizens as well as to the process of democracy. The complaints fall into several categories as noted in Table 4.

Comparing complaints against the police administration, at the provincial level, proves interesting. The biggest difference concerns the 'misbehaviour' of a policeman, which is approximately 3%. But this increases to approximately half of *all* the complaints at the provincial level. My conclusion is that complaints lodged with the Parliamentary Ombudsman are more serious than those lodged with the provincial police administration.

During the course of the year, many of the complaints about preliminary investigations are made by the same persons about the same matter. These persons are dissatisfied with the Ombudsman's decision, and they try again. Of course, in those cases the decision is that no measures are required to be taken.

Possible reactions to the complaints include: no measures taken, serving a notice of the issue involved, reprimand, and a claim for legal proceedings. The results from calculating the *content of decisions,* on the basis of the complaints *decided* each year, are:

"Serving a notice" means that the police officer has not done anything illegal or even wrong, but that s/he has, for example, been careless, impolite or lazy.

A striking feature of the 1990's are the complaints which have been made by foreigners, often from an African country. These complaints have been sensational, but their numbers have been very low. For example, during 1991-1993 there were from 5 to 6 such complaints each year. Some blacks have stated that they do not dare to lodge a complaint. Even if this were true, and even if the grounds for complaint were two or three times greater, still the number of complaints made by foreigners would remain low.

Only more general data on 'complaints' are available since 1993. A more detailed analysis would require the investigation of all documents in the office of the Ombudsman.

What is surprising is that the number of complaints against the courts in 1997 was almost 17 % of all complaints, whereas 333 complaints were made against the police (that is, 12.4 percent of the total number of 1,887 complaints) (Eduskunnan oikeusasiamiehen kertomus toiminnastaan vuonna 1997, 25).

Table 9.3 Complaints to the Parliamentary Ombudsman

Period	Number	The target of the complaint (%)					
		Govnt./ Ministry	Court	Law Enforcement	Police	Official	Other
1920-24	N= 51	27	21	13	22	10	8
1925-29	N= 127	13	31	23	3	22	8
1930-34	N= 241	3	23	37	9	19	16
1935-39	N= 479	3	34	29	8	10	16
1940-44	N= 421	2	26	37	8	15	12
1945-49	N= 1018	-	47	26	8	11	8
1950-54	N= 735	-	40	29	7	18	6
1955-59	N= 815	-	40	26	9	14	11
1960-64	N= 1001	25	7	28	10	22	8
1965-69	N= 1146	14	10	28	9	26	13
1970-74	N= 984	11	11	12	11	41	14
1975-79	N=1382	6	7	17	11	46	13

Source: Laitinen & Michelsen & Virtanen (1985, 35).

Table 9.4 The reasons for complaints to the Parliamentary Ombudsman

Reason for the complaint	Year		
	1991 (N=207)	1992 (N=207)	1993 (N=128)
Preliminary investigations made by the police	48.8%	40.1%	32.8%
The use of coercive means	18.8%	25.1%	12.5%
Licensing administration	7.7%	4.8%	4.1%
Misbehaviour of a policeman, or inadequate customer service	21.8%	27.1%	48.5%
Other	21.8%	27.1%	48.5%
In addition	100.0%	100.0%	100.0%

Source: (Eduskunnan Oikeusasiamihen kertomus toiminnastaan 1991, 1992, 1993).

Table 9.5
An Analysis of Outcomes of Complaints to the Parliamentary Ombudsman

Content of decision	Year		
	1991 (N=207)	1992 (N=207)	1993 (N=128)
Reprimand	1.9%	3.8%	1.7%
Serving a notice	1.4%	7.1%	14.5%
no measures	96.7%	89.1%	83.8%

Source: (Eduskunnan Oikeusasiamihen kertomus toiminnastaan 1991, 1992, 1993).

The Chancellor of Justice

The number of the complaints lodged with the Chancellor of Justice in 1997 was 127, but it is not possible to divide them into different complaint categories. Table 6 notes their distribution for the years 1992 and 1993.

The most apparent difference in complaints to the Parliamentary Ombudsman is the higher portion of complaints about preliminary investigations.

Complaints about the mistreatment of foreign nationals in Finland are very rare. In 1992 there were three complaints; in 1993 there was only one complaint.

The decisions were quite similar to those of the Ombudsman. The Chancellor of Justice can also check, and alter if needed, summary penal judgements given by the police.

Table 9.6 The Reasons for the Complaints to the Chancellor of Justice

Reason of a complaint	Year	
	1992 (N=151)	1993 (N=147)
Preliminary investigations made by the police	58.3%	63.3%
The use of coercive means	5.3%	9.5%
Licensing administration	7.3%	6.8%
Misbehaviour of a policeman or customer service	2.0%	-
Other	27.1%	20.4%
In addition	100.0%	100.0%

Source: (Documents of the Finnish Parliament 1992-1993).

Table 9.7 The Decisions of the Chancellor of Justice

Content of decision	Year		
	1991	1992	1993
Reprimand	3.1%	0.7%	0.7%
Serving a notice or instructions	7.1%	5.3%	9.5%
Check on summary penal judgments	10.8%	4.6%	6.1%
No measures	79.0%	89.4%	83.7%

Source: (Documents of the Finnish Parliament 1991-1993).

In addition, the number of complaints for all supervising organs was 633 in 1991, 679 in 1992, and 629 in 1993.

The reasonable conclusion to be drawn from the data is that the decisions for complaints at each administrative level, going from the local level of police administration to the Parliamentary Ombudsman and Chancellor of Justice, is that very rarely are any active measures taken. This does not mean, however, that the whole complaint system is needless. A system for appeal is a *right of citizens*, and answering appeals or complaints is a *duty of the State official* in question. At the moment - at least at the official and publicly levels - the leadership of the police take complaints seriously. They say that the decisions on complaints provide the guidelines for police operations. The most important decisions have been put together in a publication and used in police training.

Activities of the Members of Parliament

Every member of the Finnish Parliament has a right to ask verbal or written questions of the ministers. Members have frequently used this right. Some of the questions deal with the police. The number of written questions in this category has varied between 11 and 25 at the beginning of the 1990's. The number of verbal questions was a bit lower, from 5 to 9. Most of the questions have dealt with the monetary resources of the police, crime prevention, and especially crime coming from Russia and from the former Soviet area.

In recent years, the number of verbal questions has, however, decreased. For example, in 1998 there were only two verbal questions, both put forth by members of the Left Wing Alliance. They concerned a demonstration against racism, and the activities of the special unit of the police in connection with the event. The member asked why the police used a special unit for controlling a demonstration organized by young and radical persons. In 1997, there were five questions, most of which were connected with the financial resources of the police.

The number of written questions has been higher than the number of verbal questions. In 1998, there were 21 questions, 25 in 1997, and 20 in 1996. The topics were similar to those mentioned above.

Analyses of Certain Cases

This section presents some examples of the complaints, concentrating on cases concerning the constitutional rights of citizens' or human rights questions. Although the cases are typical of their own categories, the examples cannot be generalized.

- *Default of a preliminary investigation.* A citizen complained that a policeman had not started a preliminary investigation although he had left a report about an offence. The citizen suspected that the disappearance of his bonds from the safety deposit box of a bank was caused by a crime. A policeman made inquiries and decided that no crime has been committed.

According to the legislation, the preliminary investigation must be made after a report of the offence. If this is not started, the citizen must be informed of the reason. The decision-makers referred the policeman in question to the need for an appropriate compliance with the laws.

- *Detention of a citizen for too many hours.* A citizen was arrested for urinating on a public beach and spent 13 hours in a jail. Because he was, in reality, arrested for being drunk, the maximum time of arrest should - according to the law - be twelve hours. If he was arrested for urinating, the maximum time would be 24 hours. The decision-makers referred the police officers to the content and interpretation of the law.

- *The treatment of an arrested person.* A citizen was arrested and while in jail he suffered from a violent headache. He informed the duty officer, who, however, came only after two and a half hours. The content of the decision was that the duty officer at the police station had neglected his duties. The policeman reported that the arrangements in the police station was poor and that was the cause for his negligence. The decision-makers demanded that the arrangements in the police station had improved. Every 'customer' had to get the services that they immediately needed.

- *Inappropriate behaviour of a policeman.* Using a car, a citizen tried to stop a boy driving an unregistered 'moped'. He caused an accident. The citizen complained that the policeman had misbehaved when he complained about him for causing an accident. In addition, according to the complainant, the policeman was arrogant, lost his temper, and wrote a report that was intentionally misleading. The policeman was advised of the importance of proper and polite behaviour in every situation.

A Discussion on Police Corruption

Discussions have arisen, from time to time, about the corruption of the Finnish police. These cases have very rarely come up in court; most of the few cases which have occurred have failed. A number of recent cases shall be described because they have more general significance.

First, the reader should be aware that the atmosphere in Finland towards illegal or corrupt behaviour of the 'top people' of society - the Finnish elite - has grown harsher during recent years. These 'top people' have included, for example, politicians, the members of the Supreme Court, some high State officials, and some Ministers or former Ministers.

A senior Ministry of the Interior police official was, at the same time, a rally driver and a chairman of a police rally club. He participated during his summer vacation in 1998 as a driver in a rally in Belgium. He and his rally club were sponsored by foreigners, mainly firms. The amount of money was a little over $ 20,000. Someone, most probably a member of a competing police rally club, made a report suggesting that bribery had occurred. The police officer was suspended during the period of the investigation, although he was able show a detailed statement of accounts of the financial support of the foreigners and was able to prove that he had not received any direct personal advantages for himself.

The case is currently being investigated by a prosecutor. The Minister of the Interior, at the same time, established a committee to draw up a report and a proposal on the sponsorship of the police. It became known, during the autumn of 1998, that many other police activities have been sponsored by foreigners. For example, a large Interpol international conference was sponsored (almost one million U.S. dollars) by foreigners. Such sponsoring was not unusual. The committee's published report is being awaited. According to preliminary information, the committee will suggest the need for creating clear instructions and rules for financing the police, their hobbies and clubs by foreigners. The committee will not, most probably, suggest a total ban on this kind of sponsoring. Given that the police are a part of society, and that police officers are also members of society, there is the need to guarantee the independence of the police in each situation.

In a broader sense, a question of police corruption arose in 1998 when a senior provincial police officer was suspended and prosecuted. The police officer was a member of the board of an association that owned a hotel. This hotel was used as a brothel, and the members of the board were prosecuted for pimping. In the case of the police officer the charge failed to be proven.

The Parliamentary Ombudsman has investigated a few complaints on police corruption. An entrepreneur, whose business was that of towing vehicles, complained that the police did not treat businessmen in this field equally. They were said to favour one particular entrepreneur. It appeared that several policemen had received a bottle of spirits for Christmas. The Ombudsman decided that the value of the presents was low. However, according to the Ombudsman, the behaviour of the policemen was inappropriate. He requested that the policemen not be involved in this kind of behaviour in the future. The city's police leadership subsequently announced in 1997 instructions for ordering towing services and promised to keep the situation under review.

Other Problems

Discussion about racism among Finnish police has increased at a time when the number of refugees and other foreigners in Finland has increased. Complaints have been made, but their number, as noted earlier, has been rather low. Some important cases have, however, raised the issue of racism among the Finnish police. For example, in the City of Joensuu, the police have been accused of favouring the 'skinheads' who were arrested for violence against black refugees. Politicians and the Minister of the Interior demanded an investigation of the whole matter. An investigation was made, but the conclusion arrived at was that only one police officer's behaviour was racist; and even this was a question of interpretation. Simultaneously, the police leadership made efforts to demonstrate that the police were impartial; the unfortunate case of racism being a solitary, exceptional one. It is interesting to note that the person who first accused the police was a policeman himself. He did not succeed in presenting his arguments entirely convincingly, but something was there in the background of his argumentation. On the other hand, that policeman was said to have been 'fouling his own nest'.

In another example a policeman was a columnist in a local newspaper. During the years 1997 and 1998, he wrote columns in which he insulted ethnic minorities. The Parliamentary Ombudsman asked the Ministry of the Interior to investigate the case. In the same connection, the Ombudsman expressed surprise at the attitudes of the police authorities because they reported that the response to the columns had been partly positive. It was on this basis that the authorities defended the columnist. The result was that the Ombudsman requested the Minister of the Interior to find out whether the police acted according to international agreements on racial discrimination.

Other types of criminal or 'doubtful' cases have appeared among the police forces. The most serious are those in which a senior polices officer are involved. But most of these cases concern *individual behaviour,* not that of the whole police. For example, in 1998 a senior provincial police commander was arrested for drunken driving. There was a public demand for his expulsion from office, but the punishment that he received was a serious cautionary warning only. In addition, the court sentenced him with a fine and temporarily confiscated his driving licence.

Appointment to Office

Police are a tool of the government in every country. As a result of this one may ask whether appointments to offices in the police forces are political. Such a question is important because the more political appointments there are the more loyal the appointed person has to be to the political party or parties that make the appointment. It is usual in Finland - and, of course, in other countries - for the appointments of the highest officials to be political. It is very difficult to get information about the matter because the political appointments are not totally open, and because very few police officers are members of a political party. I have studied the appointment procedure during recent years. The only clearly political appointments are those of the head of the Secret Police. It *may* be that some appointments of the most senior police leaders, and, *possibly* the appointment of Helsinki's (the capital of Finland) police commander also have a political background. The conclusion is that political appointments to offices are more the exception than the rule.

The history of policing in Finland shows a trend away from party-political pressures towards a more open relationship with the democratic institutions of the country.

Ahti Laitinen, Ph. D., is Professor of Criminology and the Sociology of Law at the University of Turku and who is currently responsible for the training of police officers in the field of criminology and the sociology of law. He has written more than 100 articles in professional journals as well as many text books on criminology, the sociology of law, white-collar crime and juvenile delinquency; has participated in tens of international conferences and meetings, and organized international contacts and research projects in the Faculty of Law of the University of Turku.

His books include: An Introduction to the Legal Ethics; Crime, Risk, Security; Car Thefts; Economic crime: a Theory and Practice; A Childhood without Permission; Juvenile Delinquency and Crime Prevention; Approaches to the Crime; Crimes of Power.

Laitinen

References

Eduskunnan oikeusasiamiehen kertomus toiminnastaan vuonna 1997 (A report on the activities of the Parliamentary Ombudsman in 1997) (1998). Helsinki.

Jousimaa, Kyösti (1986): The History of the Finnish Police. The Police of Finland. Helsinki.

Kanteluita, valituksia ja kysymyksiä poliisin toiminnasta vuosina 1991-1993 (Complaints, appeals, and questiona about the activities of the police in the years 1991-1993) (1994). Sisäasiainministeriön poliisiosasto (The Police Department of the Ministry of the Interior). Helsinki.

Laitinen, Ahti & Michelsen, Allan & Virtanen, Antti (1985): Eduskunnan oikeusasiamies ja perusoikeuksien loukkauksista tehdyt kantelut (The Parliamentary Ombudsman and complaints of the violation of citizens' constitutional rights). Turun yliopiston oikeustieteellisen tiedekunnan julkaisuja. Julkisoikeuden Sarja A 27. (A publication of the Faculty of Law, University of Turku. Publication Series of Public Law, A 27). Turku.

Sinisalo, Kari (1971): Poliisin toimivallan määräytyminen (The determination of the competence of the police). Unpublished paper.

Wasastjerna 1998: Jyrki (ed.) The Police and the Police Training in Finland. Helsinki.

Legislation material on the Police Act.

Documents of the Finnish Parliament.

Glossary

The Chancellor of Justice: Supervises the legality of the of the Council of State's actions and provides the President of the Republic and the Council of State with information and opinions on request. He supervises the actions of the authorities and the law.

The Parliamentary Ombudsman: The Parliamentary Ombudsman is elected for a term of four years at a time in a regular session of Parliament. The person elected shall be someone distinguished for his or her knowledge of the law. The duty of the Parliamentary Ombudsman shall be, pursuant to a statute approved by Parliament, to oversee that the courts of law, other public authorities, and public servants in the performance of their official duties, as well as public employees and other persons in the exercise of public functions observe the law and fulfil their obligations. In discharging his or her duties, the Parliamentary Ombudsman oversees the implementation of constitutional rights and international human rights (Constitution Act of Finland, article 49). He is specifically a citizens' watchdog, investigating complaints from below.

The Council of State: The Cabinet.

Resources

Public resources:

1. Ministry of the Interior, Police Department. Box 257, FIN-00171 Helsinki, Finland. Telephone: +358-9-1601; fax: +358-9-1608270; http://www.poliisi.fi.

Information concerning all police affairs, police organisation, police administration, and police statistics.

2. The Chancellor of Justice. The Office of the Chancellor of Justice, Box 20, FIN-00023 . Valtioneuvosto, Finland.Helsinki, Finland. Telephone: +358-9-1601; fax: +358-9-1603975; email: kirjaamo@okv.vn.fi.

Information about supervision of the police, and information about the complaints against the police and the e-mail will be:

3. The Parliamentary Ombudsman. Ombudsman, FIN-00102 Eduskunta, Finland. Telephone: +358-9-4321; fax: +358-9-4322268; email: eoa-kirjaamo@eduskunta.fi; http://www.eduskunta.fi.

Information about supervision of the police, and information about the complaints against the police.

Private resources:
1. The Institute for Human Rights, ?bo Akademi University, Getzeliuksenkatu 2, 20500 Turku, Finland. Telephone: +358-2-2154322; fax: +358-2-2154699; http:www.abo.fi/instut/imr.

Information about the scientific studies concerning, among other topics, the police activies and human rights.

10 Analysis of Japanese Police from the Viewpoint of Democracy

*Minoru Yokoyama**

Abstract

Japanese police were a militaristic State police prior to World War II whose main interest was to maintain order for the emperor and his government. Maintenance-of-order and the law enforcement activities were performed very efficiently, while the peoples' rights to "due process" were neglected. The police, then, already carried out some kind of community policing. However, it aimed to supervise people rather than to provide them with service.

The Japanese police system was democratized, following the American model, after their defeat in World War II. However, an autonomous local police system did not take root in Japan. Subsequent to the revision of the Police Law in 1954 Japan's police system was replaced by a new system composed of the National Police Agency and the prefecture (regional) police.

Under this current system the National Police Agency has gradually strengthened its supervisory power over all prefecture police. Contemporary Japanese police have many democratic features. However, having served the conservative government for a long period, they are prone to lose their political neutrality. In addition, some serious police corruption caused by the police structure, and some structural problems of police practices in the process of law enforcement, have been noted.

Key words: Koban, Chuzaisho, due process, community policing, National Police Agency, Prefecture Police

Introduction

Contemporary Japanese police are well-disciplined. They perform functions efficiently in a hierarchical bureaucracy. They especially carry out their law enforcement activities with an extremely high rate of adjudicated guilty sentences under the principle of the 'the rule of law', and provide good services to persons in need of aid in the community. However, they are not completely immune from corruption. We expect the police to resolve these problems from and within a democratic paradigm.

Undemocratic State Police Prior to World War II: An Historical Perspective

The Meiji Restoration was declared, in 1868,under an emperor after overthrowing the Tokugawa Shogunate. In order to catch up with western countries, the centralized national government took measures to enrich and strengthen the country. It introduced modern western systems. However, Japan was not completely democratized, because the Meiji Restoration, initiated by low-class warriors, was not a civil revolution akin to those carried out in western countries. Under the Constitution of 1889 the sovereignty was assigned to an emperor. The authoritarian regime under an emperor continued until its World War II defeat in 1945.

Immediately after the Meiji Restoration chaos ensued, some leaders of the national government were assassinated. To secure the public order, the national government decided to introduce the western police system into Japan. Toshiyoshi Kawaji and seven officers were dispatched to European countries for this purpose in 1872. Japan, at the initiative of Kawaji, established the centralized State police under the jurisdiction of the Ministry of Home Affairs following the example of the French system.

In England people were afraid of the abuse of police power. Therefore, it was not until 1829 that a uniformed, armed standing police force was founded for the first time in the Metropolitan London area. The Japanese, in contrast, were a people who were bound under [12] the system of feudal rigid statuses during the Edo Period (1603-1867). Liberated from these statuses after the Meiji Restoration, they could not understand democracy. The national government succeeded in establishing the State police without any public protest. Thereafter, we saw the high-tide of movements for democracy in the early 1880's and in the early 1920's.

However, the undemocratic features of Japanese police were not changed until the end of the World War II.

Prior to World War II, people were defined as *subjects* of an emperor by the Constitution. Therefore, the security of an emperor and his regime was superior to the guarantee of the people's fundamental rights. The centralized State police performed both their crime fighting and maintenance-of-order functions efficiently for the emperor and his regime. Even the purpose of policing in the community was to supervise citizens rather than to provide them with services. Following is an analysis of the undemocratic characteristics in the main functions of the Japanese State police system.

Law Enforcement for Crime Fighting without Restraint

Subsequent to the Meiji Restoration, many former warriors were employed as police officers. They behaved authoritatively when they came in contact with people. Usually they challenged an unknown person or a suspect by scornfully shouting: *"Oi! Kora! (Hey! Halt!)"*. S/he had to prove his/her innocence, even against a charge of committing a misdemeanor such as spreading rumors and loitering. Each police station chief had the discretionary power and authority to impose a penal detention or a minor fine on him/her on the accused, or not to.

The Japanese adopted the principle of "due process" subsequent to the introduction of western criminal procedures. For example, torture was prohibited in 1879 by the proposal of, the French scholar Gustave E. Boissonade who took the initiative to create a draft of the Code of Criminal Procedure of 1880 (Okubo, 1977:1 10). The Constitution of 1889 guaranteed people some rights to 'due process' in the criminal procedure.[1] Japanese police, however, often violated these rights because of the following reasons.

- Prior to World War II the police respected the maintenance-of-order under the imperial regime more than they respected people's rights to 'due process'.

- Eager to catch suspects, they often abrogated people's rights. For example, the police were inclined to violate people's right not to be arrested and detained without a writ by abusing the process of administrative detention.[3]
- Police interrogators often tortured a suspect in jail in order to get him/her to "confess"; since a judge could declare a guilty sentence only on the basis of a confession (Aoki, 1979: 1 6). Given their authoritarian power, the police efficiently performed the crime fighting facet of law enforcement at the expense of the people's due process rights.

Although the police were powerful, their law enforcement activities were put under the direction of public prosecutors. As the public prosecutors were also proud of their responsibility to the emperor for the maintenance-of-order, they never checked illegal activities committed by police officers during the criminal procedure. They occupied many important posts in the Judicial Ministry, which was given the authority of personnel management and budgets for all judges. Therefore, they influenced judges, who also respected the maintenance-of-order as loyal subjects of the emperor. Judges scarcely criticized police officers for their abuse of power in the criminal procedure.

During the early 1880's the defense counsels embarked on working actively for the defendant who participated in the movement for people's rights and freedoms.[4] Some of them continued to work for the guarantee of due process in the criminal procedure. However, their activities for the defendant were usually neglected by judges, who were in collusion with public prosecutors. The defense counsels could not make the police stop abusing their power.

Maintenance of Order for the Imperial Regime

Since the Meiji Restoration the national government was most interested in maintenance-of-order for the emperor. Many laws, enacted for this purpose, were used and misused by the police to control anti-government movements. These included the early 1880's use of espionage by the police to suppress the movement for the people's rights and freedom; regulating the organization of political parties and meetings and censoring the press (Obinata, 1987:77). In 1886 the Tokyo Metropolitan Police Headquarters founded a specialized police force to be in charge of this task, which was called "High-Grade Police"[4]. Laborers began to organize their unions in the late 1890's with the development of industries. The socialists and communists then became a new target for police suppression. The Tokyo Metropolitan Police Headquarters founded the "Special High-Grade Police" in 1911 whose mandate was to suppress the labor movements, the left wing and censorship (Ibid.:134).

'Manhood Suffrage' was achieved in Japan in 1 925 as a result of the movements for democracy during the early 1920's However, at the same time the 'Maintenance of the Public Order Law' was enacted; its main purpose being to defend the imperial regime from communist movements. The Special High-Grade Police, organized all over the country, arrested communists, and tortured them in order to eradicate their organization. Some of them were killed by severe torture. In 1935 Japan's Communist Party, an underground movement, was dissolved. Japan waged war on China in 1931, after which the Special High-Grade Police widened their target of suppression. Neglecting the principle of due process in criminal procedure, they arrested believers in religions such as Christianity and Omoto-kyo, who did not admit the godhood of the Japanese emperor, and even ordinary people who were critical of the emperor or of a war (Social Department of "Red Flag", 1981). This suppression by the Special High-Grade Police greatly contributed to the establishment of the authoritarian military regime under the emperor Hirohito, which made war on the United States in 1941.[4]

Supervision in the Community

Police in a democracy are expected to provide some selected services to people in the community who are in need of immediate aid. However, before World War II Japanese policing in the community was carried out mainly for the purpose of maintenance-of-order under the imperial regime.

Immediately after the Meiji Restoration, the national government was eager to introduce western culture into Japan. The police, therefore, regulated old manners and habits such as walking in the semi-nude and bathing promiscuously. They actively played the role of "morality- police" prior to World War II.

Under the jurisdiction of the Ministry of Home Affairs the police were so powerful that they could deprive local governments of many tasks. For example, in 1876 the Tokyo Metropolitan Police Headquarters deprived the Tokyo Prefecture Government of 22 tasks such as gun control, regulation of drugs and prevention of contagious diseases (Obinata, 1987: 4) The police could and did supervise and control people in the community through their broad authority.

In 1874 police officers were assigned to supervise their small territory (Ibid.: 37). Their main duty was to maintain information about all residents in their territory by door to door investigation. After the investigation they "ranked" residents according to their threat to the rulers. They supervised low-ranked residents more carefully.

In 1888 the hierarchy of the State police was established (Ibid.: 87). At the bottom of this hierarchy we saw the *Hashutsujo* or the *Koban* (a police box) in a city and the *Chuzaisho* (a police house) in a village. A police officer and his family lived in a *Chuzaiso*. Although his main duty was to supervise villagers, he and his family often provided them with services when the latter were in need of aid. Therefore, villagers usually respected a police officer at a *Chuzaiso* as a community leader as they did their village chief and a school master.

Approximately half of police officers worked at the *Koban* and *Chuzaiso,* and were in charge of foot patrol and the collection of information. Their tasks, however, were not formally considered as being specialized ones (Murayama, 1990: 6).

Democratization of Japanese Police after World War II

After their defeat in World War II (August, 1945) Japan was governed by the General Headquarters of the Allied Powers (GHQ), in which the officials coming from the United States took the initiative. Japan's fundamental system was reformed toward democratization-under the direction of GHQ. Following the dissolution of Japan's armed forces, the Special High-Grade Police was abolished in October, 1945. The officers of the Special High-Grade Police, who had abrogated people's fundamental human and civil rights, were discharged[5].

GHQ guided the Japanese national government to democratize its police. The Government Section of GHQ had a plan to democratize Japanese police thoroughly by introducing local autonomous police following the U. S. model (Furukawa, 1980: 193). Japan was in a chaos immediately after the World War II. During this period many crimes, especially property crimes owing to poverty, were committed and Japan's labor movements became active. Japan's weakened police was barely able to maintain public order. The Public Safety Division of GHQ, fearing this situation, supported maintaining a powerful centralized police which the Japanese national government wanted. The Police Law was enacted in 1947 as a result of a compromise between the Government Section and the Public Safety Division.

The preamble of the Police Law of 1947 declared that in order to organize a democratic system for people, according to the spirit of the 1946 Constitution, sovereignty was given to the people. Under this law the authority of the State police was reduced. It was called "*the State-Local Police*". On the other hand, an autonomous police was created in local governments in all cities, towns and villages with a population of over 5,000. Local police were given the authority of personnel management and budgets and they were expected to perform functions as independent law enforcement agencies. In addition, the system of a Public Safety Commission was introduced following an American model in order to check police activities. However, these democratic systems of the police had to be changed soon.[5]

Abolishment of Autonomous Local Police

As was previously noted, many democratic reforms were carried out under the guidance of GHQ after World War II. These reforms, however, were not necessarily based on the needs of Japanese people. For example, older people, especially, were too conservative to understand the democratic local police. They wanted to restore the powerful centralized police.

GHQ guided Japan to create the autonomous democratic local government system. However, people were not so actively involved in activities for their local government as are citizens in the United States. In addition, the financial base of the local government was weak. Therefore, many local governments could not pay the expenditure for maintenance of their own police. Thus, in 1948, many municipal assemblies decided to "return" their local police to the State-Local Police, although it was not admitted under the Police Law (Hironaka, 1968: 82).

During the late 1940's the Socialist Party and the Communist Party became influential with the upsurge of labor movements[6]. This was the era - the 1950's - of the the Cold War between the United States and the communist countries. In such a situation national government, headed by the Liberal Party, tried to restore the strong centralized police. It was encouraged to do so by the U. S. government. It was decided at that time that it was more important to support the Japanese capitalistic system against the communist movement than to democratize Japan.

In 1951 the Police Law was revised, by which the "return" of a local police to the State-Local Police was admitted. The police system was finally drastically changed by an amendment to the Police Law in 1954, which was enacted against severe opposition by the left wing. By this revised law the autonomous local police were completely abolished before they would be rooted as a democratic system. The police system was replaced by a new one composed of the National Police Agency and the Prefectural Police.[7]

The Current Situation of the Japanese Police

More than 50 years have passed since the introduction of many democratic systems in Japan by following American models. These systems have been adjusted to Japanese culture. Many Japanese people believe that Japan has become a democratic society. Even in a democratic society the police are considered to be an undemocratic organization with the lines of a military command structure (Adler, Mueller and Laufer, 1991: 383). The following is an analysis of both democratic and undemocratic features of the contemporary Japanese police.

- Structure of the Japanese Police

- Police Organizations

Under the current Police Law, the National Public Safety Commission and the Prefecture Commission are an administrative committee and counseling body responsible for supervising the National Police Agency and the Prefecture Police. The police are expected to be politically neutral. Therefore, political balance is a consideration in the appointment of the members of a Public Safety Commission.[8] The Public Safety Commissioners are expected to check the activities of the police in their roles as the people's representative. However, the Public Safety Commission is not given the power to direct the police. The activities of the National Police Agency and the Prefecture Police are too many and too complicated for them to supervise efficiently. The posts of the Public Safety Commissioners have become an honorary post (Suzuki, 1980: 228). More often than not Public Safety Commissioners' discussion and deliberations are based on materials offered to them by the police staffs. They rarely challenge the police bureaucrats.

The power of the National Police Agency is not as strong as the power manifested by the State Police under the jurisdiction of the Ministry of Home Affairs prior to World War II.

The National Police Agency is responsible for the following tasks:

- planning of laws concerning the police, the standards of police activities and various police systems;[8]

- supporting Prefecture Police activities with both "hard-ware" and "soft-ware"; and

- coordinating Prefecture Police activities (National Police Agency, 1995: 2).

The National Police Agency does not have its own police forces to perform functions such as enforcing laws, maintaining order, and the provision of services in the community, for which the Prefecture Police are responsible. In principle the National Police Agency cannot direct the Prefecture Police on an individual case to perform these functions. Under the Police Law the Prefecture Police seem to be autonomous of the National Police Agency. However, in reality, they are put under the control of the National Police Agency through budget and personnel management control.

In principle the local or regional prefectural governments pay the expenditures of their Prefecture Police. The substantial rate of these expenditures are, however, paid and subsidized by the national government via Article 37 of the Police Law. The activities of the Prefecture Police are limited by the budget allotted to the National Police Agency. By controlling the budget, personnel management, and information, the National Police Agency substantially governs *all* Prefecture Police.

The current system of the Prefecture Police, controlled by the National Police Agency, is more undemocratic than the system under the Police Law of 1947, although the former performs the police functions more efficiently than the latter. The National Police Agency has strengthened its power over all the country under the pretext of promoting efficiency.

After World War II, the left wing and intellectuals who remembered the abuse of power by the police prior to the war, criticized the police, above all the National Police Agency, for strengthening their power. However, their criticism has become weak in the prevalence of an ongoing atmosphere of conservatism since the late 1970's. The police have gradually succeeded in strengthening their power.

For example, the Law to Cope with the Boryokudan (i.e., the organized crime gang known as the "*Yakuza*"), which gave the police more power to regulate Boryokudan activities, was passed unanimously at the Diet in 1991. There was no opposition to this law even by the Socialist and Communist Parties, parties which had always opposed a plan to widen the police power (Yokoyama, 1994). Another important example was the revision of the Police Law in 1996. In March, 1995, several members of the Aum Truth Religion killed many of Tokyo's subway riders with a toxic gas (White Paper on Police in 1996). The police, as a result, carried out massive searches in order to arrest many leading members of the Aum Truth Religion, using charges of several offenses. Escaping members were helped by "believers" all over the country. It was difficult for Prefecture Police, particularly the smaller-sized ones, to catch them. In order to cope with such an organized crime group in a wide area, a revised Police Law was passed without serious Diet debates. Under this revised law - passed for the purpose of searching for and investigating organized crime - a Prefecture Police, above all, powerful ones such as the Tokyo Metropolitan Police and the Osaka Prefecture, is allowed to enter into the jurisdiction of another Prefecture Police (Nihon-Keizai Newspaper, Ma 1996). In this case the Commissioner-General of the National Police Agency is authorized to direct the Prefecture Police concerned.

System of Recruitment and Promotion of Police Officers

Japanese police have a good system for educating and training officers at the police school. [9] Graduates from a senior high school, and those from a university who have passed recruit examination by the Prefecture Police, enter the Prefecture Police School to receive basic education and training for ten and six months respectively. They learn laws and police practices. In addition, they are physically trained through some sports such as traditional Japanese martial arts. After completing this initial pre-service training course they work at a *Koban* as on-the-job training for eight months. During this period they learn actual duties as community police officers under the person-to-person personal supervision of senior officers. This training system is evaluated highly from the viewpoint of democracy. Next, all fledgling officers are enrolled in the comprehensive training course for three months at the Prefecture Police School.[9]

During this education and training at the Prefecture Police School the newly recruited officers have to reside in dormitories. They begin to share the police subculture through limited interaction with the "outside".[10] They are, for example, especially expected to develop loyalty to both the police and to the government, as well as a spirit, or sense, of unity through a disciplined group life.[11]

The police administer promotion examinations to three higher ranks for ordinary officers. If they pass the examination for promotion to a police sergeant and to an assistant inspector, they receive their education at the Regional Police School for four and five weeks respectively. The former are expected to acquire the knowledge and skills required of a "core" officer at the police station, while the latter are educated to become a section chief at the police station. Those who pass the promotion exam to a police inspector receive their education at the National Police Academy for two months. Further, at the National Police Academy a supervisors' education course is provided for candidates with a rank of superintendent before they are appointed to a higher position such as a division chief in the Prefecture Police headquarters on as a chief of a police station. The Japanese training and education system for police officers is well organized and is regarded as being a democratic system.

In addition to the above-mentioned system, the police have developed a special system for recruitment and promotion of "elite" police officers. About 20 - in all of Japan - of those who pass the first-class recruit examination for the elite candidates of national government are employed by the National Police Agency. They are called "career officers". These career officers receive their training at the police school for only three months (Isayama, 1992: 171). Then they start their careers with the rank of an Assistant Police Inspector, a position to which the non-career police officers can be appointed only after 15 years of police work, on the average. Usually, career officers change their position every two years.[10, 11] They are often assigned to some high-ranked position in the Prefecture Police. Almost all high-ranking important positions of the Prefecture Police are occupied by these career officers.

Non-career officers, in contrast, are promoted to a higher rank from the bottom, if they pass the promotional examination. It takes 30 years, on average, for them to be appointed to the rank of superintendent, during which time they have had to pass three promotion examinations.[12] When the non-career officers are appointed to the rank of superintendent their status is transferred from a Prefecture Police officer to a National officer by Article 56 of the Police Law. In addition, some middle-aged non-career officers with outstanding job performance are transferred to the National Police Agency and work there as a National Public Officer for several years. They then return to a high position in their Prefecture Police. The high-ranking administrative officers, above all, career officers, in the Prefecture Police are more anxious about the policy presented by the National Police Agency, and about their promotion in the police organizations than the policy by their prefecture government and the public opinion in their prefecture (Suzuki, 1980: 219). It may have a undemocratic tint.

The system of promotion by achievements is regarded as being more democratic than that by ascribed characters of officers. Judging from this viewpoint, Japanese police are appreciated because they adopted the examination system.[13] However, the promotion of the career officers is exceptional, as already noted. Previously, most police officers did not receive a higher education. At that time the special promotion for career officers contributed to recruiting capable youngsters as potential candidates for "elites" who, in practice, went on to become part of the police leadership and/or policymakers at the national level.

In addition, career police officers, who often change their position, are expected to supervise non-career police as well as not to have corrupt relations with persons of power in [12, 13] the community. However, the trust in career officers was seriously damaged by the exposure of about thirty scandals during the autumn of 1999. The most serious case involved the covering up of an assistant police inspector addicted to stimulant drugs in December, 1996, who worked at the International Liaison Division of Kanagawa Prefecture Police Headquarter (Asahi Newspaper, November 2, 1999). This 'cover-up' was committed by at least nine high-ranking officers including, three career officers. The principal of this crime was the chief of Kanagawa Prefecture Police, a career officer with the rank of superintendent supervisor. The addicted officer was "protected", through the Chief's direction, at a hotel until his urine tested 'clean', acquiring for him a state of innocence re his addiction. During this process none of the officers who were involved, including a chief in the Inspection Office, did not oppose the 'direction' coming from the top. Because they feared that their Prefecture Police might lose its good name and that they, especially the three career officers, might lose a chance to be promoted to a good position. The exposure of this scandal made Japan's public aware of the existence of serious problems in Japan's rigid hierarchical organization which was led by a total of 520 career police officers.

Presently, many able youngsters who graduate from a university are employed as non-career police officers.[14] The gap in ability between the career and non-career officers has been reduced. In addition, the latter have rich experiences as practitioners. Therefore, the special promotion course for career officers becomes more undemocratic.[15] It will cause, and perhaps maintain, frustration in many capable non-career officers.

Individual Corruption and Preventive Measures in Japan's Police

Japan's police take many measures to prevent individual officers from committing a misdeed, or a crime. First, they investigate the backgrounds of those who have passed the[14, 15] recruit examination.[16] If the applicants have a tainted background, the police do not employ them as police officers. This contributes to the low rate of scandals among police officers, although it has an undemocratic tint, that is, a tint of discriminative screening.

The system of educating and training the newly recruited police officers is also a useful measure to prevent corruption among police officers. At the police school and its dormitory, recruits assume ethics as law-abiding professional police officers. After completing a pre-service comprehensive training course, younger officers work under the informal personal supervision of a chief with a higher rank and several colleagues in a team. If these novice police officers were to commit some misconduct, their chief would also receive some disciplinary punishment. [17] Therefore, a chief always endeavors to prevent the misconduct of his/her subordinates.

The police do not allow officers to occupy the same post for many years,[18] in order to prevent corruption. In addition, the police do not assign an officer to a post in which s/he has interests. For example, an officer cannot work at some post in a police station, in the same territory of which his/her parents live. This personnel management, which a small-sized municipal police could hardly adopt, is effective in preventing the development of corrupt relations between police officers and persons of power in the community.

Under the police subculture, police officers become well-disciplined conformists. They work diligently in the large-sized hierarchical bureaucracy with a military command structure. [19] The control over police officers in the bureaucracy is too strong. [20] Therefore, police officers and their families are separated from other Japanese (Ames, 1981:190). This contributes to a low incidence of deviant behavior among police officers. However, the pressure from the top of the police force hierarchy on police officers is too strong for the latter to not express their opinions in Japanese society. For example, when under pressure, some police officers at the Aich Prefectural Police were compelled to discontinue revealing scandals on illegal accounts[21] (Asahi Newspaper, June 6, 1997). This example documents an undemocratic feature of Japanese police.

Since most Japanese police officers are well-disciplined, the Japanese police system is high efficient in performing its functions. However, were the system to 'fall' into patterns of *ritualistic functioning*, as Merton pointed out (1968:203-207), Japan's police system's efficiency would be diminished. Having noted this possibility it is important to refer to Ames' analysis (1981:189). He noted that Japanese police are responsive to suggestions from below in the decision-making process concerning everyday operations, although they reject critical opinions from below. In addition, they adopt the fair promotion examination for non-career officers. These mechanisms are useful for police officers to maintain high morale. However, a Japanese police composed of an effective hierarchical bureaucracy would become a danger to democracy, if they would be directed by a dictator.

Structural Corruption

Under the Police Law the police should perform their functions for people from the standpoint of political neutrality. In reality, Japanese police continued to serve the conservative national government ruled by the Liberal Democratic Party during the period from 1955 to 1993. They continue to more severely supervise and regulate activities by the left, above all, those by the Communist Party. Their illegal supervision was explicitly exposed in the case of wiretapping by several police officers in 1986. [22] The police maintained a serious corrupt relationship with the political right wing and with the Boryokudan, as Kaplan and Dubro described (1986). However, in 1991 the Law to Cope with the Boryokudan was enacted after the upsurge of public opinion against the Boryokuda in the late 1980's (Yokoyama, 1994:9-14). Since the enforcement of this law, the police have more severely regulated activities of the Boryokudan, above all, their violent intervention in civil conflicts. I guess that the police do it earnestly, isolating themselves from the corrupt relations with the Boryokudan (Yokoyama, 1999:149). On the other hand, we still doubt whether the police severed their close relation with the right wing. [23] The Police supervise and regulate movements of the left wing much more earnestly in spite of the decline of these movements in the recent conservative mood.

Another structural corruption is the illegal diversion of a budget; spending money for private purposes, above all, for the purpose of drinking and eating as a private association. The police are especially inclined to misuse money under the budget item of secret funds, as Matsuhashi, a former career officer with the rank of a superintendent supervisor, pointed out (1984;494-495).

An individual police officer is protected under the umbrella of the police bureaucracy. If s/he would commit some deviant behavior or even some offense, the police would hide it. It is also structural corruption. This mechanism was documented in the case of embezzlement by a police officer, in which the police suspected an innocent female in his place (Yomiuri Newspaper, 1992). During the autumn of 1999 it was conspicuously revealed in scandals at the Kanagawa Prefecture Police. At the beginning the mass media exposed a few scandals in early September. In order to hide these scandals, a chief of the Inspection Office, a chief of the Police Administration Department and a chief of the Kanagawa Prefecture Police told a lie in succession at a press conference. The mass media then exposed more and more scandals of the police all over the country. One of them involved the hiding of an assistant police inspector addicted to the stimulant drug by several high-ranking officials in collusion under the direction of a chief of the Kanagawa Prefecture Police.

Control over the Police

The police have some systems to check their malfunctions by themselves. Under the Police Law, the National Public Safety Commission and the Prefecture Commission are the supreme organizations to supervise police activities, above all, structural corruption in the police from their politically neutral position. However, as I have previously mentioned, these commissions do not supervise their police in reality. Every time some scandal in the police is revealed, the commissions simply apologize to the public for it, and caution their police to take the preventive measures against such a scandal.

The prefecture Police have the Inspection Office, at which several officers work as an inspector in charge of coping with corruption within the police. As other law enforcement agencies hardly investigate this corruption, they should inspect it fairly. However, we witnessed several cases in which their fairness was doubted. The hiding of the addicted officer at the Kanagawa Prefecture Police was the most serious case, in which even a chief of the Inspection Office responsible for investigating him was involved in this hiding. We hear that the police do not announce a scandal, even a crime by a police officer, unless it would be exposed by the mass media.[24]

The Kanagawa Newspaper on November 24, 1999, reported that in March, 1991, the Inspection Office of the Kanagawa Prefecture Police published a manual on how to cope with a scandal. About two hundred copies of this manual were distributed to high-rnaking officials at an important position, such as a chief of a section or a department of the police headquarters, and a chief and a vice-chief of a police station. By the manual they were instructed that they should share information on a scandal with as feww other officers as possible, and that they should not announce a scandal actively in fear of conflicting with the mass media, because the announcement of the scandal would damage citizens' trust in the police and lower the morale of all police officers.[25] They were also advised to endeavor to find a new job for a police officer having committed an unpublished scandal in order to supervise his/her "voluntary" designation.[26]

The policy suggested by the manual must be adopted in all police organizations, as career officers moving every two years occupy all the important positions within these organizations. Therefore, we can not expect the police so much to check corruption by themselves. To cope with corruption in the police, we need to establish a mechanism of democratic control over the police from the outside.

According to Bayley's research, in the early 1970's Japanese police officers behaved so well that there was no movement among the public for the creation of a new mechanism of supervision and investigation as to their misconduct (1976:3). He thought that transformation to the better direction in police behavior was associated with the development of democracy in the postwar period.

Recently, some citizens' groups working voluntarily as ombudsmen have exposed scandals that many national and local public officers reserve money for drinking and eating by cheating on accounts. In response to their movement, some police officers at the Aichi Prefecture Police, the Nagasaki Prefecture Police, and the Akasaka Police Station in Tokyo revealed scandals on accounts. However, the Board of Audit has never published such scandals of the police (Asahi Newspaper, June 6, 1997). Nevertheless, citizens' groups continue to search for scandals by the police. They have demanded the prefectural government to give them access to information on expenditures, above all, ones for eating and drinking by the Prefecture Police. By 1999 their demand was partially admitted only in two prefectures: Shiga Prefecture and Miyagi Prefecture. The citizens' groups working as ombudsmen will contribute to checking scandals on accounts, although it would be difficult for them to expose other scandals in the police.

The mass media have played an important role in checking scandals in the police, although they are anxious to maintain friendly relations with the police. In general they are very sensitive to scandals committed by individual police officers. As Bayley has pointed out, the police misdeeds are reported as major news by the mass media (1976: 3). The mass media single-out the crimes and misdemeanors committed not only by police officers on duty but also by off-duty and retired police officers.[27] Such reports by the mass media are regarded as being one of the available democratic controls over the police, although they may me too sever on the reported person. We expect that the exposure of many police scandals by the mass media during a half year since September of 1999 will contribute to reforming the rigid police system into the democratic one

Law Enforcement Activities for the People

The new Constitution enacted in 1946 includes several articles which prescribe peoples' rights to due process during criminal procedures; modeled after the American paradigm. In order to guarantee these rights, the new Code of Criminal Procedure was proclaimed in 1948. Post-World War II officers, within the democratized police system, should perform crime fighting law enforcement functions under this Code of Criminal Procedure. Immediately after the enforcement of this law we still saw many illegal police activities carried out mostly by older officers who did not understand the principle of 'due process'. There were serious police illegal activities against the movements directed by the Communist Party around 1949.

Every time that illegal law enforcement activities were revealed, the police were severely criticized by the public. As time passed, police officers increasingly respected the principle of the 'rule of law'. The police have provided the newly recruited officers with an education program, in which laws are taught as an important subject. Generally speaking, contemporary Japanese police perform their duties efficiently for people under the principle of the 'rule of law'. They have contributed to Japan's becoming the safest developed society in the world. However, we still see some problems in the law enforcement activities by the police.

Problems Associated with the Process of Law Enforcement

The collection of information has become increasingly more important for law enforcement activities. The Prefecture Police system, coordinated by the National Police Agency, is more efficient in the collection of information than the local autonomous police. On the other hand, as previously noted in the case of wiretapping in 1986, police officers are prone to collect information, above all, about left wing activities; by any means, legal or illegal. For example, the Asahi Newspaper (June 13, 1997) reported that a person was charged with the sale of information stealing from the data base of the National Federation of Credit Centers, and that he did not regard the sale as a crime because he had often offered such information free to police officers who had requested it. The police may often use such illegal ways to collect information, as Japanese people are less sensitive about the invasion of their privacy than are people in western developed countries.

Some undemocratic features are associated with police investigations. Japanese detectives are not necessarily morally committed to aggressive criminal investigation without neglecting procedural restraints (Miyazawa, 1992:234). However, the police put pressure on police officers, above all, detectives working in teams in order to raise the productivity rates in catching criminals. Recently some serious illegal activities by police officers have been witnessed under such organizational pressure.

The most serious incident was revealed in Tokyo in 1997. First, a senior police officer was arrested on a charge of possessing 1 gram of a stimulant drug at his *Koban* (Nihon-Keizu Newspaper, April 27, 1997). After the investigation it was revealed that this principal officer and his three colleagues had arrested two innocent persons illegally on a charge for an offense under the Stimulant Drug Control Law by using this stimulant drug.[28] Then, four[28] officers were arrested for a misfeasance by a special public officer (Asahi Newspaper. May 22, 1997). At the trial, one of those four officers stated that he committed this crime because he would be negatively sanctioned in the Jyoto Police Station if he would fail to raise the productivity in 'catching a criminal.[29] This misfeasance was committed by police officers working diligently under the police's "structural pressure". However, high-ranking officers did not want to admit their organizational defects.

Thereafter, the National Police Agency issued a directive to all Prefecture Police (Nihon-Keizai Newspaper, May 23, 1997). This directive was aimed at alerting all police officers to their duties by keeping strict discipline. In addition, and above all, it placed an emphasis on their cultivation and enhancing of the respect for human rights, and on improving the supervisory administration by middle-class managerial officers. The Superintendent-General of the Tokyo Metropolitan Police was fined by the National Public Safety Commission[30] for this incident and, in turn, he fined his subordinates for their improper supervision of over four officers who had committed the crime. The Chief of the Jyoto Police Station quit after a heavy sanction was imposed on him.

Pressure within the police structure caused another recent problem concerning the seizure of fire arms. After the enforcement of the *Law to Cope with Boryokudan*, in

1992 the police established a policy of strengthening the regulation of illegal activities by *Boryokudan* members. Under this policy police officers have been urged to seize fire arms.[31] Several scandals followed in which police officers wanted to perform firearm seizures as part of 'team policing'. In 1995 and 1996 at least three incidents of such a scandal were documented.[32] Even in 1997 the scandal about police officers at the Kuramae Police Station in Tokyo was reported as being major news.[33]

The National Police Agency designates a certain week or month as the period for raising the productivity for catching a certain kind of criminal. For example, in 1997 it designated July as the month for strengthening investigations of sexual offenders. During this period police officers are put under great pressure to meet their work quota, that is, to catch at least one " targeted" criminal. They sometimes resort to illegal ways of doing so.

Criticized for the structural-organization 'causes' of the above-mentioned scandals by the mass media, the police have to improve their current system of rating police officers' achievement by merits, that is, by a total number of criminals caught. The National Police Agency declared that police officers' achievement should be rated not only by the *quantity* of their catching criminals, but also by the *quality* (i.e. the means) of their work performance (Asahi Newspaper, July 25 1997).

Structural-Organizational Problems in the Process of Law Enforcement

All Japanese uniformed police officers began to carry a pistol under the guidance of GHQ after World War II. However, their use of a pistol is strictly regulated by the Police Law. Therefore, the problem about use of deadly force by police officers is a rare one. Under Article 36 of the Constitution police officers are prohibited from torturing and imposing a cruel punishment. Today we rarely hear news about police officers using physical violence. These are some of the democratic features of the Japanese police.[34]

Japan's police are expected to investigate and search in fair and legal ways under the principle of 'due process'. For example, in principle they are prohibited from using 'entrapment'.[35] Another example is the prohibition of making 'a deal' with a suspect. These prohibitions contribute to preventing the development of corrupt relationships between police officers and members of Japan's criminal underworld.

The Police were deprived of their arbitrary power to catch a suspect by abusing the system of administrative detention after World War II. Today they can not place a suspect under some compulsory measures without a writ issued by a judge. This mechanism was designed to enable judges to check the law enforcement activities of police officers. All too often, however, this expectation is betrayed. Usually, judges issue a writ automatically in response to a request by a police officer or a public prosecutor, since they believe in the efficient law enforcement activities carried out by police officers. A suspect can be detained for less than 23 days when police officers interrogate him/her under the Code of Criminal Procedure. However, if the police want to interrogate a suspect charged with some serious offense for a longer period, they usually must get a writ for arrest and one for detention. The suspect is charged with a minor offense prior to a requested writ for the charge of the targeted serious offense. This permits the police to "legally" interrogate the suspect charged with the targeted serious offense for more that 23 days. Japanese criminal law scholars and defense counsels have criticized the police for using this approach, regarding it as an illegal practice which invade peoples' basic right to 'due process'. Article 38 of the Constitution proscribes that noone shall be compelled to confess in order to avoid being incriminated, that the confession of a suspect acquired by illegal methods shall not be adopted as evidence at the trial, and that noone shall be sentenced as guilty only on the basis of his/her confession without any other evidence. Although interrogators stopped using physical violence after World War II, they are still intent upon acquiring a confession from a suspect. Usually, Japanese suspects confess their offense voluntarily as an expression of their repentance immediately after being caught by the police. Therefore, interrogators are prone to "invade" the suspect's right to remain silent. The suspect who keeps silent is severely interrogated, for long hours, without a break, from morning through night in a police jail.[36] It is legitimate to consider this a form of psychological torture. More often than not, the confession acquired by such psychological torture is adopted as acceptable evidence by judges.

Another problem which has recently come to light is that of sexual harassment carried out by police officers, above all by interrogators. Japan has been a male-dominant society, in which people are not sensitive to "sexual harassment". However, with the advent of various feminist movements, police officers have begun to be charged with sexual harassment.[37] As a result the police have begun to take measures to prevent such behavior. For example, the police have begun to employ more female police officers [38] and offer them more important roles in treating female suspects and victims . This is especially so for the female police officers working with rape victims.[39]

Article 32 of the Constitution prescribes people's right to a judicial court trial. As a consequence, the chief of a police station lost the traditional discretion of whether or not to impose a penal detention or a fine on a person charged with some minor offense.

Under the Constitution, courts are guaranteed their independence from the government. In addition, the adversary system was introduced by enforcement of a new Code of Criminal Procedure. Therefore, judges are expected to play more important roles in checking illegal investigations and searches by police officers. However, it is the rare case in which judges decide to release a suspect or a defendant because of illegal investigation and/or search. In 1995 the total number of defendants sentenced at courts was 1,031,716, of which only 52 were adjudicated as being innocent [40] . (White Paper on Crime in 1996: 120).

Community Policing

Police officers became "public servants" in Japan under the 1946 Constitution. Today they do not behave in their "traditional" authoritarian manner in the community, as they had done in their role as loyal subjects to the emperor prior to World War II. In Japan officers working at *Koban* and *Chuzaisho* play an important role in community policing. Subsequent to World War II the National Police Agency established a policy for modernizing both the system and police equipment. Under this policy the total number of *Koban* and *Chuzaisho* decreased; the police preferred patrolling by car - the modern way - rather than by to foot. However, following Bayley's (1976) research on Japanese policing, functions performed by police officers at *Koban* and *Chuzaisho* were highly criticized in foreign countries.[41] Therefore, by changing the policy, the National Police Agency has promoted the development of community policing at *Koban* and *Chuzaisho* in order to prevent crimes and to make neighborhood residents feel secure.

The total number of *Koban* and *Chuzaisho* amounted to 6,500 and 8,400 respectively in 1995 (White Paper on Police in 1996:71). Four teams of more than three police officers work in rotation at a Koban.[42] The main job of the police officers at *Koban* and *Chuzaisho* is to visit *all* houses and offices in their territory regularly in order to get information; above all, information about residents [43], and to give them crime prevention advise. In their role as law enforcement officers they patrol by mini-car, by bicycle and on foot, carrying a mobile telephone in order to question a person who is behaving strangely. When working at *Koban* and *Chuzaisho*, police officers provide services such as giving directions and act a "lost-and-found" service. Many citizens stop by the *Koban* and *Chuzaisho* with various needs and requests. For example, in 1995 the total number of citizen's "lost-and-found" service requests to the police amounted to 2,800,000 (Ibid. :72). In addition, 96.6% of *Koban* and *Chuzaisho* police officers publish a mini-newspaper to let residents in their territory know the police activities and crime prevention measures. Their jobs contribute to enhancing contact between citizens and the police. These are additional democratic features of the contemporary Japanese police.

Japanese police have played a role in organizing community crime prevention. Due to the initiative of the police, many citizen's houses have become a liaison house for crime Prevention. 'The Society of Crime Prevention' facilitates people functioning as 'neighborhood Watchers'. In addition, the police have succeeded in organizing and supporting private organizations for crime prevention activities such as the *Society of Crime Prevention*, the *Traffic Safety Association* and the *Center for Promoting the Movement to Expel Violence*. These organizations function as if they were auxiliary police agencies.

Japan's police have earnestly performed many activities designed to prevent juvenile delinquency. For example, they have many guidance volunteers patrolling on foot with police officers, whose main activity is to warn pre-delinquents. In addition, the police perform many campaigns and activities to prevent juvenile delinquency by use of human resources in schools, work places and neighborhoods (Yokoyama 1981). They even carry out activities for the sound rearing of children, which educational and child welfare agencies should perform in principle (Yokoyama, 1989:45).

Conclusion

The authoritarian Japanese State Police was dissolved Immediately after the World War II. An autonomous local police system was introduced, modeled after American systems, in order to democratize the police. This system, however, did not take root in Japan. The current system is composed of the National Police Agency and the Prefecture Police. Under this system the National Police Agency has gradually expanded its supervisory power over all Prefecture Police. A giant, hierarchical, police power-structure, presented, has been created with a Commissioner-General of the National Police Agency at the top and plain police officers at the bottom. In addition, the policy of the National Police Agency penetrates all over the country through private associations under the umbrella of the police. This system has contributed to raising the functioning efficiency of Japan's police. Today most police officers respect the ethic of democracy prescribed by the modern Japanese Constitution. However, as a caveat, we should take note that the current police hierarchical system could become a danger to Japan's democracy by suppressing people's human and civil rights if it would be directed by a dictator.

Crimes, especially those by adults, have decreased in Japan. However, the police have succeeded in their campaign for expanding their "social service" work. In addition to broadening their crime and juvenile delinquency prevention activities, they also carry out social welfare activities more seriously. For example, police officers frequently visit the elderly or the handicapped in their homes; activities traditionally done by social workers. Using the human resources of the *Koban* and *Chuzaisho,* the police may provide people in need of aid with better services than social workers at the social welfare agencies.[44] However, since police officers have a duty to work as law enforcement officers first of all, their role as "social worker" is obviously limited. The proliferation in Japanese police should not be toward the restoration of the authoritarian police system which existed prior to World War II.

---

*Professor **Minoru Yokoyama** completed his B.A. in Law and M.A. in both Criminal Law and Sociology at Chuo University, Tokyo. He is a professor and the former Dean of the Faculty of Law at Kokugakuin University. He is the former 2nd Vice President of the Research Committee for the Sociology of Deviance and Social Control of the International Sociological Association. He is a member of the board of directors and the former president of the Japanese Association of Sociological Criminology. He is the president of the Tokyo Study Group of Sociological Criminology and a member of the board of directors of the Japanese Association of Social Problems. He has presented numerous papers at national and international conferences and symposia, and has published many articles in professional journals.*

Notes and References

Adler, Freda, Gerhard O. W. Mueller and William S. Laufer (1991). *Criminology.* New York: McGraw-Hill, Inc.

Ames, Walter L. (1981). *Police and Community in Japan.* Berkeley: University of California Press.

Aoki, Eigoro (1979). *Japanese Criminal Trial* (written in Japanese). Tokyo: Iwanami-shoten.

Bayley, David H. (1976). *Forces of Order—Policing Modem Japan.* Berkeley: University of California Press.

Furukawa, Jun (1980). "Reform of Police" (written in Japanese). Special Feature of ogaku Seminar, Modern Police. Tokyo: Nihon-Hyoron-sha.

Hironaka, Toshio (1968). *Japanese Police After the War* (written in Japanese). Tokyo: Iwanami-shoten.

Igarashi, Futaba (1989). "Coerced Confessions and Pretrial Detention in Japan". Paper presented at the 41 st Annual Meeting of the American Society of Criminology held in Reno.

Isayama, Hiroshi (1992). *Challenging the Police* (written in Japanese). Tokyo: Shin-nihon-sha.

Kaplan, David E. and Alec Dubro (1986). *Yakuza*. Reading, Massachusetts: Addison-Wesley Publishing Company, Inc.

Matsuhashi, Tadamitsu (1984). *There Is Always My Sin Before Me* (written in Japanese). Tokyo: Original Publishing Center.

Merton, K. Robert (1968). *Social Theory and Social Structure* (Enlarged Edition, 1968). New York: The Free Press.

Miyazawa, Setsuo (1988). "Scandal and Hard Reforsm". Paper presented at 10th International Congress on Criminology held in Hamburg.

Miyazawa, Setsuo (1990). "Learning Lessons from Japanese Experience in Policing and Crime". *Kobe University Law Review*, 24:30-61. Kobe: Kobe University.

Miyazawa, Setsuo (1992). *Policing in Japan*. New York: State University of New York Press.

Morinaga, Eizaburo (1984). A Series of Biographies of Japanese Counsels (written in Japanese). Tokyo: Shakai-Shiso-sha.

Murayama, Masayuki (1990). *Study on Police in Charge* of Patrol (written in Japanese). Tokyo: Seibun-do.

National Police Agency (1995). The Police of Japan, 1995. Tokyo: National Police Agency.

Obinata, Sumio (1987). *Imperial Police and People* (written in Japanese). Tokyo: Nihon-Hyoron-sha.

Obinata, Sumio (1990). "Process of Establishment of Japanese Modem Police and its Thought (written in Japanese). In Sumio Obinata and Masaomi Yui (eds.), *Bureaucratic System—Police*. Tokyo: Iwanami-shoten.

Okubo, Yasuo (1977). Boissonade (written in Japanese). Tokyo: Iwanami-shoten.

Ohno, Tatsuzo (1995). Japanese Police (written in Japanese). Tokyo: Shin-Nihon-Shuppan-sha.

Saito, Toyoji (1988). "Substitute Prison". *Konan Journal of Social Sciences*, 2:51-65. Kobe: Konan University.

Shikita, Minoru and Shin-ichi Tsuchiya (1990). *Crime and Criminal Policy in Japan from 1926 to 1988*. Tokyo: Japan Criminal Policy Society.

Social Department of "Red Flag" (1981).*Evidences on Special High-Grade Police* (written in Japanese). Tokyo: Shin-Nihon-Shuppan-sha.

Suzuki, Takuro (1980). Secret in Japanese Police (written in Japanese). Tokyo: Chobun-sha.

Tezuka, Chisako (1990). *Sexual Harassment by Police Officers* (written in Japanese). Tokyo: San-ichi-shobo.

Yokoyama, Minoru (1981). "Delinquency Control Programs in the Community in Japan". *International Journal of Comparative and Applied Criminal Justice*, 5(2):169-178. Wichita, U. S.A.

Yokoyama, Minoru (1989). "Net-Widening of the Juvenile Justice System in Japan". *Criminal Justice Review*, 14(1):43-53.

Yokoyama, Minoru (1994). "Change in Japanese Organized Crime and the Enactment of the Law to Cope with Boryokudan in 1991". Paper presented at the 13th World Congress of Sociology of the International Sociological Association held in Bieleteld, Germany.

Yokoyama Minoru (1999). "Trends of Organized Crime by Boryokudan in Japan". *Organized Crime: Uncertainties and Dilemmas.* Chicago: Office of International Criminal Justice, The University of Illinois at Chicago.

Yomiuri Newspaper, Osaka Bureau on Society (1992). Embezzlement Case by a Police Officer (written in Japanese). Tokyo: Kodan-sha.

Glossary

National Police Agency: National Police Agency is an organization of the Japan's National Government under the cabinet ruled by a prime minister. Although it does not have its own police forces, it makes out the draft of a law on police activities, and supports and coordinates activities of all *Prefectural Police.*

Prefecture Police: The Prefecture Police is a regional or local unit of Japan's police forces. It is, however, substantially controlled by the National Police Agency through budget and personnel management control.

Koban: Koban is a base of the community policing in the urban area. more than three police officers work at the *Kooban* in a rotation all year around.

Chuzaisho: Chuzaisho is a house, at which a police officer and his family live. It is scattered throughout Japan's rural area for community policing.

Notes and References

1 Article 23 of the Constitution prescribed that Japanese people, as subjects of an emperor, shall not be arrested, detained and punished without a legal, statutory basis. Similarly Articles 24 and 25 prescribed the right to a trial by a judge, and the rights against invasion of privacy in ones home as well as not to be searched.

2 Article 1 of the Administrative Execution Law prescribed, and limited, administrative detention for one day, which could be imposed on a person behaving strangely such as being drunk and mentally disordered. By abusing this prescription, the police detained a suspect in a police jail continuously for a long period (Aoki, 1979:12.).

3 After the enforcement of the Penal Code and the Code of Criminal Procedure in 1882, the counsels were first permitted to work for defendants in criminal trials. (Morinaga, 1984:190). It is interesting to note that many leaders of the movement for people's rights and freedom were former warriors who became conservative statesmen after the establishment of the Diet in 1890.

4 The term *"High-Grade Police"* means that the police who maintained order for an emperor and his regime were superior to the police for "the people" (Obinata,1990:500).

5 The total number of the discharged police officers amounted to 4,958 by October 22,1945, (Hironaka, 1968:41).

6 The term "prefecture police" includes the Tokyo Metropolitan Police.

7 For example, with the consent of the Diet a prime minister appoints five members of the National Public Safety Commission, of which three or more shall not belong to the same political party.

8 On the other hand, the career officers are appointed to be Superintendent 3 1/ 2years after graduating from police school without taking any promotion examination.

9   The police officers must prepare themselves for the promotion examination by
     learning some academic subjects. Therefore, officers who are good at learning the
     academic subjects, have a greater possibility to pass the examination than police,
     such as detectives, who are more involved in their duties. This is a disadvantage
     of the Japanese police promotion examination system. The rank of Senior Police
     Officer is provided to older police officers who cannot pass the police sergeant
     promotion.

10   In fiscal year 1993 approximately 87,000 applicants took the prefecture police re-
     cruit examination; only 5.1% passed (National Police Agency, 1995: 12).

11   Recently the National Personnel Commission issued a recommendation that all
     ministries should establish the system to promote more non-career officers to
     higher positions (Nihon-Keizai Newspaper, August 4, 1997).

12   Most of teachers at the police school are the specialist police officers with higher
     ranks. University Professors, above all, those who criticize the police, are rarely
     invited to teach at the police school.

13   Ames, in addition to other elements, pointed out three main elements regarding the
     development of Japanese police subculture: the heavy demands of loyalty and
     solidarity from the police establishment; a certain similarity in the newly recruited
     youngsters; and the extended socialization process for them within the police
     organization(Ames, 1981:153).

14   The mechanisms which the police use to maintain solidarity and hierarchy, are the
     promotion system, physical arrangement of the work environment in police of-
     fices, decision making processes, transfers, police housing complexes, the pursuit
     of leisure by police officers, marriage and family life, and retirement assistance
     (Ames, 1981:180-181).

15   It was revealed ,in 1986, that several police officers of the Tokyo Metropolitan
     Police and the Kanagawa Prefecture Police wiretapped the telephone at the private
     house of a director of the international department of the Communist Party
     (Miyazawa, 1988:10-23). They were not prosecuted in a criminal court, because
     leaders of the national government, the ruling Liberal Democratic Party and the
     police put pressure on public prosecutors (Ohno, 1995:86). However, the director
     and his family won a compensation in a civil suit against the national government
     and the Kanagawa Prefectural Government (Asahi Newspaper, June 26,1997).

16   Three mysterious tragedies caused by a train7 occurred during the summer of
     1949. The police arrested several innocent members of Japan's National Railway
     labor union - which was affiliated with the Communist Party -on a charge of killing
     by a train in conspiracy. Thereafter, the communist movements waned.

17   The typical way of cheating on accounts is to pay for travel expenses, requested
     formally by officers who do not travel in reality, and to place such funds into secret
     accounts. High-ranking officers enjoy drinking and eating wastefully with these
     funds. Low-ranked officers, above all, those participating in cheating on accounts,
     feel frustrated with this.

18   Three scandals; rape committed by an off-duty senior police officer (Asahi News-
     paper, December 21, 1996), extortion of a bribe by a police sergeant (Nihon- Keizai
     Newspaper, December 20,] 996), and acceptance of a bribe by a police sergeant
     (Nihon-Keizai Newspaper, June 8, 1997) have been reported recently. The third

case was especially reported as being major news. In this case a police sergeant at a section of investigation in the Osaka Prefecture Police Headquarters received a bribe as a reward for divulging information about a fraud investigation from the company executive being charged with the fraud.. The National Public Safety Commission imposed a warning as a sanction to this crime for the first time against the Commissioner-General of the National Police Agency, who had been a chief of the Osaka Prefecture Police Headquarters at the time of this crime being committed (Nihon-Keizai Newspaper, July 24, 1997).

19 The investigated backgrounds of applicants are family and relatives, a criminal record, mental illness, political learning and leanings.

20 Police officers with a rank higher than sergeant are usually transferred to a new post every two or three years.

21 The police hierarchy is maintained both by the formal rank structure based on merit, and by seniority among police officers (Ames, 1981:181)

22 On the other hand, an individual police officer is protected under the umbrella of the police bureaucracy. If s/he would commit some deviant behavior or even some offense, the police would hide it. This mechanism was documented in the case of embezzlement by a police officer, in which an innocent female was charged in his place (Yomiuri Newspaper, 1992).

23 Asahi Newspaper, reported August 21, 1 997, that some on duty police officers drove a car all day for a representative of ultra-rightists' groups, who wanted to see beforehand places where the groups would run their cars for demonstration against the summer seminar held by the Communist Party.

24 In the first case a senior police officer, a principal, questioned a person carrying a rucksack, at midnight, into a pocket of which another senior officer slipped 0. 1 gram of a stimulant drug. In the second case the principal officer and his two colleagues slipped 0.3 gram of a stimulant drug into a car in the early morning in order to arrest an innocent car owner.

25 During the autumn of 1996 the Jyoto Police Station established the following sanctions against officers with poor achievement in catching criminals (Asahi Newspaper, August 1 1997). First, if plain police officers would not perform well, they would be compelled to present a paper on the reason for their poor achieve-ment. Second, if a senior police officer or a police sergeant would have subordi-nates with poor achievement, s/he would be admonished by a chief of his/her section. Third, the poorly achieved officers working at *Koban* would be compelled to patrol without taking a rest and even after their working time.

26 It was the second time. In the first case the Superintendent-General of the Tokyo Metropolitan Police was fined in 1978 for his responsibility for an incident in which an on-duty police officer killed a innocent female college student.

27 Firearms are severely regulated in Japan under the Firearms and Swords Control Law. However, Boryokudan members seemed to have finished arming themselves with smuggled firearms before the peak of fighting each other in 1985 (Yokoyama, 1997:3)

28 The police officers involved in these three incidents were an assistant police inspector and his subordinates at a section for coping with Boryokudan in the Nagasaki Prefectural Police Headquarters, a police inspector and his subordinates

at a section for coping with firearms and illegal drugs in the Ehime Prefectural Headquarters, and a sub-chief at a section for securing life at the Maebashi Police Station in Gunma Prefecture. They illegally seized firearms as specialist officers during an investigation.

29 In this case some interrogators made a deal with a former member of Boryokudan charged with possessing 33 grams of a of stimulant drug, even though police officers are prohibited from making any deals with a suspect. They requested him to present them with a pistol by promising him to mitigate punishment and by offering a portable telephone for him to talk with his wife (Nihon-Keizai Newspaper, June 22, 1997). Accepting their request, he asked his friend to hand over a pistol to the interrogators. Receiving a pistol, they buried it in a cemetery. After digging up it, they forged "evidence" with the suspect's consent. Their success in performing this feat- seizure of a pistol, illegally, was revealed by the suspect for whom a five-year prison sentence was demanded by the public prosecutor. The police inspector and an assistant inspector, who had played the responsible role in this conspiracy, were charged with the forgery of public documents. It is more than likely that police officers made this kind of deal more frequently with a member of Boryokudan before the enactment of the Law to Cope with Boryokudan in 1991.

30 Recently, a police sergeant and a senior police officer were charged with beating a boy who did not answer their questions (Nihon-Keizai Newspaper, May 24, 1996). The Japanese people have become very sensitive to physical violence attributed to police officers -with the decrease in use of violence in general. The total number of body injuries reported to the police deceased from 73,985 in 1958, a peak in our history, to 17,482 in 1995 (Shikita and Tshuchiya, 1990:357 and White Paper on Police in 1996:382)

31 Recently, the police begin to use entrapment formally to catch drug control law offenders. Entrapment was legalized by a majority of three Supreme Court judges with two judges opposing (Nihon-Keizai Newspaper, October 20, 1996).

32 The Prison Law of 1908 prescribes that a police jail can be temporarily used as a substitute for a detention house. Many suspects, above all, those who choose to remain silent, are detained in a police jail. They are compelled to confess by being tormented (Igarashi,1989:3). Lawyers and criminal law scholars criticize police jails as being a hotbed of false criminal charges (Saito, 1988:60-61).

33 Tezuka (1990) reported many cases of sexual harassment by police officers. Asahi Newspaper, January 19, 1996, reported that a police sergeant who had sexually harassed a female suspect in an interrogation room was arrested for the assault by a special public officer.

34 The total number of female police officers increased from 4,100 in 1985 to 7,100 in 1996, while that of all police officers was raised from 217,023 to 226,307 for the same period (White Paper on Police in 1986:272 and in 1996).

35 The jobs of female police officers expanded from -traditional works such as traffic regulation, guidance of juveniles and supervision over female suspects. For example, in April, 1996, the Kanagawa Prefecture Police appointed three female police officers to be specialists in charge of coping with sexual offenses. In their roles as counselors, they also received a special telephone "hot line" for calls from sexual harassment and offense victims. If necessary, they work as detectives to

catch the offender. During the month for strengthening investigation of sexual offenders in July, 1997, the police received 847 calls from the special telephone "hot line" from victims and persons in need of aid all over the country (Nihon-Keizai Newspaper, August 29, 1997). The police succeeded in arresting 10 sexual offenders by clues gathered from these "hot-line" calls.

36 If an innocent person was sentenced, police officers and public officers who have treated this case, would be negatively assessed in their bureaucracy Therefore, police officers earnestly seek to acquire a confession from a suspect, and to compose a story on the basis of it in order to persuade a judge. In addition, public prosecutors strictly screen the cases referred from the police from the viewpoint of whether or not they can persuade a judge by the story on the basis of a suspect's confession and other evidence. Japanese judges are more interested in finding offenders, while judges in the United States check for 'due process' more severely.

37 Miyazawa (1990:38-39) insisted that our knowledge on the effectiveness of *Koban* and patrol activities are inconclusive, as no one has ever designed an experimental evaluation on it.

38 Police officers, working in rotation, have difficulty becoming acquainted with residents in their territory. Therefore, the Tokyo Metropolitan Police began to appoint an Assistant Police Inspector to be chief of a *Koban*, who works flexible working hours in order to create and to keep contact with residents (Asahi Newspaper, July 3], 1997). *Koban* Counselors, assigned to a large-sized *Koban*, are also expected to play an active role in maintaining good contact with residents For example, in Kawasaki City the retired police officers work as *Koban* Counselors from 9 a.m. to 4 p.m. in services such as the lost-and-found and giving directions (Kanagawa Newspaper, April 2, 1996).

39 Most residents voluntarily give information about their family to police officers visiting from *Koban* and *Chuzaisho*.

40 In 1995 there were 475,725 liaison houses all over the country (White Paper on Police in 1996:81). The rate was one per every 93 households in all Japan.

41 The Center for Promoting Movement to Expel Violence was established to cope with Boryokudan (Yokoyama, 1997).

42 For example, an office of a district branch of the Traffic Safety Association, in which retired police officers work as staffs, is located in a building of a police station. Although most directors of the Traffic Safety Association are the community leaders, the activities of this association are dependent on the traffic safety policy established by the police.

43 The police have three kinds of guidance volunteers, whose total number amounted to 58,400 in 1995 (White Paper on Police in 1996: 118).

44 In Japan social welfare agencies do not have enough specialist social workers and resources to respond to requests of people in need of aid.

* Kokugakuin University E-mail: <minoruyo@kokugakuin.ac.jp>

Section III
Introduction
Policing in Countries in
Transition Towards
Democracy

Policing in Countries in Transition Towards Democracy

After offering examples on policing in stable democracies we move towards new types of democracies, or budding democracies. Searching to understand the relationship between police, security and democracy, we could not overlook those societies which are undergoing a change, a transformation, from a totalitarian regime (on the 'right' and on the 'left' as well as other kinds) to a democratic political system and/or from a centralized economic system to a market economy. This section once again portrays policing processes in such societies in terms of the following three main issues:

- police and democracy;

- democratic police, and

- democratic policing.

There are other differences which we can not discuss in this volume - due to lack of space - regarding the processes and outcomes of such transformations, e.g. abrupt changes, slow ones or those occurring after bloody civil war or a war of independence.

The authors in this section tell us that policing in totalitarian regimes are characterized by:

- police being part of the security and armed forces;

- policing being repressive, violating human and civil rights;

- policing which lacks *transparency* and *accountability* to the civil society (if it exists at all);

- the *equity* principle of democracy not existing, while the members of the ruling elite are exempt from criminal charges, unless the politicians or those in of the police and security forces decide to punish recalcitrant members as part of the recurrent campaigns against the 'enemies of the State' or "sacrifice" them as a general deterrent effect.

An extensive use of informal control mechanisms exist in these systems, both against the people and against those whom the rulers define as being the 'enemy of the State'. This is, in a sense, a special kind of operating 'community police' or 'community policing'. The State's security system also allows - even encourages - *vigilante polic-ing*. This 'community' and 'vigilante policing' continues during the political transformation. This is so because:

- the transformation brings an increase in street and violent crimes which were previously repressed or not reported to the public;

- the deterrent effect of the police which previously was based on fearing them has now weakened and the media is more free to report on the issue of crime, of the public fear of crime, of police inefficiency and corruption;

- police professionals representing the 'ancient regime' are discharged, or leave on their own, whilst some join organized crime groups - as in the former

Russian regime. Others are employed in the growing number of private police or security agencies, and

- those 'veteran' police who do remain or the newer recruits are less trained, lack resources and are not yet imbued with the democratic value of policing;

- the transformation hardly, if at all, changes the *nature* of police non-democratic organization, nor the old style of law enforcement.

The memories of the past heritage, the inefficiency, the corruption and repressive law enforcement of the past and the present, continues to deprive the police of the trust and legitimacy which are basic, necessary pre-requisite components of democratic policing. Furthermore, police can not influence the nature of the democratic and social changes which are part of the political transformation. The economic and social status of the population worsens, poverty continues and spreads The social net of basic social security (housing, health, employment and minimum income) disappear. Unemployment, especially of youth and young adults, increases, while many of them emigrate from the rural areas to urban areas. The political-economic changes led to the belief and expectations of a better future. With the increase in expectations and aspirations there are greater disappointments and frustrations which result from failures. Crime is one 'solution' for the quest for income and social mobility, especially with the rise of the former suppressed organized crime and the advance of newer types of organized crime because of the globalization of both legitimate and illegitimate world economy.

Positive changes do however occur in the processes of democratization:

- First, the police are separated from the security and military systems. But, as in Brazil, police remain controlled by the military police and the army. The security systems are often called in to exercise law enforcement duties in event of mass disorder.

- Police are now accountable, often supposedly, to democratically elected politicians in the government and the Parliament.

- The media assume one of its main functions; being the 'watch dog' of and for the democratic process, documenting and reporting on police deviance (mainly corruption) and monitoring police policies and their effects on crime and the protection of human and civil rights.

Within this scenario, especially of the crime scene, the populace continues to want more policing in terms of a visible presence of the police - the solution to the increase of crimes which threaten personal security, robbery and burglary. But the emerging civil society also wants fair, honest and an accountable police.

For Ugljesa Zvekic *democracy* means mainly monitoring police policies and their effect on crime and the protection of human and civil rights. His paper is based on the results of comparative victim surveys on reporting crime and evaluation of police uses "reporting of crime" as an index of improvement in police-community relationships. Notwithstanding some variation among the reporting States we learn that the trust of and in the police did not change mainly because of public accountability and transparency.

Zvekic concludes that the more the democratic and market economy were part of the totalitarian regimes in the past, the less police were corrupted and the more that police were ready to accept a new style of policing. Legitimization that is conferred on to the police is connected to, confidence in, and satisfaction with proper police behavior.

Alexander Yelin describes the situation in the former Russian Republics, but the article can represent, with some variations, other States of the former Eastern bloc. His analysis of the process of transformation contains the above-suggested points that we gleaned from other sources. What is important, and intriguing, in his paper is the public demand for a strong police and even nostalgia for the sense of security which they had in the former totalitarian regime. We found that this occurred not only in the Eastern Bloc but also in other countries and areas which underwent.or are still undergoing the democratization change. In addition to the increase in crime there is also a greater increase in the fear of crime and in the perceptions of insecurity. The nostalgia for the feeling of security and safety may mean the readiness to barter security for freedom. But as President Abraham Lincoln said, *Those who are ready to sacrifice freedom for security ultimately will lose both.*

China, unlike Russia, is still undergoing a change from being only, or mainly, a communist, centralized, controlled economy to an open market economy with continuing strong repressive policies against aspirants for political freedom. The police and the security forces continue to work together against 'political deviants'.

Hualing Fu discusses the outcome of these processes in terms of the police. Mainland China's police is still politically controlled, but is also asked to police the increasing (non-political) street crimes. Within the process of transformation Chinese police are now accountable to new, less political authorities - the courts and the law. Fu posits that this and a freer, more accessible printed media tends to weaken police authority.

The police is accused of inefficiency, corruption and violations of human and civil rights, of 'zero tolerance' campaigns (the *yanda),* by special police units who are assigned to 'special difficult areas'. Similar to what is happening in Russia, the increase in crime, at a time in which there is also an increase in the growth of private - often foreign - business companies, led to the flowering of private security and policing agencies. There is also a revival of a type of 'community policing' from the past - i.e. an informal social control under the guidance of the Party. Citizen units are assigned to patrol the streets and to impose 'people justice'.

Brazil underwent a process of political democratization from a right wing military regime towards a liberal-representative political system and towards a freer market economy. De Mesquito Neto portrays these changes. Again we observe the separation of the police from the army and security forces. In this transformation, military police actually become a 'blue' law enforcement system but which continues to be controlled by the political-military elite. The 'civilization', or 'civilianizing' of Brazilian police did not obliterate the old behaviors and patterns of corruption and the support for vigilante policing. But against this background there are pressures by the emerging civil society, the media and political parties towards accountability and transparency; towards weakening the army's and the military police's resistance towards the democratization of policing to the necessary respect for the democratic rule of the police.

In Brazil, as in other countries reported about in this volume, and in other places which we know about, the march towards democracy can be and is temporarily deferred

- and even at times repressed - in situations and conditions which are deemed to be dangerous to the State. When this happens this interferes with police attempts to regain the trust and legitimization which is so necessary for democratic police and policing. Rising crime rates, both petty and serious ones, that stop the democratization process, can and do lead to the public's identification of democratization with an increase in crime and insecurity - even panic - and perceiving the police, as before, as being a brute, but now also an inefficient force. Now, however, the police is a power (often lethal) organization but with a weakened authority and deterrence ability which it previously had.

Mesqito Neto raises an important and challenging subject which exists within all societies which are in transition towards democracy: what to do with former policemen and security agents, mainly commanders, who served the regime in the past and who now find themselves discharged from their jobs and roles, being brought to justice or even facing citizen's private justice/revenge against them. Various policies and trends have emerged as a result of pressures from the civil society as well as from victims of the past persecutions:

- outright dismissal from their posts without criminal charges, sometimes retaining them in the police force;

- trials (as in Argentina) or 'truth commissions' (as in South Africa);

- leaving the public service and joining the emerging private security or policing agencies, and

- others who join the re-emerging or newly appearing organized crime groups.

Mark Shaw's title of his paper reveals what he interprets to be the process of democratization in the South African society: "Democracy's Blues".

Democratization does not change the police. Police structure and behavior remains as it was in the past - corrupt and violent and impinging upon human and civil rights. But now it is a weakened apparatus because:

- of the retirement or expulsion of the 'old', veteran professional police;

- the remaining police (veterans as well as new recruits) are as yet untrained to effectively deal with the increase in street and violent crimes;

- the new crime scene - local, cross border and transnational crime - is beyond the ability of South African police's control.

It also suffers from corruption and retains the undemocratic styles of forceful and repressive 'sweeps' against crime.

South Africa is in many ways a special case for exploring the interface between policing, democracy and transition. This is because of the:

- relatively rapid separation of the police from the security forces;

- the emphasis on transparency and accountability to the civilian representative government;

- the new civilian government included former 'enemies of the State', who were therefore, by definition, enemies of the police;

- revenge towards former police officers, along side of trials and activities of the 'truth commission' were integral parts of the transition.

As in other societies which undergo a democratization process, there were changes in South Africa's laws to guarantee human and civil rights. But notwithstanding South Africa being a 'formal democracy', the remnants of the old regime, including the police, continue to cling to the old policies. Police culture has yet to change. Moreover, the demand by the South African business community and middle class for a more forceful and efficient policing results in issues such as *accountability* and *transparency* being deferred for the 'war on crime'. This 'war' can and does give rise to a lobby of police and some social groups against democratic principles which are considered as hampering necessary police efficiency. Danger looms: infringement of rights, militarization of the police and even help to the spread of vigilante policing.

These documented processes in South Africa tell us, as in other places, that political democracy does not necessarily change police structure and operations, nor does it necessarily give rise to democratic police and democratic policing. This does not happen in existing democracies and it is even harder to establish in new democracies and police which are in transition.

It should also be mentioned that in South Africa, as with all 'democratized' police, the established Western democracies donate resources and training to these States. This generally means making the police more technologically efficient but not necessarily more democratic in their structure, organization or operations. A review of the literature teaches us that the helping hand from the West - mainly England, Holland and the USA - emphasizes policies in training and deployment against corruption and the violations of human rights. It is, however, suspected that the hidden agenda of such assistance is to strengthen the police in its war against transnational organized crime.

11 Citizens and Police Relations in Countries in Transition

*Ugljesa Zvekic**

Abstract

This chapter presents the key findings related to citizen-police relationships in countries in transition (20) which took part in the International Crime Victim Survey (1996/97). Citizens rank low on reporting crime to the police and the majority of them still exhibit dissatisfaction with police treatment once the incident is reported, as well as with police performance in controlling/preventing crime.

Key Words: Countries in transition/ex-communist countries, Victim survey/International Crime Victim Survey, Crime reporting, Police performance, Citizen evaluation, Police corruption

Introduction

Policing is at the beginning of the criminal justice system. Policing encompasses the routine provision of administrative services to citizens, patrolling, criminal investigation, recovery of stolen property, and bringing suspects to justice; it also encourages certain punitive functions such as detention and administration of fines. Obviously, the police have different statuses and sometimes function in different criminal justice systems as well as in different poltical systems and contexts. Thus, it is often claimed that in totalitarian systems the police serve first and foremost the political agenda of the regime. Similarly, in political contexts in which there are internal conflicts or external treat, police tend to take over the functions of military. Yet, even in totalitarian regimes or conflict-ridden contexts most of the time policing is a mixture of preventive, administrative and repressive functions.

The police are usually the first criminal justice agency with which citizens come into contact, and they will shape opinions about the justice system as a whole. No other agency of justice is under such continuous public scrutiny and the object of such frequent political debate regarding powers of control, issues of privacy, crime prevention, and control priorities. Often, the real or perceived failure of the police to meet real or perceived community interests leads to the development of alternative policing styles (Findlay and Zvekic, 1993).

This evaluative process is based either on direct experience or on expectations as to what should be done. It is almost always an intrinsic interplay between experiences and expectations. Experience is not the exclusive domain of crime victims. Rather, experience of the police comes mainly from routine contacts with them as they administer public services: daily observation of policing in the local area, mass media reports about policing activities, or knowledge of the policing experiences of family members, friends and neighbours. Obviously, criminal victimization itself gives more opportunity for informed evaluation, though the particular position of the victim may result in biased generalizations. On one hand, having suffered damage or harm victims might be prompted to generalize about crime and offenders on the basis of their very personal experience, while on the other, attitudes based on personal experience with crime are more informed than those based on stories, rumors, etc. Yet, being more informed does not make them, ipso facto, unbiased since informed decisions or attitudes are not necessarily the most objective and rational ones.

The International Crime Victim Survey in Countries in Transition

There have been three rounds of the International Crime Victim Survey (ICVS). The first was carried out in early 1989, the second ICVS took place in 1992/94, and the third in 1996/97.[1]

The third round of the ICVS was carried out in 1996 and 1997 and encompassed eleven industrialised countries, thirteen developing countries and twenty countries in transition. The volume by Zvekic (1998) and the accompanying volume (Hatalak, Alvazzi del Frate and Zvekic, 1998) report the findings related to countries in transition, while the results of the 1996 ICVS for industrialised countries are reported in Mayhew and van Dijk (1997) and, for developing countries, in Alvazzi del Frate (1998).

All in all, with the 1996/97 ICVS, more than 130,000 people were interviewed in 40 languages around the world. Regarding countries in transition, six countries participated in the 1992-94 ICVS, while twenty countries took part in the 1996-97 sweep. Only Poland (Warsaw) participated in the first sweep (1989) and from then on in both the second and third sweeps of the ICVS. Six countries in transition participated both in the second and third sweeps. It should be noted that using the conventional classification of industrialised countries, developing countries and countries in transition, the latter group is the largest in terms of number of participating countries. It is also the group that increased threefold from the second to the third sweep of the ICVS.

This is very much the result of the interest of the international community and donors in the reform process toward a market economy and a democratic political system. Moreover, in many communist countries crime statistics were either not available to the public or indeed to the international community, or were considered inadequate. Nor was there much experience with victimization surveys and in particular citizens' experience with law enforcement and crime prevention. These and other reasons prompted an emphasis on countries in transition, a term which groups together ex-communist countries (Central-Eastern Europe and Central Asia). Furthermore, the fall of the communist system was accompanied by the dismemberment of the USSR, Czechoslovakia and Yugoslavia, and consequently the creation of a number of newly independent states. The only example of integration following the fall of the Berlin Wall (1989) is that of East Germany into the Federal Republic of Germany.

Table 11.1 Overview of participation, methodology and languages used in the International Crime Victim Survey in countries in transition

Second ICVS (1992-94)	Date	Sample Size	Urban*	Rural	Method	Language
Czechoslovakia: Czech**	1992	1,262	237	1,025	F/F	Czech/Slovak
Czechoslovakia: Slovak**	1992	508	21	487	F/F	Czech/Slovak
Estonia	1993	1,000	457	543	F/F	Estonian
Georgia	1992	1,395	-	-	F/F	Russian
Poland	1992	2,033	666	1,367	F/F	Polish
Russia (Moscow)	1992	1,002	1,002	-	F/F	Russian
Slovenia (Ljubljana)	1992	1,000	1,000	-	CATI+CAPI***	Slovenian

* Largest city in the country or urban area over 100.000 inhabitants.
**Sample from the survey carried out in the former Czechoslovakia was broken down into Czech and Slovak.
*** Computer Assisted Personal Interview.

Table 11.1 Continued

Third ICVS (1996–97)	Date	Sample Size	Urban	Rural	Method	Language
Albania (Tirana)	1996	1,200	983	217	F/F	Albanian
Belarus (Minsk)	1997	999	999	-	F/F	Belorussian, Russian
Bulgaria (Sofia)	1997	1,076	1,076	-	F/F	Bulgarian
Croatia (Zagreb)	1997	994	994	-	F/F	Croatian
Czech Republic	1996	1,801	717	1,084	F/F	Czech
Estonia	1995	1,173	364	809	F/F	Estonian, Russian
Georgia	1996	1,137	567	570	F/F	Russian
Hungary (Budapest)	1996	756	756	-	FF	Hungarian
Kyrgyzstan	1996	1,750	1,494	256	F/F	Kyrgyz, Russian, Uzbeck
Latvia	1996	1,411	1,011	400	F/F	Latvian, Russian
Lithuania	1997	1,176	656	520	F/F	Lithuanian, Russian
FYR Macedonia (Skopje)	1996	700	700	-	F/F	Macedonian
Mongolia (Ulan Baatar)	1996	1,200	1,053	147	F/F	Mongolian
Poland	1996	3,483	2,410	1,073	F/F	Polish
Romania (Bucharest)	1996	1,091	1,000	91	F/F	Romanian
Russia (Moscow)	1996	1,018	1,018	-	F/F	Russian
Slovak Republic (Bratislava)	1997	1,105	1,105	-	F/F	Slovak
Slovenia (Ljubljana)	1997	2,053	1,107	946	CATI	Slovenian
Ukraine (Kiev)	1997	1,000	1,000	-	F/F	Ukrainian, Russian
Yugoslavia (Belgrade)	1996	1,094	1,094	-	F/F	Serbian

Face-to-face interviewing was used in the developing countries and countries in transition, with the only exception of Slovenia (1992 and 1997).

Eleven main forms of victimization are covered by the ICVS, three of which allow for further grouping. Household crimes are those which can be seen as affecting the household at large, and respondents report on all incidents known to them. For personal crimes, they report on what happened to them personally.

In the surveys in developing countries and countries in transition, consumer fraud and corruption were also covered. Consumer fraud was asked about in the industrialised countries in 1992 and 1996, and corruption in 1996/97.

The respondents are asked first about their experience of crime over the last five years. Those who mention an incident of any particular type are asked when it occurred, and if in the last year, how many times. All victims reporting incidents over the past five years are asked some additional questions about what happened.

In countries in transition, samples of 1,000 respondents were generally drawn from the population of the largest city (see Table 1), although in a few countries the survey covered either several cities with or without the addition of a small rural sample (e.g. Estonia) and in Poland in 1996 the national sample was used. Sampling generally started with the identification of administrative zones in the cities, followed by a step-by-step procedure aimed at identifying: 1) areas; 2) streets; 3) blocks; 4) households; and 5) the respondent (a person aged 16 or more whose birthday came next). On average samples reflected basic demographic parameters in terms of gender, age, education and income. For the data analysis a weighting procedure was applied.

Fieldwork included the undertaking of feasibility/training missions and the carrying out of pilot studies in the countries which were participating in the ICVS for the first time, as well as the carrying out of the full fledged surveys in all participating countries.

Furthermore, meetings were held at the Ministry of the Interior or Ministry of Justice of the participating countries, with the police and other authorities, to describe the project, its requirements and potentials in terms of developing crime prevention strategies. Either professional public opinion poll companies or research institutes/universities carried out the survey including the training of interviewers. Interviews were held in households of an average duration of 30 minutes.

As regards countries in transition, on average the response rate was 81.3%,[2] while the refusal rate was 10.1%. The highest rates of refusal were observed in the Slovak Republic (23.9%), Lithuania (21.3%), Hungary (19.3%), the Czech Republic (17.5%) and Bulgaria (15.3%). It was observed that in some countries in transition the refusal rate was higher due to the vicinity of recent war conflicts, which may have increased the general level of suspicion. In some countries, fear of strangers was so widespread that the national co-ordinator suggested including a series of questions dealing with attitudes towards opening the door to strangers and the use of entry phones.

Reporting to the police

The "*police crime story*" is the amount and type of crime known to them. It will differ from the "*real crime story*" depending on citizens' propensity to inform the police about crime. To this reported crime, the police can add crimes detected by them but not reported, and they can deduct some criminal activities which do not figure in the "police crime story" because of specific investigative, technical, procedural, social and political reasons. There are, however, important variations across countries as to the volume and type of crime known to the police and admitted into police administrative records. The ICVS[3] provides considerable information as to differences across countries in crimes experienced by victims, and those reported to the police. It does not, however, provide information on the way in which reported crimes are officially admitted into police records.

Not surprisingly, the propensity to report to the police depends heavily on the seriousness of the crime, whether tangible or intangible. However, reporting is also influenced by other factors: previous personal experiences of reporting; other acquired experience with, or attitudes, to the police; expectations; factors related to the particular victimization experience in hand; the existence of alternative ways of dealing with this (e.g.reporting to public prosecutors directly; buying-back or recovery of stolen goods on the illegal market; reporting to consumer protection authority); the relationship with the offender; and the "privacy" of the issue.

Crime reporting, as mentioned above, differs according to the crime in question. It is evident that car theft is more often reported than any other crime, while sexual incidents, corruption and consumer fraud are, on average, the least reported. However, reporting rates also differ from country to country as well as depending on the developmental level. It is also claimed that the reporting rates have to do with the crime level in the society irrespective of the above-mentioned factors or as a baseline from which other factors influence the levels of reporting.

For illustrative purposes, reporting rates for burglary, robbery and assault based on all sweeps of the ICVS are presented in Table 2.

Table 11.2 Percentage of burglary, robbery and assault reported to the police in six global regions, 1989, 1992 and 1996 ICVS (1 year)*

	Burglary	Robbery	Assault
Western Europe	79.6	45.5	28.5
New World	85.3	75.9	45.3
Countries in transition	63.2	25.1	20.4
Asia	40.8	33.3	31.0
Africa	57.7	33.5	20.4
Latin America	44.1	20.7	23.6
Total	**61.8**	**39.0**	**28.2**

Average rates were used for sites participating in more than one sweep of the ICVS.

Among the three crimes, the highest reporting level is for burglary followed by robbery. Less than one third of the victims of assault reported it to the police. For all three crimes the highest reporting levels are in the industrialised world, both Old and New. From among the group of non-industrialized countries, burglary is reported the most in countries in transition and in Africa, and the least in Asia; while from among the non-industrialised group less than one third of the victims reported assault and somewhat more than a third reported robbery to the police. Therefore, in terms of the "reporting ranks" countries in transition rank third on burglary, fifth on robbery and fourth on assault. There is then a clear difference in reporting levels between, on the one hand, the industrialised world and, on the other, the rest of the world.

Comparing the two data sets (victimization rates and reporting rates) it becomes clear that the highest level of correspondence between the victimization and reporting rates for all three crime types is found in Asia. From a comparative perspective, Asia has both the lowest victimization as well as the lowest reporting rates. On the other hand, the highest reporting rates of the New World do not correspond to the victimization levels reported for the New World. Generally speaking, it appears that the reporting levels do not reflect the victimization levels. This seems to support the hypothesis that the victimization level is not the most important factor in conditioning the reporting practice and that it cannot be considered even a solid baseline for predicting propensity to report to the police. High crime does not automatically and necessarily lead to high disclosures of crime. Other factors appear to have more weight on the propensity to report to the police.

It is more difficult to reach such oversweeping generalizations if one looks at the regional and/or country level details.

From among the 20 countries in transition, most of them (12) exhibit high reporting rates for burglary; four very high rates (> 75) and three low reporting rates (< 50). High burglary reporting countries are Romania, the Czech Republic, Hungary and Latvia. Regarding the reporting of robbery, it averages half of the reporting rates for burglary with the Czech Republic, having the highest rate followed by Hungary, the Slovak Republic, Lithuania and Macedonia. The lowest reporting rates are found in Russia and Albania. As noted above, assault is the least reported crime type from among those analysed. In Georgia, assault is very frequently reported to the police (69) and it is also relatively frequently reported in the Slovak Republic, Macedonia, Yugoslavia and the Czech Republic. It is least reported in Estonia, Latvia, Albania and Belarus.

As noted above, it is difficult to establish a clear correspondence pattern between the victimization experience and reporting practice, which further supports the earlier mentioned observations regarding the relationship between crime occurrence and crime disclosure.

Several countries participated in both sweeps of the ICVS, as mentioned above. As regards burglary, the most significant changes in terms of more burglaries being reported to the police are found in the Czech Republic; in all the other countries with, the exception of Russia, the reporting levels for burglary decreased, but not to any significant degree. Therefore, on average, the propensity to report burglary to the police has not changed in the period under observation. Reporting of robbery to the police increased significantly in the Czech Republic and Slovenia. It also increased somewhat in Russia and Poland, while it decreased in Estonia and Georgia. Only in

Table 11.3 Reporting rates in countries in transition: burglary, robbery and assault, 1989, 1992 and 1996 - by country

	Burglary	Robbery	Assault
Albania	47.4	22.9	20.0
Belarus	47.1	26.2	19.5
Bulgaria	62.8	37.1	20.3
Croatia	61.4	30.1	25.5
Czech Republic	84.1	74.7	27.2
Estonia	66.5	31.0	16.5
Georgia	51.7	27.4	68.9
Hungary	78.9	45.8	18.1
Kyrgyzstan	59.4	27.4	13.6
Latvia	74.4	25.2	16.0
Lithuania	58.3	43.7	24.5
Macedonia	64.8	40.7	33.0
Mongolia	69.4	33.2	21.3
Poland	57.7	29.9	26.9
Romania	86.3	30.9	23.0
Russia	62.5	21.1	21.2
Slovak Republic	61.8	44.4	33.3
Slovenia	67.1	27.2	28.4
Ukraine	49.8	32.2	20.7
Yugoslavia	70.5	36.9	28.6

Russia did the number of assaults reported to the police increase significantly; while it remained more or less at the same level in the other countries.

It would appear that the propensity to report to the police has not increased in most of the countries with the exception of the Czech Republic for both burglary and robbery, and Russia for all three types of crime considered here. It can be also noted that, on average, the propensity to report robberies has increased most.

Why do people report crimes to the police? The reasons are divided into: sense of civic duty (*"should be reported"*; *"to stop it"*); need for assistance (*"to get help"*); recovery/compensation of damage (*"recovery of property"*; *"insurance"*). *"Want the offender caught/punished"* lies somewhere between means for recovering property and damage and expectation for the law enforcement agency to effectively deal with offenders.

Civic duty related reasons are prominent across the board independently of crime type and developmental groupings. While this is true for *"should be reported"*, reporting crime for preventive purposes *"to stop it from happening again"* is of particular significance for threats/assaults or robbery while less so for burglary. This is quite a rational attitude on the part of the victims who also consider that reporting violent crimes has more chances of inducing preventive action by the police while burglary prevention is becoming much more the citizen's own prevention activity.

"To get help" as a reason for reporting is more frequently mentioned with relation to threats/assaults and robbery.

Recovery of property and insurance are both mentioned with respect to burglary and robbery. It is interesting to note that reporting for the reason of recovering property for both crimes is much more present among victims from countries in transition and the developing world than from the industrialised world. Inversely, insurance reasons are much more important in the industrialised world. There is a very clearly established pattern, according to which high insurance coverage results in high reporting rates in order to get the insurance premiums. Where insurance coverage is low, expectations related to reporting are to *"recover"* stolen property. Since the level of insurance coverage is much higher in the industrialised world than in countries in transition, the reasons for reporting in order to compensate for damage will reflect this discrepancy. *"At the individual level, those without insurance are less likely to report burglaries to the police... At the aggregate level, there is always a strong association between the insurance coverage and reporting of burglaries to the police"* (van Dijk, 1994). Indeed, the countries and regions with low insurance coverage tend to display low reporting rates of burglaries to the police.

"Want the offender caught/punished" as a reason for reporting figures prominently for all three crimes. However, the differences in the importance of this particular reason between the regions are less pronounced when it comes to assault and robbery, and more pronounced when it comes to burglary. Most probably, the level of insurance coverage again is at play in a sense that for the victims of insured households to get the offender caught/punished is of less importance in terms of reporting to the police. On the other hand, if there is no household insurance, in order to recover property it is also important to find and punish the offender. In addition, there is a more punitive orientation in the developing countries and countries in transition (Zvekic, 1997) which also indicates the importance of this reason for reporting crime to the police.

It was noted that, on average, there are more non-reported crimes - in particular robberies and threats/assaults - in all the regions of the world and especially in countries in transition.

That the *"police could do nothing"* was frequently given as a reason for not reporting property crimes - thefts of personal property, thefts from cars, etc. This may signify a belief that the police would be unable to recover property, find the offender, or do anything else of benefit. It could also signify a fairly realistic judge-

Table 11.4 Reasons for reporting crime to the police, 1996

	Recover property	Insurance reasons	Should be reported	Want offender caught	To stop it	To get help	Other reasons
Burglary							
Western Europe	31.2	43.2	46.0	31.9	18.2	8.4	1
New World	17.4	22.8	51.1	27.2	13.0	8.7	1
Countries							
in transition	57.5	15.0	37.4	51.4	27.0	12.5	2
Asia	82.2	4.4	18.9	64.4	64.4	26.7	-
Africa	72.6	13.1	26.8	53.9	20.8	16.7	1
Latin America	53.2	26.2	19.5	42.9	34.8	8.6	3
Total	52.4	20.8	38.3	45.3	29.7	13.6	6
Robbery							
Western Europe	35.2	13.6	40.9	36.4	21.6	17.0	1
New World	13.3	13.3	56.7	46.7	26.7	20.0	1
Countries							
in transition	43.2	12.4	33.9	54.1	33.6	21.1	7
Asia	80.6	2.8	47.2	69.4	41.7	25.0	2
Africa	57.6	10.1	36.4	55.6	20.2	17.2	2
Latin America	39.0	32.0	23.0	54.0	40.5	17.0	3
Total	46.5	14.0	39.7	52.7	30.7	19.6	8
Assault/threat							
Western Europe	4.5	5.6	35.0	32.2	31.6	22.0	2
New World	6.9	6.9	36.2	39.7	39.7	24.1	2
Countries							
in transition	8.5	12.2	31.8	41.1	44.0	25.6	7
Asia	16.2	10.8	43.2	48.6	73.0	40.5	-
Africa	3.5	-	34.1	56.5	45.9	17.6	3
Latin America	18.0	42.4	18.7	38.8	44.6	22.3	7
Total	9.6	15.6	33.2	42.8	46.5	25.4	1

ment about the liability of the police to do much about something on which they have little information to act. In essence, though, it is an expression of resignation. In contrast, "*the police wouldn't do anything*" may carry a more explicit criticism that the police would be reluctant to take action, even though they might be expected to do so. "*Fear/dislike of police*" certainly signifies a negative attitude towards the police, either of a general nature, or related in some way to the particular offence in hand. As might be expected, fear and/or dislike of the police was often mentioned in relation to violent crimes and sexual incidents. These might involve a close relationship with the offender(s), or sometimes even a lifestyle that may lead the police to treat the victims as accomplices, or people *"who deserve what they got"*. That female victims of sexual incidents are often treated unsympathetically by the police is also now well recognised.

Table 5 presents reasons for not reporting. Crimes are mainly not reported because they are not considered "serious enough". Since this section deals with the police, it is worth looking more clearly at police related reasons: *"police could do nothing"*; *"police won't do anything"* and *"fear/dislike of police"*.

It should be noted that around 30% of the victims of burglary from the New World and even 52% from Asia thought that the burglary which took place in their household was *"not serious enough"*; this reason, together with *"inappropriate for police"*, indicates the characteristics of the event itself. As regards robbery, *"not serious enough"* is mentioned as a reason for not reporting by 36%, 30% and 23% of the victims from Western Europe, Asia and countries in transition respectively. On the other hand, 22%, 26% and 15% of victims of assault/threats from Latin America, Africa and countries in transition mentioned the *"inappropriateness"* of the case for the police as reasons for non-reporting.

The resigned attitude towards the police (*"police could do nothing"*) is particularly prominent among the victims of all three crimes dealt herewith from all but the industrialised world. As will be seen later, this has much to do with the expectations citizens have about the police as well as with satisfaction with the police in controlling and preventing crime.

The two more implicit criticisms of the police are also more pronounced reasons for not reporting the three crimes provided by victims from countries in transition. This is, however, more related to *"police won't do anything"*. It should be noted that the implicit criticism that the police would be reluctant to take action is on average more highly related to robbery and assault/threats than to burglary.

"Fear/dislike" of police is mentioned significantly as a reason for not reporting robbery in Latin America and the New World as well as for assault/threats in Asia.

Satisfaction with the police

The ICVS also indicates the strength of police-community relations in showing: 1) the degree of satisfaction victims feel when they report to the police; and 2) the reasons why victims were dissatisfied with the way the police handle cases once reported.

Among the reasons for dissatisfaction with the police once burglary was reported, the most frequently mentioned were *"the police did not do enough"* and *"were not interested"*. The first reason was identified by more than 40% of the burglary victims in countries in transition and up to 75% of those from the New World. Disinterest on the part of the police was mentioned by 41% of the victims in Latin America and one third of the victims in countries in transition and Western Europe.

A substantial portion (ranging from one third to more than a half) of the victims of burglary from the countries in transition also highlighted that the police *"did not find the offender"* or *"did not recover goods"*. Indeed, in countries in transition *"want offender caught/punished"* and *"recovery of property"* were among the principal reasons for reporting burglary to the police. Therefore, if these expectations are not met by the police, victims who reported burglaries express dissatisfaction highlighting unmet expectations. As mentioned earlier, in this part of the world, where insurance

Table 11.5 Reasons for not reporting burglary, robbery and threats/assaults (1996)

	Not serious enough	Solved it myself	Inappropriate for the police	Other authorities	My family solved it	No insurance	police could do nothing	Police won't do anything	Fear/ dislike of police	Didn't dare	Other reasons	Don't know
Burglary												
Western Europe	26.2	21.4	4.8	-	7.1	4.8	16.7	2.4	-	2.4	21.4	8.1
New World	30.8	15.4	7.7	-	-	7.7	-	15.4	-	-	38.5	-
Countries in transition	27.0	13.3	13.2	6.6	9.0	6.5	28.4	16.7	5.6	6.8	8.6	9.4
Asia	52.4	13.3	14.3	2.9	3.8	2.9	14.3	5.7	11.5	-	3.8	3.8
Africa	17.4	12.3	10.7	7.1	5.5	2.4	35.2	12.3	2.8	6.3	14.2	4.3
Latin America	24.0	10.8	2.9	-	5.9	5.3	21.1	42.1	7.7	2.6	13.7	2.4
Total	**29.6**	**14.4**	**8.9**	**5.5**	**6.3**	**4.9**	**23.1**	**15.8**	**6.9**	**4.5**	**16.7**	**5.6**
Robbery												
Western Europe	35.7	10.7	17.9	1.8	5.4	-	25.0	7.1	5.4	7.1	16.1	2.7
New World	5.9	41.2	11.8	11.8	-	-	5.9	-	11.8	17.6	23.5	-
Countries in transition	23.4	12.7	10.3	1.7	6.4	8.0	30.9	27.7	13.5	9.9	9.7	6.5
Asia	30.4	10.1	18.8	4.3	10.1	1.4	30.4	17.4	9.1	10.1	4.3	-
Africa	14.7	9.6	10.9	-	1.9	0.6	46.8	14.7	5.1	12.2	16.7	1.9
Latin America	18.1	6.3	5.5	0.5	0.5	2.0	34.0	53.9	24.4	3.9	3.9	0.9
Total	**21.4**	**15.1**	**12.5**	**4.0**	**4.9**	**3.0**	**28.8**	**24.2**	**11.6**	**10.1**	**12.4**	**3.0**

	Not serious enough	Solved it myself	Inappropriate for the police	Other authorities	My family solved it	No insurance	police could do nothing	Police won't do anything	Fear/ dislike of police	Didn't dare	Other reasons	Don't know
Threat/Assault												
Western Europe	38.6	13.6	8.0	4.7	2.7	-	15.0	10.9	2.9	7.4	16.5	2.4
New World	25.6	17.9	7.7	6.4	2.6	-	6.4	15.4	5.1	5.1	28.2	5.1
Countries in transition	26.2	19.5	14.5	6.3	6.8	6.7	21.1	18.2	23.1	9.6	7.8	3.8
Asia	36.4	33.9	8.3	8.3	17.4	0.8	31.4	20.7	33.3	20.7	3.3	3.9
Africa	22.5	18.1	25.2	2.5	6.0	-	19.9	12.7	2.7	15.2	9.4	1.6
Latin America	17.4	30.7	21.8	0.7	4.2	1.6	14.9	26.1	6.9	9.6	6.2	1.8
Total	**27.8**	**22.3**	**14.3**	**4.8**	**6.6**	**3.0**	**18.1**	**17.3**	**12.3**	**11.3**	**11.9**	**3.1**

Table 11.6 Reasons for dissatisfaction with the police (1996)

	Did not do enough	Were not interested	Did not find offender	Did not recover goods	Gave no information	Incorrect/ impolite	Slow to arrive	Other reasons	Do not know
Burglary									
Western Europe	44.0	34.7	30.7	18.7	28.0	10.7	16.0	14.7	-
New World	75.0	25.0	25.0	20.0	25.0	10.0	20.0	20.0	-
Countries in transition	41.5	34.0	46.8	46.4	16.0	12.8	11.2	7.1	1.0
Asia	50.0	20.6	52.9	55.9	14.7	17.6	17.6	2.9	-
Africa	51.5	21.8	38.4	44.1	20.5	5.7	18.8	6.1	-
Latin America	55.8	41.4	34.5	32.1	26.1	20.9	4.8	3.6	0.8
Total	**53.0**	**29.6**	**38.1**	**36.2**	**21.7**	**13.0**	**14.7**	**9.1**	**0.9**
Robbery									
Western Europe	50.0	41.2	14.7	20.6	8.8	20.6	11.8	11.8	-
New World	40.0	40.0	40.0	6.7	13.3	20.0	13.3	6.7	-
Countries in transition	38.7	41.1	44.3	32.5	18.0	20.1	12.0	11.9	2.2
Asia	46.7	33.3	73.3	73.3	33.3	13.3	33.3	6.7	1.7
Africa	40.0	21.7	40.0	38.3	18.3	11.7	16.7	6.7	1.7
Latin America	56.0	53.6	44.0	26.4	29.6	18.4	9.6	0.8	-
Total	**45.2**	**38.5**	**42.7**	**33.0**	**20.2**	**17.4**	**16.1**	**7.4**	**2.0**
Assault/Threat									
Western Europe	21.1	15.3	9.3	1.0	9.4	5.8	7.8	13.6	-
New World	23.4	14.3	10.0	-	14.3	-	10.0	12.2	-
Countries in transition	45.3	42.1	24.2	9.5	13.5	21.7	12.7	9.8	0.6
Asia	31.3	25.0	37.5	12.5	31.3	25.0	18.8	-	-
Africa	44.7	17.0	34.0	10.6	14.9	17.0	12.8	19.1	-
Latin America	50.0	44.9	34.6	6.4	25.6	29.5	11.5	2.6	-
Total	**36.0**	**26.4**	**24.9**	**8.0**	**18.2**	**19.8**	**12.3**	**11.5**	**0.6**

coverage is low, victims will have a substantial economic stake in reporting in order to retrieve stolen property or receive some compensation from the offender who needs to be identified and brought to justice.[4]

Victims of burglary from the developed world are more sensitive to other indicators of police performance such as providing appropriate information and the speed or slowness of the police in arriving at the place of the crime.

Victims of robbery across the globe tend to emphasise that the police "*did not do enough*" (ranging from 40% in the New World and in countries in transition up to 56% in Latin America) and "*were not interested*" (from a peak of 54% in Latin America to 22% in Africa). More than 70% of the victims of robbery in Asia are dissatisfied with the police because the offender was not found and the goods were never recovered. Around 40% of the victims of robbery from Africa, Latin America and countries in transition express the same view. These two reasons for dissatisfaction are less prominent among the victims of robbery from Western Europe and the New World, although the latter gives more importance to the offender being caught rather than to the goods being recovered.

The victims of assault/threats, particularly in countries in transition, single out that the reasons for dissatisfaction with the police reaction to reporting the crime have to do with the police not doing enough and not finding the offender. In addition, victims complain that the police were incorrect/impolite, which is more characteristic of the victims' evaluation of police attitudes in countries in transition. This factor indicates certain features of police culture that lacks respect for the particular needs and expectations of victims of violence.

On the global level, less than half of the respondents are satisfied with the police in controlling crime locally, even though those who are satisfied are more than those who are not (Table 7). In the New World a large majority of the respondents (76%) are satisfied with the police in controlling crime; this is also the case with citizens from Western Europe (54%) and Asia (58%). On the other hand, more than half of the respondents from Africa (52%), 40% from countries in transition and as many as 70% from Latin America are not satisfied with the police job in controlling crime locally.

It should be noted that the lowest levels of citizens' satisfaction with the police are exhibited in Latin America and in countries in transition. However, it should also be noted that the largest percentage of "don't knows" is found in countries in transition. This can be explained by the fact that, during the period in which the 1992 ICVS was carried out, and - in some countries - during the period when the 1996 ICVS was administered, the police were undergoing changes as to their mandates and organisation.

Table 8 shows that in the countries in transition that participated in both sweeps of the ICVS, the general level of satisfaction with the police controlling crime locally has, contrary to expectations, either decreased or remained at the same level. There were indeed some slight improvements in the citizens' evaluation in Estonia, Russia, and the Slovak and Czech Republics, but there was also a decrease in satisfaction both in Poland and Slovenia. As a matter of fact, what is really surprising is the still very high level of those that could not or refused to evaluate police performance in controlling crime locally. In both sweeps of the survey, with the exception of Slovenia in 1992, there was no country in transition in

Table 11.7 Satisfaction with police in controlling crime locally, by regions (1996)

	Yes, good job	No, not a good job	Don't know
Western Europe	54.0	25.6	20.4
New World	76.0	15.1	8.9
Countries in transition	23.2	40.0	36.7
Asia	58.3	30.7	11.0
Africa	41.1	51.7	7.2
Latin America	21.9	69.6	8.5
Total	**45.8**	**38.8**	**16.8**

Table 11.8 Police do a good job: countries in transition, 1992-1996

	Good job		Not a good job		Don't know	
	1992	1996	1992	1996	1992	1996
Czech Republic	11.6	16.9	32.8	32.7	55.6	50.4
Estonia	9.4	15.9	54.3	46.1	36.3	38.0
Georgia	1.0	25.5	12.5	47.1	86.4	27.4
Poland	24.8	18.3	49.4	49.0	25.7	32.7
Russia	7.5	10.2	44.7	47.7	47.8	42.1
Slovak Republic	19.2	20.2	27.3	28.7	53.5	51.1
Slovenia	55.3	41.3	20.3	35.7	24.4	23.0
Albania	-	44.2	-	15.9	-	39.9
Belarus	-	19.1	-	33.5	-	47.3
Bulgaria	-	23.0	-	37.0	-	39.2
Croatia	-	37.9	-	29.5	-	32.6
Hungary	-	21.5	-	35.4	-	43.1
Kyrgyzstan	-	12.0	-	52.1	-	35.9
Latvia	-	14.6	-	36.0	-	49.3
Lithuania	-	14.1	-	65.7	-	20.2
Macedonia	-	34.7	-	39.0	-	26.3
Mongolia	-	24.7	-	36.4	-	39.0
Roumania	-	28.1	-	53.0	-	18.9
Ukraine	-	15.6	-	37.7	-	46.3
Yugoslavia	-	25.5	-	42.7	-	31.7

which the majority of the citizens were satisfied with the police, averaging some 23% of satisfied and some 40% of dissatisfied.

In 1992, apart from Slovenia, the highest level of satisfaction was expressed in Poland (one quarter). In 1996, again Slovenia was followed by Albania (the survey was carried out before the most recent Albanian crisis), Croatia, Macedonia (above 30%) and then Romania, Mongolia, Bulgaria, Yugoslavia and the Slovak Republic (above 20%). However, it should be noted, that among these countries, more than half of the respondents in the Slovak Republic did not evaluate the police performance. This was the case in Albania, Bulgaria and Mongolia with some 40%, and in Croatia and Yugoslavia with some 30%. Around half of the respondents did not evaluate police performance in the Czech Republic, Latvia and Ukraine. In other countries the "don't knows" are also high (averaging 20%).

Other factors related to police performance also have a lot to do with citizens' satisfaction.

According to the results of ICVS corruption is widely spread out in particular in developing world and countries in tranistion. Consequently, the citizens in those parts of the world are at a higher risk of being victimized by corrupt public administration. Obviously, it should be noted that corruption is a process and a relationship in which citizens are involved in different ways but most frequently in two of them. First, in order to effect their legitimate rigths and interests which, due to the malfunctioning of the public administration and/or complexity of regulation, they are not able to realise through normal channels and on time. Second, to realise their specific interests, which may not be legitimate, they tend to utilise corruptible public administration. In countries in transition corruption ranks as the third most common form of citizens' victimization after consumer fraud and theft from car. Sites from the Commonwealth of Independent States such as Tbilisi (Georgia), Bishkek and Osh (Kyrgyzstan) and Moscow (Russia) exhibit the highest levels, followed by Belgrade (Yugoslavia), Riga (Latvia), Tirana (Albania) and Kiev (Ukraine). The lowest levels of bribary are recorded for Budapest (Hungary), urban Estonia and Ljubljana (Slovenia).

Two patterns appear evident. First, the levels of corruption in public adminis-tration are lower (on average) in those countries in transition that have reached notable levels of change of both political and economic character and most prob-ably have improved on their public administration, too. Second, from an interna-tional comparative perspective the average reporting level for corruption is the lowest in countries in tranistion. This has much to do with the type of public officials involved in bribery and the relationshiop between citizens and public administration. Among the public officicals involved in corruption in countries in transition the most frequently reported are police officers, particularly in Russia, Bulgaria, Georgia, Yugoslavia, Croatia, Lithuania and the Slovak Republic. Conse-quently, there is a rather substantial correlation (0.426) between the level of citizen's satisfaction with police work and the level of police officials' involvement in cor-ruption. In other words, the higher the level of police involvement in corruption the lower the level of citizens' satisfaction with police performance.

There is a moderate positive correlation between satisfaction with the police in controlling crime locally and frequency in local patrolling (0.349), although it is higher in both the developing world (0.382) and countries in transition (0.376) than in the industrialized world (0.165). In all likelihood, respondents in those parts of the world attach more importance to the presence of police locally in evaluating their performance in controlling crime locally. It might be the case that the citizens of the developing world and countries in transition consider that frequent police patrolling would deter crime and meet a number of their expectations such as finding and arresting offenders, recovering stolen goods and arriving speedily at the place of the crime. In addition, the citizens in countries in transition to a larger extent than citizens from the industrialised world are concerned that a burglary will occur within the next year. Therefore, fear of burglary in the near future also contributes to dissatisfaction with the police in controlling crime locally and supports the view that more frequent patrolling might be both deterrent as well as effective in "stopping crime", finding the offender and recovering the stolen property.

Discussion

The lowest levels of citizens' satisfaction with the police are exhibited in countries in transition and Latin America. Furthermore, reporting to the police of cases of robbery and assault is among the lowest in the comparative perspective although this is not the case for burglaries; the propensity to report to the police has not increased in most countries in transition. Moreover, corruption in public administration, including the police, is still widespread in countries in tranistion, and the levels of citizens' satisfaction with police are also negatively affected by police involvement in corruption. Thus, the two very important and most powerful indicators of changes in terms of confidence building between citizens and the police in countries in transition (satisfaction with police and reporting to police) do not provide a satisfactory picture.

The evaluation of police performance seems to be a rational process within a given context. Victims' expectations of interested and efficient treatment from the police in the developed world reflect a concern with citizens' rights, good service delivery by the police, and reliance on insurance mechanisms for damage recovery. The recovery of stolen property and bringing offenders to justice is the rational response of victims in less affluent, less "insured" and more crime-ridden societies. There is no doubt that satisfaction with the police is higher in the developed world and in the more affluent regions. Here, other public services are also probably more accessible and of a better quality.

In terms of crime prevention and control, the ICVS confirms that public safety is still very much police business, and that citizens in countries in transition expect more police presence and more police efficiency, as a minimum. Seeking safety, less crime and less fear of crime is a process in which all parties have a role to play.

There appears to be a substantial relationship between satisfaction with police performance, crime reporting, frequency of patrolling and corruption. These findings strongly support the idea that an elementary requirement for good policing in crime prevention consists in systematic police presence and less-corruptibility of public administration, which increase both the feeling of safety among citizens and satisfaction with the police. Needless to say, these are both in turn important for public security. An increased feeling of security that has to do with police presence increases public satisfaction with police as a reduced corruptibility of police increases public confidence in the police. This is not a matter of more investment in the number of personnel and/or equipment, or rather not only that. It is much more a matter of a more rational policy for the allocation of resources, and it is very much a matter of a general democratisation of public institutions and services to be made sensitive to the needs of the clients and accountable to the public. It is also a matter of changes in the culture of the police-citizen relationship. Such a change requires, at the same time, both more and less than what conventional skill-related training, better equipment and other types of assistance are able to provide for.

There is still much dissatisfaction with the police, particularly in terms of the ways in which they deal with reported cases and control residential areas. The fear that a burglary will occur in the near future is widely diffused. Despite investments in police reform, the overall results as evaluated by citizens and victims are far from satisfactory. Citizens are concerned with outcomes, everyday police behaviour and the police culture in general. All these take place in a wider context of the socio-economic and political changes and the development of service orientation and practice of public administration, including the police. The results of the ICVS clearly indicate that democratization process calls for higher levels of accountability of public administration, police included. Therefore, police reform must include mechanisms to provide both for the internal (within police) and external (vis-à-vis the public) accountability. Needless to say police need to develop new criteria for measuring its own performance one of them being the level of citizens' satisfaction and trust.

The police should concentrate on improving outcomes of the organization: lowering the victimization rate, improving the perceived safety and the level of safety problems experienced by the population, preventing public order problems and improving confidence in the police. Reaching these objectives is a rational measure of police performance and evaluation. The citizens' evaluation of the police is a rational reflection of crime concerns and police behaviour in servicing the community. For crime prevention and control and for justice in society it is at least no less important than any other device developed for the internal measurement of police success. There is still much to be desired in changing the police culture and improving police-community relations in countries in transition.

Ugljesa Zvekic, Ph.D., Criminologist, Regional Advisor, Crime Prevention and Criminal Justice, UN Office for Drug Control and Crime Prevention, S. Africa; Scientific Counsellor, Institute of Criminological and Sociological Research, Belgrade, Yugoslavia, Honorary Professor, University of Hull, UK , Visiting Professor, Faculty of Law, University of Belgrade, Yugoslavia; author and editor of publications related to the judicial profession, informal crime control, policing, alternatives to imprisonment, probation, and international victim survey in countries in transition and developing countries.   Zvekic

References

Alvazzi del Frate, A. (1998). *Victims of Crime in the Developing World.* Rome: UNICRI.

Findlay, M. and Zvekic, U. (1993). *Alternative Policing Styles: Cross-cultural Perspective*. Deventer, Boston: Kluwer.

Hatalak, O., Alvazzi del Frate, A. and Zvekic, U. (Eds.) (1998). *International Crime Victim Survey in Countries in Transition: National Reports*. Rome: UNICRI.

Mayhew, P. and van Dijk, J.J.M. (1997). *Criminal Victimisation in Eleven Industrialised Countries*. The Hague: WODC.

Van Dijk, J.J.M. (1994). 'Who is afraid of the crime victim: criminal victimisation, fear of crime and opinions on crime in an international perspective'. Paper presented at the World Society of Victimology Symposium. Adelaide, Australia, 21-26 August 1994.

Van Dijk, J.J.M. and Mayhew, P. (1992). *Criminal Victimisation in the Industrialised World: Key Findings of the 1989 and 1992 International Crime Surveys*. The Hague: Ministry of Justice of the Netherlands.

Van Dijk, J.J.M., Mayhew, P. and Killias, M. (1990). *Experiences of Crime Across the World: Key Findings from the 1989 International Crime Survey*. Deventer: Kluwer Law and Taxation.

Zvekic, U. (1997). 'Les attitudes des victimes envers la police et la punitivité: résultats des sondages internationaux de victimisation'. *Revue internationale de criminologie et de police technique, /*' Attitudes of victims of crime towards police and punishment: the results of the International Crime Victim Survey. International review of Criminology and Police Technique/, Vol. I, Janvier-Mars /January-March.

Zvekic, U. (1998). *Criminal Victimisation in Countries in Transition*. Rome: UNICRI.

Zvekic, U. and Alvazzi del Frate, A. (1995). *Criminal Victimisation in Countries in the Developing World*. Rome: UNICRI.

Notes

1   Fifteen countries took part in the first (1989) ICVS, including the cities of Warsaw (Poland) and Surabaya (Indonesia). The second (1992/94) ICVS covered eleven industrialised countries, thirteen developing countries and six countries in transition. Full details of the 1989 and 1992 surveys in industrialised countries are reported in van Dijk *et al.*, (1990) and in van Dijk and Mayhew (1992). Further information and reports on the 1992 ICVS, including six countries in transition, are presented in Alvazzi del Frate *et al.* (1993).

2   The lowest response rates were observed in Lithuania (53.9%) and the Slovak Republic (55.9%). In all the other countries in transition the response rates were above 73% (Croatia).

3   For the results of the 1992-94 ICVS related to policing, see Zvekic (1997).

4   For the preliminary analysis related to a restricted sample of countries in transition, see Zvekic (1996).

*   Regional Advisor, Crime Prevention and Criminal Justice, United Nations Office for Drug Control and Crime Prevention, 527 Church Street, P.P.Box , 26088, Arcadia 0007 Pretoria, South Africa. Tel: +27 12 41 8971 Fax: +27 12 341 8969; E-mail: "Ugi Zvekic" <uzvekic@hotmail.com>

12 Police, Security & Democracy: A Police Perspective of the Russian Experience During Times of Transition

Alexander Yelin

Abstract

This paper presents current problems in the development of the police force in Russia since Perestroika from the practitioner's point of view and outlines key areas where urgent measures need to be taken in order to ensure further democratization of policing. In the early '90s some radical changes were made to the law-enforcement system of Russia, but later on the system slipped back into stagnation. The way to more democratic policing is through ensuring openness in police work, its availability for public scrutiny, and community involvement.

Key Words: Organized crime, corruption, democratization of police work, reforms, criteria for evaluating the performance of police, human rights, public opinion

Introduction

Prior to presenting and discussing issues facing Russian police during this difficult period of transition, its important to provide some preliminary explanations. First, this article is essentially a critique. It would, of course, be easier and safer to write about achievements and successes in combating crime in the context of developing democracy in Russia rather than talking about unresolved problems and contradictions. However, *the ship of Russian police* is so much decayed and worn out that it would be unethical for a professional who does care for his work to pretend that nothing serious is happening and by doing so follow the mainstream official policy. What we need is an informed discussion of the reasons for the crisis and what emergency measures need to be taken in order to overcome it. But it is not my intention to cast a shadow on the Russian police, most of whom are honest and brave professionals despite the difficulty of their lives.

Secondly, I am not a representative of the Federal Ministry of the Interior (MVD) or any of its research divisions. The reader is offered a practitioner's view of the problems existing in law enforcement and policing in a provincial, fairly typical region of Russia. Most of the factual material in this paper is, thus, of a regional character. This makes it necessary to introduce briefly the region of Sverdlovsk Oblast of Russia.

Sverdlovsk Oblast is located in the central part of Russia, in the Ural Mountains separating Europe from Asia. Its area is 194,300 square kilometers. The region is highly urbanized, with about 90 % of its population (4.5 million people) living in urban areas. The largest cities are Ekaterinburg (the region's administrative center with a population of 1,350,000 people), Nizhni-Tagil, and Kamensk-Uralsky.

The region is one of the country's industrial strongholds (it ranks third in industrial output after Moscow and St.-Petersburg), a center of mining, metallurgy and machine-building industries in Russia. The region is rich in mineral resources, including iron, copper, nickel ores, bauxites, gold and platinum; it boasts one of the largest deposits of emeralds.

Sverdlovsk Oblast possesses a high research and cultural potential. Thus, in Ekaterinburg alone there are 16 higher educational institutions and the Ural branch of the Russian Academy of Sciences.

Internationally, Sverdlovsk Oblast is sadly known for the fact that in 1918 the Bolsheviks killed the royal family in Ekaterinburg. Also, it is the home of Boris Yeltsin, the first democratically elected President of Russia.

A Summary of the History of Russian Police

Peter the Great is considered to be the founder of police in Russia. In 1718 he introduced the position of Police General, determined the numbers, structure and functions of the police forces, and set a regulation stating the rights and duties of police ranks. The specific feature of the Russian police of that time was that they performed not only policing functions (maintaining law and order, detecting criminals) but also investigation and imposition of punishment for some of the offences. The police system was then regularly reviewed and adapted to allow for new realities. In 1802 a Ministry of the Interior was set up, which incorporated the police force as well.

One of the landmarks in the development of the Russian police was the setting up of a political police in 1826, the so-called "Third Department of His Imperial Majesty's Office". This is how the Tsar responded to the December 1825 uprising of the guardsmen regiments in St. Petersburg who demanded the introduction of a constitutional monarchy.

Radical changes in the Russian law enforcement system were brought about by the 1858-1862 Reform whereby the police forces were separated from investigation and criminal justice functions. The task of the police was limited to detecting and detaining criminals and gathering preliminary evidence. The job of further investigation was placed on independent criminal justice investigators. The police itself was divided into two parts: general police forces and detective forces. The first of them had their own tasks within their assigned geographic boundaries. The second were subordinated to the central police agency and were engaged in investigating serious crimes using operational techniques. In 1890 the first criminological units were set within the investigation branch of the police.

Normal development of the Russian police was interrupted by the 1917 revolution. During the years preceding that event the police forces had been used to combat revolutionary activities, which provoked a negative attitude towards the police amongst the public. Thus, after the dethronement of the Tsar the first democratic government (February to October 1917), the communist regime (after October 1917) took measures to liquidate the old police forces and set up new ones.

The starting point for Soviet police (called 'militia') is considered to be November 19th, 1917 when Lenin, the Bolshevik leader, signed the document "On Setting Up Workers' Militia". This date is now an official police holiday in Russia.

The first period of Soviet power was dominated by Utopian ideas as to the contents, forms and methods of policing. It was believed that armed units of workers and peasants were able to cope with the task of policing if released from work for a certain period of time. But life proved necessary to set up a professional police. In October 1918 the People's Commissariat of the Interior was re-formed into the Main Police Department. Structurally it had units responsible for crime detection and detention, information, criminology, patrolling, etc.

As the scope of work increased new police forces were set up such as railway police (1919), factory guards (1924), juvenile delinquency prevention (1935), traffic police (1936), and economic police (1937). In 1963 the police were given authority to do most types of investigations, ranging from work at the scene of the crime to the presentation of the case to the court; and corresponding investigation units were set up.

During the Soviet period, policing had its own specific features such as:

- being politically directed and actually managed by the communist party;

- being secondary as compared with the KGB;

- being dually subordinated: vertically, to the Ministry of the Interior, and horizontally, to local authorities.

The peak of development of Soviet police was reached in the early 1980's. The Ministry of the Interior then was a powerful, well organized mechanism whose leaders were connected with the top officials of the country by personal friendship (Minister Nikolai Shchelokov was a friend of Leonid Brezhnev, Secretary General of the Communist Party) and family ties (Yuri Churbanov, First Deputy Minister of the Interior, was married to Galina Brezhneva, Leonid Brezhnev's daughter). It was considered to be prestigious to work in the police, and they were well paid.

However, as often happens, power based on personal ties proved to be weak. The chiefs of police had a lot of enemies who were waiting for an opportunity to get even. The opportunity presented itself in November 1982 when Leonid Brezhnev died. The defeat was quick and effective. In 1983, Shchelokov and his team were removed from office and their places were occupied by people from the KGB led by Vasily Fedorchuk. These leaders took a lot of prompt but thoughtless action, and serious damage was caused to the organizational structure of the police, which, admittedly, was fairly good. Thus, they reduced patrol forces and closed the crime prevention service. Therefore when in 1986 Mikhail Gorbachev removed Fedorchuk from office and appointed professionals to manage the police, it was generally received as a belated but correct decision.

In general, it should be stated that by the beginning of *Perestroika* a sufficiently effective system of crime prevention had been developed, which was evidenced by low crime rates (from 1981 to 1998 the number of reported crimes increased by only 12.2 %).

Approaching the Critical Line

Cardinal changes in the dynamics and structure of crime in Russia began in the late 1980's. After 1988 the number of recorded crimes increased by an average of 25 % every year to 2,760,000 in 1992. Growth in crime was observed in other republics of the USSR as well. In Ukraine, for instance, the number of crimes increased from 242,974 in 1988 to 480,478 in 1992, an increase of 97.7 %; in Byelorussia the increase was from 48,755 to

96,637 or by 98.5 %. However, Russia was worse off in terms of the number of crimes per 100,000 population. In 1992 it amounted to 921 in Ukraine, 937 in Byelorussia and 1,856.5 in Russia (Crime and Offences: Collection of Statistics, 1992).

Within the context of that general increase in crime, the proportion of serious and violent offences grew at a faster rate. Thus, over that period of time the number of aggravated assaults and robberies increased 3.8 times (Crime and Offences: Collection of Statistics, 1992).

There were also qualitative as well as quantitative changes in crime. The growing gap between the rich and the poor brought about what can be called "crimes of the poor" and "crimes of the rich." Increasing social deprivation was accompanied by an obvious growth in domestic violence, hooliganism, and alcohol-related offences. Well-off citizens found themselves under a serious threat. Material wealth became an object of criminal intent not only for petty criminals, but for master criminals, different sorts of swindlers, corrupt officials, and organized crime as well.

Throughout the country and in its industrial centers in particular, organized criminal groups were emerging, which very soon started fighting for influence and for a share in the 'property'. As early as 1990 organized crime was responsible for 3,315 criminal offences in Russia. In 1992 the police of Sverdlovsk Oblast had information on 59 actively working organized criminal gangs, totaling up to a thousand members. The year 1992 proved to be the bloodiest in the years of fighting between the clans, and the number of victims of armed clashes reached several dozens. What follows is my brief review of the main developments in organized crime in Sverdlovsk Oblast.

During those early years of the transition period of three large criminal gangs emerged in the region. The most influential was the gang nicknamed "Central" by the police (led by Oleg Vaguin, Nikolai Shirokov and Mikhail Kuchin). In addition to using criminal methods for making money (racket, fraud, prostitution, etc.) this gang was establishing extensive contacts with authorities in order to set up lawful businesses. The interests of the gang covered insurance, banking, and trade. One of the first Russian casinos, "Katarinenburg", was also controlled by the Centrals.

The second gang, in terms of influence, was the Uralmash, named after the major factory "Uralmash" located in the same district where the gang was operating. It was led undividedly by Grigory Tsyganov, who had gathered together his friends with whom he had grown up and played sports with. The structure and ideology of the grouping was strongly reminiscent of the Sicilian mafia clans with their strict discipline and absolute authority of the leader combined with mutual help and care for each member of the organization.

The third place was occupied by the "Blues" as nicknamed by the police. It was headed by the people who stuck to the traditions and rules of criminal leaders of the past, the so-called "thieves-at-law". These were engaged in purely criminal activities, including robberies, 'banditism', and extortion. To be able to provide support to members of the organization the Blues set up and are still running a special pool of funds ("obshchak"), which is formed from deductions from criminal gains.

In the early 1990s an armed fight for influence began between the Centrals and the Uralmash. It started in July 1991 with the killing of Grigory Tsyganov, who was shot through the window in his flat on the ground floor. It is believed that the killing had been organized by Oleg Vaguin. The killing did not destroy the Uralmash gang. On the contrary, they reorganized and got stronger. They set up an effective attack force armed with automatic weapons and shoulder-fired rockets. It was headed by Kurdyumov and Terentyev. Konstantin Tsyganov, Grigory Tsyganov's brother, took over general leadership.

In 1992-1994 nearly all the leaders of the Centrals were killed. On October 26, 1992 Oleg Vaguin himself and his three bodyguards were gunned to death in the elite housing estate located close to the regional administration and police headquarters. In 1993, in Budapest, Nikolai Shirokov was gunned to death in his own house and his plane blasted at the airport. In February 1994, Mikhail Kuchin was shot dead from in Ekaterinburg when driving out of his house.

As a result, the Centrals lost their influence in the criminal world and the gang broke up. The Uralmash gang, on the contrary, occupied the dominant position and felt so strong that in 1993 members of the gang fired grenades at the building of the organized crime police force and the regional administration in response to the temporary detention of their leader Konstantin Tsyganov.

Over the same years:

- the new kinds of crime such as murder, racketeering, kidnapping, and criminal bombings became widespread;

- the non-public sector of the national economy was affected by crime at birth and

- corruption was growing at an unprecedented pace.

All this threw the people into a state of shock. In a public opinion survey carried out in Ekaterinburg in March 1993 by the Institute of Social Studies and Technologies, 83 % of the respondents named growth of crime as their main concern and 74 % stated that power in the city belonged to the mafia who, they said, had bought all the officials (Mafia in Ekaterinburg). People demanded that urgent measures be taken to establish law and order.

The Answer is Modernization and Democratization.

Realizing that crime was becoming a real threat to the country, the government, somewhat belatedly, took a number of legislative, organizational, and financial measures to restructure the law enforcement mechanism. This was made possible to a great extent by Boris Yeltsin, who succeeded in the early 1990's in consolidating the democratic forces of Russia and led them towards further democratic reforms in the country and in its state machinery. Western countries, where respect for human rights is the main principle in police work, provided useful support.

First, efforts were made to bring legislation into conformity with the basic international documents such as the 1948 General Declaration of Human Rights, the 1984 Convention Against Torture and Other Cruel, Inhumane or Humiliating Treatment and Punishment, the 1979 Code of Behaviour for Law Enforcement Officials, and the Code of Principles of Protection in Case of Detention or Imprisonment in any Form.

Thus, in May 1992 amendments were made to the Criminal Justice Code of Russia ensuring protection of personal rights and freedoms in the criminal justice process. It is now a law that a person placed under arrest has a right to appeal and to demand a judicial check of his or her detention for lawfulness and validity.

The atavistic provisions of the Criminal Code and other legislative acts dating back to the old command system were abolished. Specifically, criminal liability for commercial intermediation and private business was cancelled.

The president of Russia used his law-making powers extensively. Thus, for instance, his decree of April 4, 1992 "On the Struggle against Corruption in the Civil Service System" officially recognized, for the first time, the presence of corruption in the state apparatus, described forms of corruption in civil service and formulated preventative measures. During that period of time the practice of developing federal and regional anti-crime programs was started. Those programs were aimed at co-ordination primarily.

The former Soviet system of law-enforcement and supervision, dominated by the communist party, was radically reformed. Specifically, communist party committees and the People's Supervision Committee, which had held great power in the area of law enforcement, ceased to exist; and the KGB was profoundly restructured. New agencies were not established (tax inspection and tax police, and Counting Chamber). in parallel, and the customs forces were strengthened. All of these reforms created favorable conditions for further democratization of police work.

The police force itself was significantly modernized

In April 1991 the Federal Law "On Police" was adopted. It proclaimed a new hierarchy of priorities in policing, the first priority being personal safety and protection of all forms of property rather than only state property. According to the new law the police were divided into two main parts: criminal investigation police and public security police. The first one was to be financed from the federal budget and it was assigned special functions, including serious crime prevention and detection, and criminal investigation. The public security police service was to carry out a wider spectrum of functions, including the enforcement of law and order, traffic policing, crime prevention, managing minor and administrative offences and a number of others functions. This service was to be financed by regional and local authorities. The law determined the rights and duties of the police, set a legal framework for their activities and for the use of weapons and other special means such as handcuffs, batons, and gas. It should be noted that it was a very progressive and democratic act for that period of time.

In response to the challenges posed by crime, the law-enforcement system had to restructure its police force, and new divisions were established. In 1988 the Federal Ministry of the Interior set up special police forces (OMON in Russian abbreviation) and organized anti-crime squads to deal with public disorder and to conduct special operations. In 1990 Interpol opened its national bureau in Russia. The following year the Federal Ministry of the Interior ordered that drug squads and technical intelligence services be set up in all regional divisions of the country. The police strength was thus increased drastically. For example, in 1993 an additional 118,000 policemen were recruited on the funding provided by the federal government. Thus, the organized crime service was increased 3.5 times and it was provided with rapid response forces for conducting operations and dealing with armed resistance in all of Russia (A.P.Mordovets). The technical facilities and equipment were improved, and salaries and wages were also appreciably raised.

All of these measures had a positive effect on 'law and order' - the crime rate remained stable for several years and from 1992 to 1996 the number of recorded crimes in Russia was reduced by 6.3 % (from 2,760,652 to 2,625,081). The work of the police became more dynamic and more effective. From 1993 to 1996 the number of detected crimes increased by more than 500,000 943/4 %), and the number of sentenced criminals increased from 1,262,737 to 1,618,394 (by 355,000) (1996 - Crime and Offence).

The police were liberated from the stifling communist influence. In 1991 political departments and communist party committees were closed. The police had to adapt to working in a new, more democratic legal system characterized by a growing power of courts, lawyers and other democratic institutions.

It was, nevertheless, essential to continue reforms. Specifically, it was vitally important to update the legal framework in order to combat crime effectively and introduce changes to the law-enforcement and judicial systems in order to ensure persisting democratic changes.

Bureaucratic Revenge

Unfortunately, in the mid-90s reforms in the law-enforcement system were, in fact, suspended, and in many areas of law enforcement a return to the old practices took place. Mistakes in the economic policy and exorbitant expenses as a consequence of the military conflict in Chechnya resulted in a reduction in the funding made available for anti-crime programs to a minimum. An additional negative effect was brought about by a crisis in the implementation of democratic reforms in Russia as a whole. Of the major events that have taken place in recent years in the law enforcement system the two that are worth mentioning are:

- the introduction on January 1, 1997 of the new Criminal Code, and
- the transfer of the penitentiary system from the realm of the Interior Ministry to the Ministry of Justice.

In the Shadows of the Old Laws

Reforms in legislation have practically been stopped. As a result, the old legislative framework continues to impede an effective struggle against highly organized crime and corruption. On the other hand, the adoption of relevant laws is repeatedly postponed. In my opinion, there are two reasons for this:

- the supreme law-making body of Russia, the Federal Assembly, spends too much time on sorting out political struggle between various factions and fails to pay sufficient attention to law-making;
- the development of an effective law-enforcement framework is counteracted by influential forces, including organized crime, 'shadow' business, and corrupt government officials who make every effort to slow down the law-making process or stop it completely.

To illustrate this, in 1996 the draft laws "On the Struggle Against Corruption" and "On the Struggle against Organized Crime" were presented to the Federal Parliament (Duma), and since then these draft laws have been going through the vicious circle of endless consultations. In July 1997 the Criminal Procedures Code of the Russian Federation was adopted in its first reading. The second reading was planned for the first quarter of 1999 but has not yet been adopted. In October 1998 the Federal Parliament (State Duma) adopted the Law "On Counteracting the Legalization (Laundering) of Ill-Gotten Income." However, it was rejected by the upper house of the Legislative Assembly in the same year.

In the parliamentary portfolio of draft acts there are many other documents prepared by the law-enforcement agencies: the Draft Administrative Code of Russia, a draft law on state protection of witnesses and victims in organized crime cases; a draft law on the system of crime prevention, and a number of others. However, the police have to be guided by archaic, outdated acts, and, in particular, by the Fundamentals of Criminal Procedures Legislation of Russia adopted in 1958. In spite of the numerous amendments that have been made to it, this document remains essentially the same.

In their daily activities the police face various contradictions caused by outdated regulations, from which criminals benefit. Consider the following:

- The Criminal Procedure Code and the Code of Administrative Offences provide that "search and forfeiture" can be carried out in the presence of only two witnesses only. In many cases, however, it proves difficult to fulfil this requirement. For instance, it is dangerous to include witnesses in the attack groups during raids where weapons are likely to be used. Also, it is difficult to find two witnesses to carry out a search at night. In these and many other everyday situations the police are compelled either to waste time and effort on finding witnesses or to resort to falsification in which they put themselves at risk of prosecution.

- Problems are also posed by the regulation requiring that the accused and his or her lawyer be acquainted with the files of their criminal case upon the end of the investigation. Frequently this procedure allows serious criminals to extend the judicial process for many months and use this time to their advantage in order to take action and destroy the evidentiary base of the accusation.

- The word 'victim' is not part of Russian legislation. Instead, use is made of the word that translates into English as 'person who has suffered from an incident', and the legal status of such a person is insufficiently defined. Part 3 of Article 30 of the Federal Law "On Property" provides that "damage caused to the property owner as the result of a crime shall be recompensed by the state based on court decision". Assuming that this was true, people, full of hope, started claiming such damages from the state. The government, however, did not allocate any funds for this purpose; nor did it work out a mechanism for paying damages to victims. As a result, thousands of court resolutions have remained unsatisfied.

- The law does not stipulate protection for victims, witnesses, law-enforcement workers and judges who participate in proceedings against organized crime.

- The economic police also have much to complain about regarding current legislation. Consider, for instance, the law on banking activities in the Russian Federation.

In the Soviet Union, before Perestroika, there were only 5 banks, which were controlled by the state. With the development of a market-economy in the country the number of banks soared and reached 2,500 on March 1, 1995. However, such rapid development of the banking system was not offset by a corresponding legal framework for banking activities. *"From the very outset the law-makers set very liberal conditions for setting up commercial banks with the introduction in parallel of a limited system of controls over the registration or expansion of the share (charter) capital. At the same time, their investment, lending and deposit activities were not regulated by any clearly defined legal framework and antitrust law"* (A.I.Peshkov: 1996, p.64). The criminals were prompt in taking advantage of this situation and started using banks for money laundering, conducting fraudulent operations, obtaining never-to-be-repaid loans, and other criminal activities. Thus, between 1991 and 1994 the police and other law-enforcement agencies put a stop to the operation of 310 organized criminal gangss in the banking system of Russia (A.I.Peshkov: 1996, p.26). In 1997, the banking system of Russia fell victim to 9,051 crimes, including 2,793 frauds and 1,602 embezzlements (O.P.Stepanov: 1998, p.52).

The Russian banking law is still full of flaws which complicate the decriminalization of the banking sector for the police. Thus:

- the law does not oblige banks and other financial institutions to report on all suspicious transactions and large deposits in cash; nor does the law provide for a process for following up cash flows. As a result, it is virtually impossible to detect crimes connected with money laundering (Article 174, Criminal Code of Russia).

- the law does not define unambiguously the notion of confidentiality in banking operations. Article 25 of the Federal Law "On Banks and Banking Activity" contains but a short list of information that shall be considered confidential.

- confidential information can be requested from banks only *after* a criminal investigation has been started. However, such information is often necessary at the pre-investigation stage or for intelligence purposes. Banks, however, refuse to provide information referring to the letter of law.

- the law does not protect bank staff from prosecution for disclosing information on offences in banking activities to law-enforcement agencies.

- There are many contradictions between the various acts. For instance, the Criminal Code of Russia does not stipulate responsibility for the use of illicit drugs without prescription. At the same time, the new Federal Law "On Narcotic Drugs and Psychotropic Substances" adopted on 08.01.98 contains such a clause (item 40), and two years after its adoption this inconsistency has not yet been eliminated.

The Reform is Slipping

Russia's law enforcement crisis continues to worsen. This worsening situation is not only, or simply, a function of the State's lack of attention needed in order to effectively combat crime. There are many internal defects within the police system and today that threaten to reach critical mass.

Changing Interior ministers and chiefs of regional divisions, a typical Russian phenomenon, is having a negative effect on the continuity of management. Over the last four years (1996-1999), three federal Ministers and four heads of Sverdlovsk Oblast Interior Department have been replaced. Reasons for replacement are often associated with personal loyalty to the head of the regional executive authority rather than with with business, moral or managerial qualities. In Sverdlovsk Oblast the governor's resignations in 1994 and 1996 automatically led to resignations of the chiefs of police, experienced professionals, who now work elsewhere in equivalent or even higher posts.

Corruption scandals are getting 'louder' at all levels of the Interior system. In 1997 and 1998, as many as 44 cases of bribery and abuse of office were recorded in the police, mainly among senior and middle officers. (Statistical Report: Information Center of the Main Department of the Interior for Sverdlovsk, Oblast, NZSH3, 1998).

The Federal Ministry of the Interior has no reasonable long-term reform strategy. In 1996 it issued (Order No. 145 of 20 March 1996) a Conceptual Framework for Developing the MVD System of Russia, a draft strategy designed until the year 2005. That document did not 'survive' even two years as it became outdated and cannot be used as a guiding document now.

Being politically dependent, the police chiefs cannot allow themselves to take an objective, critical view of the problems that interfere with normal development of the police forces, a well documented characteristic of any inflexible, bureaucratic system that fears change. The way the above draft strategy was discussed is a vivid illustration of this. In its variant of the October 1995 draft strategy daringly declared that one of the basic reasons for the existing state of affairs in relation to crime was *"the low effectiveness of the law-enforcement agencies resulting from their fragmentation, loss of support among the public, outflow of professionals, low professionalism and performance discipline among the staff, legal, material, financial, personnel and social problems, and growing corruption in the state apparatus, including law-enforcement agencies. It should be stated that the MVD system of Russia has failed to adapt to new economic and social conditions of the transition period. Within the MVD system there are numerous problems whose resolution cannot be delayed any further. Its work demonstrates negative features that should be subject to decisive eradication"* (Discussion Document Prikaz Conceptsiya razvitiya organov vn del na period). However, the final version of the strategy approved in 1996 lacked the sharpness of these formulations, and self-criticism was reduced to one or two meaningless phrases which admitted corruption among individual employees.

Furthermore, it would be no exaggeration to conclude that the MVD system of Russia is becoming inundated in paperwork and bureaucracy. The passion for gathering information is turning into a mania. Thus, the Main Department of the Interior for Sverdlovsk Oblast used to send to the Federal Ministry of the Interior 4 monthly reports containing 1340 various items in 1994. Five years later, in 1999, the reporting volume increased to 7 reports containing 2717 items. In addition to this excessive but, nonetheless, systematic information, the MVD demands a lot of additional information, reports on the implementation of regulations, preventive operations, etc. The main burden of preparing such reports is borne by operational staff, who are distracted from their direct policing duties. Often reports are prepared formally, some of the figures may be made up; as a result, generalizations at the federal level provide a distorted view of the state of things in the regional divisions. There is no less bureaucracy at the regional level, where chiefs of police are involved in a turmoil of co-ordination conferences, board meetings, etc.

Resources are a growing problem. In 1994 the MVD supplied the Main Department of the Interior for Sverdlovsk Oblast with 112 motor vehicles; in 1998 this figure fell to

18. In 1999, a real petrol crisis affected the fleet. Centralized petrol supplies fell down to one tenth of the need, and the prices for petrol soared up 2-3 times. Because of the shortage of petrol all motor vehicles had to be withdrawn from operation excepting 24-hour services, and operational and patrol services.

The provision of police forces with means of communication has been halved in recent years. In 1992 the number of radio stations amounted to 63.8 % of the need, and in 1999 this figure fell to 38.3%. Moreover, up to half of the radio communication facilities have outlived their service life. This is creating insoluble problems in the management of police patrols.

Problems with equipment and consumables, and even stationery, compel chiefs of police to seek help from local magnates (who are not always on good terms with the law) or create and personally supervise various foundations which also provoke abuse and corruption. In 1997-1998 the regional branch of the police force (the public security police) in Sverdlovsk Oblast and in the majority of other regions of Russia were not getting their salaries for months on end. Those salary debts have not yet been fully paid up.

The dominance of bureaucracy, difficult working conditions and inadequate pay have almost destroyed the recruitment policy in Russia's MVD system. In Sverdlovsk Oblast, in 1998, one out of ten staff left the police and over the last five years almost half of the personnel were replaced. Ten years ago this would have been unimaginable for the Oblast that had always featured stable personnel (Stat otchet o sostave personala za 98 g).

The first to quit were professionals from lead services such as investigators, criminal detectives, economic crime detectives (who easily found jobs in the private sector); many of them joined criminal gangs and today they operate against the police ("Non_Governmental Security Structures" Kursiv Information Bulletin: 1997, No. 8, p.9).

These were replaced by people who educationally, morally or psychologically fail to meet the requirements set for the police. For example, according to the existing regulations, police inspectors should have a higher legal education only. Today, however, only 45 % of the inspectors in Sverdlovsk Oblast meet this criterion (82 % in 1988). A similar picture is observed in other services. (Statistical Report of the Main Department of the Interior for Sverdlovsk Oblast on Staffing Structure, 01.12.1999).

Poor training, the lack of practical experience in policing combined with the popular idea that the police enjoy unrestricted power, and the placing of the interests of the state and the police above the interests of ordinary people bring about malpractice and violations of human rights. From 1992 to 1998 there was a fivefold increase in reported cases of abuse of power (from 110 to 559) in Sverdlovsk Oblast. The actual number of such cases, however, is likely to exceed the above figures considerably (Statistical Report: Information Center of the Main Department of the Interior for Sverdlovsk, Oblast, NZSH3, 1998).

A Race Without Rules

One of the pitfalls that the Russian police force has fallen into is competition for formal performance indicators, a harmless thing at first glance. It is, however, most dangerous where the detection rate becomes the main criterion for judging performance.

During the Soviet period 'detection rate' was also number one amongst parameters describing police performance, and at that time detection rates soared to cosmic heights of 95-98% of reported crime (State of Crime and Organization of Struggle with It in Dnepropetrovsk, Sverdlovsk, Cherkassy and Novgorod". 1973: 126). The 'restructuring' (Perestroika) made adjustments to the official policy, and chiefs of regional divisions were allowed to show real figures. As a result, by 1992 detection rates in the country had fallen down to 46.9 %, and to 37.2 % in Sverdlovsk Oblast. (Stat sbornik 1986 and 1992)

However, common sense did not triumph for long, and the MVD system of Russia began to recoil back to the former practice. As a result, very soon detection rates started rapidly growing, and in 1998 it reached 74.4 % (an increase of 27.5 % against 1992), and in some regions, for instance in Tambov Oblast, it exceeded 90 percent (Statistical Book "State of Crime and Results of Struggle with it in the Russian Federation": 1998, No.12).

Regions in Russia are now in fierce competition for high detection rates. This competition is consciously encouraged by the MVD of Russia. Those who 'underperform' suffer powerful administrative pressure in the form of special controls, frequent inspections, hearings, and sanctions on police chiefs. Moreover, local features, crime rates and operating conditions are completely disregarded. It is, for instance, considered quite normal to compare the tiny North-Caucasian Republic of Karachayevo-Cherkessiya and industrially advanced Sverdlovsk Oblast.

The result of this policy is obvious. Today Russian police forces show little interest in quality, crime prevention, or public opinion. It is sufficient to have the detection rate above the Russian average or regional average in order to live in peace.

But this aspect of the problem presents only the top of the iceberg. The issue of criteria for evaluating performance is not internal to the police; it affects human rights. This manifests itself primarily in how crimes are detected. Struggling to expose criminals, the police often resort to falsifications, use unlawful methods for obtaining evidence, and allow other infringements (Report of the Human Rights Watch Representative for Sverdlovsk Oblast for 1998. Oblast Gazeta, 11 March 1999). This 'malpractice' often comes to light during the criminal justice process and renders the body of evidence inapplicable. In 1998 alone the courts of Sverdlovsk Oblast had to acquit 148 persons (102 in 1997); one out of ten cases submitted to the courts had to be discharged from criminal prosecution; 14 % of all criminal cases were returned for additional investigation because of the poor quality of evidence. Of equal, if not greater, concern is the fact that no one can tell how many guiltless people have been sent to prison?

This race for high detection rates provokes such gross violation of personal rights as concealing reported crimes from record. In fact, according to regulations the police are obliged to register each reported crime, but they may create all sorts of pretext in order to shirk from carrying out this mandated duty. As a rule, they would register crimes where criminals are known and there is no need to make an additional effort in order to raise the detection rate. Other crimes reported to the police may not be so fortunate. A range of clever tricks have been developed over the years for deceiving 'victims', Following are two of them:

- An officer on duty can convince the victim that the sum of damages is insignificant, the case will not be prosecuted anyway and there is, therefore, no need to spend energy and time on investigating the offence.

- In other cases the victim can be accused of having been imprudent (or reckless), which resulted in the crime or in its investigation being rendered impossible. The victim is thus discouraged from reporting the crime in writing. This occurs particularly frequently where the victim was drunk during the criminal attack or comes to the police station to report the crime after some time has already elapsed.

There is an even more widespread institutionalized negligence through the sheltering of undetected crime from records by making unjustified resolutions not to initiate a criminal investigation. In accordance with Russian criminal justice practice and legislation, some behaviors are not categorized as crime and do not lead to criminal investigation. For example, in cases where damages are small the police are allowed not to register misbehavior as a crime and, accordingly, criminal investigation is not started.

This 'legal' norm is widely applied. Thus, in 1998 there were 101,000 reported crimes not followed by any criminal investigation relative to 96,000 officially recorded crimes in Sverdlovsk Oblast. Often this loophole leads to violations of the law. Unethical officers would resort to all sorts of tricks to obtain a written statement from the victim that the damage was not serious and that the victim does not want the investigation to be initiated. In 1998 the prosecutor for Sverdlovsk Oblast, whose job is to supervise policing, had to intervene and reverse 3,307 such unfair decisions (2.9 % of all 'dishonored' cases) and initiate criminal investigation (Statistical Report: Information Center of the Main Department of the Interior for Sverdlovsk Oblast KAJDAL1, 1998).

There are many other ways to artificially raise the detection rate. All of them, however, result in violation of personal rights to protection and damages, unpunished crime; hypocrisy and permissiveness in the police. The Ministry of the Interior cannot (or, possibly, does not want) to correct this state of affairs. Mr. Sergei Stepashin, appointed as Interior Minister in 1998, formulated the task of adopting new criteria for evaluating performance in the police in accordance with democratic standards as his priority but he failed to implement it. One of the reasons for this could be the complexity of the issue of developing new approaches. However, the time that it is taking to move things forward creates a strong impression of unwillingness to change the existing state of things.

Boomerang

Considering the above noted problems, and the existence of many other problems as well, it becomes clear why the Russian police fail to do their job properly. This is, unfortunately, an indisputable fact despite growing police numbers! Between 1992 and 1998 the number of police officers in Sverdlovsk Oblast increased by 60.6%. Added to this is a considerable army of private guards and private security services (about 20,000 licensed and non-licensed people), who not only prevent various crimes, ranging from theft to fraud, but also help the police combat street crime by joint patrolling ("Non-Governmental Security Structures" Kursiv information Bulletin 1997 No. 8, p.8).

But all of these forces have failed to contain crime and protect the public from violence on top of the burden of political and social problems. In the autumn of 1998 the crime rate began to grow further, and in 1999 it increased by one fifth across Russia (Statistical Book: State of Crime and Results of Struggle with it in the Russian Federation 1999, No. 12).

It should be admitted that law-enforcement agencies can no longer control organized crime, which, according to the statistics, grew 8.5 times (from 3,315 to 28,500 offences) from 1990 to 1997 (Statistical Book: State of Crime and Results of Struggle with it in the Russian Federation: 1999, No. 12). The Russian government took unprecedented measures to suppress the Mafya but failed. For example, the President of the Russian Federation issued decree No. 1226, "On Urgent Measures to Protect Population Against Gangsterism and Other Manifestations of Organized Crime," on 14.06.1994, in which he authorized the law enforcement agencies to detain persons suspected to participation in organized crime for up to thirty days against three days of detention according to the prevailing law. This suppressive measure was applied to 2,000 suspects in Sverdlovsk Oblast between 1994 and 1996 but it did not do any harm to the local criminal gangs. Moreover, it was recognized that 138 persons, or 6.9 % of all such cases, were detained unnecessarily and had to be released (Temporary reports form, 66, 1996).

As a result, according to analysts from special services, not only has organized crime established control over the major industries of Sverdlovsk Oblast, but it has also made itself conspicuous on the political arena. For example, in May 1999 an influential political organization, "*OPS Uralmash*", was registered in Ekaterinburg. Among the founders of the organization there were individuals who either had a criminal record or were wanted for crimes, including Konstantin Tsyganov, suspected of a number of crimes. In the intelligence records they appear as leaders of an organized criminal gang. Alexander Khabarov, a representative of this clan, stood for the Federal Parliament of Russia (Duma) and failed to be elected by a narrow margin.

Other problems that the public is worried about and which the Russian police fail to resolve in spite of their apparent power and repressive measures made available to them is illegal production of alcohol, corruption in the state apparatus, and some others.

However, in the mid-90s the Russian government "*overlooked*" the need to continue work on creating an effective police force. Again, one is left with an impression that the authorities did not want any changes. Professional, technically well-equipped police could put a stop to criminal fights for influence, prevent people with a criminal record from entering power structures, and undermine corruption in the state apparatus. It is quite probable that certain circles are not interested in seeing the police forces and other law-enforcement agencies strengthened. The responsibility for the failure of the federal anti-crime programs and for the failure to adopt relevant laws rests with the supreme authorities of Russia - the President and the Federal Assembly as the supreme law - making body.

'*Inactivity*' returned as a boomerang and provoked a new upsurge of crime, leaving the public even less protected. In 1999 the number victims of crime in Sverdlovsk Oblast increased by 15.9 % (Statistical Book: State of Crime in Sverdlovsk Oblast, 1999, No. 12).

The inability of the police to achieve positive changes in their struggle with criminality has resulted in further loss of respect for them, which is confirmed by regular population attitude surveys conducted by the Main Department of the Interior for Sverdlovsk Oblast since 1997. Typically, the sample size of such surveys amounts to 5,000 respondents. These are internal regional police department surveys designed to provide management with a picture of what ordinary people think about the police and other facets of the criminal justice system. Though being rough and politically biased, these surveys nonetheless show that trust in the police is steadily going down, and discontent is growing. In 1997 more than half (52.4 %) of those who contacted police for help were satisfied with the action taken. Two years later this indicator went down to 43.7%. Over the same period of time the number of people who did not want to report crimes to the police increased by eight percent (from 29.4 % to 37.4 %). The number of people who witnessed wrongful action on the behalf of the police in performing their official duties remains high from year to year (around 40 %) Results of Population Surveys in Sverdlovsk Oblast for 1997 and 1998).

It is not surprising then that in answering the question *"Do you have trust in law-enforcement agencies?"* in 1997 20.3 % of the respondents said 'no' and in 1999 the number of such answers rose to 23.1%. People with a higher educational background grew even more distrustful - from 23.2 % to 31.6%.

In light of the above resultsone could question the Russian Interior Minister's statement at a multilateral conference in Strasbourg (France) in November 1998: "... *I can responsibly state... that the law-enforcement agencies of the Russian Federation are tackling the task of combating crime and maintaining law and order in the most effective way."*

Conclusion: No Alternative to Reforms

In assessing the condition of the Russian police, experts state that the extensive development option chosen by the Russian government as a priority had completely exhausted itself by the mid-90's, and the system slipped into a state of stagnation ("Cbornik mterialov por red: Abramkina 1997).

Discussions around the future of the MVD continue. There are two basic, irreconcilable positions on this issue. The first view is supported by the MVD officials and their supporters in various branches of state power. In short, they suggest giving the system a facelift without implementing any profound structural changes. The second position was formulated by A. Lopatin, member of the State Duma of Russia. In his opinion, the MVD in its present form is a weak, unguided organization squandering public money and being ineffective in carrying out the functions assigned to it. The US law-enforcement system is suggested as a model to follow, with its decentralization of the police forces and fragmentation of the law-enforcement system into functional services.

Mr. Lopatin suggests splitting up the MVD system into several parts; transferring the fire-fighting service to the Ministry of Emergencies and the passport service to the Ministry of Justice; and setting the MVD troops, the investigation service, and the organized crime service as independent federal agencies. At the city and district levels, the patrol services, traffic police, and area police inspectors should be reformed into municipal police forces subordinated to local authorities.

There is logic to Mr. Lopatin's approach. The Interior Ministry currently performs many functions that have nothing to do with combating crime and ensuring 'law and order'. In the MVD system, there are, for instance, sobering-up services, which duplicate public health services, or divisions of guards which are similar to private guard firms, etc. We should, however, be realistic. It would be impossible to implement such costly reforms within a short time considering the acute financial deficit problem that has affected the state budget of Russia. This could be a long-term goal.

In my opinion, the way towards a reformed MVD of Russia lies midway between the above extreme approaches, through optimizing the existing system and making it more effective and adapted to modern-day conditions. What needs to be done first is to develop a state strategy for combating crime and to adopt the laws that were mentioned above in order to create a normal legal framework for the operation of law-enforcement agencies.

In parallel, it would be essential to modernize and democratize all the components of the law-enforcement system, the criminal justice system and the penitentiary institutions. This is vitally important for the criminal justice system of Russia. Consider the following: currently there are only 15,700 judges and 31,000 assistant staff in Russian courts against the 35,700 budges and 225,000 assistant staff needed (Rossiyskaya Yustitsiya, 1999, No. 2, p.3). The lack of judges and assistant staff results in the inability of the criminal justice system to cope with increasing volumes of work, violating the right of citizens to effective protection and producing a negative effect on the functioning of the entire law-enforcement system.

It is essential to set up a national crime monitoring service that would be independent from the police and other law-enforcement agencies. This service should be empowered to control MVD statistics.

It is important to carry out a critical, in-depth, comprehensive and, most importantly, independent analysis of contemporary criminality in the country and of the performance of the MVD of Russia. The results of such analysis should be made available for a discussion between various interested parties (including the MVD, independent research institutions, parliamentary commissions, prosecutors, courts, etc.) with the aim of defining methods and means for overcoming the crisis. New criteria should be developed for evaluating the performance of police forces.

A number of organizational and structural changes need to be made as well. Thus, it would be reasonable to reduce support services (financial, maintenance, personnel management, etc.). Recently these services have been increasing more rapidly than operational staff directly involved in combating crime - between 1990 and 1996 the support services increased 1.9 times, whereas the detective services only 1.6 times; economic police grew 1.1 times (Statistical book of the Ministry of the Interior of Russia, 1997). Such disproportion has a negative effect on the ability of the police to combat crime.

Measures need to be taken to reduce the amount of unnecessary paperwork and the number of statistics and reports circulating between various levels of the MVD system.

It is essential to make reductions in the patrol police and traffic police service, however difficult this could be. The main rationale behind this suggestion is quality at the expense of quantity. There is no doubt that patrols and patrolling are an essential element of policing and western democratic policing in particular. Patrolling forces are often the first point of contact with the police for people. However, because the level of pay in Russian patrol services is, in fact, below any imaginable minimum, it is practically impossible to recruit proper patrolling staff that would meet statutory requirements. That is why negligence, oft times institutionalized, and corruption are so widespread in these services, whilst performance is very low. The limited resources that are allocated for patrolling need to be channeled into improving patrolling by reducing those who are not suitable for the service, and recruiting less but better-qualified staff who are offered higher salaries.

There is a need to create and maintain effective, flexible intelligence and information-gathering groups in operational divisions whose job would be to provide operational staff with required information. Currently, such information is fragmented between various services, and access to it is difficult.

In additional to the above technical and staffing issues, police work in Russia needs to be democratized further through making more open and available for public scrutiny, and empowering the community to exercise control over police activities.

To ensure openness, a range of measures need to be taken, including periodic parliamentary inspections with subsequent parliamentary general or committee hearings. Also, supervision boards could be set up, including representatives of the community and respected people who could control police forces at municipal and regional levels but also provide help in resolving social and financial problems in the police. It would be essential to carry out a review of the list of information relating to various aspects of police work, such of violations of human rights, police numbers, budgets, etc.

Community involvement in maintaining 'law and order' needs to be expanded. In the past communities were actively involved in combating crime. Thus, in March 1959 voluntary law-enforcement teams were set up at enterprises and district areas. People participating in such teams on a voluntary basis would patrol the streets together with the police in their free time. The main incentives for them for doing this type of work are ideological and organizational (pressure from local communist party committees) but also there are material incentives, including three additional days to annual holidays. After Perestroika this form of community involvement collapsed as soon as state support was withdrawn.

But life shows that without help from the community the police cannot do their work effectively. In response to the report presented by the Main Department of the Interior for Sverdlovsk Oblast, on March 19, 1996 the Legislative Assembly of Sverdlovsk Oblast adopted the law "On the Participation of the Population in Law-Enforcement in Sverdlovsk Oblast", an attempt to revive voluntary support. The law specified the status of such voluntary law-enforcement teams, the rights and duties of its members, and incentives. The law, however, failed to achieve its goal, primarily because the incentives stipulated in the law were purely declarative. Thus, for instance, local authorities do not have funds to be able to exempt voluntary supporters from municipal utility payments or to provide them with free fuel (in rural areas), or to make travelling in public transport free for them; private enterprise refuse to give additional holidays to their employees doing this work.

Thus, contrary to official reports stating a large number of voluntary teams and members, in reality these do not exist. For instance, in January 2000 Sverdlovsk Oblast reported to have about 300 voluntary law-enforcement teams totaling over 4000 members. However, the results of their work proved poor. In 1999 they only detained 7 criminals, whereas in 1980 the number of detainees was 608 (Report of the Main Department of the Interior for Sverdlovsk Oblast for 1999, p.10).

The above suggests that other forms of community involvement in the maintenance of 'law and order' need to be developed allowing for the new economic circumstances and the modern-day realities of life in Russia. Models can be provided by such western programs as "neighborhood watch", "call and get", etc.

The above is just a short list of changes that need to be made in the law-enforcement system of Russia. Without reform, without further steps towards democratization, openness, and community involvement, the police will not be able to overcome internal contradictions and rise to a new qualitative level in combating crime.

Lieutenant Colonel Alexander Yelin was born on 27 January 1958 in Kamchatka Peninsula, Russian Far East. In 1984 he graduated from Sverdlovsk Law School, and in 1996 from the Russian Interior Ministry's Academy (Moscow). A. Yelin joined the police in 1984; in 1996 he was appointed Deputy Chief-of-Staff of the Sverdlovsk Oblast Regional Interior Department. His current job is essentially around information analysis and organization at the Sverdlovsk Oblast Regional Interior Depart-

ment, one of the largest regional divisions in the law enforcement system of Russia. Lt.Col. Yelin has a number of publications on police management in special periodicals published by the Interior Ministry of Russia. He has also published many articles in local periodicals, including a series of articles under the heading "Police from A to Z", which was awarded a prize as the best material devoted to the work of the regional police in 1996. Lt.Col. Yelin is engaged in community work as well. Together with his colleagues he set up an NGO called "Center of Law Education", which conducts educational work among young people on preventing drug use and delinquency. Personally he

Yelin

has delivered hundreds of lectures at school in Ekaterinburg. His favorite pastime is reading fiction, and his favorite authors are Bulgakov, Dostoyevsky, and Russian poets of the 'Silver Age'. In painting his preference is French Impressionism. Married with a daughter of 14, Natasha.

Address: Lenin Prospekt 17, Ekaterinburg, 620022, Russia.
Telephone: 007(3432) 588518, 580513.
Fax: 007(3432) 587070

Notes and References

The Russian law defines the following terms for detention of people accused of crime for the period of investigation: up to two months with the sanction of the procurator of the city or district; up to 6 months with the sanction of the procurator of the Oblast; and up to 18 months by the Procurator General of the republic. However, the terms of confinement for the period of court proceedings is not regulated, and people can wait for the court to pass a decision for years. For instance, the Concept provided that by the end of 1996 municipal police should have been set up, subordinated to local authorities and funded by the latter; however, municipal police still has not been set up. And there are many more examples like this. For instance, unlawful detention based on the suspicion of a criminal offence; violation of terms of investigation set for criminal investigation; falsification of evidence, etc.

Botashev, K.H., 'To Raise the Effectiveness of the Struggle against Illegal Arms Trafficking', Operativno-Rozysknaya Rabota, 4(1998): 25-31 (in Russian).

Mordovets, A.P., 'On the State of Things and Measures in the Struggle against Organized Crime in the Russian Federation', Operativno-Rozysknaya Rabota, 1(1999): 8-23 (in Russian).

Opanasyuk I.V., 'Legal and Organizational Problems in the Struggle Against Corruption' in Issues in the Struggle Against Organized Crime and Corruption, Moscow, VNII MVD RF, 1996: 69-77 (in Russian).

'Report by Goryacheva S.P., Deputy Chair of the State Duma of the Federal Assembly of the Russian Federation', Vestnik MVD Rossiiskoi Federatsii, 2(1999): 27-30 (in Russian).

Demidov Yu.N., Mozzhukhin, A.V., 'UN Standards and Norms as a Basis for Law Making', Vestnik MVD Rossiiskoi Federatsii, 5(1994): 46-50 (in Russian).

Cherkashina Ye.I., 'Victims of Crimes Need Protection', Rossiiskaya Yustitsiya, 3(1999): 30 (in Russian).

Lopatin V.N.. 'On Reforms of Law-Enforcement Agencies of Russia' in Criminal Law Policy of Russia. Past, Present and Future, Vyp. 1, V.Abramkin (ed.), Moscow: Public Center for Facilitation of Reforms in Criminal Law, 1997: 39-40 (in Russian).

'Soviet Militia, History and Modernity', Moscow: Yuridicheskaya Literatura, 1987.

Vlasov B.I., Goncharov N.F., 'Organization of Crime Detection in Russia in the 9th – 20th Century', Parts 1-2, Moscow: MVD RF Republican Institute for Police Development, Domodedovo, 1997.

'Crime and the Organization of the Struggle against it in Dnepropetrovsk, Sverdlovsk, Cherkassy and Novgorod', Vestnik Shtabnoi Raboty, 9(1973): 123-148

Veselyi V.Z., Zhelezonv Yu.A., 'On the Results of Struggle against Theft of State and Public Property and Personal Property', Vestnik Shtabnoi Raboty 1(1972): 172-184.

'Mafia in Ekaterinburg. Public Opinion and Press about Organized Crime', Ekaterinburg: AO Novaya Ghildiya Institute of Social Studies and Technologies, 1993.

'A Concept for the Development of the Interior Agencies and the Troops of the MVD of Russia', Vestnik MVD Rossiiskoi Federatsii 5(1996): 3-20.

'Crime and Offence. Statistics for 1992', Moscow: Interior Ministry, Ministry of Justice of the Russian Federation, Statistics Committee of the Commonwealth of Independent States, 1993.

'Crime and the Results of Struggle Against It in the Russian Federation' Statistical Monthly, Moscow: Main Information Center of the MVD of Russia.

'Data on the Results of Struggle against Organized Crime in Russia. Statistical Review', Moscow: Main Department for Struggle Against Organized Crime and Main Information Center of the MVD of Russia, 1999.

'Non-Governmental Security Structures', Kursiv Information and Analysis Bulletin. Ekaterinburg, 8(1997).

Peshkov, A.I., 'Operational Detective Measures of Economic Crime Agencies in the Banking System', Moscow: All Russian Research Institute of the Ministry of the Interior of the Russian Federation, 1996.

Stepanov O.P., 'Organization of Operational Detective Activities in the Financial System', Operativno-Rozysknaya Rabota, 3(1998)

'Conclusion on the Results of the Parliamentary Hearings "On the Implementation of the Conceptual Provisions for Reforming the Judicial System of the Russian Federation', Rossiyskaya Yustitsiya, 2(1999): 2-4.

13 After Dictatorship: The Nature and Function of the Police in Post-Mao China

H. L. Fu

Abstract

The economic modernization and political liberalization since the early 1980s has caused dramatic changes in Chinese society. Chinese police, like the society in which they operate, are experiencing a process of slow but fundamental change. Yet, China remains a one party Communist state and all the reforms and changes are occurring within this larger political structure. The police are coping with the shift from revolution to modernization and redefining their roles in a new political economy. In post-revolutionary society, the police are re-negotiating their relations with the Communist Party, the law and the community.

Key Words: Community Policing, Hard Striking, Mass Line, Party Leadership, Police Professionalism, Security Company, Socialist Legality

Introduction

The military suppression of the 1989 student movement in Beijing is a good starting point to examine the changing nature and function of the people's police in China. University students in Beijing occupied Tiananmen Square, the center of the capital city, for weeks, demanding further political reform and tougher government action against corruption. The rally was a peaceful exercise of civil disobedience. This was the first time that the police were confronted with a massive scale of peaceful demonstrators in post-Mao China. Politically, Chinese police were, and still are, regarded as an instrument of the Chinese Communist Party (the Party). As such they had to follow the Party's instruction to clean the Square and to disperse the crowd. But at the same time, the police needed to justify their action in law. Most importantly, the people's police were expected to deal with the demonstrators in a "democratic" way, and no force could be contemplated against the students, as long as they were still regarded as "the people". It is conceptually impossible to use tear gas against the people which the Party purports to represent. In the Communist ideology, the people's police serve the people, only the Fascist police would use force against their own people. In Tiananmen Square of 1989, the police faced conflicting interests of political responsibility, legal accountability and expectations of the general public. What we witnessed on the streets of Beijing in 1989 was a public play between the police and the students. There was pushing, shuffling and, occasionally, booting and belting. But the use of force was minimal and, at the same time, the students, by and large, were able to maintain the order in the Square. Before June 4th, there seemed to be no deep animosity and hostility between the police and the students. Both sides made efforts to maintain order within the disorder. It was expected by the students and the general public that once this is achieved, the government would have no excuse to suppress the students as an enemy of the state.

The prolonged occupation of the Square exacerbated the political crises generated by the student movement. With the intensification of a power struggle between different factions within the Party, the demonstration was classified as a turmoil, and the students became the counter-revolutionaries. The Party was concerned that civil disobedience on the part of the students in Beijing and other large cities might spread further and eventually shaken the foundation of the Communist rule. The army moved in, together with their tanks and assault rifles. Soldiers dealt with crowd in the only way they know: shooting. The police were reprimanded by the Party for their incompetence, and senior officers, including the Minister of Public Security, Mr. Wang Fang, were removed from their positions for their lack of action in the days prior to the shooting. To a degree, the 1989 military crackdown and the bloodshed could have been avoided if the police:

- had followed the Party line and were constantly vigilant against student movements;

- were detached from society and were willing to take measures to control the demonstration;

- were rationally organized and professionally trained in riot control and public order policing; or

- were equipped with the necessary instruments and weaponry, and were prepared to use them against the demonstrators.

The killing in Tiananmen Square compelled the Party and its police to take a serious look at the role and function of police in the post-revolutionary society. Immediately after the crackdown, two national soul-searching conferences of chiefs of police were held to draw lessons from the crackdown and to design remedial measures for the future (Editorial Group, 1996: 394). The economic modernization and political liberation since the early 1980s have caused dramatic changes in Chinese society. Chinese police, like the society in which they operate, are experiencing a process of slow but fundamental change. Yet, China remains a Communist state and all the reforms and changes are occurring within this large political structure. How the police cope with the shift from revolution to modernization and re-define their roles in a new political economy, and how to reconcile the drive toward professionalism and the need for political loyalty have posed serious questions for the Party and the police. The purpose of this paper is to discuss the change and continuity in the nature and function of Chinese police in a post-revolutionary society.

Policing a Revolutionary Society, Policing the Enemy

"*Class justice*" was an essential feature of justice in Maoist China (Brady, 1982). China was, and continues to be, a state under the people's democratic dictatorship, which has been interpreted as the dictatorship against the enemy and democracy for the people. Police occupied a unique position in the Communist theory of the State, and was instrumental in this dictatorship/democracy dichotomy (Fu, 1994). Law in general was identified with dictatorship against the class enemy and the police stood in the front line of this class struggle.

In a society divided into classes, there were *"two types of social contradictions—those between ourselves and the enemy and those among the people themselves"* (Mao, 1977: 80). The former was seen as antagonistic, the latter as non-antagonistic. Mao defined *"the people"* in broad terms, as *"the classes, strata, and social groups which approve, support and work for the cause of the socialist construction"* and the enemy as *"the social forces and groups which resist the socialist revolution, and are hostile and try to sabotage socialist construction."* The primary tasks of the police, according to the 1959 *People's Police Regulations*, were to investigate counter-revolutionary offences and to control counter-revolutionaries. As an instrument of state violence, police bore a special responsibility of securing the internal peace of the state, and were expected to take a class point of view in their work and to differentiate the two contradictions. As Dutton and Lee (1993) put it: *"policing is the means by which the despotic state sits above, controls and ultimately crushes the self-activity of civil society. Policing, then, is little other than the repressive arm of the totalitarian state which unreflectively does its bidding."* *Who are the enemy?* became the crucial question. In the early years of the Communist rule, "enemy" included spies, saboteurs, and assassins sent by the Taiwan government, members of secret societies, bandits, career criminals, landlords and capitalists who were hostile to the new government. Once they were eliminated, their positions were replaced by landlords, rich peasants, counter-revolutionaries, bad elements, and rightists. The most important feature in China's class system was that once the "enemy status" was ascribed with became inherit and permanent (Billeter, 1985; Kraus, 1981).

The class enemies were considered extremely dangerous and were prepared to topple the Communist power at any moment. It was the police which shouldered the sacred and historical duty to safeguard the new political order. This sense of eminent danger not only created a collective consciousness which united the society in its struggle against the enemies, but also necessitated mechanisms of dictatorship over the class enemies, and consequently a dictatorial police power and dictatorial mentality among the police. As the two contradictions were fundamentally different, the methods for solving them also differ. There was a two-tiered system of justice. Criminal law was reserved to suppress the enemy. A crime was not simply a violation of criminal law but a challenge to the established political order, and any act which challenged the prevailing political order was a crime. A guilty verdict had a meaning far beyond a mere conviction for it transformed the convicted person into the enemy of the state. Consequently a police station was not merely a place to enforce the law, it was also a place of dictatorship. Criminalization principally meant repression. As Leng (1977: 365) noted, members of *"black"* elements were always the *"convenient targets of class hostility and abuse and persons of good background are reported to have received lenient treatment even in serious cases"*. Mao's ideology provided a bifurcated system: democracy for the people and dictatorship for the enemy, with the enemy serving as a negative example as the enemy of the state.

Policing the People

The repressive aspect of Chinese police was often overdrawn, however. Policing in China was a polarized system, the treatment received depended on the class status of the perpetrator. In this polemical symbolism, criminal justice was regarded as the hard end of social control, reserved for the enemy who was beyond redemption. But the repressive approach did not apply to the "people". Conflicts among the people were to be dealt with by the methods of democracy, that was didactic, informal and rehabilitative methods, that is through discussion, criticism, persuasion and education (Fu, 1992; Palmer, 1987).

Bowden (1978) has noticed "dualism" in the Chinese police. On the one hand, the police were one of the instruments of the Party to fulfil its political goal, and the Party was *never averse to using them as an instrument of repression.*" On the other hand, as Chinese police were a critical element in building a new government, their intimate relationship with local communities was crucial for integrating the masses and mobilizing public support for the government. The Maoist ideology emphasized the police relationship with the public and required the police to conform to the mass line and to maintain constant contact with residents (Johnson, 1983). Policing in Mao's China relied upon the closer relationship between the police and the community (neighborhood, school, factory, etc.). The neighborhood police station (*Paichushou*) (PCS) played a fundamental role in maintaining public order. It was responsible for most of the police services and certain civil administration except for the serious political and criminal cases, which were handled by the police at higher levels. It was believed that assigning the PCS officers to work as generalists in certain neighborhoods could stabilize police/community relations and thus secure order at the maximum level. Residents' committees in the jurisdiction supported the neighborhood police officers, which, under the leadership of the police, were authorized to mediate local disputes, maintain public order and provide welfare services. The function of the neighborhood officer was to make the neighborhood visible and therefore more controllable. With many "KGB in small foot" working as his eyes and ears in the neighborhood, police were omnipresent in neighborhoods and work places, and also omnipotent, ready to stamp out any incorrect political, moral or economic manifestations, be it bourgeoisie or feudal. Community policing served another function which frequently overshadowed crime prevention, that was to articulate and apply the ideological principles of the Party and mobilise the public to increase their commitment to Party policies and goals (Fu, 1992; Li, 1978; and Lubman, 1967). There was a built-in mechanism of thought control in the Chinese community policing. Community police worked as an ideological apparatus of thought control. Neighbourhood police and community activists were cogs in the macro-control machine. Their duty was to find out the locus of the problem, to classify the deviance into a particular category and to attach to it a particular of ideological wrong, then to mobilise the mechanism of thought reform (Kamenka and Tay, 1978; Lifton, 1961). Allied with the coercive power of criminal law, community policing, armed with its thought control mechanism, protected the ideological basis of the Communist rule.

This type of police/community relationship was essentially paternalistic. As the moral authority in the community, one function of Chinese police was to educate the masses and reform deviants. The community, while used and made useful by the police, remained subordinate to the police. Bowden (1978: 200) argues that, despite the Maoist rhetoric, "*It is, in the last analysis, not the people who control the police, but the police who tightly control the people.*"

Police Powers

Because of the crucial position occupied by the police in the people's dictatorship, it is not surprising to find that the police enjoyed tremendous powers (Bowden, 1978). Before the 1980s, the police were a dominant political force in Chinese society. The Ministry of Public Security had been given a high profile in national politics and the Minister had been, until the late 1970s, an important political figure. Very senior military officers and members of the Party's Political Bureau had held the position. When Hua Guofeng, Mao's successor, was the Premier, he also took the position of the Minister of Public Security. Those Ministers kept a close and personal tie with the charismatic Chairman Mao and other top Party leaders. They were trusted by senior leaders and had special access to them. This special relation further strengthened the political status of the police and, at the same time, allowed senior Party leaders to participate in police decision-making.[1] The Ministry of Public Security was at the same time the security department of the Party and bodyguards of the paramount Party leaders.[2]

The police were important to both the conservative and radical factions of the Party. When Mao and his radical followers called for the destruction of law and the legal system in 1967, the police, as an institution, remained largely untouched. It was true that the police suffered disruption after the radical students, the Red Guards, were incited to "*smash the police, the procuratorates and the courts*" (Wang, 1992: 21), however, the disruption of police was brief and the police was called to maintain order immediately afterwards. While many of the police officers, including very senior ones, were purged, they were replaced by new blood. In April 1968, for example, the Party recruited 47,482 demobilized soldiers into the police to rejuvenate the force (Editorial Group, 1996: 446). While the court, procuratorate and other legal institutions suffered fatal blows in the radical years of Cultural Revolution, the police survived the assault and remained powerful. The police and the army were regarded as the two pillars of the Communist rule and were not dispensable even for the radicals (Fu, 1994). When the Cultural Revolution ended in 1976, the police were at the peak of its power. It dominated the legal system.

The police had substantial power in the process of education and rehabilitation. While the criminal law was reserved for the enemy only, Chinese police designed a number of preventative and punitive measures to punish or reform the people. Two measures were popularly used and proved crucial to social control in Chinese society. One was preventative detention for investigation which allowed indefinite detention of certain persons, "shelter for examination" being the most popular type of such detention. The other was administrative detention which allowed police-imposed incarceration for up to four years without judicial process. "Re-education through labour" has been representative of the administrative power of the police. In suppressing the enemy and protecting the people, the police became a law unto themselves (Hsia and Zeldin, 1992; Biddulph, 1993).

After Dictatorship: Policing a Post-revolutionary Society, Police and the Party

Before discussing the reform of Chinese police in the post-Mao era, it is necessary to state the relationship between the Party and the police. China is a one-party state and the Party's control over the police is said to be absolute and direct. The Party exercises its immense power in three principal ways. First, it controls a vast array of powerful entities with specific political responsibilities. In law, the Party's Political and Legal Commission (PLC) at the national and regional levels is the ultimate authority to which the court, procuratorate, and police and other law related institutions are directly responsible. The Party controls the police by controlling the Party members who run the police (Lieberthal, 1995). Second, the system of *Nomenklatura* ensures that important posts in the police are filled by high ranking Party members (Burns, 1987). Thirdly, there is a parallel structure of a Party Group within the police at each level, forming the core of police management. The control of the Party entities themselves ensures that the Party has a comprehensive control over policy matters. Control over key positions in government, through the Party Group within a government department, provides further assurance that Party policies will be faithfully implemented. Through these mechanisms, Chinese police are made subservient to the Party.

The police, being the instrument of the Party, are expected to serve the central task decided by the Party at a particular period of time. Standard official statements say that police work must serve the central task of the Party, police policies must be approved by the Party, and important cases must be reported to the Party. Otherwise, as the experiences have shown that the police would lose their political direction without following the direction of the Party. It has become a routine pledge of the police that they submit themselves to the absolute leadership of the Party and actively seek political guidance in their operation (Wang Fang, 1992; Xu and Xu, 1997). The priority of police work fluctuates according to the political priority of the day. As the central task of the Party oscillates from time to time, so does the priority of police work. For most of the last five decades, the police have responded to different political demands, thus unable to initiate a consistent plan for police development.

The Party leadership is fragmented, however. As China does not have a nationalized police force, there is no centralized political leadership. Police at each region, province, city, prefecture or county is semi-independent from each other and Party leadership is exercised through the Party Committee at the regional level (Wang Fang, 1992). While, theoretically, control is divided between the local Party Committee and the central police authority, the Ministry of Public Security, a regional police force is subject to the dual leadership of both the superior police station and the local Party Committee. The control exerted by a local authority is more substantial and indeed overwhelming, negating the centralized command at a national level (Xu and Xu, 1997). The vertical leadership of the Ministry of Public Security is limited to issuing guidance on professional matters, making regulations and providing coordination among different regional forces (Fu, 1994; Ma, 1997:116).

The localized control is possible largely because of the substantial personnel and financial powers of the local Party Committee. The local chief of police is appointed and removed by the local Party Committee. The chief of police is part of the local political elite, and until very recently, he holds three key positions: a member in the Standing Committee of the local Party Committee; the Chairman of the local PLC; and one of the deputy Mayors/Governors in the local government. *He is the law of the place.* A regional police force is wholly financed by the local budget, and receives no contribution from the central authority. Given the size of the manpower, which is second only to that in the education sector, and given the size of its budget, which is the largest in a locality, this total reliance on local resources puts the local Party Committee in a special position in police decision making. The control over police personnel and budget ensures a localized political accountability.

Depoliticization: toward an apolitical police in China?
China is moving from a radical political context to a conventional political context, in that the Party has gradually changed from *"quasi-totalitarianism"* to *"consultative authoritarianism"* and even *"pluralistic authoritarianism"* (Skilling, 1970). Correspondingly, the nature of the police is being shifted from dictatorship to law enforcement and related services, and their function shifted from suppression to criminalization and accommodation (Brewer *et al*, 1996). *De-politicization* has taken place not only in the economic field, but, to a lesser degree, also in the political/legal field, such as in the legislative arena (Tanner, 1999), the judicial arena (Finder, 1993), and also in the law enforcement arena. After the Party shifted its priority from revolution to modernization, the police were bound to play a supporting role of protecting the program of economic reform.

The close and personal ties between the police and the paramount Party leaders have shifted and the police have become a less powerful institution within the one-party state. The first Minister of Public Security in the post-Mao era was a professional policeman, with a lower political profile in national politics. This policy has been kept in the last two decades. Within the Party's political and legal portfolio, power is being re-distributed. The status of the police has been declining, especially at the national level. One is witnessing a corresponding increase of power of the court and the procuratorate relative to that of the police. The promotion of Mr. Ren Jiangxin to the Chairmanship of the Party's PLC at the national level when he was the Chief Justice symbolized the important shift of power within the legal system. Most importantly, the Party has also started to distance itself from the police in the regional levels, to the effect that the chief of police in a region may no longer hold key positions in the local Party Committee and Government.

The rhetoric of police as a dictatorial instrument is openly challenged by liberal reformers, including many police officers. Indeed, the whole theory of law representing the will of a ruling class has been dismissed as ultra leftist. There have been certain calls for a more apolitical and "neutral" police in China (Research Group, 1997: 158). While these views are attacked by the Party as fundamentally bourgeoisie and irrelevant in the police reform agenda, there is a consensus that police have other functions in addition to class struggle and dictatorship. Police are not only to dictate, they are also to keep peace, serve the community and enforce the law (Fu, 1991). The traditional understanding of Chinese police is said to be a creation of leftist ideology and planned economy, which now has to be abandoned. As society becomes more pluralistic, the nature and function of the police become multi-faceted.

The making of the *People's Police Law* 1995, which repealed the 1959 *People's Police Regulations*, is illustrative of this process. The Police Bill was proposed by the police, who wanted to maintain the privileged political status. Article 2 of the Bill largely reproduced the 1959 Regulations and stated: *"People's police are a public order administration and judicial force with a military characteristic under the people's democratic dictatorship."* During the deliberation of the Bill, some deputies raised the following three challenges to Article 2.

- First, it is not appropriate to identify police as a judicial force because the principal function of the police is to keep social order and to enforce laws.

- Second, most of the police work, such as household management and traffic control, is not of a military characteristic.

- Finally, as the Bill clearly stated the functions of the police, the assertion of people's democratic dictatorship does not add anything new.[3]

As a result, Article 2 in the Bill was deleted. The deletion is significant in demystifying the police. The exploiting class as a class has been eliminated under China's socialist system, the class struggle between the "*enemy*" and "*us*" is no longer the principal conflict in an age of economic modernization. *Class enemy*, while they still exist, no longer pose a serious threat to the security of the state. Police-maintained dictatorship no longer makes sense. Under the new political economy, police perform certain functions according to the ordinary division of labor. Like any other government departments, the position of the police is not unique.

Does the police remain as a dictatorial instrument? The rhetoric of police as an instrument of dictatorship continued, especially at times of crisis. The police never abandoned the rhetoric of dictatorship because it could put the police in a special status and empower the police politically. As the Ministry of Public Security stated in its official publication, "public security organs could only be strengthened, and should never be weakened" because of their position in the people's dictatorship (Wang Fang, 1992: 44). Police are still insisting that the economic reform in post-Mao China has not changed the nature of policing in China. The argument is: despite the fact that the exploiting class as a class has been eliminated, and that class struggle as it was understood is no longer the main conflict in post-Mao China, the struggle continues to exist in different areas and in different forms and could intensify under certain conditions. For the police, the separatists, political dissidents and other domestic and overseas hostile forces will continue to subvert the government. Violent crimes and religious cults are also on the increase which pose serious threats to the existing social and political order. They are the new enemies of the State which the police need to stamp out. As such, the police should still occupy a special status in China's political life and given special powers (Xu and Xu, 1997).

The dictatorial power of the police has been gradually taken away or restrained. During the late 1970s, the unfettered police power was largely blamed for the unlawfulness which occurred during the Cultural Revolution, and it became clear to the Party that the police were too powerful. When the power was centralized in one institution, it could, as it happened, be easily manipulated by those who were in control. If the monopoly of power was the problem, separation of power and mechanisms of checks and balances were the solution.

Since the late 1970s, a large proportion of power was transferred from the Ministry of Public Security to other institutions. In 1979, the investigation of crimes committed by government functionaries in their official capacity was given to the Procuratorates. In 1983, the function of espionage and anti-espionage, including surveillance of overseas dissidents, was transferred from the Ministry of Public Security to the newly established Ministry of State Security. The control over prisons was also transferred to the Ministry of Justice in the same year. In 1999, to combat the massive smuggling in the coastal regions, Premier Zhu Rongji ordered the transferring of the anti-smuggling function from the police to the Customs, and it is expected a Tax Police would be established in China in the near future to take over the investigation of taxation related crimes, thus depriving the police of another important power.

Toward Police Professionalism

Police professionalism is becoming the new source of police legitimacy in China while direct political support from the Party is declining. The first step toward professionalism taken by the police was to create a distinctive identity. The outward image of the police has been given serious attention. In Mao's China, symbolic inequality was under attack. The Communist government had taken efforts to lessen the gap between the different social groups. Police uniform and rank was not an issue of concern because cadres in general were required to merge with the officers and the public, and resemble them in appearance. A uniform, and especially a rank system, was regarded as a symbol of social inequality in a society where egalitarianism was officially imposed. For example, in 1956 Mao vetoed a police proposal to set up a rank system in 1956, on the ground that police officers would not be able to carry water and food for the people if they wear epaulettes. One of the first actions taken by the police was to change the color and style of the police uniform and to enforce a uniform dress code.[4] A more significant attempt to was the establishment of police rank system. The rank system is expected to establish the distinctive identity of the police and to assert their autonomy. The police proposed a ranking system in 1949, 1956 and 1983, without success. It was not until after a rank system was set up in 1988 in the military that the Party endorsed the police rank system. A national law on police rank was passed by the National People's Congress Standing Committee in 1992. In addition to its symbolic value of making the police distinctive from the rest of the society, the rank system is expected to assist the police to assert police independence. The establishment of rank system is an attempt to formalize the internal hierarchical structure and to ensure certain police independence from local government. It reflects a larger movement in post-Mao China to overcome egalitarianism which is now regarded as inconsistent with modernization and professionalism. The Ministry of Public Security has repeatedly claimed that the rank system is important in exerting the unified, militarized, efficient and scientific leadership over the police.

The police in China are a system of lateral entry; a lay person may become a police officer, a patrol officer or the Minister, as the Party sees fit. The rank system intends to prevent this practice, so that senior officers can only be promoted from the rank and file of the police. For the police, a single entry system is the first step to create a truly national police force and strengthen the central police authority. Indirectly, the police are challenging the existing arrangement of police governance to weaken the firm grasp of regional police forces by regional Party Committees. The dual leadership structure in general creates a fragmented structure of authority in the Chinese political system (Lieberthal and Oksenberg, 1988). For the police, the professional guidance from the superior department and even that from the Ministry of Public Security is often compromised by the intervention of the local government. The division of control builds unnecessary barriers, thus limiting the capacity of the police to fight crime, hindering the development of police professionalism, and undermining police-public relations (Fu, 1994).[5]

Despite the strong protest from the Ministry of Public Security and the reiteration of the unique position of the police and the necessity of centralization of management, especially personnel management, local governments will retain substantial control over the police. Zhang Zhaodan (1998) from the police department of Hubei Province noted that local government officials continued to pressurize the police to recruit their unqualified relatives or friends into the police force. As long as the local government has total control of the budget and the personnel appointment of the police, the role of professional control exercised by a police force at the next higher level can only be peripheral. So far, calls to centralize police have been firmly rejected by local Communist Parties. While the Ministry of Public Security is calling for unified and centralized leadership, the chief of police in the northeastern Heilongjiang province stated firmly that Party leadership means the leadership of the local Party Committee[6] (Xu and Xu, 1997).

Police under Socialist Legality

Law and legality have become increasingly relevant for the police since the late 1970s. The Maoist revolutionary ideology has become harmful and divisive and has lost its appeal. The crisis of faith among the general public seriously undermined the legitimacy of the regime. The revolutionary activism had to give way to proceduralism and legality. The recurring emphasis on *"socialist legality"* is expected to alleviate the crisis faced by the Party and justify its continuing ruling during the post-Mao period (Potter, 1994). The post-Mao leadership has been seeking a legal rational authority to create a new order (Teiwes, 1984).

The elementary requirement of socialist legality is that police power has to be derived from law and is exercised through properly defined legal procedures. Police powers of interrogation, detention, arrest, search and seizure in the criminal process were first regulated with the enactment of the Criminal Procedure Law in 1979. The Criminal Law, also passed in 1979, placed further constraints on the police. Since 1979, police powers were increasingly given a legislative basis and incorporated into the legal process. Other important police legislation includes the Police Law 1995 (Ma, 1997) and the Regulations for Public Order Administrative Punishment 1986 (Yang, 1993). While there is a very large gap between the formal law and police practice, the legalization have provided a mechanism to highlight police abuse of powers and made the exercise of police power more public and visible (Fu, 1994a).

At the same time, the police have also examined their internal rules and regulations to ensure their compatibility with national laws. The Ministry of Public Security ordered the police in the country to review their local regulations and internal rules and to amend or repeal them if they are found to be incompatible with national laws. According to the Minister of Public Security, by the end of 1990s, police regulations have been systemized, rationalized and made law-compliant (People's Public Security Daily[7] (PPSD), 5 November 1991). Police powers with dubious legal grounds, such as the power of indefinite detention, are now abolished in law and, gradually. The infamous *re-education through labor* remains, but it is only a matter of time for this police penalty to be limited by national legislation (Xu and Fang, 1997).

Police power is increasingly under the supervision of other legal institutions and mechanisms. The Peoples' Procuratorate, in addition to its general supervisory power of other state organs, is authorized to approve *every arrest* made by the police. The wide ranges of police administrative powers are now reviewable by the court. Judicial review of police administrative decisions has passed a tortuous road in China since it was authorized by the legislature in 1986 and met hostile reactions from the police. The police were concerned that judicial review would promote judicial authority, thus upsetting the balance of power between the police and the court. More importantly, a court might find a police decision unlawful and invalid, and further damage the image of the police. But by the time the National People's Congress (NPC) enacted the Administrative Litigation Law in 1989, the power of the court to review police administrative decision was widely recognized and reluctantly accepted by the police (Fu, 1994a; Finder, 1993; Song, 1994). In 1991, the NPC passed the State Compensation Law, which extends the court's jurisdiction to review police decision in the criminal process (Lin, 1995). The Amendment of Criminal Procedure Law in 1996 allows lawyers to offer legal assistance to any person interrogated, detained or arrested by the police (Fu, 1998). The NPC and the local people's congresses are exercising their constitutional power of supervising government work and are instrumental in restricting police power. The power of the NPC is broadly recognized in Chinese politics. The deputies have developed the sense, willingness and capacity to represent certain popular interests and criticize the work of the executive government and the judiciary (Tanner, 1999). The NPC has exercised its power with vigor in reviewing the country's crime and social order problem and in criticizing the expansive police power of administrative detention. Du Jinfeng (1997: 91) states that, whenever the congresses are in session, the deputies "*always express their concern about the severe situation of public security and the need to fight crime*". The police at national and regional levels are taking the views of the deputies very seriously. Law is also used to legitimize the police. The police attitude toward law and legal control is also changing. Instead of treating legal rules as a hurdle to police work, which binds the hands of the officers, the police are discovering the *enabling* aspect of law. There is a limit as to what socialist legality may be able to achieve in post-Mao China. The legal reform in China in the last two decades may have made China move closer to a country of rule by law, but not rule of law. Both the Party and the public are looking at the police with suspicion. They are demanding more police services and are ready to criticize the police if the services are not delivered to their satisfaction. In particular, the public are no longer prepared to accept the dictatorial manner and style of the police, and ready to make complaints against the police in media and other forums or take legal actions against the police if their rights are violated.

The police need justifications and they found law as a powerful resource. Legal rules are actively used and made useful to the advantage of the police. Naturally, police officers are becoming more conscious of the legal justification for their activities and decisions. For example, a Law Unit has been set up in police stations at each level to review police decisions and this unit has gained a high status within the force. In addition, the police have successfully lobbied the NPC in legislation concerning the police. For example, it succeeded in lobbing the NPC to loosen the rules of self-defense in amending the Criminal Law in 1997, in legalizing extensive police power of pre-trial detention, and in limiting the right to lawyers to persons under police detention (Fu, 1998).

Policing as Crime Control

The function of the police changed accordingly. By the late 1970s, class discrimination had officially ceased. Most of the "class enemies" had their names cleared and in 1981 the Party claimed the successful accomplishment of the historical task of reforming the "class enemy" (Dittmer, 1987; Meaney, 1987). Jiang Hua, former Chief Justice of the Supreme People's Court, reported to the NPC in 1983, that, while most of the crimes were committed in the early 1950s by the counter-revolutionaries and the remnants of the old society, the percentage of counter-revolutionary offences had dropped to only 0.5% in 1982. By the end of 1970s, the Chinese realized that the most serious danger was no longer the class enemy but *their own children*. It shocked the Party leadership to discover that more than 95% of the prison population were the sons and daughters of the "people" (Wang Zhongfang, 1992). The Party was entrapped by its own ideology that their state instrument was reserved for the enemy only, failing to take notice of the fact that by the late 1950s and 1960s, about 80% of China's prison population were "people" who committed ordinary offences, particularly theft (Gu, 1986: 170-1). By the end of 1970s, the Party's attention was clearly directed to the control of these "people" and crimes they commit. Official national crime statistics, which is largely unreliable—under-estimating the crime problem in China—documents that crime has been steadily increasing since the early 1980s (See Table 1).

The number of public order offences, that is the minor offences which are directly punished by the police, almost tripled in the last decade (See Table 2).

Street crime is more difficult to control. The class enemy in Mao's China was visible and known to the community. No matter how "evil" they are and how "dangerous" they may be in the long term, they did not present any present and clear danger to the society. On the contrary, they were held as the negative example. The living symbol of the class enemy served to create community solidarity. Street crime is perpetrated by anonymous strangers, whose identities are not known. There is no clearly defined target group against which the community can be united. Street crime is predatory and can do real harm to the individual. Murder, rape and robbery can generate real fear and inflict real pain. The danger presented by street crime is immediate and faced by all residents in their daily life. In addition, given that street crime targets its victim at random, it can "*undermine support for law enforcement, stimulate withdrawal from community life, and at best favor individualistic, self-protective action*" (Skogan, 1988). While reported crimes have been increasing, the fear of crime is increasing at a speedier pace. The survey studies by sociologists in China and press reports unequivocally indicated that crime and disorder has become the leading concerns of the urban residents in China (Dutton and Lee, 1993; Zheng Yongnian 1999). The public felt helpless about crime which tyrannizes the streets. According to the police, there is a *wall syndrome* in Chinese society, a thick wall which keeps the public silent when facing crime, and an accompanying *iron bar syndrome*: urban Chinese are barricading themselves in their home fortresses. The lack of vigilantism, which was essential for community policing in the Maoist era, eventually encourages the spread of crime, and as the police claim, it makes the society resistance-free and turns the public into by-standers (PPSD, 22 July 1995).

Table 13.1 Criminal Cases as Filed by the Police in China 1981-1997.

Year	Homicide	Assault	Robbery	Rape	Fraud	Theft	Total Cases Filed
1981	9,576	21,499	22,266	30,808	18,6657	43,1058	90,281
1982	9,324	20,298	16,518	35,361	17,707	608,501	748,476
1983	-	-	-	-	-	-	610,478
1984	9,021	14,526	7,273	44,630	13,479	394,840	514,369
1985	10,440	15,586	8,801	37,712	13,157	431,323	542,005
1986	11,510	18,364	12,124	39,121	14,663	425,845	547,115
1987	13,154	21,727	18,775	7,225	14,693	435,235	570,439
1988	15,959	26,639	36,318	34,120	18,857	658,683	827,594
1989	19,590	35,931	72,881	40,999	42,581	1,673,222	1,971,901
1990	21,214	45,200	82,361	47,782	54,719	1,860,793	2,216,997
1991	23,199	57,489	105,132	50,331	60,174	1,922,50	2,365,709
1992	24,132	59,901	125,092	49,829	46,991	1,142,556	1,582,659
1993	25,380	64,595	152,102	47,033	50,644	1,122,105	1,616,879
1994	26,553	67,864	159,253	44,118	57,706	1,133,682	1,660,734
1995	27,356	72,259	164,478	41,823	64,047	1,132,789	1,690,407
1996	25,411	68,992	151,147	42,820	69,688	1,043,982	1,600,716
1997	26,070	69,071	141,514	40,699	78,284	1,058,11	1,613,629

Sources: China Law Yearbooks (1987-1998).

Table 13.2 Public Order Offences Filed by the Police 1986-1997

Year	Total no.of cases received	Year	Total no.of cases received
1997	3,227,669	1991	2,414,065
1996	3,363,636	1990	1,965,663
1995	3,289,760	1989	1,847,625
1994	3,300,972	1988	1,410,044
1993	3,351,016	1987	1,234,910
1992	2,956,737	1986	1,115,858

Sources: China Law Yearbooks (1987-1998).

Hard Strike: the Party's Response to Crime

Common crimes and the fear of them have been perceived as threats to the Party's political order and challenge the Party's legitimacy. To restore public confidence, the Party resorted to the periodical campaigns against crime, called hard strikes (*yanda*). It started in 1981 and became institutionalized in 1983. In July 1983, paramount leader Deng Xiaoping met the Minister of Public Security and ordered the police to lunch several mass campaigns against violent crimes and to solve the crime problems within three years (Editorial Group, 1996, 372). Under political pressure, the police rendered swift and brutal justice to ensure political stability. It was expected that the legitimacy deficit could be compensated by an effective crime control. *Yanda* did not stop in 1986, it continued and has become a permanent feature of China's criminal justice system (Stern, 1997).[8]

Over the last decade, *yanda* has become more aggressive. The term *campaign* has been replaced by *war* or *battle*. The soldiers and armed police have become more visible in the operation. The period of the operation is prolonged, from "*short, sharp assaults upon particular types of crime*" (Dutton and Lee, 1993: 323), to a war with different battlefields with well planned phases. It took three years to accomplish the national war on theft. The war multiplies; there are different battles on different crimes organized by different levels of government, often carried out simultaneously. Rights of the accused and the procedural requirements as provided by the laws are routinely bypassed and ignored by the police during *yanda*. Police, prosecution and judges are required to work in a streamlined fashion in order to speed up the process. Criminal defense is virtually suspended and capital punishment is encouraged. Justice is rendered as speedily and as severely as possible. *Yanda* has been "*harsh, arbitrary and extra-legal*" (Dutton and Lee, 1993). Those who committed violent crimes are regarded as the new class enemy and treated as such. Where the *yanda* approach on crime could temporarily suppress the impetus of crime and ensure the psychological safety of the public, the police paid a high price for this problematic method of crime control. The military style of policing resulted in high casualties among the officers,[9] prolonged work hours of the front line officers, degenerated public relations, and more importantly, subverted routine law enforcement. The success in controlling crime is highly exaggerated (Du, 1997; Dutton and Lee, 1993; and Fu, 1994). Each *yanda* creates a wave of arrests and convictions. But when it is over, another crime wave is soon recorded, causing another *yanda*. The periodic crackdown on crime created a vicious circle of crime and policing in post-Mao China. As a recent police news says: the Winter Campaign has been accomplished successfully, but a Spring Campaign is imperative. Wang Fang (1990), the Minister of Public Security, admitted, when he reported about social order problems to the NPC Standing Committee in 1990, that despite the repeated campaigns on crime, "public order is not good. The People's Deputies are not happy, masses are not happy, and police are not happy".

Yet *yanda* was so entrenched in China's crime control strategy and has become an important part of "law and order" politics. Neither the Party nor the police can discontinue it. For the Party, *yanda* has become a ritual through which it regularly demonstrates to the people its strength and ability to rule. *Yanda* also provides psychological comfort to the Party that things are not totally out of control. For the police, it provides an occasion to demonstrate its importance and powers.

Each *yanda* leads to a detection of a great number of crimes and the arrest of a great number of suspects. It demonstrates the seriousness of crime, the urgency for a solution and the indispensable position of the police.[10] Since the early 1990s, a high crime rate and deteriorating social order has been strategically used by the police to bargain for more powers and resources. Yet the same set of statistics is also used by the police to prove that police is effective in combating crime. Streets are safer immediately after a terror of *yanda*, and the public feels more satisfied with social order. *Yanda* thus becomes the self-fulfilling prophecy that the police are indispensable to the legitimacy of the Party and the security of the state.

By the late 1980s, it became abundantly clear to the police that *yanda* was not the solution to the problem of crime and public disorder. Without *yanda*, society becomes ungovernable, but *yanda* relies on internal warfare to maintain order. While *yanda* continues, two other strategies have gained primary importance since the late 1980s. One is the creation of police patrols in the cities to normalize crime control; the other is the institutionalization and commercialization of public participation in crime control.

The police patrol is an important recent invention of policing strategy. In the past, the police were not readily available. Until the late 1980s, there were no uniformed officers patrolling streets in most of the cities[11]. Chinese police were uncharacteristically bureaucratic, with a substantial minority of the officers working in offices. It was commonly criticized that the Chinese police was a deformed body, with a big belly and two very slim and weak legs. Facing a more mobile and dynamic socioeconomic structure, the old system of neighborhood policing became fundamentally fragile. The old community policing was disorganized and not capable of policing a more mobile and dynamic society. As Dutton and Lee (1993: 317) put it: "certain structural alterations undertaken to facilitate economic reform have progressively weakened the old methods and strategies of policing." The old style policing, which stressed the visibility quality of a community, a division between insiders and strangers, and solidarity between the police and the residents, is now dismissed as being static. The introduction of a market element in the economy allowed millions of rural population to work and live in the cities. These "floating populations" who are subject to no particular police jurisdiction, fundamentally undermined the old style of governance. The community appeared to be paralyzed in facing changes to the social system, unable and unwilling to take any responsibility. A society of mobile strangers necessitates a more mobile and visible police presence. To have uniformed police patrolling the streets and to increase their visibility is regarded as an essential part of a dynamic policing. As early as 1984 and 1985, a number of small and medium sized cities initiated police patrol in their jurisdictions. In 1986, the Ministry of Public Security authorized the practice and called for a nation-wide exercise of putting limited police resources on the streets. Office bureaucrats were seconded to neighborhood police stations and were ordered to walk the beats. New patrol units were set up with new recruits. The underlying logic is that an increasing visibility of police on the street will increase the sense of safety. Senior police managers made many trips overseas to observe and study police patrols in some Western countries, and determined that a random patrol system in Chinese is a resolution to the Chinese problem. As a senior police officer reflects his trip to the United States: "*I visited many public places in New York and Washington. My impression is that public security is tight there and I*

*came cross police patrols frequently. Although their crime rate is higher than
ours, you feel safe when you are on the street. This is because the police who are
visible everywhere can give you strength"* (PPSD, 21 June 1993).

By the early 1990s, the uniformed police patrol system was set up in most cities in
China. By the end of 1994, there were 18,000 patrol officers.[12] A police emergency
telephone service was also set up to provide additional service to the public. The trend
of development in urban China is that, increasingly, the patrol police will be mobilized
by telephone calls and by radio dispatch. Police patrol has become a permanent feature
of Chinese policing.

Morgan (1989: 218) has argued that the quality of policing can be measured by
both the police operational style and public behavior. Policing methods mirror public
attitudes toward police and are *"indicative of public deference to their authority* (ibid.
219). Abusive police meet a hostile public. Chinese police have gradually lost their
moral authority for many reasons. While the tradition of political justification, that is to
invoke the doctrine of police as a dictatorial instrument, has been fundamentally weakened, the present justification of legality and rationality is still at its very beginning and
is far from taking root. At a more practical level, Chinese police are well-known for their
rudeness, sloppiness, and other misconduct, largely reflecting the manner and style of
government bureaucrats. Police corruption, not different from that in other state organs, is out of control and has involved high ranking police officials at both regional
and local levels. Without a sufficient control mechanism and a sense of accountability,
many police officers, armed with dictatorial powers and dictatorial mentality became
common thugs, abusing their powers against the rights and interests of the ordinary
members of the society.

It has become a common complaint among the police that the public does not
respect them. Popular support, which was vital to police work in China, was no longer
forthcoming. The public has withdrawn from participating in community policing, and
became indifferent and even hostile to the police. It is now common grievance that "it
is difficult to investigate a case, difficult to collect evidence and difficult to solve a
case" (PPSD, 24 August 1995). An Assistant to the Minister of Public Security, Luo
Feng, mentioned the deteriorating law enforcement environment. According to Luo,
"The public in our country lacks a sense of police. They not only refuse to cooperate
with the police, but also take a hostile stance." Luo describes the common violence
against the police: "they grab the insignia on the cap, tear the uniform, and smash
police cars. In some places, police officers are taken hostage. What is worse, the
officials also lack the sense of police just as the ordinary people". The police chief in
Chongqing city admits that obstruction of police law enforcement is common in his
city and is increasing. According to him, police in China are becoming a power *without*
authority (PPSD, 5 November 1991).

Community policing no longer appeals to the police in a time of police modernization, although lip service is still paid to it. Police expertise and the ideology of police
professionalism have symbolic superiority over informal community policing in China.
Informal justice in general has lost its ideological appealing and is regarded ill equipped
to tackle crime and disorder (Fu, 1992). The faith of the police and society in general
rests with the increase in police manpower, a bigger budget and more advanced equipment. According to the deputy chief of police in Anhui province, the traditional com-

munity policing has fully or partially lost its usefulness. The existing programs are a mere formality and are becoming increasingly superficial (Yun and Li, 1997: 29). Chief of police of Heilongjiang province was concerned that many police stations have started to refer to themselves as "police", instead of "people's police", in official documents (Xu and Xu, 1997: 6).

To engage the community in crime control while facing an indifferent and even hostile public presents a new challenge. One solution is to institutionalize and formalize community policing. Since the late 1970s, a civilian force, called the Joint Defense Team (JDT), was set up to control "high crime areas", such as parks, commercials centers and traffic centers. Gradually, it was expanded to all parts of the cities and finally to rural areas. The JDT members are "drafted" from the enterprises' organizations located in the jurisdiction of the respective police station. They work in the JDT for one or two years. Their salaries, bonus and other types of welfare are provided by their original employers. The general principle is "who benefits, who pays". The JDT members have no formal training. The team is attached to a specific police station at the basic level, so that a neighborhood police station would normally have a group of civilians attach to it. The JDT was successful in the early period when it was initially mobilized to control the public areas. However, with the institutionalization of the JDT as part of the conventional police force, and especially with the deepening of economic reform in the industrial sector, the internal dilemma of JDT became apparent. With the gradual separation of enterprises from government, enterprise managers started to challenge their contribution as being an illicit levy, an infringement into the enterprise's autonomy. While there were approximately 2 million JDT members working for the police in 1988, complaints of a shortage of JDT members were also common at that time. When compelled to contribute, the enterprises tended to send the "bad apples" or the "old, weak, sick and handicapped" to the police. The Ministry of Public Security conducted a nation-wide investigation on JDT in 1988, and concluded that, despite the problems, the JDT was an indispensable force in China and should be maintained. The Ministry of Public Security suggestion was approved by the State Council, which called upon the government at local levels to be supportive of the JDT (PPSD, 13 February 1992). The call to disband or reduce the JDT has been vocal and consistent, but the government has been reluctant to replace them with the formal police. The police, under a separate budget from the government now directly hires many of the JDT members. (Zheng Xunwu, 1999). Community participation is also commercialised. The traditional form of public involvement in a neighborhood is losing its function and is being replaced by a more institutionalised form. One of the significant development is the creation of Security Service Companies (SSC) to institutionalize the popular participation. The SSC provides a wide range of security-related services to the growing businesses enterprises, especially for Sino-foreign joint ventures. It is an independent entity, bestowed the status of a juridical person, and enjoys civil law rights and assumes civil law duties. A SSC works on a fee-for-service basis by contracting with clients (Fu, 1993; Ni and Chen, 1997).

The creation of SSC coincides with the privatization and securitization of State Owned Enterprises (SOEs). Chinese police was a creation of a socialist planned economy, and the shift to a more market oriented economy necessitates a re-division of labour and re-distribution of police resources. Under a market economy, the private sector is equally important to the public sector and deserves equal police protection. The police is in a process of withdrawal from direct involvement in policing SOEs, gradually leaving these enterprises to maintain their own security.

The SSC fills in this gap by providing a great range of security services to enterprises, neighborhoods and other public areas. The clients determine the nature and the scope of the function. But the work SSC does has a wide public dimension. It patrols in the premises of SOEs and residential areas. It assists police in criminal investigations and traffic regulations. While security guards cannot be armed and do not enjoy police powers (to search, detain and arrest), they could be armed with "non-offensive" weapons and, with the authorization from the police, interrogate criminal suspects. The police control the SSC by appointing senior managers regulating the service. And indeed the very idea of SSC has been criticised as factories without chimneys, another venue for the police to enrich themselves. So far, the semi-private security services are tightly controlled by the police, and are not posing a serious challenge to the public police. However, it is the very success of the SSC that makes it difficult for the police to interfere. Clients pay because they could control a SSC in a way which they cannot control the police. Private security works according to its own logic which is very distinctive from the public police. By creating a "client-oriented" security force, the police are losing the control over community policing.

Conclusion

The control of the police is becoming less political. As China is moving away from the radical political context, policing has shifted from suppression to accommodation. In law, the police are no longer the instrument of the Party's dictatorship. In a socialist market economy, the police are designated to serve the country's economic construction. After decades of dictatorship, the priority of policing now becomes conventional crime control and police modernisation. While political policing continues, and dissidents remain a target of police surveillance, the scope of the target is narrowed, and the measures are softened. Despite the occasional relapses, the police are normalized and their political function is marginalized. Police control is increasingly framed in the discourse of "law and order". Although law is still not central to Chinese police work, it is becoming increasingly relevant. Laws are replacing the Party directives to legitimize police work. Police tasks and powers are now provided and regulated by laws. Police are to enforce the law and at the same time to abide by them. As a result, police accountability is diversified. In addition to the Party, the police are also made accountable to the legislature, the court and other institutions and mechanisms lawfully created.

Policing control is more external and is increasingly imposed on the community, which is disorganized, divided, disparate, and in any sense, unable to maintain its internal order. The traditional community policing no longer exists; it either died a natural death under the market economy or is being replaced by the commercialised semi-private policing. Police and public relations are more estranged. The moral consensus disappeared together with the withdrawal of public participation and the paralysis of mass organisations. The police have lost their power to motivate and to normalise. Police professionalism in China symbolises the transformation from control of mind to the control of body, resulting in the weakening of control itself and the decline of the authority of the police. As the police become more professional, technical and geared more to law enforcement, the future relationship between police and community is more like that between consumers and service providers.

China's Police and Policing Continues their Paradoxical Nature

In a sense this review documents a continuation of institutionalized paradoxes. Consider:

- Chinese police have changed in many ways during the last two decades, and many of the changes are significant. But at the same time, there is also a sense of sameness about the Chinese police.

- The Party is distancing itself from the control of the police, but the police are still in its firm grasp.

- The police have become less powerful, but the powers are potentially there.

- The police are more accountable to the law, but when they decide to put themselves above the law, there is still no legal consequence.

- While political demands, legal requirements and public expectations intersect at police, it is, at the end of the day, the politics which takes command.

The police are now a bird in a bigger cage.

H.L. Fu is Associate Professor of Law at the University of Hong Kong. His research interests include criminal justice and criminal law, along with Constitutional and human rights in China.

E-mail: "H L Fu" <hlfu@hkusua.hku.hk>

References

Biddulph, Sarah (1993), "Review of Police Powers of Administrative Detention in the People's Republic of China", *Crime & Delinquency* 39: 337.

Billeter, Jean-Francois, (1985), "The System of 'Class Status'", in Schram, Stuart R. (ed.) *The Scope of State Power in China*. London: School of Oriental and African Studies, University of London.

Bowden, Tom (1978), *Beyond the Limits of the Law*. Middsex: Penguin.

Brady, James (1982), *Justice and Politics in People's China: Legal Order or Continuing Revolution?* London: Academic Press.

Brewer, John, et al (1996), *The Police, Public Order and the State: policing in Great Britain, Northern Ireland, the Irish Republic, the USA, Israel, South Africa and China*. London: Macmillan Press.

Burns, JP (1987), "China's Nomenklatura System", *Problems of Communism* Sept-Oct 1987: 36.

China Association of Police Studies, Basic Theories Sub-Committee of Public Security Committee (eds.) (1997), *Public Security with Chinese Characteristics*. Beijing: Mass Publisher (in Chinese).

China Law Yearbook, 1987-1998. (in Chinese)

Clarke, Donald C. and Feinerman, James V. (1995), "Antagonistic Contradictions: Criminal Law and Human Rights in China", *China Quarterly* 141: 135.

Dittmer, Lowell (1987), *China's Continuous Revolution: The Post-Liberation Epoch 1949-1981*. Berkeley: University of California Press.

Du, Jinfeng (1997), "Police-Public Relations—A Chinese View", *The Australian and New Zealand Journal of Criminology* 30: 87.

Dutton, Michael and Lee, Tainfu (1993), "Missing the Target? Policing Strategies in the Period of Economic Reform", *Crime and Delinquency* 39: 316.

Editorial Group of "History of the People's Public Security of China" (1996), *History of the People's Public Security of China*. Beijing: Police Education Press (in Chinese).

Epstein, Edward J. (1993), "Instrumental and Ideological Forms of Law: Implications for China's Transplants of Hong Kong Law", in Wacks, Raymond (ed.) *Hong Kong, China and 1997: Essays in Legal Theory*. Hong Kong: Hong Kong University Press.

Finder, Susan (1989), "Like Throwing an Egg Against a Stone? Administrative Litigation in the People's Republic of China", *Journal of Chinese Law* 3: 1.

Finder, Susan (1993), "The Supreme People's Court of the People's Republic of China", *Journal of Chinese Law* 7: 145.

Fu, H L (1991), "Police Accountability: The Case of the People's Republic of China", *Police Studies* 14: 140.

Fu, H L (1992), "Understanding People's Mediation in Post-Mao China", *Journal of Chinese Law* 6: 211.

Fu, H L (1993), "The Security Services Company in China", *Journal of Security Administration* 16: 35.

Fu, H L (1994), "A Bird in the Cage: Police and Political Leadership in post-Mao China", *Policing and Society* 4: 277.

Fu, H L (1994a), "A Case for Abolishing Shelter for Examination: Judicial Review of Police Powers in China", *Police Studies* 17: 41.

Fu, H L (1998), "Criminal Defence in China: The Possible Impact of the 1996 Criminal Procedure Law Reform", *The China Quarterly* 153: 31.

Gu, Yingchun (1986), *Introduction to the Comprehensive Treatment of Juvenile Delinquency*. Beijing: Mass Publisher. (in Chinese).

Hinton, W. (1972), *Hundred Day War: The Cultural Revolution in Tsinghua University*. New York: Monthly Review Press.

Hsia, Tao-tai and Zeldin, Wendy I. (1992), "Sheltering for Examination (Shourong Shencha) in the Legal System of the People's Republic of China", *China Law Reporter* 7: 95.

Johnson, Elmer (1983), "Neighborhood and the Police: The People's Republic of China", *International Journal of Comparative and Applied Criminal Justice* 7: 207.

Johnson, Elmer (1984), "Neighborhood Police in the People's Republic of China," *Police Studies* 6: 8.

Johnson, Elmer (1986), "Politics, Power and Prevention: The People's Republic of China Case", *Journal of Criminal Justice* 14: 449

Kamenka, Eugene and Tay, Alice (1978), "Socialism, Anarchism and Law", in Kamenka, Eugene, Brown, Robert and Tay, Allice Erh-soon (eds.), *Law and Society: The Crisis in Legal Ideals*. London: E. Arnold.

Kraus, Richard C. (1981), *Class Conflict in Chinese Socialism*. New York: Columbia University Press.

Leng, Shao-chuan (1977), "The Role of Law in the People's Republic of China as Reflecting Mao Tse-Tung's Influence", *Journal of Criminal Law and Criminology* 68: 356.

Leng, Shao-chuan, and Chiu, Hungdah (1985), *Criminal Justice in Post-Mao China: analysis and documents*. Albany: State University of New York Press.

Li, Victor (1978), *Law Without Lawyer: a comparative view of law in China and the United States*. Colorado: Westview Press.

Lieberthal, Kenneth (1995), *Governing China: From Revolution Through Reform*. New York: W.W. Norton & Company, Inc.

Lieberthal, Kenneth and Oksenberg, Michael (1988), *Policy Making in China: Leaders, Structures, and Processes*. Princeton: Princeton University Press.

Lifton, Robert, J. (1961), *Thought Reform and the Psychology of Totalism: A Study of 'Brainwashing' in China*. New York: W.W. Norton & Company Inc.

Lin Feng, (1995), "An Examination of the State Compensation Law 1995", *Hong Kong Law Journal* 25: 401.

Lubman, Stanley (1967), "Mao and Mediation: Politics and Dispute Resolution in Communist China", *California Law Review* 55: 1284.

Lowenthal, Richard (1970), "Development vs Utopia in Communist Policy", in Johnson, Chalmers (ed.), *Change in Communist Systems*. Stanford: Stanford University Press.

Ma, Yue (1997), "The Police Law 1995: organization, functions, powers and accountability of the Chinese police", *Policing: An International Journal of Police Strategy and Management* 20: 113.

Mao, Zedong (1977), "On the correct handling of contradiction among the people," in *Selected Works of Mao Tse-tung* (Vol. 5). Beijing: Foreign Languages Press.

Mawby, R.I. (1990), *Comparative Policing Issues*. London: Unwin Hyman.

Meaney, Constance Squires (1987), "Is the Soviet Present China's Future?", *World Politics* 39: 203.

Morgan, Rod (1989), "'Policing by consent': legitimating the doctrine," in Morgan, Rod and Smith, David (eds.), *Coming to Terms with Policing: perspective on policy*. London: Routledge.

Ni, Minle and Chen, Guanfu (1997), "Strategic Considerations for the Speedy Development of Security Services Business", in China Association of Police Studies, Basic Theories Sub-Committee of Public Security Committee (eds.), *Public Security with Chinese Characteristics*. Beijing: Mass Publisher (in Chinese).

Pei, Minxin (1997), "Citizens v. Mandarins: Administrative Litigation in China", *China Quarterly* 152: 832.

Potter, Pitman (1994), "Riding the Tiger: Legitimacy and Legal Culture in Post-Mao China", *The China Quarterly* 138: 325.

Palmer, Michael (1987), "The Revival of Mediation in the People's Republic of China: Extra-Judicial Mediation", in Butler, W.E. (ed.), *Yearbook of Socialist Legal Systems 1987*. New York: Transnational Books.

PPSD (People's Public Security Daily): 12 June 1990; 7 December 1990; 20 December 1990; 5 November 1991; 13 February 1992; 21 June 1993; 22 July 1995; 24 August 1995, 20 January 1996. (in Chinese)

Research Group, Basic Theories Sub-Committee of Public Security Committee, Guangdong Province (1997), "New Characteristics of Public Security Work under the Economic Conditions of Socialist Market Economy in Guangdong's practice", in China Association of Police Studies, Basic Theories Sub-Committee of Public Security Committee (eds.), *Public Security with Chinese Characteristics*. Beijing: Mass Publisher (in Chinese).

Skilling, H. Gordon (1970), "Group Conflict and Political Change", in Johnson, Chalmers (ed.), *Change in Communist Systems*. Stanford: Stanford University Press.

Skogan, Wesley G. (1988), "Community Organizations and Crime", in Tonry, Michael and Morris, Norval (eds.), *Crime and Justice: A Review of Research (Vol. 10)*. Chicago: The University of Chicago Press.

Song, Bing (1994), "Assessing China's System of Judicial Review of Administrative Actions", *China Law Reporter* 8: 1.

Stern, Russell H. (1997), "China: A most favored nation or a most feared nation — the PRC's latest anti-crime campaign and a possible US response", Geo. Wash. J. Int'l L. & Econ. 31: 119

Tanner, Murray Scot (1999), *The Politics of Lawmaking in Post-Mao China: institutions, processes and democratic prospects*. Oxford: Clarendon Press.

Teiwes, Frederick C (1984), *Leadership, Legitimacy and Conflict in China: from a charismatic Mao to the politics of Succession*. London: Macmillan.

Wang, Fang (1990), "Report on Current Conditions of Public Security Work and Social Order" (Presented at 14th meeting of the 7th session of the National People's Congress Standing Committee). *Gazette of the National People's Congress Standing Committee*. March 1990: 65 (in Chinese).

Wang, Fang (ed.) (1992), *Public Security in Contemporary China*. Beijing: Contemporary China Press (in Chinese).

Wang, Zhongfang (ed.) (*1992*), *Comprehensive Management of Public Order in China*. Beijing: Mass Publisher (in Chinese).

Xu Yongzheng and Fang Shijiao (1997), "A Characteristics of Public Security Work of Our Country: The System of Re-education through Labour", in China Association of Police Studies, Basic Theories Sub-Committee of Public Security Committee (eds.), *Public Security with Chinese Characteristics*. Beijing: Mass Publisher (in Chinese).

Xu, Yandong and Xu Zhixin (1997), "Insisting on Constructing the Police through Politics", in China Association of Police Studies, Basic Theories Sub-Committee of Public Security Committee (eds.), *Public Security with Chinese Characteristics*. Beijing: Mass Publisher (in Chinese).

Yang, Cheng (1988), "Criminal Procedure in China: Some Comparisons with the English System", *International and Comparative Law Quarterly* 37: 190.

Yun, Shusheng and Li, Wencheng (1997), "Mass Line is the Fundamental Characteristics of China's Public Security Work", in China Association of Police Studies, Basic Theories Sub-Committee of Public Security Committee (eds.), *Public Security with Chinese Characteristics*. Beijing: Mass Publisher (in Chinese).

Zhang, Zhaodan (1998), "Irregular Tendency in the Construction of Public Security Forces and the Solutions", in Personnel Bureau of the Ministry of Public Security (ed.), *Theories and Practices of Normalization of Public Security Forces.* Beijing: China University of Public Security Press.

Zheng, Xunwu (1999), "Brief Analysis of the Problems in Public Security Recruitment and the Solutions", *Public Security Studies* 3: 51. (in Chinese).

Zheng, Yongnian (1999), "From Rule by Law to Rule of Law: A realistic view of China's legal development", *China Perspective* 25: 31.

Notes

1 It was said that the Ministry of Public Security was the third most important Ministry in Mao's time, following the Ministry of National Defense and Ministry of Foreign Affairs (Fu, 1994), and the two matters for which Mao took personal responsibility were foreign affairs and public security (Editorial Group, 1996:338).

2 One typical example was that the first Minister, Luo Riqing, learned to swim when he was over 50 years old so that he could personally test the flow of water in the Yangzhi River to ensure it was safe for Chairman Mao to swim.

3 Article 2 of the Police Law states that tasks of the police are to "*safeguard national security, maintain social order, protect citizens' personal safety, personal liberty, and lawful property, protect public property, prevent, stop, and punish unlawful and criminal activities.*" These functions certainly do not necessarily mean the leadership of the Communist Party, nor the nature of "dictatorship".

4 To enforce a dress code proves to be very difficult. Uniforms are worn both by on duty and off-duty officers, and even officers on their holidays. Officers on duty are not dressed properly. They wandered on the street in partial police uniform and partially civilians clothes and invoked a strong reaction from the public (PPSD, 20 December, 1990). In 1996, the police in Danian city of the same province conducted its eighth inspection campaign on unlawful use of police uniform. The result is shocking: one out three persons in a police uniform is not a police officer (PPSD, 20 January 1996). The fundamental reason for the failure to stop the misuse is that the uniform is readily available for a price, and the profits go to the police. An investigation in Nanjing city found 37 factories making police uniform unlawfully (PPSD, 7 December, 1990), with the police being the chief beneficiary of such abuse (PPSD, 12 June, 1990). The police not only sell their uniforms, but also other police instruments, such as insignias, sirens, police cars and plates.

5 In presenting the Police Bill to the National People's Congress, the Minister of Public Security complained: "*In recent years, police officers encounter some unlawful interference in the execution of their duty. Some asked the people's police to intervene in economic disputes; some demanded the police to exceed their authority to levy fees and issue fines unlawfully. Those activities not only violated the lawful rights and interest of citizens and organisations, and damaged the police/public relations, but also caused some police officers to bear legal liabilities because of enforcing orders which violate laws.*"

6 Nevertheless, there are indications that local governments at some places are taking the opinions of superior police station seriously when filling the positions of the local chief of police. The Ministry of Public Security is said to have success-

fully blocked attempts by some regional governments to promote lay persons into senior management positions.

7   The newspaper is the official publication of the Ministry of Public Security.

8   In a most recent National Conference of Chiefs of Police which was held on 8 January 2000, the Chairman of the Party's PLC stressed that *yanda* will be continued in the new millenium to secure social stability (Wen Wei Po, 8 January 2000).

9   The increasing number of police officers killed or injured on duty demonstrates this tension.

Year	Injury on duty	Death on duty
1997	8,142	522
1996	10,102	423
1995	8,526	395
1994	8,702	331
1993	8,121	275
1990	6,492	243
1983-1990		1,298

Sources: China Law Yearbooks (1990-1998).

10 The crime rate was regarded as the index of public order in a locality and was used to evaluate the competence of the local government leaders. Having vested interests in keeping the crime rate low, local leaders applied various pressures on the police to maintain low figures. One viable resolution was to "cook the book" to satisfy the concern of local governments for their local image. The Ministry of Public Security also added to the pressures by imposing a high clearance rate. It was the traditional requirement that for serious crime, the clearance rare should be above 80% and for ordinary crime 60%. But clearance rate was calculated on the basis of the number of crimes recorded. The lower number of crimes recorded, the higher the clearance rate. The police were under the pressure from both the government, which wanted to see less crimes in the statistics and from the Ministry of Public Security which wanted a higher clearance rate. Since 1988, this dark figure issue received some serious attentions from the police authorities. The former Minister of Public Security, Wang Fang, warned that the crime statistics were so inaccurate that they could no longer reflect public order and the true tasks facing the police. He noted that this mistake must be rectified. Police are urged to ignore the 'face' of a locality and file a case if it satisfies the filing standard. To encourage the accurate report and record of crime, the Ministry of Public Security abandoned its imposition of clearance rate on local police stations. The measures taken produced some results, which were clearly shown in the 1989 statistics.

11 Patrol was carried out by the soldiers in the early 1950s. In the 1960s, the workers' militia were involved in patrolling streets (See Hinton, 1972 for example).

12   The latest police manpower was published in 1991, according to which, there were
     854,000 regular police officers. Among them, 82,000 were detectives, 122,000 were
     traffic officers and 349,000 were public order officers (China Law Yearbook, 1993).
     Police manpower is concentrated in cities, and police presence in rural areas is
     rare. As police are financed through the budget of local government, the level of
     economic development of a region determines the ratio of police in the region. The
     national ratio of police remained 0.06% until 1990s when it is increased to 0.09%.
     But in the more prosperous southern cities, the ratio has jumped to approximately
     0.5 to 0.7% (Research Group, 1997: 179).

The author would like to thank Professor Gary T. Marx and the editors for their
comments on the paper and Ms. Pinky Choy for her research assistance.

14 Police, Armed Forces and Democracy in Brazil*

Paulo De Mesquita Neto

Abstract

This chapter examines the role of the police and the armed forces in the public security system in Brazil. It focuses on the separation and differentiation between the police and the armed forces and the establishment of civilian and democratic control over the police since the transition to democracy in 1985. The chapter posits that democratic governments have failed to separate and differentiate the armed forces and the police and to consolidate civilian and democratic control over the police. Civil society has played an important but still limited role in the reform and demilitarization of the public security system. The incomplete separation and differentiation between the armed forces and the police and the uncertainty regarding civilian and democratic control over the police have contributed to the persistence of police violence and police ineffectiveness in law enforcement and order maintenance and have undermined the policies and programs to control crime and violence and consolidate the democratic regime.

Key Words: Democracy, armed forces, police, crime, Brazil

Introduction

Many countries in Latin America completed the transition from authoritarianism to democracy in the 1990s and began to focus attention on the tasks of democratic consolidation. The decline of the ideological and political polarization that marked the Cold War facilitates the consolidation of democracy in the region. However, other trends make this process problematic or at least difficult: the fiscal crisis of the State and the programs of economic stabilization and reform in Brazil, Argentina and Mexico in the 1980s and 1990's; the rise of crime and violence in Brazil, Mexico, Colombia and Peru, associated with the problems of poverty and inequality and with the problems of organized crime, drug-traffic and arms trade.

A review of the literature suggests that the process of democratic consolidation has been more difficult in Latin America than in Southern Europe. Among the main obstacles to democratic consolidation in Latin America include a high degree of social and economic inequality, weak party systems, weak states, low degree of respect for the rule of law and human rights, and a low degree of civilian and democratic control of the armed forces and the police.[1]

This article examines one problematic area for democratic consolidation in Latin America that has been relatively understudied: the role of the armed forces in the public security system and the relations between the armed forces and the police. In Latin America, there are many studies on the role of the armed forces in politics.[2]

However, there are few studies on the role of the armed forces in the public security system and on the relations between the armed forces and the police, particularly from the perspective of democratic transition and consolidation.[3]

The separation and differentiation between the armed forces and the police, the limitation of the role of the armed forces in the public security system and the civilian and democratic control of both institutions are central characteristics of consolidated democratic regimes.[4] In Latin America, however, the military still plays a central role in the public security system, undermining the civilian and democratic control of the police, particularly in countries where the armed forces established authoritarian regimes and assumed control of the government and the police in the 1960s and 1970s.[5] A fundamental challenge of the new democracies in the region is the limitation of the role of the armed forces in the public security system and the development of institutions and practices to ensure the civilian and democratic control of the police.[6]

This article focuses on the experience of Brazil, a country in which the military still participates extensively in the public security system, the armed forces and the police are not clearly separated and differentiated and the civilian and democratic control of the police is not yet consolidated. It examines the legacies of the authoritarian regime and the efforts by democratic governments to limit the participation of the military in the public security system, to separate and differentiate the armed forces and the police and to establish civilian and democratic control over the police. The article highlights the impact of institutional and political factors on the structure and functioning of the public security system. It also highlights the ways in which the nature of the preceding authoritarian regime and the mode of transition to democracy have shaped institutional and political arrangements and the structure of the public security system under the democratic regime.

Brazil is not a model or an example for other countries in Latin America. The countries in the region have very different histories, institutions and cultures. However, the analysis of the Brazilian case highlights some of the problems in the area of public security that, to a greater or lesser extent, are faced by many countries in the region as they try to consolidate democratic regimes.

In Brazil, during the authoritarian regime, both the armed forces and the police joined forces in the repression of political groups and social movements. The armed forces participation in political repression was justified and sustained by the doctrine of national security formulated and disseminated by the Superior War College, which focused attention on the problems of internal security and national development rather than external security.[7]

The police were influenced, controlled and often directed by the military.[8] Under the influence of the military, the police were also influenced by the national security doctrine. The police were organized and prepared mainly for the maintenance of social and political order and the repression of social movements and political groups, not to control crime, maintain public order and protect communities and citizens.[9] The police – particularly the military police but also the civilian police – were more concerned with the maintenance of internal security than with the maintenance of public security.[10] The problems of police violence[11] and crime and violence in the society[12] became major obstacles to the processes of democratic transition and consolidation.

Facing growing problems of crime and violence in the society and police violence during the 1980s and 1990s, reformers in civil society and more recently in the Federal Government and in State Governments, insisted on two basic changes in the public security system[13]:

- the separation and differentiation of the armed forces and the police and the limitation of the role of the military in the area of public security; and

- the expansion of the civilian and democratic control of the police.

The military, however, insisted on the maintenance and redefinition of the role of the armed forces in the area of internal security, assigning to the armed forces the responsibility for supporting police organizations in the area of public security, particularly organized crime, drug traffic and arms trade.[14]

The compromise was to accept the participation of the armed forces in the area of public security only in emergency situations, temporarily, while police organizations are reformed and better prepared to protect communities and citizens against crime and violence.[15]

This article develops the following argument regarding the role of the armed forces in the public security system and the relations between the armed forces and the police since the transition to democracy in Brazil:

- Democratic governments have failed to separate and differentiate the armed forces and the police, limit the role of the armed forces in the public security system and to consolidate civilian and democratic control over the police;

- In the process of reforming the public security system, democratic governments confronted serious crises in the system and relied on the support of the armed forces to maintain public order during these crises;

- The Federal Government and State Governments established compromises with the armed forces and the police limiting the direct participation of the armed forces in the public security system to emergency situations. These compromises allowed the containment of crises in the short run but rendered more difficult the separation and differentiation between the armed forces and the police and the consolidation of civilian and democratic control over the police in the long run;

- Civil society has played an important, but still limited, role in the reform of the public security system, supporting and proposing policies and programs with the objective of separating and differentiating the armed forces and the police, limiting the role of the armed forces in the public security system and consolidating civilian and democratic control over the police;

- The incomplete separation and differentiation between the armed forces and the police and the uncertainty regarding civilian and democratic control over the police contribute to the persistence of police violence and undermine the policies and programs to control crime and violence and to consolidate the democratic regime.

These propositions help to explain the crises in the public security system, the containment of these crises and the difficulty to resolve these crises in Brazil. They also help to explain the changes and the continuity in the relations between the armed forces and the police, which have facilitated the transition from authoritarianism to democracy, but have rendered difficult the consolidation of the democratic regime.

In the first part, the article describes the structure of the public security system in Brazil. The second and third parts describe the organization of this system during the authoritarian regime and the changes and the continuities in the system during the transition to democracy. The fourth part analyses the obstacles to reform. The last part focuses on the prospects for reforms in the public security system and the relations between reforms in the public security system and democratic consolidation in Brazil.

The Public Security System and the Federal State

Brazil is a federal State, formed by the union of 26 States and the Federal District. The structure of the public security system is closely linked to the federal structure of the Brazilian State. Even though Brazil had six constitutions (1891, 1934, 1937, 1946, 1967, revised in 1969, and 1988) and different types of political regimes since the proclamation of the republic in 1889, the basic structure of the public security system did not change dramatically.[16]

Brazil has a pluralist and decentralized public security system. It is formed by many police organizations (as in the United States, Canada, Germany, United Kingdom, Mexico and Argentina) rather than one police organization (as in Japan, Israel, Sweden, Norway, Finland, Denmark, Island, Ireland, Greece, Bolivia, Peru and Colombia) or two police organizations (as in France, Italy, Spain, Portugal and Chile). It has police organizations controlled by different governments (as in the United States, Canada, Germany, United Kingdom, Mexico and Argentina) rather than by the same government (as in France, Italy, Spain, Portugal, Chile, Bolivia, Peru and Colombia).[17]

In Brazil, however, both the pluralism and the decentralization of the public security system are moderate rather than extreme. The pluralism is moderate to the extent that Brazil has dozens of police organizations (as in Germany and the United Kingdom) rather than hundreds of police organizations (as in Canada) or thousands of police organizations (as in the United States). The decentralization is moderate to the extent that the police organizations are controlled by the Federal Government and by State Governments (as in Germany) not by city or local government (as in the United States, Canada and United Kingdom).

Brazil has a relatively small federal police, with approximately 7,000 agents and non-uniformed civilians under the control of the Federal Government responsible for crimes within the federal jurisdiction, drug traffic and border control.[18] Contrary to Argentina, for example, which also has a federal State, Brazil never had a large federal police and a federal military police.[19]

Brazil also has municipal guards responsible for the protection of municipal property, but these guards do not have police authority. Contrary to the United States and Canada, Brazil does not have local police organizations controlled by local governments.

In Brazil, the States in the federation have the primary responsibility for the organization of the police and each State has two police organizations. The military police, which has more agents and more resources, is a uniformed, administrative police, responsible for maintaining public order.[20] The civilian police is a non-uniformed judicial police responsible for criminal investigation. Contrary to France, Italy and Spain, however, which have two police organizations with different territorial responsibility and similar functional responsibility, the federal States in Brazil have two police organizations with the same territorial responsibility and different functional responsibility.

Each one of the 26 federal States and the Federal District has a military police and a civilian police. Brazil has, therefore, 54 State police agencies, in addition to the federal police, with a total number of 472,803 police officers.[21] The total number of officers in the military police is 368,900 whereas the total number of officers in the civilian police is 103,903. In the State of Sao Paulo, which has the largest police agencies, the military police has 82,021 agents and the civilian police have 36,883 agents.[22]

In Brazil, while the State governments are responsible for the organization of the police, the federal Government is responsible for the organization of the armed forces: the Army, the Navy and, since 1941, the Air Force.

However, there is not a clear separation and differentiation between the police and the armed forces, regarding their organization and function in the political system. The armed forces are responsible for external defense and internal security. The police are responsible for public security and internal security.

The military police is considered to be an auxiliary force and reserve of the Army and maintains a highly centralized organization similar to the Army. Furthermore, in the military police, as in the armed forces, officers and soldiers have very different backgrounds, educations, training, careers, wages, benefits and rights. The inequality and authoritarianism within the military police has reproduced and reinforced the inequality and authoritarianism within the armed forces and the Brazilian society. In the military police, as in the armed forces, education and training have historically emphasized the function of internal security.

The reason for this overlapping of military and police organizations and functions, as the reason for the duality of police agencies in the States, is not the strengthening of the systems of national defense and public security or the civilian and democratic control over the armed forces and the police. The duplication of roles is an instrument through which the Federal Government and the armed forces can balance the power of the State governments and the police, and vice-versa. It is also an instrument through which the Federal Government and the State Governments can join forces for maintaining the political and social order.

Historically, even though revolutionary guerrilla or terrorist organizations never had a strong presence in Brazil, internal security, rather than external defense and public security, has been the main role of the armed forces and the police. The armed forces and the police have been organized to protect the State against political opponents and social movements, to repress political and social conflicts, not to protect the State against threats and attacks from other States or to maintain law and public order or to protect the citizens. The authoritarian regime in 1964-85 simply accentuated and led to the extreme of this tendency.[23]

The Authoritarian Regime

In 1964, the military assumed control of the federal Government and expanded the role of the armed forces in politics. An important part of this process was the expansion of the role of the armed forces in the area of public security. This expansion was supported by institutional arrangements and government policies that sustained the direct participation of the armed forces in the maintenance of law and order and the subordination of the police to military control.[24]

The 1967 Constitution established that the armed forces were responsible not only for national defense but also for the maintenance of law and order and the protection of the three constitutional powers, the Executive, the Legislative and the Judiciary (1967 Federal Constitution, article 92, paragraph 2).[25] The 1967 Constitution also established that the military police in the States was an auxiliary force and reserve of the Army responsible for maintaining order and internal security (1967 Federal Constitution, article 13, paragraph 4).

This institutional framework generated four types of problems for the public security system:

- ambiguity and vagueness regarding the role of the armed forces and the police;

- conflict between the armed forces and the police regarding their respective roles;

- difficulty of coordination between the armed forces and the police; and

- difficulty of coordination between the military police and the civilian police in the States.

During the authoritarian regime, these problems were minimized through the expansion of the military control over the police. Through law-decrees 317/1967 and 667/1969, the military government reorganized the military police and subordinated the military police to the Ministry of Army. It established a special division in the Army General Staff to supervise and control the military police (law-decree 667/1969, articles 1 and 2) and establish the norms regarding the organization and mobilization of the military police (1967 Constitution, article 8). The same law-decrees established that the Minister of the Army had to approve the appointment of the commandant of the military police, which, according to the 1967 Constitution, was made by State governors (law-decree 667/1969, article 6).

This institutional arrangement was reinforced by national security laws, which also emphasized the role of the armed forces in the area of internal security and subordinated the police to the Army.[26] Furthermore, during the authoritarian regime, the State governors systematically appointed military officers to direct not only the military police but also the Secretariat of Public Security, which was responsible for public security policy and directed both the military police and the civilian police.[27] In the late 1960s and 1970s, special unit were formed by the military and the police, under military command, to repress the opposition to the regime.[28] In 1978, the authoritarian regime took to the extreme the tendency towards the military control of the police and the insulation of the police from civilian and democratic control. The Supreme Federal Court transferred from the Criminal Justice system to the Military Justice system the competence to judge military police officers accused of crimes against civilians.[29]

The centralization and concentration of power in the armed forces minimized the problem of coordination between the armed forces and the police. However, this process produced serious distortions in the role of the armed forces and the police and in the organization and functioning of the public security system. On the one hand, this process subjected the police to military and authoritarian rather than civilian and democratic forms of control. On the other hand, this process virtually eliminated the separation and differentiation between the armed forces and the police. The armed forces were organized not for external defense, but mainly for internal security. The police forces were organized not for public security but mainly for internal security.

The result of this militarization of the public security system was a reduction in police effectiveness, from the perspective of law enforcement and order maintenance, and an increase in police violence. The police became more concerned with, and more focused on, political and social control rather than with law enforcement and order maintenance. To maintain the political and social order, the police relied systematically on the use and threat of violence, particularly against members of the lower classes and the black and *mestizo* groups.

To be clear, the public security system was already militarized before the authoritarian regime in 1964-85. However, the authoritarian regime sustained and increased to the highest degree the militarization of the system.[30] Furthermore, the militarization of the public security system did not happen only in Brazil. It happened also in Argentina, Chile, Peru, Mexico and other countries in Latin America that, like Brazil, had authoritarian regimes during the 1960s and 1970s. Even though there were significant differences from one country to another, the militarization of the public security system in one country facilitated, and was facilitated by, the militarization of the system in other countries.[31]

The Transition to Democracy

In Brazil, the transition from authoritarianism to democracy began in 1974, when President Ernesto Geisel began to lift the press censorship and initiated a process of political liberalization that became known as "opening" [*abertura*]. In 1982, for the first time since 1964, there were direct and free elections for State governments and the opposition to the authoritarian regime won the elections in nine States, including the central States of Sao Paulo, Rio de Janeiro and Minas Gerais. In 1984-85, the opposition won the indirect election to the Presidency of the Republic and a civilian, José Sarney, assumed the Presidency, after the death of the elected President Tancredo Neves. The Constituent Assembly met in 1987-1988 and the new Federal Constitution was promulgated in 1988. The transition to democracy ended only in 1990, when Fernando Collor de Mello, the first president elected directly since 1960, assumed the Presidency of the Republic.[32]

A major challenge during the process of democratic transition was the demilitarization of the political system[33] and particularly the demilitarization of the public security system, a complex process that involves three different, but interdependent processes:

- the separation and differentiation of the armed forces and the police, with the specialization of the armed forces in external defense and the specialization of the police in public security;

- the limitation of the role of the armed forces in the area of public security; and

- the establishment of civilian and democratic control of the police.

The demilitarization of the public security system began during the authoritarian regime and gained force with the promulgation of the 1988 Federal Constitution. However, the scope of this process has been limited due to the opposition by the armed forces, the military police and conservative parties and groups. Further-more, and perhaps more important, this process happened during a period of rising crime and violence, particularly in large urban centers, which sustained and even strengthened the pressures for the preservation of the role of the armed forces in the area of public security.

The first step in the limitation of the role of the armed forces in the public security system was the strengthening of the police, particularly the military police. From 1981 to 1991, the number of soldiers in the military police grew from 185,000 to 243,000, while the number of soldiers in the armed forces grew from 272,550 to 296,700.[34] In 1994, there were ,600 soldiers in the military police and 336,800 soldiers in the armed forces (219,000 in the Army, 58,400 in the Navy and 59,400 in the Air Force).[35]

From 1981 to 1994, the number of people in the military police grew 208% while the number of people in the armed forces grew 139%. The military police, which was 24% smaller than the armed forces in 1981, became 14% larger than the armed forces in 1994. This change reflected and contributed to the expansion of the role of the police and the State governments and the limitation of the role of the armed forces and the Federal Government in the area of law enforcement and order maintenance.

In 1986, President José Sarney established the Afonso Arinos Commission to draft a project for the new constitution. The Commission presented a project for the new constitution that, if approved, would radically alter the structure of the public security system. The Federal States would be able to maintain the military police, but there would be a clear separation between the military police and the armed forces. The military police would be an auxiliary force to the civilian police, not an auxiliary force to the Army. The civilian police would have the responsibility for public security and the armed forces would have the responsibility for external defense and the maintenance of the constitutional order. Furthermore, the federal Govern-ment and the Army would have the authority to establish control over the police only in exceptional circumstances, after declarations of war, federal intervention in the States or states of emergency.[36]

However, the reforms proposed by the Affonso Arinos Commission were rejected in the Constituent Assembly. They were systematically opposed by the armed forces, the military police and the conservative parties, with the argument that the police were not sufficiently strong required the assistance of the military to contain the rise of organized crime and particularly illegal drug and arm trade. [37]

The 1988 Federal Constitution established the institutional basis for the new demo-cratic regime and for the organization and functioning of the public security system. The 1988 Constitution, for the first time in Brazilian history, introduced the concepts of national defense and public security, separating and differentiating the roles of the armed forces and the police. There is a special chapter on public security, which fo-cuses on the federal police, the civilian police, the military police and the municipal guards. There is a separated chapter on the armed forces and another chapter on states of emergency. These three chapters are grouped under a title dedicated to the defense of the State and democratic institutions (1988 Federal Constitution, articles 136-144). The Constitution also expanded the prerogatives of the Judiciary, the National Con-gress and the Presidency regarding the control of the armed forces and the preroga-tives of the Judiciary, Legislative Assemblies and State Governments regarding the control of the police. In addition, the Constitution assigned to the public prosecutors the responsibility for the external control of police activities (1988 Federal Constitution, article 129, VII).

The 1988 Constitution, as the previous constitutions, assigned to the armed forces the responsibility not only for national defense but also for maintaining law and order and protecting the constitutional powers (1988 Federal Constitution, article 142). The difference is that the 1988 Constitution explicitly established that the armed forces are authorized to participate in the maintenance of law and order only by request of the constitutional powers. Furthermore, the complementary law 69/1991, and subsequent complementary law 97/1999, explicitly established that this participation can happen only under the direction of the president and after the police forces have demonstrated their incapacity to preserve public order.

Furthermore, the 1988 Constitution explicitly assigned the responsibility for public security to the Federal police, the civilian police, the military police and the municipal guards. In addition, the Constitution explicitly assigned the responsibility for controlling the civilian police and the military police to the State Governments.

Yet, the Constitution also maintained the clauses establishing that the military police is an Army reserve and auxiliary force and that organization and functioning of the military police is regulated by the Federal Government (1988 Federal Constitution, article 144, paragraphs 1 and 8). The armed forces are still responsible for public security, regularly, not only, as proposed by the Affonso Arinos Commission, in exceptional situations like war, Federal intervention and states of emergency. The president can determine the mobilization of the armed forces to maintain law and order independently of the National Congress or the Judiciary, as long as the police is incapable or is perceived as incapable to preserve public security.

Thus, the 1988 Constitution reflected and sustained a very gradual process to separate and differentiate the armed forces and the police, to assign the responsibility for public security to the police and the responsibility for national defense to the armed forces. Furthermore, the majority of the personnel in the police are in the military police, which continues to be an auxiliary force and reserve of the Army, therefore subject to military regulations and military control, normally, not only in exceptional situations. In many States, Army generals or colonels are still appointed to direct the military police and the secretary of public security.

In 1996, President Fernando Henrique Cardoso began to implement policies designed to enforce the new constitutional norms and limit the role of the armed forces in the area of public security announcing the National Defense Policy. The National Defense Policy directed the role of the armed forces to the problems of external defense and international peacekeeping. It limited the role of the armed forces in the area of public security to exceptional and temporary situations, under the control of civilian authorities, to support rather than control or direct police operations, particularly in the Amazon, and to control the international trade of illegal drugs and arms. In 1999, President Fernando Henrique further strengthened this policy thorough the creation of the Ministry of Defense and the subordination of the Army, Navy and Air Force to Ministry of Defense in June 1999.

Since the transition to democracy, the armed forces have become more focused on national defense and the police have become more focused on public security. Both the armed forces and the police are more subject to the control of civilian and democratic governments. The participation of the armed forces in the public security system is more limited than it was during the authoritarian regime. However, this participation directly and indirectly supports the police and is still frequent, not exceptional, but temporary as in the consolidated democracies.

From November 1994 to May 1995, the Federal Government and the State Government developed "Opertation Rio", in which the armed forces were deployed to support police operations against organized crime and drug traffic and to control police corruption and violence in the State of Rio de Janeiro.[38] From 1985 to 1997 the armed forces were deployed at least 50 times in different States, mostly to support police operations but also to contain police crises and riots - as in the strikes in the federal police in 1994 and the strikes in the military police and the civilian police in 1997. Table 1 shows that the direct of participation of the armed forces in the area of public security has increased, not diminished, from 1985 to 1997. The participation of the armed forces in the control of strikes diminished, but the participation of the armed forces in law enforcement, order maintenance and the control of mass demonstrations increased – particularly in rural areas. Furthermore, the armed forces have participated in the crises and rebellions by the police, which started when police agents, who are not allowed to strike, engaged in demonstrations and rebellions protesting against government policies and demanding wage increases. From 1994 to 1997, the armed forces intervened to control police crises and rebellions at least four times during the Itamar Franco Government (1993-94) and nine times during the Fernando Henrique Cardoso Government (1995-97).

Table 14.1 Participation of the Armed Forces in Public Security, Brazil, 1985-1997

Law Enforcement	Order Maintenance	Demonstrations	Strikes	Police Crises
1985				
1986		1	1	
1987			1	
1988			1	
1989				
Total Sarney 0	**0**	**1**	**3**	**0**
1990 1				
1991 1				
1992	1			
Total Collor 2	**1**	**0**	**0**	**0**
1993	1	1		2
1994 1		2		2
Total Itamar 1	**1**	**3**	**0**	**4**
1995 1			1	1
1996 5		2		1
1997 7	3	6		7
Total Cardoso 13	**3**	**8**	**1**	**9**
Total 16	**5**	**12**	**4**	**13**

Source: Folha de S. Paulo, O Estado de S. Paulo, O Globo, Jornal do Brasil, Veja and IstoÉ.

Institutional Obstacles to Reform

There has been a significant change toward the separation and differentiation between the armed forces and the police and the establishment of civilian control of the police since the transition to democracy in Brazil. However, the armed forces still play an extensive role in the public security system and still exercise a significant influence over the police, particularly the military police.

There are at least four institutional rules that make the demilitarization of the system difficult.

- First, the rule according to which the armed forces are responsible not only for national defense but also for the maintenance of law and order (1988 Federal Constitution, article 142, and Complementary Law 69/1991). This rule, despite the limitations imposed upon this participation, still allows ample room for the armed forces in public security, as is demonstrated in Table 1.

- Second, the rule according to which the States have military police forces and the military police forces are auxiliary forces and reserve of the Army (1988 Federal Constitution, article 144, specially paragraphs 5 and 6).

- Third, related to the second rule, the rule according to which the military police forces have their organization and functioning subject to federal and military rules (article 22, item XXI; law-decree 667/1969).

- Fourth, the rule according to which the States in which the military police has more than 20,000 agents can have a Military Justice to judge military police officers. In 1996, the National Congress approved, and President Fernando Henrique Cardoso enacted, a law transferring from the Military Justice to the Criminal Justice System the responsibility for judging the officers accused of homicide. However, this law still leaves to the Military Justice the responsibility for judging the officers accused of other crimes, contributing to sustaining the expectation of impunity regarding the military police.

These four rules make it quite difficult to reform the public security system. They limit the scope of the reorganization and redefinition of the role of the police and the integration of the military police and the civilian police. They also undermine the civilian and democratic control of the police. Finally, they make it difficult to reduce police violence and increase police legitimacy and effectiveness in law enforcement and order maintenance.

The homicide rate in Brazil increased from 11.7 homicides per 100,000 habitants in 1980 to 22.0 in 1990 and 23.70 in 1996. Homicide rates reached 35.2 in the State of Sao Paulo, 37.2 in the Federal District, 39.9 in Pernambuco, 41.0 in Espirito Santo, and 53,6 in Rio de Janeiro in 1996.[39]

The average annual homicide rate in Brazil increased from 14.8 homicides per 100,000 habitants in 1980-84 to 18.3 in 1985-89 and 22.6 in 1990-95. In the same period, the average homicide rate by firearm increased from 5.4 in 1980-84 to 7.6 in 1985-89 and 11.7 in 1990-95.[40]

In the State of Sao Paulo, the only State that regularly collect and publicize information on police violence, the number of civilians killed by the police declined from 1086 in 1991 and 1458 in 1992 to 420 in 1993, 550 in 1994, 661 in 1995, 436 in 1996. However, the number of civilians killed by the police is still extremely high compararcd

Table 14.2 Homicide Rate*, Brazil, 1980-1996

YEAR	1980	1981	1982	1983	1984	1985
	11.7	12.9	12.9	14.1	15.6	14.9
YEAR	1986	1987	1988	1989	1990	1991
	15.5	17.1	17	20.5	22.0	20.8
YEAR	1992	1993	1994	1995	1996	—
	19.1	20.3	21.3	23.9	23.7	—

Source: Catao 1999. * Homicides/100,000 habitants.

Table 14.3 Homicide Rate*, Sao Paulo, 1980-1996

YEAR	1980	1981	1982	1983	1984	1985
	13.8	16.4	16.0	21.9	25.8	25.1
YEAR	1986	1987	1988	1989	1990	1991
	25.2	27.2	25.2	30.2	30.8	30.7
YEAR	1992	1993	1994	1995	1996	—
	28.2	28.3	30.2	34.3	35.2	—

Source: Catao 1999. * Homicides/100,000 habitants.

Table 14.4 Homicide Rate*, Rio de Janeiro, 1980-1996

YEAR	1980	1981	1982	1983	1984	1985
	26.1	22.0	18.8	15.9	20.8	21.3
YEAR	1986	1987	1988	1989	1990	1991
	20.2	30.9	24.7	34.2	56.1	39.5
YEAR	1992	1993	1994	1995	1996	—
	35.0	41.1	48.7	61.8	53.6	—

Source: Catao 1999. * Homicides/100,000 habitants.

Table 14.5 Number of Civilians Killed by the Police, State of Sao Paulo, 1990-1999

YEAR Civilians Killed	1990	1991	1992	1993	1994
	595	1086	1458	420	550
YEAR Civilians Killed	1995	1996	1997	1998	1999
	661	436	466	546	647

Source: Sao Paulo, State Secretary of Public Security.

to the number of civilians killed by the police in consolidated democracies and has increased again to 466 in 1997, 546 in 1998 and 647 in 1999.[41]

The continuity of reforms in the public security system will require significant changes in constitutional rules. There are at least four major proposals in the National Congress.

Hélio Bicudo, a federal deputy from the State of Sao Paulo, proposed a constitutional amendment in 1991 that, if approved, would demilitarize the public security system by abolishing the military police and Military Justice, separating and differentiating completely the police and the armed forces. Bicudo proposed the amendment in 1991.[42]

In April 1997, the governor of the State of Sao Paulo, Mario Covas, proposed another constitutional amendment that, if approved, would transfer from the military police to the civilian police the responsibility for maintaining public order.[43] It maintains the military police in States with a smaller size for policing public events, mass demonstrations, prisons, schools and forests, and also for traffic control, fire brigade and civil defense. Furthermore, this proposal would make the military police responsible not only for public order but also for "internal security".

In August 1997, President Fernando Henrique Cardoso and Minister of Justice Iris Rezende proposed a constitutional amendment which would give to the States autonomy to decide on the maintenance or extinction of the military police.[44] However, according to this proposal, the military police, if maintained by the States, would continue to be an Army reserve and auxiliary force, organized in accordance with federal and military rules, and, as in the proposal made by Governor Mario Covas, would be responsible not only for public order but also for "internal security".

Zulaiê Cobra Ribeiro, a federal deputy from the State of Sao Paulo and rapporteur of the Chamber of Deputies' Special Commission to Examine the Question of Public Security, proposed another constitutional amendment in June 1998. As the constitutional amendment proposed by Bicudo in 1991, Ribeiro's constitutional amendment, would, if approved, eliminate the military status of the uniformed police in the federal States and their linkage to the Army. It would separate and differentiate the police and the armed forces. However, as the proposals made by Bicudo, Covas and Cardoso, this proposal would not change the constitutional role of the armed forces and, more specifically, it would not limit the role of the armed forces in the maintenance of law and order.[45]

The National Congress never passed the constitutional amendments mentioned above. However, under the pressure from the armed forces and the military police, the National Congress approved in February 1998 a constitutional amendment transforming the soldiers in the armed forces from "*public servants*" into "*militaries of the armed forces*" and agents of the military police from "*military police agents*" into "*militaries of the States*". The constitutional amendment reinforced the military status of the officers in the military police and made more difficult the demilitarization of the public security system.[46]

Perspectives for Reform

The consolidation of democracy requires not only the limitation of the role of the armed forces in government and politics but also the limitation of the role of the armed forces in the public security system. The existing institutional arrangements and government policies, however, have not fully supported this process. Even though there have been significant changes since the transition to democracy, these changes have not been sufficient to clearly separate and differentiate the armed forces and effectively limit the role of the armed forces in the area of public security. The result is the persistence of military influence, oversight and control over the police, the prevalence of repressive strategies of crime law enforcement and order maintenance and the continuity of police violence, particularly against the members of low income and minority groups.

The armed forces, the military police and conservative groups have successfully blocked proposals for changes in the basic structure of the public security system in the Constituent Assembly and in legislative commissions established in the National Congress and Legislative Assemblies.

In the last few years, however, the media and non-governmental organizations, such as Teotonio Vilela Human Rights Commission in Sao Paulo, Viva Rio in Rio de Janeiro, the Office of Legal Assistance to Popular Organizations in Pernambuco, Human Rights Watch, Amnesty International and Center for Justice and International Law have played a major role in exposing police violence and police ineffectiveness in the area of public security. Research centers, such as the Center for the Study of Violence at the University of Sao Paulo and the Institute for the Study of Religion in Rio de Janeiro, have studied and proposed reforms with the objective of reducing police violence and increasing police effectiveness.

The Center for the Study of Violence, with the collaboration of non-governmental and governmental organizations, elaborated the project for the National Program for Human Rights, announced by President Fernando Henrique Cardoso in May 1996.[47] It also elaborated the project for the Program for Human Rights in the State of Sao Paulo, announced by Governor Mario Covas in September 1997.[48] Both programs focus extensively on the questions of public security and support the establishment of community policing and police accountability to the citizens as strategies to reduce police violence and improve police performance in law enforcement and order maintenance.

With the support of non-governmental organizations, the States of Sao Paulo, Rio de Janeiro, Minas Gerais and Pará established an independent police ombudsman for receiving citizen complaints and monitoring police investigation of police misconduct. The State of Sao Paulo has implemented a State-wide community policing program.[49]

Despite the growing participation of, and pressures from, civil society, the changes in the organization and functioning of the public security system are still limited in scope. Democratic governments continue to seek the support of the armed forces to contain crises in the public security system, crises that either are not resolved or are generated by the police. The support of the armed forces has helped democratic governments to contain the crises in the public security system in the short run. However, it has reinforced institutional arrangements and government policies that have limited the scope of the reform and demilitarization of the public security system that are necessary to resolve these crises in the long run.

Since the transition to democracy, democratic governments have sought to limit, but at the same time preserve, the participation of the armed forces in public security. They support the reform and demilitarization of the public security system, which is necessary for democratic consolidation in the long run. However, facing crises in the public security system and conservative opposition in the National Congress and in Legislative Assemblies, democratic governments accept the participation of the armed forces in the public security system, which is necessary for their political survival.

The question is to what extent will the democratic governments be able to reform and demilitarize the public security system in the long run, if they depend on the armed forces in the short run. The reform and demilitarization of the public security system is a long-term process.

- If democratic governments limit the participation of the armed forces in the area of public security, they increase the chances of reform and demilitarization in the public security system in the long-term, but they also increase the risk of crises in the short term.

- If democratic governments accept the participation of the armed forces in the public security system, they reduce the risk of crises in the short term, but they also reduce chances of reform and demilitarization in the public security system in the long-term.

Faced with this dilemma, democratic governments have continued to rely on the armed forces to reduce the risk of crises in the public security system in the short term, and have abandoned or at least postponed temporarily the project of reform and demilitarization of the system. This strategy has not only facilitated the control of crises in the public security system during the transition to democracy, but has also made reform and demilitarization of the public security system more difficult during the consolidation of democracy.

Further research is needed on policies and strategies that democratic governments have adopted and can adopt to reconcile the conflict between the long term goal of reforming and demilitarizing the public security system and at the same time achieving the short term goal of controlling crises in the public security system. More specifically, research is needed on the opportunities and risks of police reforms in emerging democracies, particularly reforms aimed at the establishment of community policing and police accountability to the citizens. These reforms, supported by non-governmental organizations, may reduce police violence, increase police effectiveness and limit government dependence on the armed forces in the area of public security. However, they do not eliminate the need for constitutional reforms, which depend more on the support of governments and parties.

Paulo de Mesquita Neto, Ph.D. in Political Science, Columbia University 1995, is senior researcher at the Center for the Study of Violence at the University of Sao Paulo and executive secretary of the Institute Sao Paulo Against Violence. At the Center for the Study of Violence, Paulo Mesquita has developed research on the consolidation of democracy and the protection of human rights in Brazil, focusing attention on the role of the armed forces and the police on these processes. At the Institute Sao Paulo Against Violence, a non-governmental organization, Paulo Mesquita supports the development of democratic policies and

Neto

strategies to reduce crime and violence in the State of Sao Paulo. Paulo Mesquita participated in the elaboration of the project for the National Program for Human Rights and the Program for Human Rights in the State of Sao Paulo. He is member of the Comission for the Implementation of the Human Rights Program and the Commission for Community Policing in the State of Sao Paulo. He has published numerous articles in professionals journals. His areas of interest include: processes of democratic transition and consolidation; human rights policies and programs; the limitation and control of the use of force in contemporary societies, particularly by the police and the armed forces but also by individuals and social groups; his hobbies include outdoor activities, going to the movies and reading, if possible with my wife and two children.

Center for the Study of Violence-University of Sao Paulo, Av. Prof. Lucio Martins Rodrigues, Travessa 4, Bloco 2, CEP 05508-900, Sao Paulo, SP, Brazil. Tel.: (55-11) 3818-4951. Fax: (55-11) 3818-4950. E-mail: pmesquit@usp.br

References

Adorno, Sergio. 1997. "A Criminalidade Violenta Urbana no Brasil: Tendências e Características" [Violent Crime In Urban Brazil]. Paper presented at the Conference on Urban Crime and Violence, Rio de Janeiro, RJ, March 2-4, 1997.

Aguero, Felipe. 1992. "The Military and the Limits to Democratization in South America". In Mainwaring, O'Donnell and Valenzuela 1992.

Arquidiocese de Sao Paulo. 1985. *Brasil: Tortura Nunca Mais* [Brazil: Torture Never More] (Petropolis: Vozes).

Bayley, David H. 1994. *Police for the Future* (New York and Oxford: Oxford University Press).

Bayley, David H. 1985. *Patterns of Policing* (New Brunswick, NJ: Rutgers University Press).

Bicudo, Hélio 1997. "A Violência e a Estrutura Judiciária Brasileira" [Violence and the Brazilian Judicial Structure]. In *Estudos Avançados* 30: 67-78.

Bicudo, Hélio. 1977. *Meu Depoimento sobre o Esquadrao da Morte* [My Testimony on the Death Squad] (Sao Paulo: Comissao Justiça e Paz-SP).

Caldeira, Cesar. 1997. "Seguranca Publica e Sequestros no Rio de Janeiro (1995-1996)" [Public Security and Kidnappings In Rio de Janeiro] . *Tempo Social* 9:1.

Cancelli, Elizabeth. 1994. *O Mundo da Violência: A Polícia na Era Vargas* [The World of Violence: The Police in the Vargas Era]. (Brasilia: UnB).

Cano, Ignacio. 1997. *Letalidade da Acao Policial no Rio de Janeiro* [Lethal Police Action In Rio de Janeiro] (Rio de Janeiro: ISER).

Catao, Yolanda. 1999. *Mortes Violentas: Um Panorama dos Homicidios no Brasil* [Violent Deaths: An Overview of Homicides In Brazil]. Manuscript (Rio de Janeiro: IBGE).

Chalmers, Douglas A., Vila, Carlos M. and Hite, Katherine, eds. 1997. *The New Politics of Inequality in Latin America: Rethinking Participation and Representation* (Oxford: Oxford University Press).

Chevigny, Paul G. 1995. *The Edge of the Knife: Police Violence in the Americas* (New York: The New Press).

Chevigny, Paul G. 1991. *Police Deadly Force as Social Control: Jamaica, Brazil and Argentina* (Sao Paulo: Nucleo de Estudos da Violencia).

D'Arauo, Maria Celina, Soares, Glaucio Ary Dillon, e Castro, Celso. 1995. *A Volta aos Quarteis* [The Return to the Barracks] (Rio de Janeiro: Relume-Dumara).

D'Araujo, Maria Celina, Soares, Glaucio Ary Dillon, e Castro, Celso. 1994a. *Anos de Chumbo* [Gunshot Years] (Rio de Janeiro: Relume-Dumara).

D'Araujo, Maria Celina, Soares, Glaucio Ary Dillon, e Castro, Celso. 1994b. *Visoes do Golpe* [Visions of the Coup] (Rio de Janeiro: Relume-Dumara).

Diamint, Rut, ed. 1997. *La Cuestion Civico-Militar en las Nuevas Democracias de America Latina* [The Civil-Military Question in the new democracies in Latin America]. Workink Papers (Buenos Aires: Universidad Torcuato di Tella).

Diamond et al. 1997. *Consolidating the Third Wave Democracies.* Baltimore and London: The Johns Hopkins University Press.

Diamond, Larry and Plattner, Marc F. 1996. *Civil-Military Relations and Democracy.* Baltimore and London: The Johns Hopkins University Press.

Diamond, Larry, Linz, Juan J. and Lipset, Seymour M., eds. 1995. *Politics in Developing Countries: Comparing Experiences with Democracy* (Boulder and London: Lynne Rienner Publishers).

Diamond, Larry, Linz, Juan J. and Lipset, Seymour M., eds. 1989. *Democracy in Developing Countries: Latin America* (Boulder and London: Lynne Rienner Publishers).

Dominguez, Jorge I. and Lowenthal, Abraham F. (eds.). 1996. *Constructing Democratic Governance: Latin America and the Caribbean in the 1990s* (Baltimre and London: The Johns Hopkins University Press).

Fernandes, Heloisa R. 1985. "A Forca Publica no Estado de Sao Paulo" [The Public Force in the State of São Paulo]. In Boris Fausto, ed., *Historia Geral da Civilizacao Brasileira - O Brasil Republicano, Sociedade e Instituicoes, 1889-1930* [General History of the Brazilian Civilization – The Republican Brazil, Society and Institutions, 1889-1930] (Sao Paulo: Difel).

Fitch, J. Samuel. 1998. *The Armed Forces and Democracy in Latin America* (Baltimore and London: The Johns Hopkins University Press).

Flores, Mario C. 1992. *Bases para uma Politica Militar* [Basis for Military Policy] (Campinas: Editora da UNICAMP).

Fruhling, Hugo, ed. 1998. *Control Democratico en el Mantenimineto de la Seguridad Interior* [Democratic Control and the Maintenance of Internal Security]. Santiago: Centro de Estudios del Desarrollo.

Gleizal, Jean-Jacques, Gatti-Domenach, Jacqueline and Journes, Claude. 1993. *La Police: le cas des democraties occidentales* (Paris: Presses Universitaires de France).

Goodman, Louis W., Mendelson, Johanna S.R., and Rial, Juan, eds. 1990. *The Military and Democracy: The Future of Civil-Military Relations in Latin America* (Lexington and Toronto: Lexington Books)

Goodman, Louis W. and Mendelson, Johanna S.R. 1990. "The Threat of New Missions: Latin American Militaires and the Drug War". In Goodman, Mendelson and Rial 1990.

Holloway, Thomas H. 1993. *Policing in Rio de Janeiro: repression and resistance in a 19th century city* (Stanford: Stanford University Press).

Huggins, Martha. 1998. *Political Policing: The United States and Latin America* (Durham, NC: Duke University Press).

Huggins, Martha K. 1991. *Vigilantism and the State in Modern Latin America: essays on extra-legal violence* (New York: Praeger).

Huggins, Martha and Haritos-Fountouros, Mika. 1996. "Conciencia torturada: secretos y moralidad en la violência policial brasilena" [Tortured Conscience: secrets and morality of police violence in Brazil]. In Waldmann 1996.

Hunter, Wendy. 1997. *Eroding Military Influence in Brazil: Politicians Against Soldiers* (Chapel Hill and London: University of North Carolina Press).

Huntignton, Samuel P. 1991. *The Third Wave: Democratization in the Late Twentieth Century* (Norman: University of Oklahoma Press).

Kant de Lima, Roberto. 1994. *A Policia da Cidade do Rio de Janeiro: seus dilemas e paradoxos* [The Police In the City of Rio de Janeiro: dilemmas and paradoxes] (Rio de Janeiro: Forense)

Linz, Juan J. and Stepan, Alfred. 1996. *Problems of Democratic Transition and Consolidation: Southern Europe, South America and Post-Communist Europe* (Baltimore and London: The John Hopkins University Press).

Lowenthal, Abraham F. and Fitch, J. Samuel. 1986. *Armies and Politics in Latin America* (New York: Holmes & Meyer).

Mainwaring, Scott, O'Donnell, Guillermo and Valenzuela, J. Samuel, eds. 1992. Democratic Consolidation: *The New South American Democracies in Comparative Perspective* (Notre Dame: University of Notre Dame Press).

Mann, Michael. 1993. *The Sources of Social Power: The Rise of Classes and Nation States, 1760-1914* (Cambridge: Cambridge University Press).

Martinez-Lara, Javier. 1996. *Building Democracy in Brazil: The Politics of Constitutional Change, 1985-95* (New York: St. Martin's Press).

Mathias, Suzeley K. 1995. *Distensao: O Projeto Militar, 1973-1979* [Opening: The Military Project, 1973-1979] (Campinas: Papirus).

Mendez, Juan, O'Donnell, Guillhermo and Pinheiro, Paulo Sergio. 1999. *The (Un)Rule of Law and the Underprivileged in Latin America* (Notre Dame: University of Notre Dame Press).

Mesquita Neto, Paulo de. 1999a. "Violencia policial no Brasil: abordagens teoricas e praticas de controle" [Police Violence in Brazil: theoretical framework and practices of control]. In Pandolfi, Dulce et al., *Cidadania, Justiça e Violência* [Citizenship, Justice and Violence] (Rio de Janeiro: Editora da Fundacao Getulio Vargas).

Mesquita Neto, Paulo de.1999b. Policiamento Comunitário: A Experiencia em Sao Paulo" [Community Policing: The Experience in São Paulo]. *Revista Brasileira de Ciencias Criminais* 7(25): 281-292.

Mesquita Neto, Paulo de and Affonso, Beatriz Stella. 1998. *Polícia Comunitária: A Experiência em São Paulo* [Community Policing: The Experience in São Paulo]. Research report. São Paulo: Universidade de São Paulo, Núcleo de Estudos da Violência.

Mesquita Neto, Paulo de. 1995. From Intervention to Participation: The Transformation of Military Politics in Brazil, 1974-1992. Ph.D. Dissertation. Columbia University, New York.

Minayo, Maria Cecilia. 1994. "A Violencia Social sob a Perspectiva da Saude Publica" [Social Violence from a Public Health Pesrepctive]. *Cadernos de Saude Publica* 10:1.

Monet, Jean-Claude. 1993. *Polices et societes en Europe* (Paris: La Documentation Francaise).

O'Donnell, Guillermo, Whitehead, Laurence, Schmitter, Philippe, eds. 1986. *Transitions from Authoritarianism: Perspectives for Democracy* (Baltimore and London: The Johns Hopkins University Press, 1986).

Pereira, Anthony. 1998. "O Monstro Algemado?: Violência do Estado e Repressao Legal no Brasil, 1964-1997" [The Monster in Handcuffs? State Violence and Legal Repression In Brazil, 1964-1997]. In Zaverucha 1998.

Pinheiro, Paulo S. 1997a. "Popular Responses to State-Sponsored Violence in Brazil". In Chalmers, Vita and Hite 1997.

Pinheiro, Paulo S. 1997b. "Violencia, crime e sistemas policiais em paises de novas democracias" [Violence, crime and police systems In new democracies]. *Tempo Social* 9:1.

Pinheiro, Paulo S. 1996. "O Passado nao esta morto: nem passado e ainda" [The Past is not Dead: it not yet past]. In Dimenstein, Gilberto, *Democracia em Pedacos: Direitos Humanos no Brasil* [Democracy In Pieces: Human Rights in Brazil] (Sao Paulo: Companhia das Letras).

Pinheiro, Paulo S. 1991a. *Estrategias da Ilusao: A Revolucao Mundial e o Brasil, 1922-1935* [Illusory Strategies: Global Revolution and Brazil, 1922-1935] (Sao Paulo: Companhia das Letras).

Pinheiro, Paulo S. 1991b. "Police and Political Crisis: The Case of the Military Police". In Huggins 1991.

Pinheiro, Paulo S. 1991c. "Autoritarismo e Transicao" [Authoritarianism and Transition]. *Revista USP* 9.

Pinheiro, Paulo S. 1981. "Violencia e Cultura" [Violence and Culture]. In Lamounier, Bolivar, Weffort, Francisco C. and Benevides, Maria Victoria, eds. *Direito, Cidadania e Participaacao* [Law, Citizenship and Participation] (Sao Paulo: Brasiliense).

Pinheiro, Paulo S. et al. 1991. "Violencia Fatal" [Fatal Violence]. *Revista USP 9*, Dossie Violencia.

Przeworski, Adam. 1995. *Sustainable Democracy* (Cambridge: Cambridge University Press).

Przeworski, Adam. 1991. *Democracy and the Market: Political and Economic Reforms in Eastern Europe and Latin America* (Cambridge: Cambridge University Press).

Rizzo de Oliveira, Eliezzer. 1994. *De Geisel a Collor: Forcas Armadas, Transicao e Democracia* [From Geisel to Collor: Armed Forces, Transition and Democracy] (Campinas: Papirus Editora).

Rocha, Luiz Carlos. 1991. *Organizacao Policial Brasileira* [Police Organization In Brazil] (Sao Paulo: Saraiva).

Rouquie, Alan. 1987. *The Military and the State in Latin America* (Los Angeles and London: University of California Press).

Skidmore, Thomas E. 1988. *The Politics of Military Rule in Brazil, 1964-1985* (Oxford: Oxford University Press).

Skidmore, Thomas E. 1967. *Politics in Brazil, 1930-1964: An Experiment in Democracy* (Oxford: Oxford University Press).

Silva, Jorge da. 1996. "Militarizacao da Seguranca Publica e Reforma da Policia: um depoimento" [The Militarizatoion of Public Security and Police Reform: A testimony]. In Ricardo Bustamante and Paulo Cesar Sodre, eds. *Ensaios Juridicos: O Direito em Revista* [Juridical Essays; The Law in Review] (Rio de Janeiro: Instituto Brasileiro de Atualizacao Juridica).

Silva, Jorge da. 1990. *Controle da Criminalidade e Seguranca Publica* [Crime Control and Public Security] (Rio de Janeiro: Forense).

Smith, Peter H., ed. 1993. *El combate a las drogas en America* [The war on drugs in America] (Mexico, DF: Fondo de Cultura Economica).

Soares, Luiz Eduardo, ed. 1996. *Violencia e Policia no Rio de Janeiro* [Violence and Police in Rio de Janeiro] (Rio de Janeiro: ISER e Relume Dumara).

Souza, Edinilsa R. de. 1994. "Homicidios no Brasil: O Grande Vilao da Saude Publica na Decada de 80 [Homicides in Brazil: The Great Villain in Public Health In the 1980s]. *Cadernos de Saude Publica* 10:1.

Stepan, Alfred. 1988a. *Rethinking Military Politics: Brazil and the Southern Cone* (Princeton: Princeton University Press).

Stepan, Alfred, ed. 1988b. *Redemocratizando o Brasil* [Redemocratizing Brazil] (Rio de Janeiro and Sao Paulo: Paz e Terra)

Stepan, Alfred, ed. 1973a. *Authoritarian Brazil: Origins, Policies and Future* (New Haven: Yale University Press).

Stepan, Alfred. 1973b. "The New Professionalism of Internal Warfare and National Development". In Alfred Stepan 1973a.

Stepan, Alfred. 1971. *The Military in Politics: Changing Patterns in Brazil* (Princeton: Princeton University Press).

Tonry, Michael and Morris, Norval, ed. 1992. *Modern Policing* (Chicago and London: The University of Chicago Press).

Varas, Augusto, ed. 1989. *Democracy under Siege: New Military Power in Latin America* (New York: Greenwood Press).

Vidigal, Armando F. 1989. *Las Fuerzas Armadas y los Nuevos Problemas de la Seguridad* [The Armed Forces and the New Security Challenges] (Santiago: Comision Sudamericana de Paz).

Waldman, Peter, ed. 1996. *Justicia en la calle: ensayos sobre la policia en America Latina* [Justice in the Streets: essays on the police in Latin America] (Medellin: Fundacion Konrad Adenauer Stiftung, Centro Interdisciplinario de Estudios sobre Desarrollo Latinoamericano, Instituto de Investigacion sobre Espana y America Latina, Biblioteca Juridica Dike).

Zaverucha, Jorge. 1994. *Rumor de Sabres: Tutela Militar ou Controle Civil - Estudo Comparativo das Traniscoes no Brasil, na Argentina e na Espanha* [Military Guardianship or Civilian Control: A Comparative Study of Transitions in Brazil, Argentina and Spain] (Sao Paulo: Atica).

Documents and Periodic Publications

Americas Watch and Nucleo de Estudos da Violencia-USP. 1993. Violencia Policial Urbana no Brasil: Mortes e Tortura pela Policia em Sao Paulo e no Rio de Janeiro, 1987-1992 [Police Violence in Urban Brazil: Deaths and Torture by the Police in São Paulo and Rio de Janeiro, 1987-1992].

Brazil. Constituicao Federal de 1988 [Federal Constitution 1988]. Document in the Internet (www.mj.gov.br).

Brazil, Assembleia Nacional Constituinte, Comisssao da Organizacao Eleitoral, Partidaria e Garantia das Instituicoes. 1987. Relatorios e Pareceres aos Anteprojetos das Comissoes - Substitutivo [Reports and Opinions on the Projects of the Commissions – Substitute Project].

Brazil, Assembleia Nacional Constituinte, Comissao da Organizacao Eleitoral, Partidaria e Garantia das Instituicoes, Sub-comissao da Defesa do Estado, da Sociedade e da sua Seguranca. 1987. Anteprojeto – Relatorio [Project – Report].

Brazil, Camara dos Deputados. 1997a. Redacao para o segundo turno de discussao da proposta de emenda a Constituicao 338-B/1996 [Text for the second round of the discussion of the constitutional amendment 338-B/1996].

Brazil, Camara dos Deputados. 1997b. Proposta de Emenda Constituicao 514/97 [Proposal of Constitutional Amendment 514/97].

Brazil, Camara dos Deputados. 1991. Proposta de Emenda Constituicao 46-A/91 [Proposal of Constitutional Amendment 46-A/91].

Brazil, Camara dos Deputados, Comissao Especial com a Finalidade de Exminar a Questao da Segurança Pública no País. 1998. Relatorio [Report].

Brazil, Ministerio do Exercito, Secretaria de Comunicacao Social do Exercito. 1987. Temas Constitucionais [Constitutional Themes].

Brazil, Ministerio da Justica. 1997a. Medidas Minimas para Reforma da Seguranca Publica [Minimum Steps for the Reform of Public Security].

Brazil, Ministerio da Justica. 1997b. Conferencia Nacional Seguranca, Justica e Cidadania [National Conference on Security, Justice and Citizenship].

Brazil, Presidencia da Republica. 1996a. Programa Nacional de Direitos Humanos [National program for Human Rights]. Document in the Internet (www.mj.gov.br).

Centro de Estudios Legales y Sociales. 1997. Control Democratico de los Organismos de Seguridad Interior en La Republica Argentina [Democratic Control of the Organizations for Internal Security in Argentina].

CEDEC. 1997a. Mapa de Risco da Violencia - Cidade do Rio de Janeiro [Map of the Risk of Violence – City of Rio de Janeiro].

CEDEC. 1997b. Mapa de Risco da Violencia - Cidade de Salvador [Map of the Risk of Violence – City of Salvador].

CEDEC. 1996a. Mapa de Risco da Violencia - Cidade de Curitiba [Map of the Risk of Violence – City of Curitiba].

CEDEC 1996b. Mapa de Risco da Violencia - Cidade de Sao Paulo [Map of the Risk of Violence – City of Sao Paulo].

Folha de S. Paulo. 1986. Guia da Constituinte [Guide of the Constitution]. Special edition. September 19, 1986.

Human Rights Watch/Americas. 1997. Brutalidade Policial Urbana no Brasil [Police Brutality in Urban Brazil].

Human Rights Watch/Americas. 1996. Violencia X Violencia: Violacoes aos Direitos Humanos e Criminalidade no Rio de Janeiro [Violence x Violence: Human Rights Violations and Criminality in Rio de Janeiro].

The International Institute for Strategic Studies. 1994. The Military Balance, 1994-1995.

Nucleo de Estudos da Violencia and Comissao Teotonio Vilela. 1995. Dossie Direitos Humanos no Brasil 2 [Human Rights in Brazil 2].

Nucleo de Estudos da Violencia and Comissao Teotonio Vilela. 1993. Dossie Direitos Humanos no Brasil 1 [Human Rights in Brazil 1].

Ordem dos Advogados do Brasil. 1994. Proposta de Uma Nova Politica de Seguranca Publica [Proposal for a New Public Security Policy].

Revista USP 21. 1994. Dossie Judiciario [Judiciary].

Revista USP 9. 1991. Dossie Violência [Violence].

Sao Paulo, Governo do Estado. 1997. Programa Estadual de Direitos Humanos [State Program for Human Rights].

Sao Paulo. Gabinete do Governador. 1997. Proposta de Emenda Constitucional [Proposal of Constitutional Amendment].

Sao Paulo, Secretaria da Seguranca Publica, Ouvidoria da Policia do Estado de Sao Paulo. 1999. Relatorio Anual de Prestacao de Contas – 1998 [Annual Report 1998].

Sao Paulo, Secretaria da Seguranca Publica, Ouvidoria da Policia do Estado de Sao Paulo. 1998. Relatorio Anual de Prestacao de Contas – 1997 [Annual Report 1997].

Sao Paulo, Secretaria da Seguranca Publica, Ouvidoria da Policia do Estado de Sao Paulo. 1997. Relatorio Anual de Prestacao de Contas – 1996 [Annual Report 1996].

Tempo Social 9:1 - Seminario Estrategias de Intervencao Policial no Estado Contemporaneo [Seminar: Strategies of Police Intervention in Contemporary States].

U.S. Department of Justice/National Institute of Justice and U.S. Department of State/Bureau of International Narcotics and Law Enforcement Affairs. 1997. Policing Emerging Democracies: Workshop Papers and Highlights.

Washington Office on Latin America. 1998. Temas y Debates en la Reforma de la Seguridad Publica: Una guia para la sociedad civil [Themes and Debates in the Reform of Public Security: a guide for civil society].

Washington Office on Latin America. 1995. Demilitarizing Public Order: The International Community, Police Reform and Human Rights in the Americas.

World Bank. 1997. O Crime e a Violencia como Problemas do Desenvolvimento na America Latina e no Caribe [Crime and Violence as Development Problems in Latin America and the Caribbean]. Document presented at the Conference on Urban Crime and Violence, Rio de Janeiro, RJ, March 2-4, 1997.

Notes

1 Diamond et al 1997; Dominguez and Lowenthal 1997; Linz and Stepan 1996, Diamond, Linz and Lispet 1995 and 1989; Przeworski 1995 and 1991; Mainwaring, O'Donnell and Valenzuela 1992; Huntington 1991, O'Donnell, Whitehead and Schmitter 1986.

2 Fitch 1998; Diamint 1997; Aguero 1992; Goodman, Johanna and Rial 1990; Varas 1989; Stepan 1988a and 1973b; Rouquié 1987; Lowenthal and Fitch 1986.

3 Studies on the role of the military in the public security system tend to focus on the participation of the armed forces in the control of drug traffic. See Smith 1993 and Goodman e Mendelson 1990. For analyses of the armed forces-police relations, see Waldmann 1996; Huggins 1991; U.S. Department of Justice/National Institute of Justice and U.S. Department of State/Bureau of International Narcotics and Law Enforcement Affairs 1997; Washington Office on Latin America 1995.

4 Bayley 1994 e 1985; Gleizal, Gatti-Domenach and Journés 1993; Mann 1993; Monet 1993, Tonry and Morris 1992; Dahl 1989.

5 The armed forces established military governments in Brazil (1964-1985), Argentina (1966-1973 and 1976-1983), Uruguay (1973-1985), Chile (1973-1989), Peru (1968-1980), Ecuador (1972-1979), Bolivia (1964-1978 and 1980-1982) and Paraguay (1954-1989). In Guatemala, Honduras, El Salvador, Nicaragua and Panama, military leaders frequently organized coups and counter-coups and assumed control of the government.

6 Mendez, O'Donnell and Pinheiro 1999; Fruhling 1998, Wola 1998.

7 Stepan 1971 and 1973b.

8   Silva 1996; Pinheiro 1991b, 1991c and 1981.

9   Chevingy 1995 and 1991, Pinheiro 1997a, 1997b and 1996.

10 In Brazil, the concept of "public security" refers to the security of citizens and communities, in the context of conflicts in which citizens and communities are involved in a complex society. The concepts of "internal security" and "external security" refer to the security of the state, in the context of conflicts in which the state is involved with other organizations within its territory and other organizations, particularly other states, outside its territory.

11 Mesquita Neto 1999a; Cano 1997; Pinheiro 1997a, 1997b, 1996; Pinheiro et al. 1991; Chevigny 1995 and 1991; Human Rights Watch/Americas 1997 e 1996; Núcleo de Estudos da Violência e Comissao Teotonio Vilela 1995 and 1993; Americas Watch and Nucleo de Estudos da Violencia 1993.

12 Catao 1999; Adorno 1997; Caldeira 1997; World Bank 1997; Minayo 1994; Soares 1996; Souza 1994; CEDEC 1997a, 1997b, 1996a e 1996b.

13 See the project for the new constitution presented by the Affonso Arinos Commission to the Constituent Assembly in 1996, described below in the section on transition to democracy. See also Brasil, Camara dos Deputados 1997b and 1991; Brasil, Ministério da Justiça 1997a and 1997b; São Paulo, Gabinete do Governador 1997; Brasil, Presidencia da Republica 1996a; Ordem dos Advogados do Brasil 1994.

14 Flores 1992; Vidigal 1989; Brazil, Ministerio do Exercito, Secretaria de Comunicacao Social do Exercito 1987.

15 Brazil, Lei Complementar 97/1999; Cardoso 1994; Brazil, Lei Complementar 69/1991; Brazil, Constituicao Federal/1988.

16 For the political history of Brazil, see Skidmore 1988 and 1967.

17 For the structure of the police systems in advanced democracies, see Gleizal, Gatti-Domenach and Journés 1993 and Monet 1993.

18 The federal police was created as the police of the federal district in 1944 and reorganized as the federal police in the 1960s.

19 In Argentina, which is also a Federal State, there is a strong federal police, with 33,000 agents, and a military police, the Gendarmeria Nacional, with 18,500 agents, controlled by the Federal Government. The provinces have just one police organization, which is responsible for maintaining public order and criminal investigation. The only exception happens in the Ciórdoba, where there are two police organizations. The province of Buenos Aires has the largest police in the country, with 48,000 agents. See Centro de Estudios Legales y Sociales 1997: 9-12.

20 In Brazil, the term "military police" refers to the militarized police force of the federal States, not to the police of the armed forces. For the history, organization and function of the military police and the civilian police in Brazil, see Kant de Lima 1994; Holloway 1993; Rocha 1991; Silva 1990; Fernandes 1985.

21 Ministry of Justice, National Secretary of Public Security.

22 With a population of approximately 35 million, the state of Sao Paulo has 1 police agent for each 294 habitants. The ratio is comparable to the ratio in Italy, which has a population of 57 million, 199,000 police agents and 1 police agent for each 286 habitants. For purposes of comparison, Spain has a population of 38 million, 139,000 police agents and 1 police agent for each 276 habitants. France has a population of

56 million, 207,000 police agents and 1 police agent for each 270 habitants. The United Kingdom has a population of 57 million, 140,000 police agents and 1 police agent for each 407 habitants. Monet 1993: 124-125.

23   Pinheiro 1991a, Cancelli 1994.

24   Skidmore 1988; Stepan 1973a and 1971, D'Araújo, Soares and Castro 1994a and 1994b.

25   The constitutional amendment 1, in 1969, established that the armed forces were also responsible for the execution of the national security policy, a responsibility which included all the others (1969 Federal Constitution, article 91).

26   See law-decree 898/1969 and law 6.620/1978 and law 7.170/83.

27   Silva 1996.

28   Huggins 1998; Huggins and Haritos-Fontouros 1996; Arquidiocese de Sao Paulo 1985; Bicudo 1977.

29   On the military justice, see Pereira 1998 and Bicudo 1997.

30   Pinheiro 1981, 1991a and 1991b.

31   On the militarizaztion of the police in Latin America, see Waldmann 1996; Huggins 1991; Washington Office on Latin America 1995; Centro de Estudios Legales y Sociales 1997.

32   On the transition to democracy, see Linz and Stepan 1996; Marttinez-Lara 1996; Skidmore 1988; Stepan 1988b.

33   On the changes in civil-military relations during the transition to democracy, see Hunter 1997; D'Araaújo, Soares and Castro 1995; Mathias 1995; Mesquita Neto 1995; Rizzo de Oliveira 1994; Zaverucha 1994; Skidmore 1988, Stepan 1988a.

34   Mesquita Neto 1995.

35   The International Institute for Strategic Studies 1994.

36   For the text of the constitutional project elaborated by the Affonso Arinos Commission, see *Folha de S. Paulo*, September 19, 1986.

37   See Brazil, Assembleia Nacional Constituinte, Comissao da Organizacao Eleitoral, Partidaria e Garantia das Instituicoes 1987; Brazil, Assembleia Nacional Constituinte, Comissao da Organizacao Eleitoral, Partidaria e Garantia das Instituicoes, Subcomissoes da Defesa do Estado, da Sociedade e da sua Seguranca 1987.

38   Soares 1996; Caldeira 1995.

39   Catao 1999.

40   Catao 1999.

41   Sao Paulo, State Secretary of Public Security.

42   Brazil, Camara dos Deputados 1991.

43   Sao Paulo, Gabinete do Governador 1997.

44   Brazil, Camara dos Deputados 1997b.

45   See Brazil, Câmara dos Deputados, Comissao Especial com a Finalidade de Exminar a Questao da Segurança Pública no País 1998.

46   See Brazil, Camara dos Deputados 1997a.

47   Brazil, Presidencia da Republica 1996.

48   São Paulo, Governo do Estado 1997.

49   Sao Paulo, Secretaria da Seguranca Publica, Ouvidoria da Policia do Estado de Sao Paulo 1999, 1998 and 1997; Mesquita Neto 1999b; Mesquita Neto and Affonso 1998.

* This article is based on research conducted in Brazil with the support of the National Council for Scientific and Technological Development in Brazil (1995-1998) and the Open Society Institute's Center on Crime, Communities and Culture in New York (1998-2000). Earlier versions of this article were presented at the Sawyer Seminar, at the New School for Social Research, New York, November 4, 1997, and at the Latin American Studies Association XXI International Congress, Chicago, IL, September 24-26, 1998. The author thanks the participants at these meetings for their comments as well as his colleagues at the Center for the Study of Violence for their continuous support all these years.

15 Democracy's Blues: The Politics of Police Reform in South Africa, 1990-2000

Mark Shaw

Abstract

Policing under apartheid was designed for control and suppression. Thus the transformation of the police has been an essential requirement of the post-democratic order in South Africa. Achieving this has been a difficult and far from a uniform process. Initially, the challenge to policy makers, who at the time did not fully trust the police, was to acquire greater legitimacy among the public for the erstwhile policing agencies of authoritarianism who now also policed the democracy. These initiatives have been overtaken by a need to respond to increasing levels of crime in the country, which is now seen as a key threat to the democratic order. The police, in the absence of a range of skills taken for granted in most democracies, and with the urging of politicians, are assuming a much greater law and order stance in an attempt to clamp down on crime. Now the police struggle to achieve legitimacy not through political assurances that they support the new order but by reducing lawlessness on the ground.

Key Words: South Africa, Police transformation, Crime Community policing, Politics of crime control

Introduction

The public and political debate on policing in South Africa has come full circle. The new democracy saw dramatic changes — including an amalgamation of all the country's police forces into a single police service and a focus on community oriented forms of policing and human rights — being made to the policing agencies of apartheid in order to improve their accountability and legitimacy. However, increasing levels of crime in the immediate aftermath of apartheid, and the police's inability to deal with these, have prompted a new approach by government. Now crime and not the police, as was the case in the first days of the new order, are seen as a threat to democracy. The result is an increasingly harsh enforcement response, illustrated by large military style operations, to lawlessness. It is too early to tell whether this approach will dramatically reduce levels of crime. However, what is clear, is that the backlash against crime may, over time, undercut hard won civil liberties.

A system of brutal policing was central to maintaining apartheid. The majority of South Africans were policed more for control than for crime prevention — although in the eyes of white politicians, since black people were perceived to be the predominant perpetrators of crime, this amounted to the same thing. Police actions, particularly as the apartheid state, came under greater threat during the violent conflict of the 1980s were increasingly brutal.[1] By this time, there was little love lost between the majority of the country's citizens and the police. Given that policing in the country had been highly politicized, political rather than policing imperatives drove the debate around the shape of a new police agency — the result was a highly centralized, large and bureaucratic body, run from Pretoria, designed to maintain control at the center, rather than a devolved and locally orientated one.

In the immediate aftermath of the fall of apartheid, the new government's attempts at police reform were based largely on making policing more legitimate in the eyes of the public and more accountable to the new political dispensation. In effect, to transform a body responsible for policing political dissent to one which held the confidence of the majority of people in order to police the democracy. This included ensuring safety for citizens and policing crime and criminals in a way that was consistent with the human rights focus of the new democracy. Respect for the police, by those who had been subject to its brutal regime, was such, that problems of lawlessness (or more accurately the prospect that the police would not be able to control it) were not viewed initially by the new political leadership as a serious threat to the democracy.

Apartheid's police however turned out to be the wrong tool for policing the new democratic order. Not only was a lack of legitimacy replaced by contempt for poor performance, but the police seemed to have few of the investigative and other skills required to operate effectively in a democratic environment. "*The police,*" said one senior official, "*were like a rugby team playing in a game of soccer.*"[2] More seriously, these discoveries were made because the post-apartheid order was subject to some of the highest violent crime levels in the world. South Africa's homicide rate per 100,000 of the population is far higher than figures available for other countries in comparative stages of development — 55.3 homicides per 100,000 of the population as opposed to 40.4 for Brazil (In contrast, the rate for the United States is 8.2 and the United Kingdom 2.4).[3] Data on other jurisdictions in Africa remain sketchy, but on the 1997 INTERPOL figures South Africa has the highest homicide rate in the world. Growing levels of crime in the immediate aftermath of the fall of the apartheid State are central to understanding ongoing attempts at police transformation.

The issue of crime however was not viewed as a serious challenge by the government until three to four years into the new order. This was the result of some high profile criminal incidents, including a spate of cash in transit heists carried out in broad daylight by large groups of armed men, as well as a growing public outcry on the issue of crime. Particularly influential was a strong business lobby, both domestic and foreign, which argued that crime was undercutting the country's chances of attracting much needed foreign investment. The strategy at first was a defensive one. The growing recognition that crime (and the dissatisfaction with government responses to it) was being seen as a key weakness of the new government in their attempt to co-opt those groups (business and the white middle class) most critical of its performance in this regard and the forging of partnerships with a range of interest groups. This was done by engaging those critical of government performance (who were in any event eager to discuss the issue with senior Ministers) and argue that to criticize the state was not enough, people should get involved, bringing ideas and resources to the table. This approach, however, had some important implications for the building of police legitimacy — a number of innovative partnership initiatives were launched, notably in the area of victim support. These initiatives included the adopting of police stations by business and community groups, the provision of resources such as cars and phones and the provision of training and (to a lesser extent) skilled administrative and financial personnel. It did, however, subject the police to a range of (often competing) interest groups including foreign donors, leading to a proliferation of priorities, strategies and objectives. The majority of these remained paper plans, never impacting upon policing on the ground.

Crime continued to remain at high levels. Violent property crimes such as motor vehicle hijacking (a key concern of the white middle class) escalated significantly in this period. Continued prominent incidents of crime, including the hijacking and shooting dead of prominent personalities (including some foreign and local business executives) kept the issue in the public eye. This included the victimization of prominent black people, including a football and TV star, and continued politically motivated killings in KwaZulu-Natal as well as ongoing violence between taxi groups and gangs elsewhere in the country. At the time, overall levels of crime, reflected in the data collected by the police — which with some prominent exceptions like hijacking and armed robbery, were remaining stable at very high levels — was less important in changing perception than ongoing and high level media coverage of prominent (and often brutal) criminal events. Importantly, over time, it was clear that crime was not just the rantings of a white elite, vulnerable in the post-authoritarian order. The majority of victims of crime were in fact black and survey evidence suggested that issues of safety increasingly topped the list of priorities of the majority of the country's citizens. In the period immediately after the country's second democratic election in April 1999, government's stance on the issue of crime took an immediately harder and much more proactive line. Ironically, the more the democracy has matured, the easier it has become to return to a relatively harsh law and order dominated policing regime reminiscent of apartheid. Strong statements, both permitting and legitimizing a harsh policing regime, which would have been impossible in the political context of 1994, condemned crime and criminals roundly, and urged the police to deal harshly with offenders.

It may be too early to tell what the impact of this approach will be. Statements have been followed by a clearer policing strategy, which concentrates on law enforcement rather than on issues of community policing, service delivery and human rights, under the auspices of a new (black) police commissioner. It is possible that this strong operational stance will lead to a reduction in some categories of crime over time. It is clear also that, given encouragement from within the police, from politicians (including opposition political parties) and most importantly by the public to the police to deal harshly with criminals, the problem of police brutality will remain a key issue within the society.

In the space of ten years then policing in South Africa has undergone dramatic changes. The assumption is often that this has been consistent and thereby a planned process, beginning at one point and ending at another. Nothing could be further from the truth. The process of policing transformation has not been uniform. While it has often meant different things to different people, and has been controlled more strongly by some interests than others at different times, a series of distinctive phases can be identified. Each of these phases has impacted upon how the police function today.

The first phase relates to the period before 1994, when the police themselves began a series of changes that determined to some extent the foundation of much of the transformation process that was to come. The second phase is the critical first two years of the new democratic order when the focus was on achieving an accountable and legitimate police agency and the prerogatives of crime fighting took a back seat. The third phase, from late 1996 through to 1999, was one of increased partnership largely with business but also with community groups, seldom initiated by the police, but shaped by their desire to bring external players on board and acquire the resources they offered. The last phase, from the election in April 1999, has concentrated almost exclusively on an enforcement response to crime control. The paper considers each of these phases in turn and concludes with a brief examination of the future prospects for policing and crime control in the country.

Reform from within: 1990-1994

President FW de Klerk signaled a new era in South African politics with the announcement of the un-banning of the African National Congress (ANC) in February 1990. That had important implications for the police. They had been engaged in a vicious and low level civil war with the liberation movements and there is evidence that many of these activities (with or without political approval) continued for a period thereafter[4]. The perception amongst most outside observers at the time was that the South African Police (SAP) would be resistant to change. De Klerk himself at least appeared to believe this — senior police managers were called together and told that they would be required to change to accommodate the new and emerging order. In a series of purges, a number of senior generals were removed or retired early from the SAP.

At the same time, however, senior police management (drawn at the time exclusively from the old apartheid order) began to rethink their position. The reality with which they were confronted was a complex one. The country continued to be characterized by high levels of violence that they were under public pressure to contain — even though it is clear that in many incidents, they could at best be accused of selective policing and at worst of direct involvement.[5] These accusations were to have important long term implications for policing in the country — apart from militarizing the police to a greater extent than would have otherwise been the case, the direct involvement in violence led many citizens to view the police as criminal from the beginning. Many black South Africans often seem unsurprised at the high number of police officials involved in crime as though the lines between those who enforce the law and those who commit crime has always been blurred in the South African context.

Internal to the SAP, however, important debates within senior management (which was at the time exclusively white) were underway as to their future. While there may have been disagreements as to what should be changed and when, there was unanimity that change should be controlled by the police themselves. At least on the surface there seemed to be recognition that given current poor relations between the police and communities, urgent action was required in the context of the changing political environment. Change was not only necessary to ensure that the SAP would survive as a core structure, but was seen to be essential if it was to operate at all. Key interventions were made in this period that recognized the necessity for change at the same time as ensuring that capacity was maintained to fight political dissent. A 1991 internal commission headed by Hennie de Witt, an ex-Commissioner sought to restructure the SAP in a number of important ways. The creation of a visibly separate Internal Stability Division responsible for the maintenance of public order in the most violence torn parts of the country was meant to ensure that ordinary station level police officers could get on with the job of building relations with the citizenry and fighting crime. At the same time, an attempt was made to remove more visible aspects of political policing to counter accusations that the SAP was doing pretty much what it had always done — crush those in opposition to the government. The Security Branch was combined into the investigations division to form a new branch of the force.

These changes, however, did little else other than rearrange the furniture. Even in Security Branch, where the brightest and most ambitious officers made their careers, skilled personnel were in short supply. There was also little opportunities for lateral entry into the police force — it was often noted with pride that the Commissioner had once been a constable who had patrolled the streets. There was thus little infusion of skills into the police agency — most officers who completed degrees, even in support divisions such as finance, had acquired these through part time study once in the police. Most notable, given these recruitment practices, an overall shortage of analytical skills existed which would prove serious after 1994 when the SAPS re-orientated itself to focus exclusively on crime and criminal organizations. Given a history of extracting confessions from suspects, detective skills were in short supply. While the SAP had always had detectives the nature of the society had meant that 'detection' was often less about the gathering of evidence than the extraction of information from suspects. In respect of more complex issues related to organized crime and complex fraud, although these were not at the time priorities, the police force was and remains underskilled.

The police force and its management was also driven excessively by a structural response to problems. Thus, when community policing became increasingly a key component of police strategy from 1990 onwards the outcome was the appointment of a community policing division and community policing officers. At the time, there was little objection from within the police, police unions were poorly developed at the time, and most members of the SAP were happy to follow orders in a highly structured environment. This logic excluded the possibility that community policing should be carried out by all officers regardless of their position or function. Community policing then simply became a 'soft' add on to ordinary day to day law enforcement.[6] Community policing officers did not have a clear mandate, being encouraged to build better relations with communities (which was often interpreted as a requirement to extract information from the community) and to liaise with local political leaders. The country was in a high state of tension at the time and these efforts were often rebuffed by black communities who remained deeply suspicious of the SAP.

Despite these problems, the emphasis on community policing increased towards the end of 1993 when the SAP announced that "community involvement in law enforcement would be the cornerstone of its strategic plan for 1993/94."[7] It added that this was the first time a strategic SAP plan had been made public, and that 'outsiders' — a Police Board, established earlier to broaden supervision of the SAP — had been involved in framing it. But by mid-1994 the limits of the SAP's community relations thrust were still evident. Not least of the problems was that many old Security Branch members were redeployed as community policing officers.

At the time, however, the SAP were not the only police agency in the country — there were another ten police forces in each of the 'homelands', nominally black ruled parts of the country.[8] Some of these agencies, notably the KwaZulu and Bophutatswana Police, were notorious for their allegiance to their respective homeland regimes and their harsh policing of anti-apartheid activists. These police forces however were closely tied to the apron strings of Pretoria and the SAP — policing transformation at the center would effectively also mean change on the periphery.

It was against this backdrop that the SAP (under the auspices of the National Party government) entered the process of negotiations with the ANC. The negotiations around policing transformation were taking a different form from those involving the future of the South African military. Most critically there were no ANC police cadres and little thought had been given to the issue during the struggle against apartheid (apart from a few exceptions in the intelligence arm of the movement) to bring to the police. That meant that the police could remain pretty much as it had, albeit with the addition of 'service' to its name and a restructuring around the new provinces.

Indeed, it was on the issue of whether or not there should be regional police agencies that the police themselves exerted, independent of the National Party negotiators, their own interests which included ensuring that the police be retained in as close a form to its current reality as possible. Dramatic change would mean police mangers would lose control over the pace and nature of the policing transformation.[9] The ANC had a clear policy position on the issue — to regionalize policing would be dangerous as it would allow transformation to take place at different speeds across the country and would offer the opportunity for regionally based political parties to use the police for their own ends. Senior management of the police were in agreement but for different reasons — regionalizing the police would destroy national control of policing, now so effectively in their hands, and undermine their ability to control change. A deal was struck, although it resulted in a messy compromise where there would be provincial ministers responsible for policing, but who would have almost no power. The provincial Minister's could not interfere in the line command of the police, in effect they could not order the police to do anything. They were responsible for ensuring good relations between the police and communities, monitoring police performance as well as launching inquiries into issues relating to policing.

It was, in any event, in the interests of the police to delink (at least in private) from the view of the National Party. Police strategy at the time was to 'project' the SAP as a professional force independent of the ruling party which indeed, at the height of the struggle against apartheid, was exactly what it had been. But police managers could hardly deny that the SAP had been used as a brutal agency of suppression — so they didn't, simply arguing that they had acted under the orders of a past political dispensation and would act under the orders of a new one.

The outcome of these developments were that when the South African Police Service (SAPS) was created as an amalgamation of the 11 police agencies in the country, senior SAP managers were firmly in control of change, occupying the key senior positions in the SAPS. The implications of this were two folds:

1   First, there was no new blood to inject and redirect the police agency towards policing a democracy with the pace and form of change being controlled by SAP officers;

2   Second, and related to the first, there were precious few skills to accomplish this task.

Legitimacy first, all else will follow: 1994-1996

While SAP senior managers waited apprehensively in their offices in May 1994 for the new Minister, Sydney Mufumadi, to arrive, internal discussions within the ANC had shaped what his new agenda would be. Given the history of policing in the country, it was assumed that the SAP was an all powerful instrument which could be used effectively by the new government if two conditions were satisfied, namely, that:

• it could be made more accountable to those whom it policed and

• at the same time more legitimate.

Indeed, there remained very real fears at the time that the police would be used to disrupt the functioning of the new government by mounting a coup or disrupting the state in less overt ways.

A series of inter-locking challenges confronted the new government. First was the requirement to retain a degree of consistency within the leadership of the police. While it was debated whether or not to place a civilian as the new head of the SAPS, it was ultimately agreed that an 'old order' police officer who did not have a tainted record should be placed in charge. Second was to improve the legitimacy of the police in the eyes of the public. At a political level, President Mandela and other prominent leadership went out of their way to praise the police and urged citizens to accept them as their new protectors. If the police could be legitimized in the eyes of the public, it was believed a major obstacle had been cleared.

At the time the issue of crime was not viewed seriously by those with the political responsibility for policing. The governments own White Paper on Safety and Security in late 1998 stated: *"The immediate challenge of the new government in 1994 was to create a legitimate police service out of the eleven police forces constituted under apartheid. Along with this challenge, political leaders had to ensure that the police would support the new democracy, rather than oppose or undermine it. Key to this process was ensuring that the police in the future would act in ways which won the trust of citizens who had once feared them."*[10]

The real requirements at the time then remained essentially political — ensuring that the police were made accountable and legitimate in the eyes of the public. While there was a growing outcry around crime, it came mainly from the white middle classes. Indeed, government responses, including statements to this effect by President Mandela himself, around the issue often implied that blacks had always been the victims of crime and that whites should not complain if they themselves were now being victimized. The issue of crime simply was not given the same level of importance as it would assume by the year 2000.

A key mechanism to enhancing police legitimacy and strengthening accountability was a sustained focus on the implementation of community policing, building on those changes already implemented in the SAP. Indeed, community policing, in effect a strategy to legitimize the police through greater contact with the community, was seen as a central transformation strategy, not only to make the police more acceptable to citizens, but also as a tool to change the police from within. The idea of community policing was never entirely embraced in all parts of the SAPS. Its largest impact, and correctly so, was on station level policing, its effect on the large number of specialized units and other entities within the police was limited. In any event, for many police officers, community policing remained a 'soft' add on to the 'hard' aspects of real policing. Both community policing and human rights training was, however, introduced in the SAPS — however there was a moratorium on recruitment and so few new officers were trained. In-service training in the SAPS was of poor quality and may not have reached officers at the front-end of the police.

The most significant visible change in the system was the creation through legislation of community police forums at police stations across the country. Initially the forums had been stipulated as a requirement in the country's first interim constitution which indicates suggest how seriously the issue of community policing was seen to be a change-agent for the police. CPFs were unelected structures which consisted of local community representatives who had an interest in improving police performance. Members did not have to represent any constituency and it was generally expected (although this often did not turn out to be the case) that they would be people of standing in the community. The effectiveness of community policing forums have been much questioned. Within the SAPS many officers regarded them as a necessary evil, required to bring citizens in contact with the police, but having little impact on the day to day conduct of policing. A key debate which arose in this regard were disputes between community policing forum members and the local SAPS as to the operational independence of the police. CPF members demanded that the police do what they said; the police refused. Legally, the police were generally on solid ground, but that enhanced the impression that CPFs were simply 'toy telephones.' In effect, CPFs had no legal powers other than attempting to influence the police through persuasion.

Within the police agency itself, those charged with community policing and the management of transformation and change assumed growing importance. The new Minister had brought with him a group of civilians, largely lawyers and academics, with little practical experience of policing. By 1996 a civilian Secretariat had been formed, as the constitution made provision for, responsible for advising the Minister, providing civilian oversight of the SAPS and monitoring police performance. The Secretariat was headed by a civilian who had equal rank, and in theory status, to the SAPS Commissioner. This was a recipe for conflict and also sent a signal to the police that while they were in line command of policing, they were not necessarily trusted. The Secretariat, however, could not over-rule the police, or could only do so through their influence on the Minister leading to many acrimonious exchanges within the Department. Often however conflict was avoided simply by both parties lobbying the Minister separately.

By 1996, however, some serious deficiencies were beginning to show themselves. The SAPS did not have a history of criminal detection characteristic of the police in other democratic societies. While pockets of excellence were present within the Service, the general skills of collecting, collating and presenting evidence were weakly developed. This was the result both of the fact that the police had often not been required to do this in the past and that the police (despite having some talented officers) had never sought to recruit these skills. Where they were present however, was in the more distasteful aspects of political policing, which could not be easily transferred into the new democracy.

This was reflected, by among other factors, in the training and skill levels of detectives within the SAPS. In 1994, once the new police agency had been constituted, only about one quarter of detectives had been on a formal investigation-training course. While just over one in ten detectives had more than six years experience.[11] These facts were, by 1996, being reflected in the relatively low, and in some cases declining, case solving rates.[12] Research conducted in 1998 showed that some 2.2 million crimes were reported to the police, of which 259 000 cases (or 12%) resulted in a prosecution or guilty plea by the accused person[13].

Those resources which did exist within the SAPS were also orientated heavily towards areas in the country which had been classified as 'white'. Thus, in 1994, three quarters of the country's police stations were situated in (white) suburbs and business districts.[14] The vast majority of inter-personal violent crime, however, occurred in township and rural areas.[15] Very low levels of service delivery was the norm at many township and rural stations. In particular areas, such as in the province of KwaZulu-Natal where the police jurisdiction was of the former KwaZulu Police had been, policing was by 1998 virtually in a state of collapse. In KwaMashu just outside Durban, for example, the police were closely linked to crime in the area, had a close relationship with local gangs, were often drunk on duty and were closely associated with the Inkatha Freedom Party.

Public surveys conducted over the period 1994 to 1998 suggested initially that there remained a clear distinction between citizens' views of policing. Whites were more inclined to trust the police yet viewed service delivery as declining rapidly. Blacks were more likely to mistrust the police, but regarded the emergence of democratic governance as bringing some improvements in police service delivery on the ground. Over time, however, there was a convergence of black and white views, safety became a (if not the) key issue of concern to citizens and the police were viewed across racial lines as performing poorly in their fight against crime.[16] This was a significant change with critical policy implications. For the majority of the country's people it was now not enough to say that the police were legitimate — that legitimacy had to be earned.

Government did not, at first, have a coordinated response to the problem of crime. This was to emerge later in the form of the National Crime Prevention Strategy (NCPS), although even an overarching approach to controlling and preventing crime such as the NCPS did not necessarily mean a more focussed approach. For a period of time, however, government response was partly to deny that crime was a problem and partly to respond in an *ad hoc* fashion as representations were made to it on particular issues. The result was a real frustration by whites in particular with the government's inability either to concede openly that crime was a problem and then show the clear will and intention to do something about it.

Partners in crime: 1996-1999

The growing outcry against crime did not only take the form of increased protests against government, but also resulted in the mobilization of a diverse range of anti-crime groups. These ranged from vigilante organizations, which came in a variety of

guises — from small disorganized community groups to more structured and sophisticated organizations such as Mapogo a Matamaga — to initiatives launched by big
business. Government's immediate response to growing pressure on crime which could
no longer be ignored, was to co-opt those groups who were most vocal.

The most prominent initiative against crime was that formed by a powerful (white)
business group, representing local, national and multi-national business interests;
'*Business against Crime.*' While BAC originally acted as a lobby organization aimed at
pressuring government into change, it was also seen as a means to channel resources,
financial, physical and human, to the government. Initially, the relationship between
business and government was an uncoordinated one — a mixture of pressure and
resource provision. A proliferation of business interests offered resources to the police
in a range of projects — there was little strategy and in many cases few means to
determine whether or not the SAPS used the resources effectively. Over time, as both
constituencies formalized the relationship, agreements were struck as to what issues
were of priority for business intervention. This was made possible both by government's
desire to use the business skills and resources on offer and the urgency with which key
individuals within the business community viewed the problem.

The proliferation of assistance from groups outside of the police, including most
of South Africa's major corporations, multi-nationals, foreign governments (although
largely European and North America states) and funding foundations often increased
rather than reduced the pressure on the police. At first the SAPS accepted almost all
offers of assistance. The result was the initiation of an array of projects, often driven
by the requirements and expertise of donors, rather than the immediate priorities of the
SAPS. Absorbing the funding and assistance often, at least in the short term, con-
sumed rather than built capacity. "*If we spent as much time meeting people offering us
assistance*", one senior commissioner noted, "*we would [have time and energy] to be
in a position to make a difference on the street [in the fight against crime].*"[17]

The relationship between business and government peaked with the appointment to the SAPS of a prominent local business personality, Meyer Kahn from
South African Breweries in 1997. While Kahn was appointed as Chief Executive
Officer of the SAPS, this did not usurp the role of the Commissioner of Police,
George Fivaz, and Kahn's role and status, and his position in the line of command,
was never entirely clear. The appointment of Kahn however largely signaled the
end of the business outcry around crime.

Ironically, it was another anti-crime initiative which was to exert a powerful influence in government circles on the need for a tougher stance on lawlessness. A vigilante group, calling themselves *People against Gangsterism and Drugs* (PAGAD),
had been operating since the mid-1990s in the Western Cape. While originally it had
targeted drug dealers in former 'colored' townships on the periphery of the city, using
in many cases crudely made bombs, a radical Muslim group increasingly usurped the
leadership of PAGAD. The result was an increased targeting of state buildings, particularly police stations, as well as prominent tourist areas in the heart of Cape Town.

Originally, when PAGAD's targets had still been drug dealers in 'colored' townships, Fivaz had met with them, arguing that the group should work with the police
rather than against it. A similar co-option strategy was used employed against a number of other groups, which as we have seen, were mobilizing around crime. Attacks in

central (and white) Cape Town, however, using more sophisticated bombs, which received prominent domestic and international media coverage, increased the debate within the state as to the options available.

A strong lobby within the police, as well as within other security agencies, argued that the provisions of the Constitution tied the State's hands in fighting crime and now terrorism. That was because, the argument went, the Constitution limited the ability of the police to hold individuals for reasonable periods to ensure effective questioning and investigation. While the drawbacks of the Constitution in fighting remained a gripe of the police (and to some extent senior politicians), the details of what exactly was proving of dissatisfaction were seldom debated. Indeed, the argument often seemed to be an easy explanation for the failure of the police to perform their duty. In particular, it was suggested that in specific instances detention without trial for a specific period of time should be reintroduced. The problem was, however, that the police did not appear to be confronting the problem effectively within the current powers available to them. Cases appeared to be poorly investigated and, despite promises to the contrary, few suspects arrested.

A parallel lobby within government to the emergent one on law enforcement emphasized the importance of prevention. The government had adopted the NCPS in 1996 which sought to focus all of the government resources in both improving the functioning of the criminal justice system and preventing crime. The NCPS however was difficult to operationalize — given both an overly theoretical approach to the problems, the fact that it relied on various government departments (over which it had no control) to implement initiatives and because crime prevention was seen as a long term (and therefore impractical) solution to an immediate crisis — and brought little practical improvements on the ground. Where it did, given the multi-departmental nature of the structure, line function departments often took the credit. A heavy focus of the NCPS had also been a knowledge-driven approach to crime prevention — the conducting of research in the area was slow, cumbersome and difficult to justify as having immediate impacts on the ground where violent crime was seen by many citizens to be out of control. As in the case of community policing before it, crime prevention was increasingly seen as a 'soft' social approach to crime control, outside of the ambit of the police.

Perceptions played an important part in how the public viewed the success of government strategies to fight crime. As already suggested, prominent individual crime incidents continued to drive the debate and public perceptions were shaped more by these than by any pronouncements by government that most crimes had stabilized. Minister Mufumadi, who had negotiated the amalgamation of the various component forces into the SAPS, was now seen by the public at large (and particularly by whites) as weak and vacillating. Government promises after each case of serious crime was that such actions would not be tolerated and that no effort would be spared to ensure that the perpetrators were behind bars, began to ring hollow and undermined public confidence

What was needed at the time was a more focused approach to dealing with crime. Yet, under political pressure from all quarters - business, community groups, politicians including from the ruling party - a system of police priorities (laying out which crimes would be given priority and what internal organizational issues would receive concern) to do just this, became ineffective from the beginning. There were simply too many priorities. When outside interest groups complained on one issue or another, the response was to add the particular issue to the list of priorities or to argue that action was already being taken as that issue had been identified as a priority. In fact, the system of priorities was merely a paper exercise having almost no impact on the ground.

High levels of public pressure, including open criticism by politicians from all parties, and a perception within the police, particularly from the senior set of white managers, that they had little political support led to declining levels of police morale. This was reflected in increases in police corruption, (the result of both poor working conditions, low morale, few controls and weak management, and in which low salaries can be a contributing factor) police involvement in crime and an overall weakening of discipline across the police agency. The government's response was increasingly one of fire-fighting problem after problem as they emerged — bombs in the Western Cape, cash heists in Gauteng and North West province and ongoing political violence in KwaZulu-Natal. Indeed, the system became increasingly dominated by parallel forms of policing — a strong 'punching arm' deployable from Pretoria to counter particular problems and weak station level policing. But operational initiatives from the center did succeed in some cases, although problems reasserted themselves once force levels were again reduced. These led to renewed demands, particularly in KwaZulu-Natal, from local communities for national intervention.

By late 1998, problems with the police were manifest. Hardly a day went by without media coverage showing poor police performance or police involvement in crime. The police themselves were increasingly under attack, reflecting the viciousness of the battle on the streets: in 1997, 224 (approximately 0.002 of the operational police service of 100,000) police officers lost their lives, the majority while off duty.[18] While crises in parts of the country were contained through national intervention local station service delivery deteriorated. The lobbying power of business and other groups had largely been spent or extinguished by too close a proximity to the police. By associating themselves with government's efforts to fight crime, business could hardly maintain a critical stance. The stage was set for change.

From prevention to cure: 1999 - 2000
The period immediately before the election in June 1999 saw the police on the defensive in almost all areas. Policing was widely criticized in the media and the opposition used crime — arguing that while government Minister's had protection, the majority of citizens did not — as the central factor of their campaign. Softer approaches such as prevention and partnership, which had been in vogue only a few months before, were increasingly seen as limp responses to what was assuming the dimensions of a national crisis.

Overall levels of violent property crime, such as armed robbery and hijacking, peaked in October 1999 at around 8,000 reported incidents for that month. There were also reported increases in theft and ordinary street robbery. However, most categories of crime remained stable at very high levels: murder averaging between 2,000 to 3,000 incidents a month, serious assault between 15,000 and 30,000 a month, and rape between 3,000 and 5,000 incidents reported to the police each month.[19] There was no sudden and dramatic increase in crime before Tshweti took office. There was, however, a significantly better understanding of the nature and extent of organized crime in the country, and a feeling that harder action was required in this respect. It should be noted, however, that overall statistical increases and decreases in crime levels generally have little impact on political and public perceptions of the problem — it is as likely that an accumulation of high profile criminal events, such as the bombs in the Western Cape, the hijacking of prominent individuals and a spate of cash in transit heists in the country shaped these perceptions as much as any sober examination of the available crime statistics.

The most significant result of the new mood of crisis was the move to establish a new police agency outside of the SAPS altogether. In the negotiations around the new unit, the police put forward a proposal that a large new investigative structure, similar to the United State's Federal Bureau of Investigation, be created. This option was rejected by the President and Ministers who opted for a smaller highly skilled investigative body situated in the Department of Justice, as opposed to the Department of Safety and Security, which held the overall responsibility for policing. This was a significant move — it signaled to both the public and the police not only a new government commitment to fighting crime, but also a growing recognition that the police may not have the appropriate skills to win the fight.

Government statements on crime assumed a harder edge after the election with the appointment of a new Minister for Safety and Security, Steve Tshwete. The new Minister traveled widely across the country meeting police officers and speaking out harshly against crime. The thrust of his message was that criminals would be treated harshly and that police officers should use all the powers available to them to combat crime. Indeed, Tshwete went much further than this, both in public and private, urging treatment which was clearly outside of the Constitution and Bill of Rights, urging police officers to deal harshly with criminals, "like a dog would treat a bone." Criminals were to be shown no mercy. Tshwete has also raised the option of constitutional change to support the fight against crime, an issue which many police officers, at least at the senior level, strongly favor.

Tshwete's statements tapped into a deep vein of public resentment around crime. The focus on the 'fact' that criminals had more rights than victims is one which resonated particular well. What was surprising about the Minister's statements was that there was so little opposition to them. Newspapers editorialized against the worst outbursts, but public surveys suggested that citizens were entirely in agreement with the Minister, believing that a harsh response against crime was necessary.[20] If there had been any doubts before about government's commitment to ending crime, they were effectively quelled in a few months by the new Minister.

There were some casualties as the new approach took affect. For example, one was related to those charged with investigating police misconduct, including deaths in police custody or by police action. The issue of police misconduct had been a central point of concern in 1994 and a body, the Independent Complaints Directorate (ICD), reporting directly to the Minister was established. Given its role, the ICD had limited popularity in the police. The ICD was not downgraded structurally but its standing weakened through the Minister's statements, both in public and in private, which suggested not only that a harsh approach was needed against criminals, but that those who sought to protect offenders when in the hands of the police or during arrest were performing a disservice.

The issues that the ICD investigates are serious. Since 1994, there have been frequent reports of deaths in police custody, some of which resulted from torture or ill-treatment. A number of people shot dead by police may also have been extra-judicially executed. In 1997 alone 5,300 cases of assault were lodged against the police. In the first ten months of 1998, the ICD received 607 reports of deaths in police custody or as a result of police action.[21]

A second victim was the civilian Secretariat for Safety and Security. Effectively meant to advise the Minister and monitor police performance, its presence at least suggested that the police could still not be trusted. That impression required change. The post of Secretary was downgraded and the Secretariat restructured to meet the requirements of the new Minister. A key function of the Secretariat, which in any event was only performed with limited success, was to offer competing advice to the Minister to enhance the available policy choices open to him. Critical, in this regard, is to allow competing assessments of police performance between the Secretariat and the SAPS. Police assessments of performance often (for obvious reasons) overestimated progress being made giving a distorted picture to decision-makers.

What was clear from Tshwete's approach, however, was that while public statements were strongly worded, there was little strategy other than speaking out strongly. While police morale improved, there was no plan to repair the structural weaknesses of the police. Tshwete's approach has been, to some extent, balanced by the appointment of a new Commissioner of the SAPS. Jakkie Selebi is an outsider to policing, a former diplomat with a good record. He is also close to the President and thus carries significant political legitimacy and weight.

Selebi selected a limited number of priorities — in the main these include focusing on 124 police station areas which generate 50% of the country's crime. Policing actions in these areas include high profile visible deployments, roadblocks and cordon and search operations. These have been conducted in close co-operation with the military, who have assumed an important internal policing dimension. The police however remain the lead agency in such activities. One potential problem with these operations is that they will continue to disempower station level managers and not lead to dramatic improvements in police service delivery at the local level. But a politically powerful black Commissioner has options open to him which were not available to the former white Commissioner. He is in a position to confront more effectively the powerful (black) police unions - which carry much less influence now than previously, although there is substantial pressure for the promotion of black officers and criticize poor performance without being accused of racism. Equally, he can defend the police in senior political circles in a way that former policemen who served the apartheid order clearly cannot. This bodes well for some improvements in policing.

It is too early to assess progress being made since the election and the appointment of a new Minister and Commissioner. It is clear however that the discourse of human rights and legitimacy is a thing of the past. These are significant changes in police policy in the post-apartheid environment. It will in the long term be damaging if the immediate statements made by the new Minister have undermined the issue of human rights entirely. What is clearly needed is a police agency which acts with greater confidence in fighting crime, has the support of its political masters while at the same time respects the rights of those who it polices, guilty and innocent alike.

Conclusion

The South African Police under apartheid enforced illegitimate laws brutally. The coming of the democratic order required substantial changes in how the society should be policed. Initially these changes focused on ensuring that the police were more legitimate and more accountable. Oversight and other structures were established and community police forums were introduced at the local level. Such changes did have some success — for many black people policing was seen to improve, probably less in actual content than in a decline in intrusiveness and brutality. For whites, however, levels of service declined and as the police increasingly became no longer the preserve of one community. Crime among whites remains one of the key areas of dissatisfaction with the new order. Whites are also in a better position to afford private security — the industry has grown dramatically in the country with most formerly white suburbs in cities like Johannesburg now largely policed privately by armed response companies.

For their part, however, the police sought to control change from early on. This was made easier by the fact that the ANC had few available cadres with a knowledge or interest in the police to insert into the organization. The SAP and later the SAPS had throughout the transformation process retained a noticeable degree of institutional interest of its own. The disagreement with the then ruling National Party (and agreement with the ANC) about the nature and extent of devolution is a notable example. Senior managers in the SAPS were also influential in arguing that the systems of civilian oversight were no longer needed. A new black commissioner is likely to strengthen rather than weaken this process — the police are now more confident and more politically connected than ever before. Much of these are welcome developments. Questions of trust and accountability are no longer the central issues of the day. While it is likely that these would in any event have faded as the democracy matured, and the various players worked more closely together, increases in crime in the country have acted as a catalyst for this process. But increases in crime have also resulted in a strong lobby within the police to weaken not only the civilian oversight functions but also the democratic legal framework for policing the democracy. While calls to change the Constitution and the Bill of Rights are generally made only after significant incidents of crime, such as bomb explosions in the heart of Cape Town, it remains a lingering sub-text to much of the debate on fighting lawlessness. Ironically, the more successful the police and other law enforcement agencies are in the short term, the weaker the case will be for making changes to the legal framework.

Operational policing is also changing. Capacity and experience now exists (or at least is better organized) at the center to intervene in local trouble spots. There has been some success in this respect, for example, in stabilizing violence torn areas in KwaZulu-Natal and to a lesser extent the Western Cape. However, much work is still required to introduce a sustainable ethic of service delivery at the 1,200 police stations across the country. Policing a democracy requires not only legal frameworks which protect citizens from the police but also police officers responsive to the needs of citizens.

It will take perhaps another decade to instill such changes and recruit and train another generation of police officers who had no experience of apartheid. The danger until then is that the fight against crime will lead to ongoing paramilitary responses, as are currently being initiated, which while necessary in the short term, may lead to longer term damage to the concept of democratic policing in South Africa. If the latest law enforcement initiatives do not show success, and this is possible given that much crime in the country has social and economic roots or requires sophisticated investigative skills, than more forceful crackdowns are possible.

The debate on policing change is however likely to swing between two polls — as indeed it does in many democracies. Over time, should police brutality increase significantly or a number of high profile cases of corruption be exposed, institutions of civilian control will again be strengthened and more effective forms of local accountability introduced. Such developments are a long way off. The key question for the moment is whether levels of crime in South African society can be reduced. If that is achieved it will open up space for debate on how to improve policing in the context of an evolving democracy. For the moment, for the majority of decision-makers in and outside of the security environment, crime remains the biggest threat to the democratic order. Other issues, such as improving local accountability, reducing police brutality and upgrading service delivery, no matter if improvements in these areas will assist the fight against crime in the longer term by building confidence in the police, will remain secondary.

Dr Mark Shaw is a Research Fellow at the South African Institute of International Affairs based at the University of the Witwatersrand, Johannesburg. He is currently working on a research project which examines the impact of political, economic and social transitions on crime levels in a number of countries in Africa, Eastern Europe and Latin America. Before his current appointment he worked at the Department of Safety and Security in Pretoria, the Institute for Security Studies and the Centre for Policy Studies. He has written widely on issues related to crime and policing in South Africa.

Shaw

Notes

1   See Jacques Pauw, *In the Heart of the Whore: The Story of South Africa's Death Squads*, Johannesburg, 1990. Also, Patrick Laurence, Death Squads: Apartheid's Secret Weapon, Johannesburg, 1991.

2   Agar Cachalia, Secretary for Safety and Security, address for the launch of the White Paper on Safety and Security, September 1998.

3   Paulo Sergio Pinheiro, 'Democratic governance, violence and the unrule of law', in *Daedalus*, Vol 129, No 2, Spring 2000, p. 122-123.

4   See Rupert Taylor and Mark Shaw, 'The Dying Days of Apartheid', in David R Howarth and Aletta J Norval, *South Africa in Transition: New theoretical perspectives*, New York, St Martins Press, 1999.

5   *Ibid.*

6   Janine Rauch, 'Crisis of Legitimacy: The limits of police reform', *Indicator SA*, Vol 8, No 4, Spring 1991.

7   See Etienne Marais, 'Policing the periphery: Police and South Africa's homelands', paper presented to the 22nd Congress of the Association of Sociology in South Africa, 30 June 1992.

8   *Daily Dispatch*, Port Elizabeth, 20 October 1993.

9   See Mark Shaw, 'Point of order: Policing the compromise', in Steven Friedman and Doreen Atkinson, *The Small Miracle: South Africa's negotiated settlement*, Johannesburg, Ravan, 1994.

10 *In Service of Safety: White Paper on Safety and Security*, Pretoria, September 1998, p. 4.

11 *Ibid.*, p. 5.

12 See Martin Schonteich, 'Lack of conviction: Prosecutors poor performance', *Nedcor ISS Crime Index*, Vol 3, No 2, March-April 1999.

13 Martin Schonteich, Assessing the crime fighters: The ability of the criminal justice system to solve and prosecute crime, ISS papers, No 40, Institute for Security Studies, Pretoria, September 1999, p. 10.

14 *In Service of Safety*, *op. cit.* p. 4.

15 See Antoinette Louw and Mark Shaw, *Stolen Opportunities: The impact of crime on South Africa's poor*, Institute for Security Studies, Monograph Series, No 14, July 1997.

16 See, for example, Rod Alence, 'The Democratic Transition and Crime in South Africa: The record of the 1990s', *Nedcor ISS Crime Index*, Vol 3, No, 2 March-April 1999.

17 Presentation to *The Committee to investigate appropriate guidelines to deal with crime in South Africa*, November 1997.

18 *South African Survey 1999/2000*, South African Institute of Race Relations, Johannesburg, p. 79.

19 Figures obtained from month on month comparisons supplied by the Crime Information Management Centre, South African Police Service, Pretoria.

20 Human Sciences Research Council Quarterly Survey, 1999/2000, March 2000.

21 *Amnesty International, Report 1999*, pp. 304 - 307.

Appendix - Foreign Language Abstracts

Policia, Policiamento, Estado e Sociedade: Alguns Problemas Basicos na Prote,cao dos Direitos Humanos e Civis

Menachem Amir

A relacao entre policia, policiamento e democracia e cheia de conflitos e paradoxos. Isto deriva do envolvimento da policia na politica. Policia e policiamento nao sao a-politicos. A policia as vezes serve interesses politicos. Diz-se que a policia e defensora da democracia, mas as vezes a policia colabora no ataque e ate destruic,ao do sistema democratico de sociedade e governo. Este paper discute os aspectos sociais e normativos e tipos de democracia que a policia na maioria das vezes concebe como sendo um impedimento ao trabalho policial «eficiente'. A tensao entre policia e o processo democratico se torna mais nitida quando regimes politicos e sociais totalitarios estao em processo de transformac,ao para a democracia. A situa,cao da policia e do policiamento sob estas condicoes e discutida. E tambem expressa a crenc, a de que o «policiamento democratico» e a «policia democratica» serao alcancados.

La Policía: Control Social, El Estado y Democracia

Nigel Fielding

Tres modelos generales se pueden identificar en la organización y distribución de servicios de vigilancia de la policía en las sociedades contemporáneas: el modelo de ejecución de la ley, el modelo de servicio y el modelo comunitario. Cada modelo es examinado en referencia a su filosofía, estructura de organización, rendimiento, política del manejo, y su estrategia operacional y tácticas. Se consideran los méritos e inconvenientes de cada modelo, y una evaluación de la precisión entre los modelos y diferentes formas de organización política. Se incluye un glosario de términos importantes.

Depois da Ditadura: A Natureza e a Funcao da Policia na China Apos Mao

H. L. Fu

A moderniza,cao economica e a liberaliza,cao politica desde o inicio da decada de 1980 tem causado mudan,cas dramaticas na sociedade chinesa. A policia chinesa, como a sociedade na qual ela opera. esta experimentando um processo de mudan,ca lento mas fundamental. Entretanto, a China continua a ser um estado comunista de partido unico e todas as reformas e mudanas estao ocorrendo dentro desta estrutura politica maior. A policia esta lidando com a mudan,ca da revolu,cao para a moderniza,cao e redefinindo seu papel em uma nova economia politica. Na sociedade p6s-revolucionaria, a policia esta renegociando suas rela,coes com o partido comunista, a lei e a comunidade.

Policía y Democracia en Finlandia

Ahti Laiten

En Finlandia la confianza de los ciudadanos en el policía es más alta que la confianza en las cortes, la maquinaria administrativa o los políticos. Según encuestas de opinión, las personas ven a la policía como un órgano importante en su garantía, y muchas personas están listas a dar a la policía más poder, más dinero y otros recursos. La reputación de la policía en el presente es alta en Finlandia. Al mismo tiempo, en Finlandia ha habido una discusión incesante sobre el incremento de los poderes de la policía. El policía finlandés está bajo mando del parlamentario. Si alguien siente que ha sido maltratada por el policía, esa persona legalmente tiene derecho a hacer una denuncia oficial, y esta será tratada por un oficial apropiado. La posibilidad de poner una queja está en los niveles local y nacional. La corrupción entre las fuerzas de policía Finlandesas es muy rara. Según comparaciones internacionales, la corrupción de las autoridades Finlandeses es, después de la de Dinamarca, la segunda más pequeña del mundo.

Los cargos policiales en Finlandia no son políticos. Puede ser que algunos nombramientos de algunos altos puestos en la administración son a veces políticos por naturaleza. En general, la policía contemporánea Finlandesa es bastante independiente

La Vigilancia Policíaca en la Era de la Información

Peter K. Manning

Este artículo argumenta que los cambios en la estructura social son reflejados en patrones de vigilancia policíaca que no son ya mas nacionales sino transnacionales. En el pasado, fue util concentrarse en la vigilancia policíaca en estados democráticos e industrializados y examinar su historia, estructura y propiedades emergentes. La definición de vigilancia policía, obtenida de Weber y Bittner, se basa en el deber de los ciudadanos de cumplir en un orden legítimo, inclusive con ordenes implícitas; en tanto que la fuerza es limitada a asegurar su cumplimiento. Esta familia de definiciones implica la existencia de un territorio limitado designado y denominado dentro del cuál un mandato prevalece. El monopolio de la fuerza legítima, (una característica del estado según Weber) es problemático. La Vigilancia policíaca global o transnacional, significa la aplicación de la fuerza de una manera cuasi-legítima en tanto no se ha declarado un estado de guerra.

La "Vigilancia Policíaca" ya no es facilmente definida o restringida a fuerzas nacionales con mandatos nacionales, obligaciones territoriales restringidas y limitaciones legales estrechas. Nuevos intereses nacionales y patrones internacionales de control cambian las relaciones entre democracia y seguridad.

Cambios en relaciones internacionales y en la economía, asi como cambios en tecnología de la información , transporte y comunicaciones, son reflejados ahora en la vigilancia policíaca. El mandato esta siendo reformulado por consideraciones no solo de seguridad personal, pero de seguridad de la información como propiedad, asimismo como de la información como símbolo o tema de expresión. Muchos temas de vigilancia policíaca tradicional que no serán tratados aquí en detalle, tales como restricción, control de información, ocultamiento y revelación, respecto por la privacidad de los ciudadanos y cumplimiento, estan cambiando y estos cambios afectan tanto a la policía como a los ciudadanos de naciones democráticas.

Policia y Democratico

Gary Marx

Este articulo considera algunas variedades y ayudas para policia democratico y pone en contraste abreviadamente el policia en los Estados Unidos, el Reino Unido y la Francia. Policia democratico se debe ver como un proceso y no resultado. Las sociedades experimentan una tension continua entre el deseo para la orden y la libertad. Hay una paradoja en el hecho de que una sociedad democratico necesita la proteccion por el policia y de policia. La potencia de las nuevas tecnologias de la vigilancia, se dan las sociedades democraticas deben pedir continuamente " *como es eficiente quisieramos que fuera el policia y bajo que condiciones el uso de estas tecnologias apropiadas* "

Policia e Democracia

Gary T. Marx

Este artigo considera algumas variedade e apoios para uma policia democratica e contrasta brevemente o policiamento nos Estados Unidos, Reino Unido e Franc,a. O policiamento democratico deve ser visto ColllO um processo e nao como um resultado. Sociedades experimentam uma tensao continua entre o desejo por ordem e liberdade. Existe um paradoxo no fato de que uma sociedade democratica necessita protec,ao tanto pela policia quanto da policia. Dado o poder das novas tecnologias de vigilancia, sociedades democraticas devem continuamente perguntar «quao eficiente nos queremos que a policia seja e sob que condic,oes e o uso destas tecnologias apropriado?».

Policia, Foras Armadas e Democracia no Brasil

Paulo de Mesquita Neto

Este capitulo examina o papel da policia e das forc,as armadas no sistema de seguranca publica no Brasil. O capitulo focaliza a separac, ao e diferenciac, ao entre a policia e as forc, as armadas e o estabelecimento de controles civis e democraticos sobre a policia desde a transi,cao para a democracia em 1985. 0 capitulo afirma que os governos democraticos nao foram capazes de separar e diferenciar as for,cas armadas e a policia e consolidar o controle civil e democratico sobre a policia. A sociedade civil tem desempenhado um papel importante mas ainda limitado na reforma e desmilitariza,cao do sistema de seguranc,a publica. A separa,cao e diferenciac,ao incompleta entre as for,cas armadas e a policia e a

incerteza com rela,cao ao controle civil e democratico sobre a policia tem contribuido para a persistencia da violencia policial e da ineficiencia policial e tem solapado as politicas e programas para controlar a criminalidade e a violencia e consolidar o regime democratico.

Blues da Democracia: A Politica da Reforma Policial na Africa do Sul, 1990-2000

Mark Shaw

Policiamento sob o apartheid foi planejado para controle e supressao. Assim a transforma,cao da policia tem sido uma condic,ao essencial da ordem pos-democratica na Africa do Sul. Atingir isso tem sido um processo dificil e longe de uniforme. Inicialmente, o desafio dos governantes, que naquele momento nao confiavam na policia, foi adquirir maior legitimidade entre o publico para as agencias policiais do regime autoritario que agora policiavam tambem a democracia. Estas iniciativas tem sido superadas por uma necessidade de responder a niveis crescentes de crime no pais, que e agora visto como uma amea,ca chave a ordem democratica. A policia, na ausencia de uma gama de habilidades consideradas asseguradas na maioria das democracias e instigada por politicos, esta assumindo mais um postura de manuten,cao da lei e da ordem na tentativa de fazer baixar o crime. Agora a policia luta para atingir legitmidade nao atraves de garantias politicas de apoio a nova ordem mas reduzindo a ilegalidade na base.

A Transformacao do Governo da Segurana e Justica

Clifford Shearing

Este paper examina a impliea,cao de mudanc,as na maneira pela qual a seguran,ca e justic,a estao sendo promovidas para o lugar e o papel da violencia governamental na manuten,cao da ordem. O paper argumenta que a emergencia da logica de risco assim como os desafios a concepcao expiatoria e denunciatoria de justic,a estao transfigurando a maneira pela qual a violencia esta sendo utilizada como uma tatica de governo.

El Consentimiento de Los Gobernados: Policía, Democracia y Diversidad

Lawrence W. Sherman

La vigilancia policíaca democrática está fundada en el consentimiento de los gobernados. Este consentimiento require de cuatro principios de vigilancia policíaca, culminando en la necesidad de evidencia empírica sobre cuál es la mejor manera de lograr valores democraticos através de la práctica policial. El primer principio es que la misión de la vigilancia policíaca consiste mas en lograr el cumplimiento de la ley, que en administrar coerción: alcanzar objetivos mas que emplear medios específicos. El segundo principio es que diferentes democracias requieren medios diferentes para lograr el cumplimiento de la ley en poblaciones diversas. El tercer principio es que la policía puede construir en las democracias, la identidad maestra de todos los ciudadanos. El cuarto principio es, que la evidencia empírica en cómo obtener el cumplimiento de la ley a través de la persuación y las buenas maneras ("vigilancia policíaca educada"), ayudará a la policia a llevar al mínimo el uso de la coerción y a incrementar la legitimidad del Estado-nación democrático.

La Perspectiva de William Bratton sobre Vigilancia Policíaca

Eli B. Silverman

Naciones que emergen de dictaduras militares y regímenes comunistas han creado intencionalmente sistemas de justicias disfuncionales. Puede llevar años de aumento en las tasas de criminalidad antes de que se hagan los cambios necesarios en sus sistemas de vigilancia policíaca. Los medios de comunicación juegan papeles múltiples en la apertura de las organizaciones policiales y en hacerlas mas transparentes. Aunque el entrenamiento ha sido mejorado en el transcurso de los últimos 30 años, el entrenamiento sigue siendo el tobillo de Aquiles de la vigilancia policía en América.

Policía, Seguridad y Democracia: Una Perspectiva Policial de la Experiencia Rusa en Tiempos de Transición

Alexander Yelin

Este artículo nos presenta problemas actuales, desde el punto de vista de los practicantes, en el desarrollo de la fuerzas policiales en Rusia desde la Perestroika. Y esboza areas claves donde se deben tomar medidas urgentes para asegurar la mayor democratización de la vigilancia policíaca. A principio de la decada del 90 se realizaron algunos cambios radicales en el sistema de coacción de las leyes en Rusia, pero mas tarde el sistema reacayó nuevamente en el estancamiento. El camino a una vigilancia policíaca más democrática consiste en asegurar mayor apertura en el trabajo policial, su disponibilidad para el escrutinio público y la participación de la comunidad.

Analise da Policia .laponesa do Ponto de Vista da l)emocraca

Minoru Yokoyama

A policia japonesa era uma policia nao-democratica antes da Segunda Guerra Mundial cujo principal interesse era manter a ordem para o emperador e seu governo. Atividades de manutenc,ao da ordem e aplicac,ao da lei eram desempenhadas de maneira muito eficiente, enquanto o direito das pessoas ao devido processo legal era negligenciado.

A policia, entao, ja realizava policiamento comunitario. ntretanto, o policiamento comunitario tinhapor objetivo supervisionar ao inves de prestar servi,cos as pessoas. O sistema policial japones foi democratizado de acordo com o modelo americano apos a derrota japonesa na Segunda Guerra Mundial. Entretanto, um sistema policial local autonomo nao se enraizou no Japao. Subsequentemente a revisao da Lei de Policia de 1954, este sistema foi substituido por um novo sistema composto pela Agencia Nacional de Policia e a policia municipal. Sob este sistema, a Agencia Nacional de Policia gradualmente fortaleceu seu poder de supervisao sobre as todas as policias municipais. A policia japonesa contemporanea tem muitas caracteristicas democraticas. Entretanto, tendo servido o governo conservador por um longo periodo, ela esta inclinada a perder sua neutralidade politica. Alem disso, alguns casos serios de corrupc,ao causados pela estrutura policial e alguns problemas estruturais da pratica policial no processo de aplicac,ao da lei tem sido observados.

Ciudadanos y Relaciones con la Policía en Países en Transición

Ugljesa Zvekic

Importantes hallazgos relacionados con las relaciones ciudadano-policía en países en transición (20) que tomaron parte en la Encuesta Internacional de Víctimas del Crimen (1996/ 97) son discutidas. Una pequeña cantidad de ciudadanos reportan crímenes a la policía y la mayoría de ellos todavía exhiben descontento con el tratamiento policíaco una vez el incidente haya sido reportado, así como con la ejecución policíaca en controlar prevenir el crimen.

Polizia, sorveglianza, stato e società: alcuni problemi di base per proteggere i diritti umani e civili

Menachem Amir

Il rapporto tra polizia, sorveglianza e democrazia è pieno di conflitti e paradossi. Ciò nasce dal coinvolgimento della polizia nella politica: polizia e sorveglianza non sono a-politiche. La polizia talvolta è al servizio degli interessi politici e, sebbene la si pensi essere il baluardo della democrazia, a volte collabora ad attaccare e persino distruggere il sistema democratico di un società o di un governo. L'articolo discute gli aspetti e i generi normativi e sociali di democrazia, che la polizia spesso concepisce come limitanti l'efficacia del suo lavoro. La tensione tra polizia e processo democratico è massimamente distinta quando i regimi sociali e politici totalitari sono nella fase di transizione verso la democrazia; si discutono la situazione della polizia e del sorveglianza al manifestarsi di tali condizioni e processi. Si crede infine che sarà possibile arrivare a una polizia e a una sorveglianza completamente democratici.

La polizia: controllo sociale, stato e democrazia

Nigel Fielding

Nelle società contemporanee si possono distinguere tre grandi modelli per l'organizzazione della polizia e l'erogazione dei servizi di polizia: il far osservare la legge, il modello del servizio, e il modello della comunità. Ciascuno di essi viene esaminato sotto il rispetto della teoria, della struttura organizzativa, del prodotto, della politica di gestione, della strategia e tattica operativa; ne sono considerati i meriti e gli svantaggi, e viene fatta una valutazione di quanto ciascun modello si adatti alle diverse forme di organizzazione politica. Si include un glossario dei termini chiave.

Dopo la dittatura: la natura e la funzione della polizia nella Cina dopo Mao

H.L. Fu

La modernizzazione economica e la liberalizzazione politica in atto dai primi anni 80 ha generato drammatici cambiamenti nella società cinese. La polizia cinese, così come la società in cui opera, sta sperimentando un processo di lenta ma basilare modifica. Tuttavia la Cina resta parte dello stato comunista e ogni riforma e modifica occorrono entro tale ampia struttura politica. La polizia sta affrontando lo spostamento dalla rivoluzione alla modernizzazione, ridefinendo il proprio ruolo all'interno di una nuova politica economica. Nella società post-rivoluzionaria la polizia rinegozia i suoi rapporti col partito comunista, la legge e la comunità.

La polizia di cui abbiamo bisogno

Andrew Goldsmith

L'articolo si domanda come e perché stia cambiando il potere della polizia in Australia, e se nel frattempo non stia divenendo meno responsabile. Gli argomenti considerati sono: potere della polizia, legge e ordine politico; l'applicazione della legge sulla droga; concezioni di *management* di polizia; integrazione globale. Si esaminano gli obiettivi di aree di lavoro di polizia in conflitto tra loro, quali droghe illegali e rapporti della polizia nella comunità, che rendono la vigilanza più incerta. Si indagano anche le implicazioni per una maggior responsabilità e trasparenza degli approcci *manageriali*, e ci si interroga se il cittadino in una democrazia possa paragonarsi a un consumatore in un mercato.

Polizia e democrazia in Finlandia

Ahti Laiten

In Finlandia i cittadini danno fiducia più alla polizia che a tribunali, amministrazione e politici. Secondo i sondaggi, la gente vede la polizia come un importante organo di sicurezza, e molti sono pronti a concederle più potere, denaro e risorse. Al momento in Finlandia la sua reputazione è alta e di continuo si discute sull'allargamento dei suoi poteri. La polizia finnica è sotto controllo del parlamento e se qualche persona reputa di esserne stata maltrattata ha diritto di far protesta, che sarà presa in considerazione da un apposito funzionario. Si può protestare a livello sia locale sia nazionale. La corruzione tra le forze di polizia finnica è assai rara, essendo le autorità finniche al secondo posto dopo la Danimarca in una classifica internazionale di minor corruzione. In Finlandia gli incarichi di polizia non sono dati dalle autorità politiche, con l'esclusione a volte di qualche posizione di alto livello amministrativo; ma nell'insieme la polizia finnica è oggigiorno assai indipendente.

Sorveglianza nell'era dell'informazione

Peter K.Manning

L'articolo discute l'idea che i cambiamenti nella struttura della società sono riflessi in modi di vigilanza che non son più nazionali, ma transnazionali. In passato è stato utile concentrarsi sulle azioni di sorveglianza degli stati democratici industrializzati ed esaminarne storia, struttura e proprietà emergenti. La definizione di azioni di sorveglianza, riferendosi a Weber e Bittner, poggia sull'obbligo che i cittadini sentono verso in un ordine legittimo ai fini di aderire a comandi anche impliciti, laddove la forza è chiamata ad assicurare l'adesione. Tale famiglia di definizioni implica l'esistenza di un territorio identificato e a confini definiti in cui vige un mandato. Il monopolio di una forza legittima, che è una caratteristica dello Stato secondo Weber, costituisce un problema. Le azioni di sorveglianza nazionali o trasnazionali significano che la forza viene applicata in modo quasi legittimo in assenza di dichiarazioni di guerra. Il termine sorveglianza non è più delimitabile a forze e a mandati nazionali, o a ristretti obblighi territoriali e a limitazioni legali. Nuovi interessi nazionali e modalità internazionali di controllo modificano la relazione tra democrazia e sicurezza. I cambiamenti nell'economia e nelle relazioni internazionali, così come nella tecnologia informativa, nei trasporti e nelle comunicazioni, si riflettono oggi nella sorveglianza. Il mandato è stato ridefinito dalle preoccupazioni per la sicurezza personale, ma anche per l'informazione intesa come proprietà o come simbolo o materia di espressione. Molti aspetti della sorveglianza non discussi qui, quali la restrizione, il controllo dell'informazione - ambedue in grado di nascondere e di rivelare -, il rispetto della privatezza del cittadino, e la sua adesione, stanno cambiando e tali cambiamenti influiscono sia sulla polizia sia sui cittadini delle nazioni democratiche.

Polizia e democrazia

Gary T. Marx

Questo articolo considera alcune possibilita' e alcune argomentazioni a favore di una polizia democratica, procedendo ad una breve analisi comparata dell'attivita' di polizia negli Stati Uniti, nel Regno Unito e in Francia. La democraticita' dell'attivita' di polizia dovrebbe essere vista come un processo piu' che come un risultato. Le societa' sperimentano una continua tensione tra il desiderio di ordine e la liberta'. Vi e' qualcosa di paradossale nel fatto che una societa' democratica abbia bisogno di protezione tanto da parte della polizia che dalla polizia stessa. Il potere delle nuove tecnologie di sorveglianza richiede che le societa' democratiche si interroghino continuamente su quanto desiderino sia efficiente l'attivita' di polizia e sulle condizioni alle quali l'uso di tali tecnologie risulti appropriato.

Sfide quotidiane all'attivita' di polizia in una democrazia: alcune note 'dalla prima linea'

Geoffrey Monaghan

L'attenzione di questo saggio e' focalizzata in primo luogo sul processo investigativo penale in Inghilterra e in Galles. L'intenzione e' quella di esaminare alcuni aspeztti fondamentali relativi al potere e alle pratiche della polizia, in particolare il potere di fermare e perquisire, il potere di arresto, l'interrogatorio dei sospetti in stato di detenzione e l'uso degli informatori. Si procede quindi alla discussione di alcune problematiche etiche relative a tali aspetti fondamentali. Sulla base di queste premesse, l'autore punta l'attenzione sulle carenze della legislazione e sull'assenza di una chiara supervisione amministrativa, portando argomenti a favore di una maggiore attenzione nei riguardi dell'interfaccia tra l'aspetto legalistico-formale che disciplina l'interazione tra cittadino e polizia e le esigenze di una attivita' poliziesca democratica e dell'attivita' poliziesca in una democrazia.

Polizia, forze armate e democrazia in Brasile

Paulo de Mesquita Neto

Questo saggio esamina il ruolo della polizia e delle forze armate nel sistema brasiliano di pubblica sicurezza. Ci si sofferma sulla separazione e sulla differenziazione tra la polizia e le forze armate e sul raggiungimento di un controllo sociale e democratico sulla polizia a partire dalla transizione verso la democrazia iniziata nel 1985. Si sostiene che i governi democratici non sono riusciti a separare e differenziare le forze armate dalla polizia, e a consolidare un controllo sociale e democratico su quest'ultima. La societa' civile ha giocato un ruolo importante ma ancora limitato nella riforma e nella demilitarizzazione del sistema di pubblica sicurezza. L'incompleta separazione e differenziazione tra le forze armate e la polizia e l'incertezza relative al controllo sociale e democratico sulla polizia hanno contribuito alla persistenza di pratiche poliziesche violente e inefficienti e hanno minato l'efficacia delle politiche e dei programmi volti al controllo del crimine e della violenza e al consolidamento del regime democratico.

Il blues della democrazia: la politica della riforma della polizia in Sud Africa, 1990-2000

Mark Shaw

L'attivita' poliziesca al tempo dell'apartheid era stata appositamente progettata per fini di controllo e repressione. Pertanto la trasformazione della polizia e' stata una condizione essenziale per il consolidamento dell'ordine post-democratico in Sud Africa. Questo obiettivo e' stato raggiunto con difficolta' e in modo tutt'altro che uniforme. Inizialmente la sfida che i decisori pubblici, che al tempo nutrivano poca fiducia nella polizia, si sono trovati a fronteggiare e' stata quella di ottenere una maggiore legittimazione nell'opinione pubblica per gli organi di polizia che fino a poco prima erano stati espressione dell'autoritarismo e ora dovevano garantire l'ordine democratico. Tali iniziative sono state vanificate da una pressante necessita' di far fronte a crescenti livelli di criminalita' nel paese, che vengono oggi considerati una minaccia grave all'ordine democratico. La polizia, in mancanza di una gamma di competenze che vengono considerate imprescindibili nella maggior parte delle democrazie, e sotto la pressione dei politici, sta assumendo una caratterizzazione saempre piu' repressiva nel tentativo di debellare il crimine. Al momento gli organi polizieschi si battono per il conseguimento della propria legittimazione non attraverso il riconoscimento del loro ruolo di tutori dell'ordine concesso dai politici ma attraverso l'efficace lotta all'anarchia criminale sul territorio.

Il volto mutevole della gestione della sicurezza e della giustizia

Clifford Shearing

Il saggio prende in esame le implicazioni dei mutamenti del modo in cui la sicurezza e la giustizia forniscono giustificazioni all'uso e al ruolo di una violenza di stato ai fini del mantenimento dell'ordine. Si argomenta che l'emergere di una logica di rischio e di sfide aperte all'attuale concezione denunciatoria ed espiatoria della giustizia stanno riconfigurando il modo in cui la violenza viene oggi usata come tattica di governo della societa'.

Il consenso dei governati: polizia, democrazia e diversita'

Lawrence W. Sherman

La polizia democratica si fonda sul consenso dei governati. Tale consenso richiede quattro principi di orientamento dell'attivita' poliziesca che culminano nel bisogno di evidenza empirica circa il miglior modo di promuovere i valori democratici attraverso la pratica poliziesca. Il primo principio e' che la missione dell'attivita' poliziesca e' quello di ottenere il rispetto della legge, piuttosto che di dispensare coercizione: di perseguire fini piuttosto che di impiegare un qualunque specifico mezzo. Il secondo principio e' che democrazie differenti richiedono mezzi diversi per ottenere il rispetto della legge da parte di popoli diversi. Il terzo principio e' che la polizia puo' strutturare il quadro fondamentale di identita' di tutti i cittadini di una democrazia in quanto cittadini. Il quarto principio e' che l'evidenza empirica circa il modo di ottenere il rispetto della legge attraverso la persuasione e le buone maniere (polizia gentile) aiutera' la polizia a minimizzare l'uso della coercizione e ad aumentare la legittimazione dello stato-nazione democratico.

La prospettiva del Commissario William Bratton sulla polizia democratica

Eli B. Silverman

Le nazioni che stanno emergendo dalla dittatura militare e dai regimi comunisti hanno intenzionalmente costruito dei sistemi di giustizia malfunzionanti. Possono essere necessari anni di tassi di criminalita' in aumento per apportare i cambiamenti necessari in tali sistemi di polizia. I media giocano diversi ruoli paralleli nel rendere gli organi di polizia piu' aperti e trasparenti. Sebbene l'attivita' formativa sia migliorata negli ultimi 30 anni, essa resta il tallone d'Achille della polizia democratica in America.

Polizia, sicurezza e democrazia: una prospettiva poliziesca dell'esperienza russa nell'era della transizione

Alexander Yelin

Il saggio analizza gli attuali problemi nello sviluppo della forza di polizia in Russia a partire dalla Perestroika dal punto di vista degli operatori coinvolti e delinea alcune aree fondamentali in cui e' necessario prendere misure urgenti al fine di assicurare una futura democratizzazione dell'attivita' poliziesca. Nei primi anni '90 sono stati introdotti alcuni cambiamenti radicali nel sistema russo di pubblica sicurezza, ma in seguito il sistema e' tornato alla stagnazione. La strada verso una polizia piu' democratica passa dalla garanzia di una maggiore trasparenza nelle pratiche poliziesche, una maggiore disponibilita' al controllo da parte dell'opinione pubblica, e un maggior coinvolgimento della comunita'.

Analisi della polizia giapponese dal punto di vista della democrazia

Minoru Yokoyama

La polizia giapponese e' stata una polizia di stato non-democratica fino alla seconda guerra mondiale. Il suo interesse principale era quello di mantenere l'ordine per conto dell'imperatore e del suo governo. Il mantenimento dell'ordine e le attivita' di pubblica sicurezza venivano svolti molto efficientemente, mentre i diritti dei cittadini ad un equo processo erano poco garantiti. La polizia, a quel tempo, svolgeva gia' compiti di polizia comunitaria. Tuttavia essa tendeva piu' a controllare i cittadini che a fornire loro un servizio. Il sistema di polizia giapponese fu democratizzato sulla base del modello americano dopo la sconfitta nella seconda guerra mondiale. Tuttavia un sistema autonomo di polizia locale non riusci ad attecchire in Giappone. A seguito della revisione della Legge di Pubblica Sicurezza nel 1954 essa fu rimpiazzata da un nuovo sistema composto dall'Agenzia Nazionale di Polizia e dalla polizia prefettizia. Sotto questo sistema tuttora in uso l'Agenzia Nazionale di Polizia ha gradualmente rafforzato il suo potere di controllo su tutte le polizie prefettizie. La polizia giapponese contemporanea ha molte caratteristiche di democraticita'. Tuttavia, avendo servito il governo conservatore per un lungo periodo, essa tende a perdere la sua neutralita' politica. Inoltre, si e' notata l'insorgenza di alcuni gravi fatti di corruzione originati dalla struttura poliziesca, e di alcuni problemi strutturali della pratica poliziesca nel processo di tutela dell'ordine pubblico.

Relazioni tra cittadini e polizia nei paesi in transizione

Ugljesa Zvekic

I principali risultati relativi alle relazioni tra cittadini e polizia nei paesi in transizione (20) che hanno partecipato alla Indagine Internazionale sulle Vittime del Crimine vengono qui discussi. I cittadini tendono a denunciare poco i crimini subiti alla polizia e la maggioranza di quelli che lo fanno si dichiara insoddisfatta del modo in cui la polizia affronta la denuncia, cosi come dell'efficacia della polizia nel controllare e nel prevenire il crimine.

Police, maintien de l'ordre, Etat et société: Quelques problèmes essentiels au regard de la protection des droits de l'homme et du citoyen.

Menachem Amir

La relation entre police, maintien de l'ordre et démocratie recèle de nombreux conflits et paradoxes. Ceci est le résultat de l'implication de la police dans la politique. La police, tout comme le maintien de l'ordre, n'est en effet pas apolitique. Elle sert parfois des intérêts politiques. Considérée comme garante de la démocratie, la police participe pourtant, occasionnellement, aux attaques perpétrées à l'encontre de notre société démocratique et du gouvernement, voire à leur destruction. Cet article examine les aspects normatifs et sociaux, et les différents types de démocratie, souvent perçus par la police comme des limites à un travail policier « efficace ». La tension entre police et fonctionnement démocratique atteint son comble lorsque des régimes sociaux et politiques totalitaires se trouvent en cours de mutation vers un régime démocratique. La situation de la police, et du maintien de l'ordre, lorsqu'un tel processus est en cours, est également examinée. L'article exprime enfin son optimisme sur l'évolution vers les concepts de « maintien de l'ordre démocratique » et de « police démocratique ».

La police : Contrôle social, Etat et démocratie

Nigel Fielding

Dans nos sociétés contemporaines, trois modèles principaux peuvent être identifiés pour l'organisation de la police et le fonctionnement des services policiers : le modèle dit « d'application de la loi », le modèle dit « de service », et le modèle « communautaire ». Chaque modèle est ici analysé en référence à sa philosophie, sa structure organisationnelle, sa politique de gestion, ses résultats, ainsi que sa stratégie et tactique opérationnelle. Les succès et limites de chaque modèle sont examinés, tandis que l'auteur s'efforce d'évaluer la concordance entre ces différents modèles et les divers modes d'organisation politique. Un glossaire des termes essentiels est également présenté.

Après la dictature: Nature et fonction de la police dans la Chine post-maoïste

H.L. Fu

La modernisation économique et la politique de libéralisation en cours depuis le début des années 80 ont amené des changements profonds dans la société chinoise. La police chinoise, à l'image de la société dans laquelle elle intervient, est engagée dans un processus de lente mais fondamentale mutation. Néanmoins, la Chine demeure un Etat communiste fondé sur le système du parti unique, et toute réforme ou changement vient s'inscrire dans le cadre plus large de cette structure politique. La police doit composer avec cette évolution de la révolution vers la modernisation, et avec la nécessité de redéfinir son rôle dans la nouvelle économie politique. Dans cette société post-révolutionnaire, la police chinoise s'efforce aujourd'hui de renégocier ses relations avec le parti communiste, le droit, et la communauté.

Police et démocratie en Finlande

Ahti Laiten

En Finlande, la confiance accordée par les citoyens à la police est supérieure à celle accordée aux tribunaux, à l'appareil administratif ou encore aux hommes politiques. Selon les sondages, les Finlandais perçoivent la police comme un élément central de leur sécurité, et beaucoup seraient prêts à lui accorder davantage de pouvoir, de moyens financiers et de ressources. La réputation de la police est aujourd'hui très bonne en Finlande, et un débat y a cours depuis longtemps sur l'élargissement de ses pouvoirs. La police finnoise est placée sous contrôle parlementaire. Si un individu estime qu'il ou elle a fait l'objet de mauvais traitement par la police, il a le droit tout à fait légal de porter plainte officiellement, l'affaire étant ensuite traitée par les services compétents. La possibilité de porter plainte existe tant au niveau local qu'au niveau national. La corruption est extrêmement rare au sein des forces de police finnoises. A titre de comparaison sur le plan international, le niveau de corruption des autorités finnoises est, après celui du Danemark, le plus faible au monde. La nomination des policiers finnois n'est pas politique. S'il est possible que les nominations d'une poignée d'officiers de police au sommet de l'administration revêtent un caractère politique, globalement, la police finnoise peut aujourd'hui se vanter d'être indépendante.

Police et Démocratie

Gary T. Marx

Cet article s'intéresse à certains facteurs et fondements d'une police démocratique, et met en contraste les modes de maintien de l'ordre aux Etats-Unis, au Royaume-Uni et en France. Le maintien de l'ordre démocratique doit être envisagé comme un processus, et non un résultat. Les sociétés sont confrontées à une tension permanente entre le désir d'ordre et le désir de liberté. Paradoxalement, une société démocratique a besoin d'être protégée tant par la police que contre la police. Etant donnée la puissance des nouvelles technologies de surveillance, les sociétés démocratiques doivent en permanence se demander : « *quel degré d'efficacité voulons-nous pour la police, et dans quelles conditions l'usage de ces nouvelles technologies est-il approprié ?* »

Police, forces armées et démocratie au Brésil

Paulo de Mesquita Neto

Cet article analyse le rôle de la police et des forces armées dans le système de sécurité public au Brésil. Il s'intéresse plus particulièrement à la séparation et la différenciation entre police et forces armées, et à la mise en place de leviers de contrôle civils et démocratiques sur la police depuis la transition démocratique de 1985. L'article avance que les gouvernements démocratiques ont échoué dans leur tentative de séparer et différencier entre armée et police, et de renforcer le contrôle citoyen et démocratique sur la police. La société civile a joué un rôle important, mais très limité, dans la réforme et la démilitarisation du système de sécurité publique. Ce processus non achevé de séparation et différenciation entre armée et police, de même que l'incertitude pesant sur le contrôle civil et démocratique du système policier, ont contribué à la persistance des violences policières et de l'inefficacité des services de police. Ce qui a, à son tour, considérablement nui à la mise en place de politiques et de programmes visant à lutter contre le crime et la violence, et à renforcer le régime démocratique.

Le blues de la démocratie : La politique de réforme de la police en Afrique du Sud, 1990-2000.

Mark Shaw

Le maintien de l'ordre sous le régime d'apartheid avait pour but le contrôle et la répression. La transformation de la police est de ce fait apparue comme une condition essentielle de l'ordre post-démocratique en Afrique du sud. Mener à bien cette mutation s'est révélé un processus ardu et non uniforme. A l'origine, le défi qui se posait aux décideurs -qui à l'époque n'avaient pas pleinement confiance en la police- était de permettre aux organismes anciennement chargés d'un maintien de l'ordre autoritaire d'acquérir une véritable légitimité aux yeux de l'opinion pour le maintien de l'ordre démocratique. Ces initiatives ont été dépassées par le besoin d'apporter une réponse à la criminalité croissante dans le pays, qui constitue aujourd'hui une menace sérieuse pour l'ordre démocratique.
Privée d'un éventail de compétences considéré comme élémentaire dans la plupart des démocraties, et pressée par les responsables politiques, la police affirme aujourd'hui plus clairement sa position au regard de la défense de la loi et de l'ordre, s'efforçant de réprimer la criminalité. Aujourd'hui la police se bat pour renforcer sa légitimité non par la démonstration de sa capacité à soutenir l'ordre politique nouveau, mais par la réduction des troubles à l'ordre public sur le terrain.

Le visage changeant de la gouvernance de la sécurité et de la justice

Clifford Shearing

Cet article s'intéresse aux conséquences, sur l'importance et le rôle de la violence gouvernementale dans le maintien de l'ordre, des changements dans la promotion et la perception de la sécurité et la justice. L'auteur observe comment l'émergence d'une logique de risque, en même temps que l'apparition de défis à la conception traditionnelle de la justice, reposant sur la dénonciation et l'expiation, est en train de remodeler l'utilisation de la violence en tant que stratégie de gouvernance.

Le point de vue du Commissaire William Bratton sur les Organisations Policières Démocratiques

Eli B. Silverman

Les nations qui émergent de dictatures militaires ou de régimes communistes mettent en place intentionnellement des systèmes judiciaires dysfonctionnels. Il faudra des années de hausse du taux de criminalité avant que ne s'opèrent les transformations souhaitables dans les systèmes policiers de ces pays. Les médias jouent un rôle essentiel en incitant à une plus grande transparence dans les organisations policières. Bien qu'il se soit amélioré au cours des trente dernières années, l'entraînement demeure, aujourd'hui encore, le talon d'Achille du système policier démocratique en Amérique.

Police, Sécurité et Démocratie : Un point de vue policier sur l'expérience russe en période de transition

Alexander Yelin

Cet article évoque, à travers le regard d'un professionnel, les difficultés rencontrées dans le développement des forces de police en Russie depuis la Perestroïka, et identifie les secteurs-clé au sein desquels il est urgent de prendre des mesures afin de poursuivre le processus de démocratisation du maintien de l'ordre. Si des changements radicaux ont été initiés au début des années 90 dans le système de maintien de la loi en Russie, le système a pourtant régressé ensuite vers une sorte de stagnation. Un maintien de l'ordre plus démocratique ne pourra être mis en place qu'en soumettant le travail de la police à la transparence et au contrôle public, et en encourageant l'implication de la communauté.

La police japonaise: Analyse au regard des valeurs démocratiques

Minoru Yokoyama

A la veille de la Seconde Guerre Mondiale, la police japonaise était une police d'Etat non-démocratique, dont le but principal était d'assurer le maintien de l'ordre pour l'Empereur et son gouvernement. Le maintien de l'ordre et l'application de la loi étaient assurés de manière très efficace, tandis que le droit des individus à une justice équitable était négligé. La police s'inscrivait déjà, à cette époque, dans une logique de maintien de l'ordre communautaire. Cependant, cette action visait à surveiller les individus, non à leur offrir un certain nombre de services.

Le système de police japonais a amorcé un processus de démocratisation sur la base du modèle américain, à la suite de la défaite du Japon pendant la Seconde Guerre Mondiale. Pourtant, cela n'a pas permis à un système policier décentralisé autonome de prendre racine au Japon. Suite à la révision de la Loi sur la Police en 1954, s'est substitué à l'ancien système policier un nouveau système comprenant l'Agence Nationale de Police et la police de préfecture. Sous ce système, qui a toujours cours aujourd'hui, l'Agence Nationale de Police a progressivement renforcé son contrôle sur l'ensemble de la police préfectorale.

La police du Japon d'aujourd'hui présente beaucoup d'aspects démocratiques. Pourtant, ayant longtemps été au service d'un gouvernement conservateur, elle est toujours susceptible de perdre sa neutralité politique. De plus, des cas de corruption sérieuse, dus à la structure de la police, ont été récemment observés, de même que certains problèmes structurels dans l'exercice de la fonction policière, au regard de la défense de la loi.

Les citoyens et leur rapport à la police dans les pays en transition

Ugljesa Zvekic

Cet article présente les résultats inédits de l'Etude Internationale sur les Victimes du Crime menée en 1996-97 dans 20 pays en transition, et commente ses conclusions eu égard aux relations entre police et citoyens. Peu de citoyens dénoncent les actes criminels dont ils sont victimes à la police, et la majorité d'entre eux se dit insatisfaite de la manière dont l'affaire est traitée par la police lorsqu'une déposition a lieu. De même, beaucoup expriment leur insatisfaction quant aux performances de la police en termes de contrôle et de répression de la criminalité.

قوات الأمن، المحافظة على الأمن والنظام، الدولة والمجتمع
بعض المشاكل الأساسية في الدفاع عن الحقوق المدنية والإنسانية

Menachem Amir

إن العلاقة القائمة بين قوات الأمن، والمحافظة على النظام والديمقراطية ملينة بالتناقضات والصراعات نتيجة لتدخل الشرطة في السياسة. فقوات الأمن والمحافظة عليه لا يعتبران محايدان من الناحية السياسية فالأمن يخدم أحيانا مصالح سياسية، ويقال بأن قوات الأمن هي المدافعة عن النظام الديمقراطي إلا أن قوات الشرطة تقوم أحيانا بالمساهمة في مهاجمة وحتى تدمير النظام الديمقراطي السائد في المجتمع والحكومة. وتناقش هذه المقالة الجوانب الاجتماعية والمعيارية للديمقراطية وأنواعها والتي عادة ما تنظر إليها قوات الأمن عن أنها تعمل على "تقييد" العمل الكفؤ للشرطة. ويصبح التوتر بين قوات الأمن والعملية الديمقراطية أكثر وضوحا عندما تكون الأنظمة الاجتماعية والسياسية الاستبدادية في حالة من التحول نحو الديمقراطية. وتتناول هذه المقالة حالة قوات الأمن والمحافظة على الأمن والنظام ضمن هذه الشروط والعمليات التي تقوم بها. كما أن هناك الاعتقاد بأن المحافظة على الأمن بشكل ديمقراطي "الشرطة الديمقراطية" يمكن تحقيقها من خلال مناقشات هذه المقالة.

الشرطة: الضوابط الاجتماعية، الدولة والديمقراطية

Nigel Fielding

يمكن تحديد نماذج ثلاثة لتنظيم قوات الأمن وتقديم خدمات الشرطة في المجتمعات المعاصرة وهي نموذج سيادة القانون، نموذج الخدمات ونموذج المجتمع. ويتم فحص كل من هذه النماذج بناءا على فلسفته، بنيته التنظيمية، نتائجه، السياسات الإدارية له، استراتيجيات العمل والتكتيك. ثم تتم مناقشة كل من ميزات وسيئات كل نموذج كما يتم إجراء تقييم لملائمة النماذج الثلاث والأشكال المختلفة للتنظيم السياسي. ويوجد هناك أيضا قائمة بالمصطلحات ذات العلاقة.

ما بعد الديكتاتورية: طبيعة الشرطة ووظيفتها بعد حادثة ماو في الصين

HL Fu

لقد أدى التطور الاقتصادي والتحرر السياسي منذ أوائل الثمانينات إلى إحداث تغيرات جذرية في المجتمع الصيني، فالشرطة الصينية مثل المجتمع الذي تعمل فيه تمر في عملية تدريجية من التغيير الأساسي إلا أن الصين لا تزال عبارة عن دولة شيوعية ذات حزب واحد حاكم وكافة أشكال الإصلاحات والتغيرات تحدث ضمن هذه البنية السياسية الأوسع. فالشرطة تتعامل وتتدبر أمر التحول من الثورة إلى التحديث وإعادة تحديد وتعريف دورها ضمن إطار سياسي جديد. وتقوم قوات الشرطة في المجتمع الذي يشهر مرحلة ما بعد الثورة بعملية التفاوض على علاقاتها مع الحزب الشيوعي، والقانون والمجتمع.

قوات الشرطة التي نحن بحاجة إليها
Andrew Goldsmith

تتساءل هذه المقالة عن كيفية تغير قوة الشرطة في استراليا ولماذا تغيرت كما تتساءل عما إذا أصبحت الشرطة ذات مصداقية أكبر أو أقل نتيجة لعملية التغيير هذه. إن القضايا المحددة التي تتم مناقشتها هي: قوة الشرطة، القانون، سياسات المحافظة على النظام، تطبيق قانون المخدرات، الفلسفات التي تقوم عليها إدارات الشرطة، والتكامل العالمي. ويتم في هذه المقالة فحص بعض الأهداف المتضاربة الظاهرة في مجالات عمل الشرطة مثل المخدرات غير المشروعة والعلاقات بين الشرطة والمجتمع والتي تجعل من عمل الشرطة أكثر تشويشا وتشتتا. كما تفحص المقالة وجود مؤثرات ذات مصداقية أكبر وشفافية ضمن مناهج إدارية جديدة وتستكشف إمكانيات مساواة المواطن في النظام الديمقراطي بالمستهلك في السوق الاستهلاكية.

أداء مهمة الشرطة في عصر الإعلام
Peter K. Manning

تحاول هذه الورقة أن تبرهن على أن التغييرات في البنية الاجتماعية تنعكس في أنماط أداء مهمة الشرطة التي لم تعد مهمة وطنية، بل تخطت الحدود القومية. كان من المفيد في الماضي التركيز على القيام بدور الشرطة في دول ديمقراطية صناعية وفحص تاريخ تلك الدول وبنيتها وملكياتها البازغة. إن تعريف أداء مهمة الشرطة بناء على Weber and Bittner يعتمد على واجب المواطنين في نظام شرعي الإذعان حتى لأوامر ضمنية بينما تعرض القوة لضمان الإذعان. وتشير فصيلة هذه التعريفات على وجود منطقة مسماة ومصنفة وتحيط بها حدود يسود داخلها تفويض. إن احتكار القوة الشرعية، وهي إحدى سمات الدولة وفقا لما يراه Weber، أمر فيه إشكاليات. فأداء مهمة الشرطة على نطاق عالمي أو بصورة تتخطى الحدود القومية تعني تطبيق القوة بأسلوب شبه شرعي عندما لا تكون قد أعلنت حرب.

لم يعد من السهل تعريف "أداء مهمة الشرطة" أو حصرها بقوى وطنية تفويضات وطنية وواجبات إقليمية محدودة وقيود شرعية ضيقة. إن المصالح الوطنية الجديدة وأنماط السيطرة الدولية تغير العلاقات بين الديمقراطية والأمن. وأصبحت التغييرات في العلاقات الدولية والاقتصاد وكذلك العلاقات في تكنولوجيا الإعلام والنقل ولاتصالات تنعكس الآن في أداء مهمة الشرطة. وتجري صياغة التفويض باهتمامات لا تقتصر على الأمن الشخصي فحسب بل على اهتمامات بأمن الإعلام كملكية وكذلك الإعلام كرمز أو مسألة تعبيرية. إن العديد من قضايا أداء مهمة الشرطة التقليدية التي لم نتناولها هنا بالتفصيل مثل الكبت والسيطرة الإعلامية الإخفاء والكشف كلاهما واحترام خصوصية المواطنين والإذعان يجري تغييرها الآن وتؤثر هذه التغييرات على رجال الشرطة والمواطنين كليهما في الدول الديمقراطية.

الشرطة والديمقراطية
Gary T. Marx

تتناول هذه المقالة بعض أشكال الدعم للشرطة الديمقراطية وتقارن بشكل مختصر بين قوات الشرطة في كل من الولايات المتحدة، المملكة المتحدة وفرنسا. يجب النظر إلى الشرطة الديمقراطية على أنها عملية وليست نتاج ما. فالمجتمعات تمر بتجارب من التوتر المستمر بين الرغبة في النظام والرغبة في الحرية. فيوجد هناك نوع من التناقض حيث أن أي مجتمع ديمقراطي يكون بحاجة إلى حماية الشرطة وكذلك الحماية من الشرطة. وفي ضوء تقنيات المراقبة المتطورة والحديثة يتوجب على المجتمعات الديمقراطية أن تتساءل دوما "ما هي الكفاءة التي نريد أن تتمتع بها الشرطة وضمن أية شروط يجوز استخدام هذه التقنيات ؟ " .

الشرطة، القوات المسلحة والديمقراطية في البرازيل
Paulo de Mesquita Neto

يدرس هذا الفصل دور الشرطة والقوات المسلحة في نظام الأمن العام في البرازيل. كما يركز على الفصل والتفريق بين الشرطة والقوات المسلحة وبين إنشاء نوع من الرقابة والسيطرة المدنية والديمقراطية على الشرطة منذ بدء عملية الانتقال إلى الديمقراطية في عام 1985. ويفترض المقال بأن الحكومات الديمقراطية قد فشلت في الفصل والتفريق بين القوات المسلحة والشرطة وبين توثيق السيطرة المدنية والديمقراطية على الشرطة. لقد لعب المجتمع المدني دورا هاما إلا أنه لا يزال محدودا في عملية إصلاح نظام الأمن العام ونزع الأسلحة منه. إن الفصل غير المكتمل والتفريق بين القوات المسلحة والشرطة من جهة ووجود الشك وعدم الثبات والاستقرار من جهة أخرى فيما يتعلق بالسيطرة المدنية والديمقراطية على الشرطة ساهم في تزايد واستمرار عنف رجال الشرطة وعدم كفاءة الشرطة كما قلل من أهمية السياسات والبرامج المعدة للسيطرة على الجريمة ومكافحتها ومنع العنف وإرساء قواعد النظام الديمقراطي.

الشرطة الديمقراطيين: Democracy's Blues
سياسات إصلاحات الشرطة في جنوب أفريقيا
Mark Shaw

لقد كان الهدف من إنشاء قوات المحافظة على الأمن واستحداثها تحت نظام الفصل العنصري السائد السيطرة والقمع لذا كانت عملية تحويل الشرطة من إحدى المتطلبات الأساسية لمرحلة نظام ما بعد الديمقراطية في جنوب أفريقيا وكانت عملية تحقيق هذا الأمر تواجه صعوبات وبعيدة عن ما يسمى بعملية منتظمة. وفي بادئ الأمر كان التحدي لصانعي السياسات الذين في ذلك الوقت لم يمنحوا ثقتهم الكاملة للشرطة حيث توجب عليهم الحصول على شرعية أكبر لدى الرأي العام لمؤسسات الشرطة الاستبدادية السابقة والتي تقوم حاليا

بالدعوة إلى الديمقراطية. لقد سيطرت على هذه المبادرات الحاجة إلى الرد على المستويات المتزايدة للجريمة في البلاد والتي تعتبر الآن التهديد الرئيس للنظام الديمقراطي. وبغياب عدة مهارات متوفرة في معظم الأنظمة الديمقراطية وتشجيع السياسيين فإن الشرطة حصلت على مكاسب قانونية وتنظيمية أكبر في محاولة منها في مكافحة الجريمة. وتكافح الشرطة الآن لإضفاء الشرعية عليها ليس من خلال الضمانات السياسية التي تدعم النظام الجديد وإنما من خلال التقليل من حالة عدم الخضوع لسيطرة القانون على أرض الواقع.

الوجه المتغير لسيادة الأمن والعدالة
Clifford Shearing

تستطلع هذه المقالة تأثير التحولات في طريقة تشجيع الأمن والعدالة حول مكانة العنف الحكومي ودوره في المحافظة على النظام. وتذكر بأن ظهور منطق المغامرة وكذلك التحديات للمفهوم اشجبي والتكفيري للعدالة هو إعادة تشكيل طريقة استخدام العنف على أنه نوع من التكتيك في الحكم.

موافقة المحكومين: الشرطة، الديمقراطية، والتنوع
Lawrence W. Sherman

عمل الشرطة الديمقراطي نابع من موافقة المحكومين. إن هذه الموافقة تطلب أربعة مبادئ شرطية تكتمل في الحاجة لدلائل مجربة عن كيفية تحقيق قيم الديمقراطية من خلال العمل الشرطي. المبدأ الأول هو أن مهمة العمل الشرطي هي تحقيق اتباع القانون وليس استخدام الإجبار: تحقيق الهدف النهائي وليس استخدام أي وسائل محددة. المبدأ الثاني هو أن الديمقراطيات المتنوعة تطلب وسائل متنوعة لتحقيق اتباع القانون بين الشعوب المختلفة. المبدأ الثالث هو أن الشرطة تستطيع إنشاء الهوية الرئيسية لجميع المواطنين في الديمقراطيات كمواطنين. المبدأ الرابع هو أن الدلائل المجربة عن كيفية الوصول إلى اتباع القانون من خلال الإقناع والأخلاقيات الجيدة ("عمل الشرطة بأدب") سيساعد الشرطة على تقليل استخدام الإجبار وزيادة الشرعية لديمقراطية الشعب والدولة.

وجهة نظر المفوض William Bratton عن عمل الشرطة الديمقراطي
Eli B. Silverman

إن الشعوب الخارجة من أنظمة حكم دكتاتورية عسكرية وشيوعية صارمة شكلت بقصد أنظمة عدل غير فعالة ببنيتها. إن من المحتمل أن تأخذ عملية وضع التغييرات الضرورية في أنظمتهم الشرطية سنين من ارتفاع نسب الجريمة. إن الإعلام يلعب دورا متعدد الجوانب في إظهار المنظمات الشرطية وجعلها أكثر شفافية. بالرغم من أن التدريب تحسن خلال الثلاثون سنة الأخيرة , إلا أنه في أواخر الأولويات بالنسبة لعمل الشرطة الديمقراطي في أمريكا.

الشرطة، الأمن، الديمقراطية: منظور الشرطة للتجربة الروسية خلال فترة الانتقال

Alexander Yelin

تعرض هـذه الورقـة المشـاكل الحاليـة التـي تواجـه عمليـة تطويـر قـوات الأمـن في روسيا منـذ انطـلاق حركـة "بريستـرويكا" الإصلاح والتعمير وذلك مـن خـلال منظـور معالج. كما تبين النقاط الرئيسية التي تحتاج إلى إجراءات وتدابير عاجلة لتضمن استمرار عملية الديمقراطية في الشرطة. فقـد حدثـت بعض التغيرات الجذرية في التسعينات لنظام تطبيق القانون في روسيا الآن إن النظام سرعان ما علق في حالة مـن الجمـود. إن الطريق إلى الحصول على مزيد من التطبيق للديمقراطية في الشرطة هو من خلال التأكيد على الصراحة والانفتاح في عمل الشرطة وخضوعه إلى المسألة والانفتاح في عمل الشرطة وخضوعه إلى المسألة والفحص مـن قبل الرأي العام وكذلك السماح للمجتمع في المساهمة فيه.

تحليل الشرطة اليابانية من منظور ديمقراطي

Minoru Yokoyama

لقد كانـت الشرطة اليابانية عبـارة عـن شرطة الحكومـة غير الديمقراطية قبـل الحرب العالميـة الثانية وكـانت وظيفتها الأساسية الحفاظ على النظام واستمرار لسيطرة الإمبراطور والحكومة. وقد تم تطبيق قوانين المحافظـة على الأمن والنظام بشكل فعال جدا إلا أنه تم إهمال حقوق الشعب في هـذه العملية. وكانت الشرطة آنذاك تقـوم بأعمـال الشرطة المجتمعية إلا أن هدفها كـان في الإشراف علـى النـاس والتحكم بهم بـدل مـن تقديم الخدمات لهم. لقد تم تطبيق الديمقراطية علـى الشرطة اليابانية علـى شـاكلة النمـوذج الأمريكي وذلك بعـد هزيمتهم في الحرب العالمية الثانية. ومع ذلك لم يتم إرساء قواعد متينة لنظام شرطة محلي يتمتع باستقلالية ذاتية في اليابان. وبعد أن تمت مراجعة قانون الشرطة في عـام 1954 تم استبداله بنظام جديد مكون من وكالة الشرطة الوطنية وشرطة الولاية. وخلال هذا النظـام الحالي قامت وكالة الشرطة المحليـة بتعزيز مكانتها بشكل تدريجي وتدعيم صلاحياتها الإشرافية على كافة أنظمة شرطة الولاية.

ويتمتع نظام الشرطة الياباني الحالي بعدة مزايا ديمقراطية إلا أن تأثير خدمة الحكومـة المحافظة لفترة طويلة من الزمان واضح في عدم تحليهم بالحياد السياسي وكذلك لوحظ بأن هناك بعض الفساد الخطير في بنية نظام الشرطة وكما يواجه النظام بعض المشاكل التركيبية في ممارسات الشرطة في عمليات تطبيق القانون.

العلاقات بين المواطنين والشرطة في الدول التي شهدت فترات تحول
Ugljesa Zvekic

تناقش هذه المقالة نتائج الأبحاث التي تم التوصل إليها حول العلاقات بين المواطنين والشرطة في الدول التي شهدت فترات التحـول وعددها (20) وشاركت في دراسـة ضحايا الجريمة العالمية (1996-1997). فقد وجد بـأن المواطنين لا يرغبـون كثيرا في الإبلاغ عن جريمة لدى الشرطة ولا تزال تظهر الأغلبية مـن المواطنين عدم الرضى من معاملة الشرطة في حالة الإبلاغ عـن حادث وكذلك فيما يتعلق بـأداء الشرطة في مكافحة الجريمة ومنعها.

要　約

警察、警察活動、国家および社会：人権および市民権の保護における基本的諸問題
（著者：Menachem Amir）

警察、警察活動および民主主義の関係は、葛藤と矛盾に満ちたものであるのである。これは、警察が政治に巻き込まれることから生じる。警察および警察活動は、非政治的ではない。時には、警察は、政治的闘利益に奉仕する。民主主義の擁護者であることと言われている。しかし、民主主義の社会的および規範的な視点や結果であるが、それは、政府の民主的システムを攻撃したり、それを擁護することにさえある。この両文のある。民主主義の過程との間の緊張が、最も明確になるのは、全体主義の社しばしば、警察によって「主権的な」警察作用を抑制するものと考えられている。警察と民主的な過程との間の緊張が、最も明確になるのは、全体主義の社会的および政治的な体制か、民主主義へ向かう変動の過程においてである。これらの諸条件や諸過程の下での警察や警察活動の状況が、当じられる。「民主的な警察活動」や「民主的な政治的な警察」は急速に達成されたるであろうという提案も、言及される。

警察：社会的統制、国家および民主主義
（著者：Nigel Fielding）

現在の社会における警察組織と警察サービスの提供について、三つの広範囲のモデルが、認められるかもしれない。その三つとは、法執行モデル、サービス・モデルおよび地域モデルである。各々のモデルは、その哲学、組織構造、産出されるもの、経路政策、および、その使用可能な資格や戦略に関連して検討される。各々のモデルの長所や欠点が、考察される。そして、各モデルと政治組織の異なる諸形態の間の適合について、評価がなされる。主要な各警の用語集が、含まれている。

独裁の後に：毛沢東の後の中国における警察の性質と機能
（著者：H L Fu）

１９８０年代前半以降の経済的な近代化と政治的解放は、中国社会に劇的な変化をもたらした。中国の警察は、それが作用している中国社会と同じく、ゆっくりであるが基本的な変化を経験しつつある。しかし、中国は、一党独裁の共産主義国家に留まっており、改革や変化のすべては、この大きな政治的構造の中で起こりつつある。警察は、革命から近代化への転換に対処しつつあるし、新しい政治的経済の中で、その役割を再定義しつつある。革命後の社会において、警察は、共産党、法および地域との関係について、再折衝しつつある。

私達が必要とする警察
（著者：Andrew Goldsmith）

この論文は、オーストラリアにおける警察権力が、如何にして、また、何故、変わりつつあるのか、身につめている。それは、同様、変わりつつある各種の中の、文化の追及で、多少責任あるように、なってきているのであろうか。今挙される特殊な論点は、警察権力と法および治安政治、業務遂行、業務非行、不法拘留のような、いくつかの悪循している目標が結論じられるが、それは、グローバルな統合である。それは、警察作用の剥域において明らかで、ある。それは、また、新しい経営の視点で、より大きな責任と透明性を達めための合否を証明する。そして、民主主義における顧客と同等視さ、れるかどうか、身になる。

フィンランドにおける警察と民主主義
（著者：Ahti Laitien）

フィンランドにおいては、警察に対する市民の信頼は、裁判所、行政機構あるいは政治家に対する彼らの信頼よりも、一層高い。世論調査によれば、人々は、警察を彼らの安全のための重要な組織であると見ている。また、多くの人々は、一層多くの権力、金および他の資源を、喜んで警察に与えようとしている。フィンランドでのフィンランドにおいては警察権力の拡大について、継続的に論論が行われてきた。フィンランドの警察は、議会の技制の下になる、ある人が警察によって逮捕されたと、誰かが感じら、公の所をする法的権利を持っており、これは、適切な社会公器用によって、処理されるであろう。地方と国の両方のレヘルで存在する。フィンランドの警察権の中での腐敗は、極めて稀であ、る。国際比較によると、フィンランド当局の腐敗は、デンマークに次いでいる。フィンランドの警察官の任命は、反論的でない。行政の視点に立つ、ほんの一握りの最高の警察現場の任命は、時所、性格において政治的であるかもしれない。現在のフィンランドの警察は、まったく独立のである。

警察と民主主義
（著者：Gary T. Marx）

この論文は、民主的警察の多様性と民主的警察への支持を事する。そして、アメリカ合衆国、英国およびフランスにおける警察活動を団政に対比する。民主的警察活動は、一つの結果としてでなく、一つの追放としても見るべきである。社会は、彼々への願望と自由との間で、継続的な緊張を経験している。民主的社会は、警察による保護と、警察からの保護の両方を必要としているという事実において、新しい監視技術の力を所与とすると、民主的な社会は、「警察が力の過度排能本的であることを許すのか、適切であるのか、という問を、継続的に身ねているであるものか。これらの技術の使用は、どのような条件の下で、適切であるのか。そのような条件に身ねていかなければならない。

ブラジルにおける警察、軍隊および民主主義
（著者：Paulo de Mesquita Neto）

この章は、ブラジルの公共安全システムにおける警察と軍隊の改革を検討する。焦点を当てるのは、警察と軍隊との分離と分化に対してであり、また、１９８５年に民主主義に移行して以来の、警察への市民による統制の確立に関してである。この章が注目するのは、民主的政府が、軍隊と警察の分離と分化に失敗し、また、警察への市民による民主的な統制を強化するのに失敗したことにである。市民社会は、公共安全システムの改革と脱軍事化において、置き続き限定的な役割しか、演じていない。軍隊と警察との国の不完全な分離と分化、および、軍隊の市民による民主的な統制についての不確実さは、軍隊の暴力および不能率の弁解の存続に寄与してきた。また、犯罪や暴力を助長したり、民主的体制を強化したりするための、政策やプログラムを難なくしてきた。

民主主義の青：南アフリカの 1990 年から 2000 年における警察改革の諸政策
（著者：Mark Shaw）

アパルトヘイトのもとでの警察活動は、統制と抑圧のために設計されていた。だから、警察の変容は、南アフリカにおける民主化後の民衆の必須の要件であった。警察の変容を充分に保証していなかった。今も民主主義を監視する精緻な民主的な警察活動は、今もこれを成し遂げることには、一様性から見ると、困難な過程であった。初めは、当時警察を充分に信頼することにあった。これらの最初の試みは、国内のいろいろな主権を監視する精緻な民主的な省の警察組織機関に対して、民衆の中で一層大きな合法性を獲得することにあった。これらの最初の試みは、国内のいろいろなレベルでの犯罪の増大に応える必要さえによって、圧されている。警察は、大統の民主的な国では当然としされている。今や民主的な秩序への主要な貢献と見なされているのである。警察は、大統の民主的な国では当然としされている。また、政治家によって当がかされているので、犯罪を取り締まる試みにおいて、より一層大きな、送し秩序への実勢をとりつつある。今や、警察は、新しい秩序を支持するという反抗的な傾向によってでなく、場所にはひこっている無法を減少させることを通して、合法性を成し遂げようと、苦闘している。

安全と正義の統治の変化している面
（著者：Clifford Shearing）

安全と正義は、民衆維持における政府の暴力の場所で役割を促進するが、そのやり方の転換の含意を、この論文は探求する。論文は究明する、論文で主張するのは、丸幡の論理の出現は、確立された身体的で非強迫的な、正義の考えへの統戦と共に、暴力の統治の戦術として使われるやり方を、再考することにである。

被支配者の同意：警察、民主主義および多様性
(著者：Lawrence W. Sherman)

民主的な警察活動は、被支配者の同意に根拠をもつ。その同意は、被支配者の同意の方法に同じく、経験的な証拠を求める必要性においてである。第1の原理は、警察活動の4つの原理を要求する。それが頂点に達するのは、警察の実技を通じて民主的な価値を達成するというよりも、法への順応を達成することであり、何らかの特系な手段を採用するよりも、目的を達成するというよりも、多様な人々の中での順応を達成するために、多様な民主主義が、市民としての支配的な同一視を実きうることである。第3の原理は、民主主義における全ての市民の中で、市民としての支配的な同一視を同一視を実きうることである。第4の原理は、誠終と良い作法（「礼儀正しい警察活動」）を通じて、順応を保持する方法についての経験的調査の順大さと、警察に、強制の使用を最小にさせ、民主的な民族国家の合法性を増大させるのを、助けるということである。

民主的な警察活動についての William Bratton 警視総監の見解
(著者：Eli B. Silverman)

軍事的出現後中共産主義の体制から出現した国家は、単道的に逆機能的な司法システムを意図的に作り出していた。その警察システムに必要な質化をもたらすためには、数年にわたる犯罪率の増加があるかもしれない。メディアは、警察組織を公開し、より一層透明にさせるのに、多様な役割を演じる。貢献は、アメリカにおける民主的な警察活動の急所である。過去30年の間、改善されたけれども、貢献は、アメリカにおける民主的な警察活動の急所である。

警察、安全および民主主義：推移の時代におけるロシアの経験についての警察の視点
(著者：Alexander Yelin)

この論文は、ペレストロイカ以来のロシアにおける警察の見解での現在の問題を、実務家の観点から提示する。そして、警察勤の一層の民主化を確保するために、緊急に変る必要のある方策の主要な領域を敵討する。1980年代の同年には、いくつかの急進な変化が、ロシアの送帰行シ ステムに対してもした。その後、そのシステム上の変化は、停滞へと揺り落ちた。一層民主的な警察勤への送は、警察作用中の公開性、民衆による調査のその利用可能性、および、地域の関わりを、確保することをを通じてであろう。

民主主義の観点からの日本警察の分析
(著者：横　山　実)

日本の警察は、第二次世界大戦以前は、半民主的な国家警察であり、そのまたる任務は、天皇および彼の政府のために秩序を維持することでとであった。秩序の維持と法執行活動は、非常に能率的に遂行されたが、適正手続への人々の権利は無視されていた。その時、警察は、反に地域警察組織を行っていた。アメリカの占領のもとでは、人々にサービスを提供することを目的としていた。日本の警察システムは、第二次世界大戦の反成の後、アメリカのモデルに做って、民主化された。しかし、自主的な地方警察システムは、日本に根づかなかった。1954年の警察法の改定の後、それは、警察庁と都道府県警察によって構成される、新しいシステムに置き換えられた。この現在のシステムで、警察庁は、次第に、すべての都道府県警察への医視の権力を強めてきた。現在の日本の警察は、多くの民主的な特徴を持っている。しかし、長期間にわたって保守的な政府に仕えてきたので、政治的中立性を失う傾向がある。さらに、警察構造によって生じる、いくつかの官僚的な問題が、注目されている。警察構造によって生じる、送府の過度での警察の実態や、いくつかの官僚的な問題が、注目されている。

推移しつつある国の市民と警察の関係
(著者：Ugljesa Zvekic)

国際犯罪被害調査（1996年と97年）に参与した、推移しつつある国（20）における市民・警察の関係についての主要な結果が、論じられる。市民が犯罪を警察に通報する率は、低い。彼らの大半は、また、事件が通報されたときの警察の処置に不満を示しているし、犯罪の抑制や予防での警察の遂行について、不満を示している。

Index